REVEALING ANTIQUITY

· 15 ·

G. W. Bowersock, General Editor

CHRISTOPHER KELLY

Ruling the Later Roman Empire

THE BELKNAP PRESS OF HARVARD UNIVERSITY PRESS

Cambridge, Massachusetts, and London, England

2004

The map on p. 73 is reproduced with permission from A. H. M. Jones,
*The Later Roman Empire 284–602 : A Social, Economic, and
Administrative Survey* (Oxford: Basil Blackwell, 1964), Map VI (eastern half).

Library of Congress Cataloging-in-Publication Data

Kelly, Christopher, 1964–
Ruling the later Roman Empire / Christopher Kelly.
p.   cm.—(Revealing antiquity ; 15)
Includes bibliographical references and index.
ISBN 0-674-01564-9 (alk. paper)
1. Rome—Politics and government—284–476.
2. Byzantine Empire—Politics and government—To 527.
3. Rome—Officials and employees.
4. Byzantine Empire—Officials and employees.
5. Elite (Social sciences)—Rome.
6. Elite (Social sciences)—Byzantine Empire.
I. Title.   II. Series

DG83.5.K45   2004
937′.09—dc22   2004047664

For Keith Hopkins
(1934–2004)

Teacher and Friend

Contents

Acknowledgments

This book owes a great deal to Keith Hopkins, John Matthews, Glen Bowersock, Dick Whittaker, and Peter Brown. Their splendid combination of cheerful encouragement, elegant hospitality, and impressive critical acumen is well known, but no less a pleasure to confirm here. I have also benefited from discussions on a number of points with valued friends and colleagues. I particularly wish to mention Richard Lim, Averil Cameron, Takashi Minamikawa, Jaś Elsner, Neil McLynn, Jill Harries, Kate Cooper, Peter Garnsey, Rosalind Thomas, Jeremy Tanner, Rosamond McKitterick, Joyce Reynolds, Philip Rousseau, Atsuko Gotoh, Gillian Clark, Elaine Fantham, Gillian Shepherd, Justin Goddard, Elizabeth Speller, Peter Stacey, Caroline Vout, and Michael Williams. Warm thanks are also due to my editor Peg Fulton for patiently seeing this project through to its conclusion.

Prologue
First Thoughts

The later Roman empire was before all things a bureaucratic state.
—A. H. M. Jones

This book is an attempt to understand some important aspects of the exercise of power in the later Roman Empire. It aims to capture something of what it was like to rule, and what it was like to be ruled. One of its chief concerns is to trace the consequences of a shift in the way the Mediterranean world was governed. The Roman Empire in the first two centuries A.D. was marked by a relatively low level of centralized authority and a high degree of local autonomy. From the end of the third century, this long-standing pattern of power was significantly disrupted by the gradual establishment of a centrally organized and greatly expanded imperial bureaucracy. The movement from "soft" to "hard" government is one of the defining characteristics of late antiquity.[1] It is a transformation which separates the first-century empire of Augustus from the sixth-century empire of Justinian.

The imposition of a more deeply penetrating degree of control over the inhabitants of empire was fundamental to this transformation. The effectiveness of central government was markedly increased by an enhanced ability to collect, collate, and retrieve information, by the use of skilled personnel primarily dedicated to specialist administrative tasks, and by the promotion of a professional cadre of officials. Within the administration, the development of well-defined hierarchies, a strong esprit de corps, and binding departmental loyalties fostered both solidarity and identity. These factors helped to insulate bureaucrats from the conflicting interests of other powerful groups and to increase the likelihood that imperial directives would be enforced in the face of competing provincial particularities. Roman government in late antiquity was (unsurprisingly) far from perfect. Like many such systems it could get out of hand; like many such systems it had its own proclivities, inefficiencies, and dysfunctions. But its achievements are also worth noting. It was, to quote John Matthews' attractive summary, "unmatched in Graeco-Roman history in its scale and complexity of organisation, in its physical incidence on society, the rhetorical extravagance with which it expressed, and the calculated violence with which it attempted to impose its will."[2]

The first part of this book (Chapters 1 and 2) looks at the workings of later Roman bureaucracy through the eyes of one man. A series of fortunate accidents has ensured the preservation in the Bibliothèque Nationale in Paris of the one surviving early medieval manuscript which contains a copy of a treatise written by John Lydus, a high-ranking official serving in an important central government department in Constantinople in the sixth century. *On the Magistracies of the Roman State* is the only surviving description of the operation and functioning of central government in late antiquity written by someone who was actually on the inside. Behind an impressive façade of formal descriptions of the imperial administration (its duties, competence, and responsibilities), John's reminiscences provide a real and present sense of a complex system in motion. He allows a close appreciation of the combinations and possibilities which shaped officials' work practices, dominated their often bitter departmental rivalries, and affected their chances of appointment and promotion. He exposes the competing ambitions, interests, career strategies, and moral judgments which both structured and bounded this narrow bureaucratic world.

This delineation of the institutional contours of later Roman administration is framed by John's own experiences and his unashamedly personal concerns. Alongside his detailed account of the intricate workings of government in the imperial capital he incorporated a memoir of his own (ultimately disappointing) career. Here John confessed frankly to his thwarted ambitions. He roundly and often obscenely abused those superiors and colleagues whom he held responsible for impeding his progress. These various conflicts, successes, and failures are explored in Part I. Together they provide modern readers with a precious and intimate insight into the ancient world. *On the Magistracies* is a valuable text. In short, it offers us our best chance to understand later Roman bureaucracy from the point of view of a bureaucrat.

Part II shifts perspective. Chapter 3 maps the limitations on imperial power in a preindustrial superstate, outlining the dominant tactics used by those seeking to advance themselves or their causes in the first two centuries A.D. The early Roman Empire was, above all else, a highly personal world in which the successful exercise of power significantly depended on "clout" and connections,[3] on who you were and whom you knew. Chapter 4 explores the impact and implications, both practical and moral, of the intrusion in the later Empire of a range of new tactics. It looks closely at the charging of fees by officials, at the sale of offices, and, in particular, at the systematic promotion of the payment of money by central government as a means of regulating access to its judicial and administrative services.

Of course, many of these practices, if followed in a modern Western country, would rightly be regarded as corrupt and a perversion of the correct uses to which public office ought to be put. (No doubt some modern Western practices might have appeared curious, even unethical, to the Romans.) Moral codes differ, not to mention the nature of government, its size and sophistication, the means and speed of communication, the ability to gather, process, and interrogate information, and the demands, expectations, and ideals of both rulers and ruled. To say that the later Roman Empire was "corrupt" is in part to claim that there are sufficient similarities between that society and our own to make such comparative judgments worthwhile. But we should be wary of accepting that Western bureaucratic methods and morality, if followed by the Romans, would necessarily have proved more "natural," "just," or "efficient." Similarly, we should not simply assume that the practices which we might condemn would necessarily have had the same consequences in the ancient world or could have been eliminated by the same remedial strategies effective in reforming modern administrations. Corruption, as a specific phenomenon, cannot easily be abstracted or isolated from the society in which it occurs. It cannot stand apart from political structures or systems of government. In the end, few would disagree that it would be both inapplicable and ill conceived to attempt to understand corruption in any historical bureaucracy through the imposition of patterns and prescriptions derived from modern Western morality and institutions.

The chapters which follow deliberately avoid using modern, public-service-oriented bureaucracies as the standard by which later Roman administration should be judged. Rather, a discussion of "corruption" is used as a means of directing attention to those actions and attitudes which seem most at variance with our own. Corruption remains a useful collective term covering a significant complex of transactions and interrelations involving government officials. It prompts questions about those transactions and about the nature of the bureaucracy and the society of which it was part. In turn these offer a framework for testing the claim that certain administrative practices impaired the effectiveness of Roman government or damaged its authority.[4]

Yet corruption cannot easily be transformed into an analytic category. As a term it is inescapably judgmental; it inevitably involves moral condemnation; it is sometimes little more than abuse. In this sense, thinking about corruption can direct attention not only to problematic aspects of how power was exercised and how it affects others, but also to the ideals and prescriptions surrounding (and in part regulating) that exercise. Nor should it be assumed that those prescriptions are always self-evident. There is, for example, no particular reason to believe that the collective ideals of a society are always enshrined in its legal system. In some cases, and particularly in autocratic states, laws may represent attempts by rulers to institutionalize and impose one version of political morality. Illegality offers only one possible definition of corruption. The fact that we sometimes claim (and perhaps questionably too) that we have in our own society a reasonably settled view on what constitutes the correct exercise of government power does not mean that a broad consensus may be expected in all societies, even if we accept, as we must, that any such consensus may be radically different from our own. A society can equally well be made up of a series of competing ideals; ideals which impinge upon how power is—or may be—exercised appropriately. Under such circumstances, an exploration of corruption need not mask any externally imposed categories; rather it can be openly and unashamedly subjective as it seeks to reveal the various views of those involved.

In late antiquity, significant shifts in the system of rule often provoked strong opposition, the most bitter voiced by those who felt their own positions threatened. Some complained about the payment of money to bureaucrats, the sale of offices, and the immorality of allocating administrative time and resources without proper regard to traditional status and convention. These objections must be respected. They represent deeply felt reactions to a transformation in the way Roman government worked. (They are perhaps also striking testaments to the effectiveness of some of those tactics.) But they are only part of an argument. No single view should be allowed to fill the field. Rather, the actions and opinions of officials and of those who dealt with them were continually modified, reinforced, and constrained by a series of often fiercely contested moralities. These variously conflicting and complementary prescriptions offer another opportunity to understand something of the consequences of the intrusion of a centralized bureaucracy in a traditional society. By permitting these sometimes trenchant attitudes full play, it is possible to gain a better sense of the ways in which the bureaucracy functioned and of the strengths and weaknesses of government in the later Roman Empire.

Chapter 5 looks at these patterns of power and influence from an imperial point of view. It explores the limitations imposed on the unfettered exercise of autocratic power in a world increasingly dominated by the interests of officialdom. In some cases, the legislation collected in the *Theodosian* and *Justinianic Codes,* and (in a few instances) displayed in grand inscriptions on the walls of public buildings in provincial towns, sought to enforce a model of bureaucracy founded on detailed rules and strict hierarchies of promotion and command. Some imperial laws promulgated schedules of fees to be charged those seeking to litigate. By contrast, some moralized about the necessity of justice for all and against the payment of money to officials who staffed the empire's courts. Yet other legislation permitted the appointment of bureaucrats on the basis of their personal or provincial connections or permitted the purchase of office.

These seeming inconsistencies are revelatory. For emperors there remained an ever-present threat that, for all its many advantages, the strengthening of an extensive administrative apparatus might weaken their own influence and importance. The growth of bureaucracy in the later Roman Empire both enabled and enfeebled imperial power. Against the pressures to conform to regulation, standardization, and routine, emperors repeatedly emphasized their own authority and the dependence of officials upon them personally. Bureaucrats were sometimes to be supported, sometimes undercut. Emperors might deliberately disrupt established conventions, creating rivalries between departments, arbitrarily dividing responsibilities, and transferring high-ranking officials to new positions. Undoubtedly, the rational organization and efficient operation of the bureaucracy were impaired. But in a continuous tussle for control, emperors had to weigh these costs against the effectiveness and security of their own position at the very center of government.

A view of later Roman bureaucracy from these three standpoints—bureaucrats, emperors, and those attempting to benefit from, or to avoid, the imperial administration—offers a set of (not always convergent) perspectives for understanding a sophisticated system of rule. It also exposes a variety of competing tactics and trade-offs. Bureaucrats like John Lydus might strongly advocate the merits of a tightly organized administration with carefully defined duties and clear-cut lines of control. At the same time they deployed a number of often-overlapping tactics (such as the payment of money, the exercise of influence, or the claims of merit or seniority) to further themselves and their colleagues. Those seeking access to government services or to the courts likewise moved to their best advantage. Long-hallowed methods of promoting self-interest continued to be used in combination—sometimes uncomfortably, sometimes skillfully—with a range of other tactics (such as the payment of money or the purchase of office) which might seem to hold out a greater promise of success in a more centralized and bureaucratic empire. In particular circumstances, too, the available options might be circumscribed by the individual interests of officials, by the resilience of traditional ways of organizing power and influence, and by the ability of those deploying such methods either to accommodate or to counteract alternative and potentially challenging ways of achieving the same ends.

For many, the later Roman Empire remained an unstable world. Few emperors ever achieved a lasting or satisfactory resolution of the tensions between themselves and their administration. Few bureaucrats (as John Lydus' autobiography amply illustrates) were able to locate or maintain the fine balance necessary for the undisturbed and profitable holding of power they desired. Few of those wishing to use the judicial or administrative services provided by Roman government negotiated their way across this same difficult ground with ease or confidence. Such concerns again underscore some of the problems surrounding the expansion and imposition of a centralized bureaucracy, and its engagement with traditional priorities and expectations, both at the imperial court and in the provinces. Indeed, ambiguity and uncertainty—tightly encircling all those involved—often reflect more closely the conflicting pressures which characterized this new pattern of power. These irresolutions are important. In late antiquity, change was slow and refractory. There was no swift or revolutionary transition from "soft" to "hard" government.

PART I

The Bureaucrat's Tale

John Lydus

A Man and His Book

History is a conversation with the dead. We have several advantages over our informants. We think we know what happened subsequently; we can take a longer view, clear of ephemeral detail; we can do all the talking; and with all our prejudices, we are alive. We should not throw away these advantages by pretending to be just collators or interpreters of our sources. We can do more than that.

—Keith Hopkins

Sometime around A.D. 552, a thwarted civil servant wrote a polemical history of his own decline and fall. That man was John Lydus (or John "the Lydian"); his book—written in Greek, his first language—was titled *On the Magistracies of the Roman State.*[1] John was born around 490 in Philadelphia, the chief town of the province of Lydia, on the western coast of Asia Minor.[2] In 511, after an expensive education (which included learning Latin), he left home for the metropolitan magnificence of Constantinople, "the all golden city" (3.44). Arriving in the imperial capital, the twenty-one-year-old John had high hopes of a successful career. He aimed to secure a coveted position as a junior official in one of the imperial secretariats (*sacra scrinia*), whose highly privileged staff, working in the palace, dealt with administrative and judicial matters directly involving the emperor himself (3.26).

While waiting for a suitable opening, John furthered his studies by attending lectures on Aristotle and Plato given by the famous Athenian philosopher Agapias. Later in the same year he was offered a position on the staff of the eastern Praetorian Prefecture. The post was attractive for an ambitious newcomer. In the early sixth century, the Prefecture was still one of the most important and wide-ranging administrative departments in the empire. It had overall responsibility for judicial and financial affairs, army recruitment, public works, and the general oversight of around fifty provinces in an area covering (in a rough arc) the territory now occupied by the eastern Balkan states, Asia Minor, the Levant, and North Africa as far west as modern Libya.[3]

John owed his chance of a post to a fellow Philadelphian, Zoticus, who had recently been appointed prefect by the emperor Anastasius (3.26). Zoticus occupied a key position at court. As head of the eastern Praetorian Prefecture, he was rightly regarded as one of the most powerful and influential officials in the imperial administration. Under Zoticus' patronage, John started a promising and lucrative career on the department's judicial side. In his first year he undertook a variety of work, some of it connected with the prefectural court, some with the palace administration. (3.27) At the same time, prompted by Ammianus (a relation of John's father and also on the staff of the Prefecture), Zoticus was instrumental in securing an advantageous marriage for his Philadelphian protégé. John's new bride—"superior to women who have at any time at all been admired for their discretion"—also brought a substantial dowry (3.28, 3.26).[4]

All went as well as could be expected for the next twenty years. Then John the Cappadocian (a senior official on the Prefecture's financial side) was appointed by the emperor Justinian to head the department. During his two terms as eastern praetorian prefect (April 531 to January 532 and October 532 to May 541), "the Cappadocian"—as our John sneeringly called him (2.17, 2.20, 3.57)—was responsible for implementing a series of reforms which weakened both the position and the prospects of those on the judicial side. In restructuring the administration of the Prefecture, the Cappadocian openly preferred his former colleagues and subordinates, the technically competent financial staff (*scriniarii*), to the traditionally educated judicial officials (*exceptores*). John began to regret his decision to become a bureaucrat. He worried about his income, his career, and his chances of promotion. "When in all respects public affairs had reached the state which this account has recorded, and moreover, when Fortune (as never before) did not favor men of learning, I came to hate the service and gave myself up entirely to my books" (3.28).[5]

John's abilities were considerable. Sometime around 532 he was invited by the emperor Justinian to deliver an encomium praising the achievements of his reign and to compose a history of the recent military campaigns on the empire's eastern frontiers. The latter piece was not without its difficulties. In 530, thanks to the brilliant generalship of Belisarius, a large Persian force had been routed near Dara, in southern Armenia (3.28). But in the following year the Roman army was defeated and Belisarius suddenly recalled to Constantinople. An inconclusive military situation led to a negotiated peace with Persia in September 532 and the payment by the Romans of 11,000 pounds of gold in war reparations.[6] Regrettably, neither John's encomium survives, nor does his history of Justinian's ambiguously successful Persian campaign (if indeed it was ever written).[7]

Subsequently, perhaps in 543, John was appointed by the emperor to a chair in Latin language and literature at the State University of Constantinople.[8] An imperial edict which regulated the terms of his employment, a document John quoted with unabashed pride, publicly acknowledged "the extent of his education in literature, his precision in matters of language, his grace amongst the poets, and the rest of his erudition" (3.29). Later readers of John's works echoed something of Justinian's appreciation, if in slightly less enthusiastic tones. Photius, a ninth-century Byzantine bishop and bibliophile, found John a pleasing, if at times a rather uneven, stylist: "This author makes excessive use of literary devices, often to very indifferent effect and in an uncontrolled way, but in some instances appropriately and attractively."[9]

But for John, immediate imperial approval of his talents (and the commissions which resulted) mattered more than the carping compliments of later critics. In the early 540s he wrote at least two learned works, both of which survive: *On Months* (a lengthy disquisition on the festivals of the traditional Roman calendar and the reasons behind their celebration) and *On Portents* (an equally encyclopedic collection of antiquarian lore relating to divination and astrological practice).[10] Following his appointment to the University of Constantinople, John increasingly devoted himself to his academic duties while remaining on the staff of the Prefecture. In April 552, after forty years and four months of service, he finally retired, having been promoted to the post of *cornicularius*, the highest-ranking office on the judicial side (3.30).[11] At a formal ceremony, John was publicly praised in front of his colleagues by the then prefect, Hephaestus, as "the most learned, for he delights more in this title than in the recognition he has achieved as a result of the honors which have been conferred upon him" (3.30).

Amidst the splendor of the occasion, John was able to convince himself that "this honor was as good as a large sum of money" (3.30). But elsewhere, as he recalled the flourishing state of the department he had joined as a young man, and his subsequent disappointments following the reforms promoted by John the Cappadocian, he remarked with some bitterness: "I repent as I reflect so late in the day for what return I devoted myself to the court of justice for such a long time, having gained nothing from it by way of consolation" (3.25). For John, who always felt that he had been forced sideways into academe (in his view poor compensation for what should have been a profitable civil service career), Hephaestus' neatly phrased retirement speech, with its careful emphasis on titles and recognition rather than financial reward, must have seemed only too painfully accurate.

It was after retiring from the Prefecture that John devoted himself to writing a history of the empire's administration from the foundation of Rome by its first king, Romulus, to the reign of the emperor Justinian. This was a work ambitious in its scope. It aimed not only to outline developments in government over thirteen centuries, but also to argue for the continued significance of ancient Roman practices and traditions.[12] Moreover, *On the Magistracies of the Roman State* allowed John to parade his antiquarian erudition, his detailed knowledge of correct bureaucratic form and procedure, and his considerable knowledge of philological obscurities. (The digressions on such varied topics as the correct names for different types of infantry shield, why the river Ister is also known for part of its course as the Danube, on the life cycle of the sturgeon, and the hibernating habits of the scorpion are curiously fascinating in their own right.)[13] The result—at least according to the somewhat dismissive Photius, who clearly found such special-interest books rather tiresome reading—was "a not undistinguished account for enthusiasts of such things."[14]

But *On the Magistracies* was intended to be more than just an account of administrative affairs since Romulus. This book was also a vindication of John's career in the Prefecture, written in retirement as a highly personal explanation of his own disappointments and frustrations. To the detailed scholarly concerns of the first two parts of the work, which in successive sections carefully set out the origins of the Roman state and its chief offices, John added, as a third part, "a special and separate" (3.1) history of the Praetorian Prefecture. For the most part, this highly technical account was chiefly concerned with the personnel, organizational structure, and work practices of the judicial side of the eastern Praetorian Prefecture from the fourth century A.D. to the reign of Justinian.

On the Magistracies presented the Praetorian Prefecture as the key administrative department in the government of empire. Indeed, its role had been vital from the earliest times. John insisted on an etymological connection between the military post of master of the horse (ἵππαρχος), established by Romulus, and the praetorian prefect (ὕπαρχος) (2.6, 1.14–15).[15] Equally, he was ever ready to stress the inferiority of other departments and their lack of any proper tradition. Even the staff of the powerful *magister officiorum* (the head of the palatine bureaucracy) was put in its proper place: "I shall speak about that department toward the end of this work; for, since it is newer, it ought not to be reckoned along with the older magistracies, but given the place which time has assigned to it" (2.7). Only the judicial staff could claim the sanctity and privileges rightly due to a department which from the foundation of Rome (at least in John's highly inventive view of the past) had been the most important institution in the state after the monarchy (2.9, 2.20). "For like sparks from an everlasting fire, the remaining magistracies of the state are demonstrably dependent upon that which is truly the magistracy of magistracies" (2.7).

John's long and rather lopsided description of a major government department in the imperial capital was also intercut with an extensive memoir of his own career. Dedicated as "a thank offering" (1.15) to those prefects who had supported his advancement, the third part of *On the Magistracies* traced John's successes as well as the lamentable demise (under men such as John the Cappadocian) of the judicial side's responsibilities. For John, that decline was not only personally and financially damaging; it was also to be understood as a dangerous symptom of a wider administrative malaise. In the face of failure, *On the Magistracies* was also intended as both a bid and a blueprint for reform. By presenting its readers with "a faint mirrored picture" of past achievements (3.1), it stressed the importance of the restoration of antique form and order. It made a case on behalf of John's former colleagues on the Prefecture's judicial side, many of whom were probably not so fortunate as to have secured either academic posts in the capital or literary commissions from an emperor. But as a manifesto for administrative change, John's book was a signal failure. The publication of the (seemingly unrevised) work probably following his death, perhaps sometime soon after 554,[16] had no perceptible effect on the administrative policies of either Justinian or his successor Justin II.

For modern readers, *On the Magistracies* remains a difficult work. The amalgam of antiquarianism, specialized administrative minutiae, and personal reminiscence is especially problematic. Autobiography will always be a dubious form of recording or commenting upon the past. Few people can ever be trusted to tell the truth about themselves or their careers. Fewer still can be relied upon to give a dispassionate account of their failure to fulfill their own ambitions. In such personal versions of the past, what might seem to others (both then and now) as merely parochial issues inevitably dominate. Other concerns, thought by many of John's contemporaries to be the chief events of his time in Constantinople, were of marginal interest. Justinian's military campaigns in Persia, Africa, and Italy under the generalship of Belisarius, hard-fought doctrinal disputes, the Nika riots in 532, the codification of imperial legislation, the salacious gossip and intrigue which surrounded the empress Theodora, and the serious plague of 542 were all in John's view only side shows. Unless they had affected him or his colleagues, they deserved no more than a passing mention.[17]

More obtrusively, in his autobiography John was eager to air his dislikes. His book was written in the spirit of literary revenge. It was self-proclaimedly the work of an angry man (3.57) in a long tradition of invective which, if by the sixth century often rather repetitively stereotypical, was both recognized and celebrated as reaching back to the greatest orators, playwrights, and historians of the distant classical past. Like many convinced of the rightness of their own particular cause, John aimed in *On the Magistracies* "to expose the wicked and to praise the good" (3.39). In describing the policies, characters, and personal habits of those whom he blamed for ruining his once-glittering career he pulled no punches. John the Cappadocian was his prime target. Amid a long litany of lurid claims, he offered his readers a cartoonlike picture of the discharge of the Prefecture's official business under the Cappadocian's administration.

> Harlots led him on (while he was fondled by other naked harlots) with lascivious kisses which immediately impelled him to intercourse; and, when his capabilities waned, he used to seize on the delicacies and

drinks offered him by other catamites. So many and so frothy were these drinks that they made him sick. And when he could no longer keep them down, he vomited them forth, flooding the house like a torrent; and, as a result, he imposed no small danger on his flatterers, who used to slide around on the glistening mosaic floors.   (3.65)

It is precisely the explicitly personal, flagrantly polemical, and openly emotional character of John's autobiography which makes it such a fascinating text. At times, the unashamedly rhetorical force of his arguments, his often-strident and exaggerated responses to administrative change, and his carefully contrived strategies of self-presentation matter most. Above all, the importance of *On the Magistracies of the Roman State* lies in the extensive impression it offers of what it might have been like to be a later Roman bureaucrat. John's self-centered reminiscences convey something of the atmosphere and work practices of a major department in the imperial capital and of the consequences of a set of significant administrative reforms. These insights are unparalleled. As John, perhaps with rather too much evident pride, pointed out to his readers (in case they had any lingering doubts as to the authority of his account), "for, in fact, I know the Prefecture, not by secondhand report, but by having rendered service to its affairs by actual deeds" (1.15).

CHAPTER 1

All the Prefect's Men

Your duty as a civil servant is first and foremost to the Minister in charge of your department whom you must serve loyally and to the best of your ability. When a new party comes into power, your new Minister may require radical changes in the policy of your department. Your duty is to carry out the new policy with the same loyalty and commitment that you gave the old.

—*The Cabinet Office Staff Handbook*

Identity Parades

The ceremony which marked John Lydus' retirement from the eastern Praetorian Prefecture on April 1, 552, was a grand occasion. Before all his assembled colleagues on the judicial side, John received the personal congratulations of the then prefect Hephaestus, who rose to greet and embrace him. "Expressing his gratitude and after countless commendations," the prefect read out an official citation which acknowledged both John's erudition and his administrative expertise:

> When the most learned John served in our courts of justice, he maintained a certain single harmony through all things, following his own models in all cases and teaching through his deeds that a nature which is noble and able to impart what is particularly useful does not become separated from its own outstanding qualities (no matter what style of life it might adopt) but makes its virtue more worthy of respect when it adorns it with learning and with public affairs. For this reason, John, holding the rank of *clarissimus,* has earned a good reputation in all these things, and since he has reached the end both of his duties and of the succession of posts in our courts of justice he will hasten in the footsteps of our great emperor and will henceforward enjoy greater rewards.   (3.30)[1]

April 1 was a significant day for both the emperor and the staff of the Prefecture. It marked the twenty-fifth anniversary of Justinian's accession to the imperial throne, and it was the day on which the judicial side's senior officers retired and those next in line were promoted.[2] As a retiring *cornicularius* (the highest-ranking post on the judicial side), John was granted the honorary title of *tribunus et notarius* and was made a *comes primi ordinis* with the rank of *spectabilis*.[3] These were coveted honors and carried with them advantageous rights, privileges, and immunities. John's new status was conferred by the emperor in person. Having "adored the purple" (kissed the hem of the imperial robe), he received his *codicilli* (3.4), a document case consisting of two hinged plaques, each about 30 centimeters long. Those presented to the highest-ranking officials in the empire were of ivory trimmed with gold. For lesser honors—like John's—they were probably made of bronze, wood, or parchment. Their outer face displayed a portrait bust of the emperor; inside, over the imperial signature, were the necessary documents of appointment.[4]

The ceremony at which the *codicilli* were presented was memorably magnificent. Its climax is represented on the so-called Missorium of Theodosius I, a massive, shieldlike, solid silver plate, 74 centimeters in diameter, made to commemorate the tenth anniversary of the accession of that emperor in January 388. On the back, an inscription proudly advertises its impressive weight: fifty Roman pounds of silver. On the beautifully engraved front, under an elaborate pediment, Theodosius appears enthroned between his junior colleagues Valentinian II and Arcadius. Each wears a diadem of pearls; each is crowned by a halo. Unmoved beneath their gorgeous robes of state, flanked by their bodyguards, they present a powerful image of majesty. Together they sit with statuesque rigidity. Together they stare ahead, impassive, unperturbed, as if to meet the gaze of any viewer insolent enough to intrude into their imperial presence. In front of Theodosius stands a richly dressed official who, having adored the purple, now receives his *codicilli*. The official's hands are carefully veiled to prevent the sacrilege of touching an emperor's person. This figure is shown in much smaller scale than the seated emperors. Their very size underscores their superiority and the subordinate position of any (no matter how distinguished) who come before them. Here everything is shown in intricate detail: the armor and shields of the guards; the stripes and complex designs of the official's clothes; the elegant, elongated fingers of the imperial right hand holding the *codicilli;* the *codicilli* themselves decorated with the emperor's portrait and carefully tied with ribbon.

Above all, this scene has an eternal quality. Against the flat, shining silver surface of the plate, these delicately chiseled images seem almost to float: detached, isolated, remote. Only an allegorical figure dares approach this ceremonial space. In the bottom third of the plate, a half-naked woman representing the fruitful earth reclines in a field of corn. Around her, bearing gifts of fruit and flowers, three playful *putti* romp joyously. These charming personifications of prosperity and imperial beneficence emphasize the generosity of the emperors toward those who serve them. But they are also reminders of the high honors which wise rulers, wishing to promote the welfare and good governance of their realm, should grant their faithful officials. John, ever encouraging Justinian to restore the state by restoring the Praetorian Prefecture, would have strongly approved.[5]

The solid silver Missorium of Theodosius captured a central moment in imperial ceremonial, at least from a bureaucrat's point of view. Like a still from a movie, it froze in timeless splendor a newly elevated official standing before an emperor. But at court, John saw not only an emperor, but also his entourage augmented by the senior staff of the Prefecture, who, marching in carefully ordered ranks, had escorted him to the palace (3.30, 3.35). These military parallels were deliberate. In part reflecting its origins, many of the formal trappings of later Roman bureaucracy were closely modeled on the army. Service was known simply as *militia;* on appointment, officials in the Praetorian Prefecture were enrolled in the fictive *legio I adiutrix* (3.3). Some bureaucratic terminology still retained its military style. *Agentes in rebus* (a corps of imperial agents and messengers attached to the palace) advanced through five service grades with the same titles as noncommissioned ranks in the cavalry: *equites, circitores, biarchi, centenarii,* and *ducenarii.*[6] Even in the sixth century, the head of all the administrative staff in the eastern Praetorian Prefecture, the *princeps officii*—who had certainly never seen any real military service in his life—still carried a centurion's swagger stick as a badge of office (2.19). Most important, bureaucrats wore uniform. A mid to late fourth-century tomb painting from Durostorum (modern Silistra in Bulgaria) shows a provincial bureaucrat with attendant slaves carrying black leather shoes *(campagi),* a white long-sleeved tunic *(tunica),* a military-style cloak *(chlamys),* and a heavily decorated broad leather belt *(cingulum).*[7] The empire's highest-ranking magistrates were even more splendidly attired. For the passing out parade on April 1, the praetorian prefect no doubt wore full dress uniform, including a sword (2.9). In that fulsome and rather too expansive style beloved of experts, John clearly delighted in displaying his extensive knowledge of the technical details. As well as the flame-colored cloak with its golden stripes and the deep purple tunic, the prefect's *cingulum* received John's particular attention: "On the left side, it had a crescent made of gold; on the other, it had a tongue-shaped fastening or insert (it, too, gold-finished) made in the shape of a bunch of grapes . . . This insert, when drawn from the right and fastened to the crescent, girded its wearer securely because the pin (it, too, golden) bit into the strap and linked the bunch of grapes to the crescent" (2.13).

To judge by surviving representations, other prominent officials were also elaborately dressed. In Egypt, at the turn of the third century, a small hall within the pharaonic temple of Ammon in Luxor was remodeled to serve as a chapel for the imperial cult. The conversion, a few years after the emperor Diocletian's suppression of a serious revolt in Egypt in 297–298, was part of an extensive reconstruction of the whole temple complex as a fortified military camp. In the hall, the limestone blocks with their carefully carved hieroglyphs were plastered over and brightly painted. Although much of this fresco has now been hacked away (mostly by late nineteenth-century enthusiasts eager to reveal the Egyptian reliefs beneath), it is still possible to catch a glimpse of a once beautifully depicted imperial court.

On the hall's southern wall, a niche frames representations of the tetrarchs, the four co-emperors Diocletian, Maximian, Galerius, and Constantius Chlorus. They are shown standing against a light blue background, each dressed in purple robes, each of their heads ringed by a yellow halo. One emperor—perhaps Diocletian, the most senior —carries a blue globe and a long golden scepter. In front of the niche, an impressive canopy *(ciborium)*, supported on four columns of reddish-pink Aswan granite, covers a throne or perhaps an altar. On either side, skillfully frescoed officials form part of a procession which includes soldiers and their commanders. The civilian courtiers wear tunics decorated with multicolored medallions *(segmenta)*, their broad hems exquisitely embroidered. Their shoes are embossed and stamped with intricate designs. Around their waists they sport jeweled belts with finely wrought clasps. One official holds a staff of office, another gestures deferentially. Several (like the fourth-century bureaucrat standing before Theodosius) have their hands and forearms veiled. Even damaged, these fragmentary figures offer a striking image of courtly magnificence, still processing in silent ceremonial splendor toward four faded emperors on the southern wall.[8]

Both Diocletian and Galerius had led expeditionary forces to Egypt in the 290s. Diocletian visited Alexandria in late 297 and again in 302 (on the first occasion he besieged and captured the city). In the summer of 298 he sailed up the Nile, perhaps as far south as Aswan.[9] Diocletian may have stopped at Luxor. But—like Maximian and Constantius Chlorus—most later Roman emperors never set foot in the province. Away from court and Constantinople or from other great cities like Antioch, Rome, and Milan, the overwhelming majority of the empire's inhabitants could only imagine what it might be like to see an emperor, to enter the imperial presence, or to adore the purple. As in the frescos from the temple of Ammon, something of the sheer majesty of such an occasion is captured in the well-known mosaic from the apse of the church of San Vitale (consecrated in the late 540s) in Ravenna. Here Justinian stands resplendent in purple and gold, his head (like those of the painted tetrarchs in Luxor) encircled by a halo. He wears a gem-encrusted diadem and large pearl earrings. On one side of the emperor stand courtiers, their long white cloaks emblazoned with *segmenta*. On the other side stand two tonsured clerics led by Maximianus, bishop of Ravenna (whose name appears above his head, in case there should be any doubt as to his presence or his influential proximity to the emperor). Behind Justinian and Maximianus is another high-ranking official sometimes identified as the praetorian prefect of Italy. As on the Missorium of Theodosius, this representation of emperor and court has a transcendent, otherworldly quality. Against its ground of gold mosaic, the shimmering brilliance of this glittering ceremonial moment distances an emperor and his entourage from the more monochrome world of the less powerful. Before the staring, unblinking gaze of these figures the ordinary viewer is humbled, not so much looked at, as looked through.[10]

That the construction of distance was an important part of imperial ceremonial—whether enacted or represented—was also recognized by contemporaries. Thirteen years after John had kissed the hem of Justinian's purple robe and received his *codicilli,* the poet Flavius

Cresconius Corippus celebrated in four books of Latin verse the accession of Justin II in mid-November 565 and his inauguration as consul on New Year's Day six weeks later. Once a small-town teacher in provincial Africa, Corippus had moved to Constantinople, perhaps following the success of his epic poem in praise of Justinian's general John Troglita, who in the late 540s had crushed a Moorish rebellion in Tripolitania. Like John Lydus, Corippus had been attracted to the imperial capital and the chance of a post in the central administration. He seems to have realized his ambition, probably serving in the *sacra scrinia* (the palace secretariats responsible for judicial and administrative matters directly involving the emperor).[11] Like John, too, Corippus had a good eye for ceremony. His poem contained a series of virtuoso set pieces: Justinian's lying in state and his funeral; Justin's coronation, his acclamation in the Hippodrome, his inauguration as consul, and his distribution of largesse to the Senate and other officials. One scene which particularly captured Corippus' imagination was the sight of the emperor and his court in the principal audience chamber *(consistorium)* of the Great Palace in Constantinople.

> A lofty hall stands in the huge building gleaming with a sun of metal . . . The imperial throne ennobles the innermost sanctum, set with four marvelous columns over which a canopy, shining as if of liquid gold, shades, like the vault of the curving sky, the immortal head and throne of the emperor as he sits there. The throne is adorned with jewels and is proud with purple and gold.[12]

This imperial audience chamber was part of the original fourth-century palace built by Constantine. To reach it, John, on the day of his retirement, accompanied by the stately parade of his colleagues from the Praetorian Prefecture, passed through a series of impressive buildings. They entered the palace through the Chalke, or Brazen House, a vast domed structure situated at the southern corner of the Augusteion. This large square, surrounded by porticoes and dominated by a tall column topped by an equestrian statue of Justinian, lay between the rebuilt Hagia Sophia (dedicated in December 537) and the imperial palace. The interior of the Chalke was decorated with a series of fine mosaics. Completed a decade before John's retirement, they showed Justinian and his wife, the empress Theodora, standing in majesty surrounded by the Senate. Together they presided over a triumph depicting the return of Belisarius' army bearing the spoils of campaigns against the Vandals in Africa and the Ostrogoths in Italy. Gelimer the Vandal king had been brought in captivity to Constantinople in 534, Witiges the Ostrogothic king in 540. John, whose autobiography proudly noted these military successes (3.1, 3.54–56) and the capture of both kings (2.2, 3.55), and who himself twenty years before had been asked by Justinian to write a history of his Persian wars (3.28), would no doubt have strongly approved of this display of the empire's military strength.

But even these remarkable images must have been overshadowed by the grandeur which followed. Having processed through the Great Palace to the *consistorium,* there in silent wonder John and his fellow bureaucrats beheld the brilliant vision of an emperor enthroned beneath a golden canopy, flanked by his bodyguards, surrounded by the shining splendor of his court.[13] In the same imperial audience hall thirteen years later, in 565, Justin II heard an embassy sent by the Avars to demand the continued payment of subsidies in return for peace. (This tribe had first appeared north of the Caucasus in the late 550s and had been bought off by Justinian. Moving toward the Danube in 561, they had continued to exert pressure on the empire's northern frontier.) Something of the awe inspired by the august state occasion on which the Avar ambassadors were received was vividly conveyed by Corippus' panegyric. Ushered into the *consistorium,* these barbarians suddenly found themselves entering another world.

> The wide floor was wondrous with its paving; carpets were spread over it . . . Hangings covered the doors. Guards stood at the lofty entrance and kept out anyone unworthy who wished to enter . . . When the officials, with their groups arranged in order, had taken their places in the decorated palace, a glorious light shone from the inner chamber and filled the whole audience hall. The emperor came forth.[14]

The Avars' response to this imperial tableau was (in Corippus' version) equally dramatic. Like wild beasts released into the arena they were tamed by the sight which confronted them.[15]

> Tergazis the Avar looked up at the head of the emperor shining with the holy diadem. He then lay down three times in adoration and remained fixed to the ground. The other Avars followed him in similar fear and fell on their faces, and brushed the carpets with their fore-

heads, and filled the spacious halls with their long hair and the imperial palace with their huge limbs.[16]

The Avars were model viewers of imperial ceremonial. In the presence of an emperor in all his glory they knew themselves to be inferior. In their wide-eyed astonishment they were struck dumb by the gulf which separated barbarity from civilization. Gazing in wild surmise at those around the throne—at officials "in different uniforms, clothing, dress, and appearance" who stood with radiant countenances like "the golden shining stars in the curving sky"—the Avars could be forgiven for believing (at least in Corippus' imagination) that "the Roman palace was indeed another heaven."[17]

It is important to linger over these snapshots of a courtly world. They give some indication both of how senior officials saw themselves and of how they might have wished to have been seen by others. Any view of later Roman bureaucracy (in addition to the details of departments, responsibilities, and administrative procedures) must also include an image of the serried ranks of splendidly dressed officials. With due solemnity they surrounded the throne or escorted their retiring colleagues into the imperial presence so that they might kiss the hem of the emperor's robe. For John, this was the crowning moment of a long bureaucratic career, the moment when, in the elegant phrase of a law of 381, he was "associated with immortality."[18] In his own account of his retirement ceremony, he claimed the autobiographer's privilege to place himself (alongside the prefect and the emperor) at center stage. He omitted any reference to other members of staff retiring or receiving their promotions who must also have been praised in congratulatory decrees and have taken their places in the same procession.

But this imposing occasion was not a fitting moment to reiterate personal grievances, or to lament the decline of the judicial side of the Prefecture under John the Cappadocian, or to complain of the advancement of rivals. For once, silence would suffice. Rather, for John, these ceremonies marked out more significant divisions. Through their sheer grandeur and hieratic formality they helped to construct a clear difference between those involved in the administration of empire and those in the world outside. In all their deliberate exaggeration, they emphasized the close relationship between an emperor and his officials, and the powerful position enjoyed by the great departments of state. This was more than mere pomp and circumstance. The public display of proximity to an emperor mattered. The participation of bureaucrats in imperial ceremonies underwrote John's insistent claim that officials were important people. Corippus made the same point in more rococo terms, perhaps again reflecting something of his fellow bureaucrats' own idealized views of their prominence in the scheme of things.

> The imperial palace with its officials is like Olympus. Everything is as bright, everything as well-ordered in its ranks, as gleaming with light: just as the golden shining stars in the curving sky complete their movements balanced in measure, number, and weight, and remain fixed in the unchanging pattern in which they set. And just as one light shines over all, all the stars yield to its superior flames, and they feed on the fire of their monarch, by which they remain eclipsed.[19]

It mattered, too, that an emperor might personally confer honors on long-serving officials. Forty years before, John had been one of many provincials seeking advancement in the imperial capital. For those bureaucrats with similar backgrounds and ambitions, that they might join the privileged ranks of those who had adored the purple alone made these occasions worth celebrating and worth remembering. Equally memorable, particularly for those involved, was the way in which these majestic events, with their carefully contrived magnificence, their military style processions, and their impressive rituals, enforced a striking display of unity and esprit de corps. For uniformed bureaucrats on show to the outside world, what mattered most was a strong impression of strength and solidarity. In public, the organized parade of institutional loyalty and collegiality came first. For a short while, personal regrets and bitter rivalries were made to seem less pressing. Of this, too, John approved. Proudly processing through the streets of Constantinople, few could have thought him in private a disappointed man or guessed at the depth of his dislike for some of his colleagues who accompanied him to the Great Palace.

According to the Experts . . .

For John, grand ceremonies, along with a complex set of "customs, forms, and language" (*Pr.* 2.7), helped mark out the distance which separated bureaucrats from "outsiders" (3.9). John was ever eager to impress on his readers both the splendor and the strangeness of the official environment in which he claimed to move with ease. As well as describing something of the internal organization of the Praetorian Prefecture, its recruitment and promotion practices, he also carefully catalogued the details of high officials' uniforms and their "distinctive regalia" (1.7; see, for example, 1.7–8, 1.17, 1.32, 1.37, 2.2, 2.4, 2.13–14). He particularly called his readers' attention to the way both ordinary objects, such as axes, inkwells, or swords (1.32, 2.14, 2.9), and everyday procedures, such as writing or timekeeping (3.11–14, 2.16), were transformed within a bureaucratic context. Here they assumed a symbolic significance obscure to the untrained observer. Yet, with the broad exception of his long digressions on philological obscurities and matters of antiquarian interest (included principally to impress fellow *érudits*), John's account of his own department was intended neither to elucidate its structure nor to explain its practices. John was in no sense writing a user's guide to later Roman bureaucracy. Rather, his "special and separate account concerning the greatest staff of the foremost of the magistracies" (3.1) frequently underlined the bewildering and tortuous complexities of his administrative world.

For the uninitiated, later Roman officialdom must often have seemed like a foreign country with inexplicable customs and an incomprehensible language. Only a highly educated expert could hope, and then only after many years' experience, to have sufficient knowledge of the correct forms, styles, and procedures necessary for the successful conduct of administrative affairs. John had little sympathy for those who failed to grasp the technical details. He complained patronizingly that some people could not even master basic bureaucratic vocabulary. Mispronouncing the official title of one of the emperor's confidential personal secretariats as *adsecretis*—rather than correctly as *a secretis*—reflected "the usage of the uneducated who out of ignorance add to the preposition the letter 'd'" (3.20). The use by "ordinary people" of the term *priuatoriae* instead of *probatoriae* to describe an official's certificate of appointment was the result of "an illiterate guess" (3.2; see also 1.23, 2.4, 2.6, 2.9). Only once did John apparently relent. In introducing his extended and elaborate discussion of the doubling of the senior-ranking posts on the judicial side of the Praetorian Prefecture, he remarked: "So that the circumstances of the division may not escape even outsiders—for in fact the common people, because they do not understand, daily make inquiries in vain, being confused by the aforementioned designations—I shall point out in my account the reason for the partition of the one corps into two" (3.9). But in the explanation of the Prefecture's internal organization which followed, John gave little away. Many of his statements still remain as confusing and as contradictory as they must have seemed to contemporaries not themselves bureaucrats. John's technical language, like the formal grandeur of imperial ceremonies, consciously and deliberately excluded outsiders. In his description of the procedure followed in the prefect's court, he used in one short passage, without any explanation, six different terms to describe the process of recording a judgment.[20] Similarly, his listing of taxes levied by John the Cappadocian in the 530s remains as opaque and as alienating today as it must have seemed to any sixth-century reader without the necessary expertise to decode the stream of bureaucratic jargon: "*censualia, holographika, bouleutika, homodoula, homokensa, aphantika, enkataleleimmena, politika, tamiaka, deputata, recollata, relegata, refusa, keratismoi, ropai, parallagai, tokoi, endomatika, metatorika . . . meritika, suffragia, comitatensia, monoptera, monastika, apemelemena, leukochrysa*" (3.70).[21]

Technical language, distinctive military-style uniforms, correct procedures, and carefully regulated hierarchies all helped to separate the formal, highly structured world of officialdom from the less formal, private world of "ordinary people." Like the imperial images on the Missorium of Theodosius, in Luxor, and in Ravenna, later Roman bureaucrats must have appeared to many as distant and powerful figures. That was an impression John and his colleagues would have been pleased to convey. For them, formality, impenetrability, and obscurity were important protective strategies. At court (near an emperor) and in the provinces (near a governor), those outsiders jealous of the influence wielded by officials could not so easily exploit or colonize an organization with its own intricate rules and complex work practices. In many cases it was often quicker and more effective to enlist the cooperation of bureaucrats than to attempt to bypass or oppose them.

Similarly, many ordinary people faced with a set of rules and procedures which they could never hope to understand (and which they always feared could be suddenly turned against them) were forced to reach an accommodation with officials offering to perform administrative services. As John repeatedly made clear, the government of empire was not the proper concern of a private citizen. To be well executed, it required an expensive education, long experience, and above all a specialized knowledge of the relevant administrative arcana. Only an expert would know a department's "registers, titles, and duties" and the "practices, forms, and terms" to be used in drafting any necessary documentation (2.22). And in John's view, only bureaucrats could offer such a service.

The formal trappings of officialdom (on splendid display at the ceremony marking the retirement of bureaucrats in the eastern Praetorian Prefecture) were also important in promoting a strong and highly valued sense of corporate identity. For John, a feeling of belonging to a recognizably separate organization was doubly significant. It was another factor which marked out officials as different from the rest of the world. Importantly too, in a predatory administrative environment, it also helped to define boundaries between groups of officials. Faced with the need to defend their own area of responsibility against the expansionary claims of rival departments, officials with similar interests banded together for protection and mutual support. They formed close-knit, self-interested cliques. Similarities among members of a particular department were emphasized, differences between rivals exaggerated.

Something of this pattern was reflected in the less formal terms for bureaucrats sometimes used in imperial legislation: *praefectiani* (the staff of the praetorian prefect); *magistriani* (the staff of the *magister officiorum*, the head of the palatine bureaucracy); *urbaniciani* (the staff of the urban prefect of Rome, the high-ranking imperial official in charge of the administration of the city).[22] It was also evident in John's repetitive insistence on the greatness of the Prefecture and the inherent inferiority of other, more recently established departments. As John continually reminded his readers, the Prefecture's antiquity was a self-evident guarantee of its excellence. Against his careful exposition of "the perfections of former times" (3.68), the inadequacies of newer magistracies were clearly exposed. John claimed (seemingly without irony) that those who served under the *magister officiorum* were unable to escape from their own "arrogant-bundling-together-of-wordiness" (3.7).[23] Those appointed to either of the two chief financial posts in the empire (the *comes sacrarum largitionum* and the *comes rei priuatae*) were not even to be reckoned as magistrates, "for they are of recent origin" (2.27). By contrast, as John's autobiography set out to show, only the Praetorian Prefecture, which "from the beginning was subordinate to the scepter alone" (2.9), could justify its claims to superiority. In John's view, only its officials could be indisputably considered "the greatest staff of the foremost of the magistracies" (3.1).

Those on the inside also knew that these differences could be made to cut across departments. Within the eastern Praetorian Prefecture, John himself rarely missed an opportunity to illustrate the divisions he believed lay between the skilled and highly educated officials who had once competed to join the Prefecture, and the raw recruits whom the Cappadocian openly favored (2.18, 3.9, 3.14). In a convoluted play on words, John remarked that the common mispronunciation of *probatoria* as *priuatoria* (though still to be sneered at) was better suited to these newcomers. While clearly as *praefectiani* they "performed public functions," their very lack of experience and qualifications meant that they "did not differ from a private person" (3.2). In John's opinion, a similar rift separated the *exceptores* (who staffed the judicial side of the Prefecture) from the *scriniarii* (who staffed the financial side). Like the inexperienced and unqualified, the *scriniarii* were properly to be considered "private citizens," not public officials (3.31, 3.35). Until the end of the fourth century, they had not been regarded as fully part of the prefect's staff and had not worn uniform. "But under Theodosius I . . . they collected money as an inducement and petitioned the emperor to be reckoned in with the staff. And after they had succeeded in that, they obtained *probatoriae*, as they are known, and were promoted into the ranks of the *adiutores* (that is, those who assist) on an equal footing with the others" (3.35).[24]

To the skilled observer of ceremony, the inferior position of the *scriniarii* was still clearly on view, even if now, like the *exceptores,* they, too, wore the *cingulum* as part of their official dress. For, as John pointed out, whenever the prefect processed to his tribunal he was preceded by the judicial staff in all its ordered splendor, with the rest of the department, including the *scriniarii,* merely "trailing behind" (3.35).[25] Again, such ceremonial moments mattered. What to an outsider might look like a uniform procession of officials, might also display finer divisions and more subtle internal tensions visible only to the highly trained expert. In John's version, the same factors which distinguished bureaucrats from ordinary people also sharply divided experienced, established officials from new, unqualified recruits, and, most importantly of all, separated *exceptores* from *scriniarii.* And on this view, by parity of reasoning (or invective), these men, though undeniably officials offering a public service, were as unfit as any private citizen to govern an empire.

How widely shared John's opinions were among his colleagues on the Prefecture's judicial side it is impossible to say. But his attacks on the *scriniarii,* and his attempts to enforce a clear division between two sets of bureaucrats within the same department, again emphasized the significance (at least to insiders) of specialist knowledge, technical competence, and the observance of formal protocols in constructing and reinforcing group identity. Greater experience and superior expertise were a twofold shield which separated the judicial staff of the Prefecture both from the world outside and from others serving in the imperial administration. It helped to defend them against rivals, most of whom (at least ideally) lacked the necessary skills to pose any serious threat. The difficulty of effectively reallocating specialist or highly technical tasks might also reduce the risks of any loss of responsibility as a result of administrative reform. It was clearly in a well-run department's best interests that it both preserve the need for its own expertise and emphasize the importance of its own internal working practices.

John would no doubt have strongly approved of the ruling handed down in 368 by the emperors Valentinian I and Valens which reprimanded a provincial governor for allowing his officials to use *litterae caelestes* (literally "heavenly writing") in the documents prepared for onward transmission to the court. The governor was reminded that this form of script was the exclusive preserve of bureaucrats in the *sacra scrinia* (the palatine secretariats most closely associated with the emperor). Palace officials' mastery of a particular style of handwriting helped guard against forgeries. It marked out these documents as unmistakably imperial.[26] In John's opinion, too, complexity in administration was also an important guarantor of justice. It was a matter of pride that each case which came before the prefect's tribunal was summarized twice. One abstract was the responsibility of the high-ranking official known as the *secretarius,* the other (the *personalium*) of the most experienced *adiutor* (principal assistant) attached to the *ab actis,* the senior official on the judicial side in charge of civil cases and court records (3.11, 3.20).[27] Nor was the compilation of two separate summaries—both in Latin—to be seen as overly bureaucratic or needlessly inefficient. Rather, in John's view, this duplication was an important precaution against fraud, forgery, or loss. "And I myself well remember such an occurrence. For although a hearing had been held, the transactions relevant to the case were nowhere to be found. But when the *personalium,* as it is known, had been brought before the magistracy, the case was completely restored" (3.20). As John repeatedly insisted, the intricate formalities surrounding hearings in the prefect's court operated to the advantage of those seeking justice. Faced with the judicial staff's impressive qualifications, their long experience, and their detailed knowledge of correct procedure, litigants could (at least in John's version) only "marvel at the court of justice for its precision" (3.11), even if on some occasions they must have had little idea of what was going on.

Given the advantages which knowledge and experience conferred (at least on expert officials), any move to make specialist skills redundant was strongly resisted, even more so when such reforms were promoted by a praetorian prefect. John was both angered and perplexed by the decision of Cyrus of Panopolis (in office from December 439 to August 441 under Theodosius II) to issue his legal judgments and decrees in Greek rather than Latin. This was a significant change. Of course, Greek had been a fundamental part of Roman government in the eastern Mediterranean since the Republic. It was the language of court hearings, of many standard legal documents (petitions, contracts, bills of sale), and of much official paperwork (reports, tax lists, and land registers), particularly at provincial level. But Latin also had a technical and professional importance. The 2,500 pieces of legislation gathered together in the *Theodosian Code* (a consolidated collection of imperial edicts issued two years before Cyrus was appointed prefect) were all in Latin. Without it, full mastery of the law was impossible.

Cyrus' decision was part of a series of countermeasures aimed at breaking down that linguistic barrier. In 397 the emperors Arcadius and Honorius had allowed provincial governors to issue their judgments in Greek. In September 439, Theodosius II confirmed the validity of wills written by Roman citizens in Greek.[28] By the turn of the fourth century, Latin was no longer the language of instruction at the empire's most prestigious law schools in Constantinople and Berytus (modern Beirut). Legal textbooks and commentaries were written in

Greek. From the mid-530s on, most of Justinian's legislation (unless specifically directed at the Latin-speaking West) was promulgated in Greek.[29] His law of 535 ratifying the mid-fifth-century emperor Leo's regulations on the alienation of property by religious foundations set out the advantages of this change simply and clearly. "We decree that this law [of Leo] shall be valid in all these matters, and we confirm it. And for this reason we have promulgated and caused it to be written not in the language of our ancestors but in everyday speech, that is, in Greek, so that through ease of understanding it might become known to all."[30]

Imperial praise for administrative transparency, however worthy, was not echoed by John. Those on the judicial side of the eastern Praetorian Prefecture strongly objected to the gradual replacement of Latin as the specialist language of government. They took great pride in their hard-won linguistic competence. They valued those tasks which only a limited number of officials with the appropriate language skills could perform. Nor, on this view, were time-honored practices to be violated without serious consequences. Inevitably the Prefecture suffered first. John explicitly linked Cyrus' reform with the loss of a wide range of administrative responsibilities.

> For the emperor was persuaded to issue a law which relieved the Prefecture of all its power. For, although until that time it was within its remit both to reduce taxes and to grant funds to the cities for grain, lighting, spectacles, and the restoration of public facilities, thereafter it had insufficient authority, nor did it dare to allocate from public dues any assistance, no matter how small, for any of these things.   (3.42)

And this was only an indication of things to come. John regarded the displacement of Latin as the fulfillment of an oracle given long ago to Rome's first king, Romulus, "that Fortune would abandon the Romans when they forgot their ancestral tongue" (2.12 = 3.42).[31] In John's view, Cyrus' decision to use Greek as the official language of government marked the beginning of the decline and fall of the Roman Empire.

Despite Cyrus' reforms and their apparently far-reaching consequences, when John first joined the eastern Praetorian Prefecture at the beginning of the sixth century some important internal documents were still written in Latin: the papers enrolling a new member of staff in the fictive *legio I adiutrix* (3.3); the warrants issued by the *primiscrinius* (the second-highest-ranking official on the judicial side) appointing *executores* to enforce decisions of the prefect's court (3.12); the briefs for matters to go on appeal from the prefect to the emperor *(suggestiones)* (3.27); and the summaries of cases on which judgment had been entered, kept by both the *ab actis* (the *personalia*) and by the *secretarius* (3.20, 3.11). Early in his career John himself had drafted both *suggestiones* and *personalia* (3.27).[32]

The level of linguistic ability these administrative tasks required should not be overestimated. Most were repetitive and formulaic. For John, Latin was a dead language, a useful quarry for philological curiosities and pithy quotations from authoritative sources. In the course of his autobiography (as befitted the holder of a chair at the State University in the imperial capital) he discussed the proper use, meaning, and derivation of more than thirty Latin words. He also cited admiringly a range of commentaries and handbooks written in Latin, in some cases repeating the mistakes of their authors.[33] But these learned asides were intended primarily as impressive tokens of a particular technical aptitude, rather than as evidence of any wider literary or critical ability. They emphasized John's formal mastery of a complex and difficult field. They demonstrated the ease with which an expert could impose order on a seemingly confusing and unrelated set of minutiae. For John, his linguistic competence (like a detailed knowledge of ceremonial, uniforms, or correct administrative procedure) was best presented as a specialist skill. His was a very bureaucratic expertise. It was yet another factor which could be seen both to separate well-educated officials from the outside world and to distinguish those on the Prefecture's judicial side from others in the imperial bureaucracy lacking their technical accomplishment.

From this perspective, any move to reduce the importance of Latin within the Prefecture was a serious matter. If some knowledge of the language should no longer be required for the successful completion of litigation or for other administrative transactions, rival departments, whose members lacked the necessary skills or education, could more easily encroach on responsibilities traditionally the preserve of the judicial side. Once, according to John, those on the staff of the Prefecture "were eager to excel in the language of the Romans, for it was indispensably useful to them" (3.27). But now Latin was no longer a prerequisite for those seeking appointment or promotion. Among his many complaints, John cited the treatment of the diocese of Thrace as a model example of the danger faced by any department whose exclusive claim to certain tasks was based on its staff's expertise. In this administrative district (the diocese covering, until reforms in 536, six provinces to the west of the Black Sea, an area now occupied by Romania, Albania, and European Turkey) Greek replaced Latin as the official language of government. "The Cappadocian changed it into a haggish and base idiom, not because he cared for clarity (as he alleged) but so that it might be convenient and colloquial and cause no difficulty to those who, in accord with his aim, dared to complete what certainly did not concern them. For he transacted business, wrote, innovated, and in every way undermined the ancient ways" (3.68).

Normal administrative procedures were ignored. Bureaucrats from the Praetorian Prefecture were replaced by men sent out from the Cappadocian's own personal staff. The results, at least according to John, were predictable. The opening up of official tasks to the inexpert and inexperienced, who in addition knew only Greek, inevitably led to chaos and inefficiency. The crass ignorance of these careless incompetents meant that many documents were issued even though those responsible for the paperwork did not understand what they were doing. Nor was there any supervision, cross-checking, or proper recording of what had been done. The *cottidiana,* the daily registers summarizing business transacted in the department of the *ab actis* (3.20, 3.68), were no longer compiled. Without these safeguards, John alleged, it was provincial taxpayers who suffered most. "Whenever significant difficulties arose for the taxpayers because the documents had not been processed according to the proper procedures, the Cappadocian grew angry and sentenced to death those who did not understand the force of the documents which had been so carelessly and haphazardly issued" (3.68).

Given these baleful consequences, the claims made by John the Cappadocian, echoing those in Justinian's legislation, that the introduction of Greek and the simplification of procedures would result in greater transparency and increased efficiency were, in John's view, patently false (3.68). In his opinion, the Cappadocian's justifications for this reform were shallow excuses for promoting his own ill-educated men; unconvincing arguments advanced to lend a moral gloss to a bare-faced and well-judged attack on administrative tasks properly undertaken only by fully qualified officials. In the face of such threatening innovations, it was vitally important that the advantage secured through the expertise of a department's staff be maintained. As John repeatedly moralized, effective government could be guaranteed only by well-educated officials highly proficient in the difficult and complex business of administration. On this point John was uncompromisingly clear. Like many modern lawyers or accountants, many later Roman bureaucrats were strongly committed to the perpetuation of a system in which their hard-won mastery of specific technical skills helped both to protect their position and to secure their income. For experts, specialization was a strategic advantage not lightly to be surrendered.

Building Societies

Among later Roman bureaucrats, a common educational background, a shared technical expertise, and the formal trappings of a uniformed officialdom all helped to promote a sense of unity and identity. Some degree of solidarity was fundamental to the successful operation of any department or group of officials (such as *scriniarii* or *exceptores*). Only by working together could an advantageous allocation of administrative tasks be most effectively defended against rival groups eager to expand the areas over which they had control. No doubt it mattered, too, that losses in responsibility were also shared. This emphasis on mutuality was an important factor in regulating the relationship among bureaucrats. Individuals had always to weigh their own ambitions or the chances of immediate personal gain against the pressure to act in conformity with the perceived best interests of their colleagues. These choices must often have been relatively unproblematic. Many bureaucrats valued highly both the reciprocal benefits and the feeling of security which collegiality offered. Many also supported their fellow officials out of a deeply felt sense of duty and loyalty.

Mutuality was a virtue to be paraded. John continually stressed the importance of a sense of solidarity among his fellow *exceptores*. It colored his memories of his first years in the Prefecture and his account of its decline. John was proud of his colleagues' successes and affected to have shared equally in the worst of their misfortunes. In his later years, he claimed greatly to miss that feeling of camaraderie. He found his fellow professors in the State University of Constantinople argumentative and uncooperative. According to John, even an emperor had been frustrated in his attempt to accord a higher status to university teachers. Though an enthusiastic supporter of education and learning, Anastasius, "hindered by their disagreements," had abandoned his plans. Similarly exasperated at what he regarded as academics' inherent inability to act together in their own best interests (even in concert with a willing emperor), John ruefully reflected that "intellectuals are naturally prone to disagree among themselves, because of their detachment from reality" (3.47).

By contrast, in John's view, no right-thinking group of bureaucrats would ever have let internal discord impair its collective chances of advancement. Bureaucrats, despite their evident scholarly erudition, had no such overriding commitment to individuality. Their horizons were differently bounded. In attempting to ensure a successful career and a secure retirement, any group of officials was principally concerned to reconcile the sometimes conflicting claims of personal advantage and corporate benefit. The maintenance of such a difficult series of trade-offs resulted in a set of complex regulations and work practices. In part, that delicate negotiation rested on the knowledge that in a harsh competitive environment mutual support and cooperation were the best defenses against administrative rivals. In part (in addition to the various technical and formal factors promoting solidarity), it was also dependent on the balancing of a set of organizational, financial, and personal relationships. The collective interest of a group of officials had continually to be weighed against the pressing claims of ambitious, talented, or well-connected individuals. Under such circumstances, the virtues of mutuality were not only to be paraded; they were also to be enforced.

In the eastern Praetorian Prefecture, the flow of rewards was carefully channeled. At the department's most senior level, the strict annual promotion and retirement of those holding high-ranking positions ensured a steady and predictable turnover of personnel. For *exceptores* (the "entry-level" grade on the judicial side) the opportunities to secure a well-paid position within the department were also strictly regulated. An *exceptor* was eligible to be selected as an *adiutor* (principal assistant to one of the department's senior officers) only after nine years in post (2.18). The appointment was for one year. Nor, it seems, could an *exceptor* serve as an *adiutor* in consecutive years (3.13). On the much more simply organized financial side of the Prefecture, a *scriniarius* (the basic grade, roughly equivalent to *exceptor*) might serve as a *chartularius* (a chief administrative officer attached to an *adiutor*) no more than four times, with a year's interval between appointments; or as an *adiutor* no more than four times, with a two-year interval.[34] Here, too, the rules seem to have been designed to prevent any one member of staff occupying a particularly remunerative post for too long. Among colleagues, opportunities for gain were to be more widely distributed.

The restriction of access to a range of well-paid posts was also a re- current concern of many of the surviving imperial laws dealing with the appointment and promotion of bureaucrats and the internal orga- nization of their departments. The overwhelming majority of these laws, spanning the period from the emperor Constantine at the begin- ning of the fourth century to Justinian in the middle of the sixth, are preserved in the *Theodosian* and *Justinianic Codes*. Regrettably, for the most part, the circumstances surrounding the issuing of any one law or its subsequent inclusion in the *Codes* are unknown. (Where the text contained such information, it was routinely edited out as part of the process of codification.) In some cases, imperial legislation dealing with administrative issues may have been intended to do no more than reiterate or confirm long-established protocols. In other cases, one group in a department may have been protesting against an alleged unfair dominance of certain posts and seeking redress or reform. In yet other cases, the supporters or proposers of these laws (including the emperor himself or rivals in a competing department) may have had their own motives for seeking to change accepted practice. That said, setting aside the particular reasons prompting the drafting or promulgation of specific regulations, a number of laws included in the *Codes* seem broadly concerned to ensure that certain more remunera- tive positions not be monopolized—or at least, not for too long—by one set of officials within a particular group or department.

An important element in promoting that aim was the emphasis on a set of formal rules based on seniority and attention to duty (which in many cases meant little more than active service).[35] The basic principle was laid down under Constantine in a law issued to the *consularis aquarum* (the official subordinate to the urban prefect in charge of the aqueducts in Rome) for the regulation of his staff: "The order of promotion is to be so observed that the senior-ranking official in a department is he who was first in obtaining his appointment from the emperor."[36] In 404 the *magister officiorum* (the head of the palatine bureaucracy) was instructed to oversee the promotion of *agentes in rebus* (a corps of imperial messengers and agents under his direct administrative control) so that "henceforth no one shall attempt to seize the place of a member of staff who has died, but as soon as the fates have carried that person off, that official who in the regular order of those receiving salaries and through the merit of his labors followed the deceased in the ranks of the department shall succeed and take possession of his predecessor's emoluments, and all deceit shall cease."[37]

Similarly, in 424 Theodosius II instructed the urban prefect of Rome that in the case of a vacancy arising in his department following the death of a member of staff or for any other reason, "the harm arising from the customary exercise of influence shall be eliminated and that person, whose name comes next as verified by the personnel register, shall obtain the position." The same concern for the orderly advancement of officials was also made clear in many of the laws which aimed to restrict the success or privileges of those seeking preferment by relying on the favorable recommendation of well-placed friends or connections, or by purchasing a position (tactics discussed in detail in Chapters 3 and 4).[38]

Other legislation displayed an equally strong interest in establishing a regular pattern of promotion by limiting the tenure of various posts. In 416 the *magister officiorum* was informed that the heads *(proximi)* of the *sacra scrinia* were to have their time in office reduced. "We decree that officials who by the regular order and merit of those receiving salaries in the three *scrinia* (the *scrinium memoriae, epistularum,* and *libellorum*) have reached the rank of *proximus* should henceforth serve for one year instead of two." Provision was made for those in the *sacra scrinia* to retire with high honors after twenty years of service.[39] The rate of advancement was also controlled by prescribing a maximum number of established officials in each department, or the number allowed to serve as *adiutores* assisting the highest-ranking officers, or the number to be promoted in any year. In 470 the emperor Leo ruled on the size of the *sacra scrinia*: 62 *memoriales,* 34 *epistulares,* and 34 *libellenses.*[40] Under the same emperor, an upper limit was also set on the permitted numbers of *agentes in rebus*, each to be ranked in one of five military-style grades.

> In allowing the register of the *agentes in rebus* drawn up by your highness [the *magister officiorum*], we order that from now on the number of *ducenarii* in post shall not exceed 48, and the number of *centenarii* shall not exceed 200 men, and they shall admit those who are eligible on the basis of their rank as determined by seniority. And in the same way the title and reward of those serving as *biarchi* shall be limited to 250 men, the *circitores* to 300, and the *equites* to 450.[41]

The smooth operation of this system was not to be disrupted by those appointed or promoted through influence or the payment of money; nor was it to be disturbed by absentees, who were to be demoted; nor by the return of those who had once held a post, who were to be ranked again at the bottom of the staff; nor by the joint holding of posts in different departments, which (with some minor exceptions) was disallowed; nor by holding the same position twice, which was penalized by heavy fines; nor by transferring from one department to another in midcareer, which was prohibited; nor by those whose status or profession disbarred them from serving in the imperial bureaucracy.[42]

Even more impressive than this scatter of legislation was the overview of later Roman administration contained in the surviving copy of the *notitia dignitatum.* The *notitia omnium dignitatum et administrationum tam ciuilium quam militarium* is, as its full title implies, "a list of all ranks and administrative positions both civil and military." Its compilation and updating were among the responsibilities of the *primicerius notariorum,* the most senior of the *notarii* (a secretariat closely associated with the emperor which functioned independently of the *magister officiorum*).[43] The copy of the *notitia* which survives provides a fairly comprehensive picture of the organization of the military and administrative establishments in the eastern half of the empire at the end of the fourth century, and somewhat later, and more haphazardly, for the west.[44] On the face of it, like many such checklists, the *notitia dignitatum* does not make for particularly interesting reading. But in its outline catalogue of civil positions it does convey a strong impression of the meticulous classification of administrative tasks and the careful grading of imperial officials.

The basic unit of civil government in the *notitia* was the province, each under a governor (variously titled according to rank). In turn, the provinces were grouped into dioceses, each under a *uicarius*. The dioceses together made up four Praetorian Prefectures: Gaul (which included Britain and Spain), Italy (which included Africa and the western Balkans), Illyricum (roughly Crete, modern Greece, and the Balkan states to the north of Macedonia), and the East.[45] The principal officers of state—the highest-ranking provincial governors, *uicarii*, praetorian prefects, the urban prefects of Rome and Constantinople, and other senior officials such as the *magister officiorum*—were each given a separate entry in the *notitia* distinguished by a splendid illustrated panel displaying their insignia of office. That of the praetorian prefect of Illyricum shows his *codicilli* exhibited between burning tapers on a blue cloth-covered table, a sumptuous state carriage sheathed in silver, and a large ceremonial inkwell and pen case *(theca)*. The *theca* was a magnificent object perhaps well over a meter high (including its tripodlike base), and according to John it contained more than 100 pounds of gold (2.14). It was beautifully decorated in high relief. In its middle register stood figures in profile with veiled uplifted hands (like those of the bureaucrat on the Missorium of Theodosius) presenting offerings to the images of emperors shown in the panel above.[46] Other illustrations in the *notitia* included items related to the responsibilities of a particular officer. The panel depicting the attributes of the *quaestor sacri palatii,* the emperor's chief law officer, charged with the drafting of imperial legislation, and from 429 to 437 with the compilation of the *Theodosian Code,* displayed a set of scrolls; that for the *primicerius notariorum* showed a copy of the *notitia* itself; that for the *comes sacrarum largitionum,* whose remit covered the collection of indirect taxes and the administration of state mints, mines, quarries, and textile factories, exhibited (perhaps all too predictably) a number of overflowing moneybags.[47]

Each entry in the *notitia* also contained a brief outline of the administrative personnel serving each department. The staff *(officium)* of the eastern praetorian prefect is shown divided into two main branches, the administrative and judicial, and the financial. The hierarchy of senior posts in the former, described in loving detail by John Lydus, is here given in its most abbreviated form: *princeps officii, cornicularius, adiutor, commentariensis, ab actis, cura epistularum,* and *regendarius.*[48] In some cases, these sketch-maps of individual departments were elaborated by long and complex imperial laws setting out in detail the positions and responsibilities of specific officials. A law of 384 (as modified by the sixth-century compilers of the *Justinianic Code*) set out the *officium* of the *comes sacrarum largitionum*. In this schedule, 443 personnel were divided into eighteen different groups and listed within each group in precise order of seniority.

> *Scrinium exceptorum:*
> One official with the rank of *perfectissimus* second class, who is the
>   *primicerius* of the whole *schola*
> One official with the rank of *perfectissimus* (third class), who is the
>   *primicerius* of the *exceptores*
> Two officials with the rank of *ducenarius,* who are the *tertiocerius* and
>   *quartocerius*
> One official with the rank of *centenarius,* who is the *primicerius*
>   *instrumentorum*
> Two *epistulares*
> Thirty-six *exceptores* constituting the first grade
> Four *exceptores* constituting the second grade
> Three *exceptores* constituting the third grade.

And so on, following the same pattern, for another seventeen groups of officials.[49] Again, the unremitting attention to often highly technical minutiae is particularly impressive. This detailed presentation of the staff serving under the *comes sacrarum largitionum* seems to leave no room for promotion other than by seniority (on occasions accelerated by the death of superiors); to assume that the allocation of tasks and rewards will remain fixed between the various groups; and to suppose that the number of staff will remain constant.

An equal administrative concern for order also characterized a decree issued by the emperor Anastasius in the early 490s and inscribed (with some local variations) on the walls of a number of forts along the Empire's eastern frontier. These regulations set out the ranks, duties, and order of seniority of those serving on the civilian staff of a military commander *(dux),* as well as the stipends and fees they should expect to receive. The best-preserved version of the decree was cut on basalt blocks built into the side of the fortress at Qasr el-Hallabat, northeast of Amman, Jordan. Prescribing the structure of the department, the emperor ruled "that each member of the civilian staff of the military commanders [*duciani*], the financial side [*scriniarii*], and the administrative officers [*officiales*] shall serve according to their order in the personnel register, and no person, either now or hereafter, shall alter his rank except according to the established order of the register." There followed a (regrettably now fragmentary) listing of posts evidently in strict rank order, beginning with the commander's chief judicial adviser *(assessor)*, followed by the head of his civilian staff *(primiscrinius)*, and so on. In addition, the terms of office for those in various posts were fixed. The *primiscrinius* was to serve no more than five years; nor was any official permitted to move between departments.[50]

These documents, with their carefully compiled schedules of salaries, posts, and personnel, present a splendid image of later Roman bureaucracy. They offer a striking blueprint of a tightly regimented officialdom, its impressive concern for hierarchy and position beautifully illustrated in meticulously detailed lists or, in some cases, more permanently displayed on an inscribed wall.[51] Here are model administrative corps now (and hereafter) seemingly untroubled by the potentially disruptive demands of the ambitious or the talented. Like officials from the Praetorian Prefecture, proudly marching with their retiring colleagues through the Great Palace at Constantinople, or those flanking the emperors on the painted walls of the temple of Ammon in Luxor, these imperial edicts openly paraded a specific and highly formalized image of later Roman bureaucracy. Against the pressures exerted by individuals seeking to advance their careers or to take advantage of their influential connections, they clearly promoted the interests of a well-ordered administration as a whole.

We should perhaps think of John reading these laws, with their long and tedious schedules, or catalogues such as the *notitia dignitatum,* in the same way as he himself had encouraged his own readers to think about bureaucrats' participation in grand and lengthy ceremonies. In their complexity and intricate formality, both could be seen as marking out the differences in organization, identity, and work practices between later Roman bureaucracy and the world outside. Together they presented a powerful and distinctive image of a coherent and well-regulated administrative system. Both, too, could be understood as strong assertions of the importance of corporate interest in securing the wider success of any group of officials. The fact that an individual's ability or his connections continued to be factors in determining appointment or promotion did not mean that legislation stressing the formal aspects of the administration was either ignored or rendered ineffective, any more than it made the ceremonies surrounding John's retirement meaningless shams. Rather, these repeated affirmations of the benefits of order and mutuality staked out a significant position in a continuing series of trade-offs. They isolated and underlined particular moments in a disputed balance between the competing claims of individual bureaucrats and the collective advantage of their colleagues. Enshrined in the legislation of empire, and sometimes displayed on its walls, the formal and detailed regulation of a department through the careful prescription of its personnel, posts, and administrative tasks—like the serried, ceremonial ranks of an official procession—forcefully emphasized a set of highly visible "fixed points" in a complex set of negotiations.

Getting On in the World

A concern to reconcile personal advantage with mutual benefit was also an important theme in John's own account of his career in the Praetorian Prefecture. In his early years he had been greatly helped by a network of influential connections. He owed much to his hometown of Philadelphia (a debt he acknowledged in his works by the inclusion of much miscellaneous information on its history and traditions, as well as a special account of its sufferings under the Cappadocian).[52] After John's arrival in Constantinople in 511, and his initial failure to join the *sacra scrinia,* the praetorian prefect Zoticus prevailed upon him to join his staff. The offer of a position was an attractive one, for, as John explained, the new prefect was "a fellow countryman of mine and liked me immensely" (3.26). Thanks to Zoticus' support, John's career got off to a flying start, "as though I were equipped with wings" (3.27). He had little apparent difficulty in securing a wide range of well-paid work, and, exceptionally in his first year in post, he was selected as a *chartularius* (chief administrative officer) to the *adiutores* assisting the *ab actis.* He also seems to have undertaken work for the *a secretis* (one of the emperor's confidential secretariats, entirely separate from the Praetorian Prefecture in its staffing and administration).

Another Philadelphian, Ammianus, "a lover of learning and wisdom throughout his life," who was also an *exceptor* on the judicial side of the Prefecture and a relation of John's father, arranged (again with Zoticus' help) an attractive and profitable marriage which brought John a dowry of 100 pounds of gold (3.28, 3.26).

Although John never again seems to have been so closely connected to another prefect, nor so rapidly advanced in so short a time, he wrote warmly of several others who benefited him in various ways. He strongly approved of "the renowned" Sergius, "respected for his learning," in office in 517, when John served a second annual stint as a *chartularius,* this time to the *adiutores* assisting the *commentariensis* (the third-highest-ranking official on the judicial side, primarily responsible for the conduct of criminal cases) (2.21, 3.17, 3.20). He was even more lavish in his praise of Phocas, in office in 532 (in the brief period between John the Cappadocian's two terms as praetorian prefect). In John's view, Phocas was a man "surpassing as a result of his countless gifts those who have ever yet been admired for the greatness of their soul" (3.72). It is possible, too, that Phocas had been instrumental in securing John's commission to compose an encomium in praise of Justinian and to write a history of the recent campaigns against Persia. Last, John offered a neatly turned antiquarian compliment to the prefect who presided at his retirement ceremony in April 552 and had ensured that John received the honors which as *cornicularius* he felt he merited. The prefect Hephaestus, John opined in a learned aside, "in his name alone displayed the nobility he possessed, for he was reputed to be a descendant of that Hephaestus who, according to the Sicilian historian, had ruled as the first king of Egypt" (3.30).[53]

But John was also aware that his pride in the successes of his early career and the parading of his personal connections with various prefects could be seen as running counter to the strong emphasis he placed on departmental solidarity and the importance of collegiality. No doubt some of John's peers had seen his rapid advance, especially at the start of his career, as both unfair and disruptive of good departmental order. John attempted to forestall similar criticism from his readers, not by denying his connections or the benefits which they had brought, but by seeking to demonstrate that his own individual good fortune had not in any way disadvantaged his colleagues. Indeed, John took great pains to show that his personal concerns had always been congruent with the corporate interest of those on the judicial side. He insisted that in his first year in post his broad range of duties (including the *a secretis*), far from taking work away from others, had helped his fellow *exceptores* cope with their heavy load (3.27). More generally, John claimed that he had prospered in his early career along with many of his colleagues, just as later he had suffered with them under the Cappadocian.

The importance of that shared experience was underlined by the way in which John chose to construct his autobiography. He carefully interleaved the account of his own time as a bureaucrat with detailed, technical descriptions of the Praetorian Prefecture: its long history, its expert personnel, and its complex administrative responsibilities. In his own version, John's tale of a shattered career was always to be read alongside the story he told of his own department's ruination in the face of John the Cappadocian's reforms. His individual experience was often merged indistinguishably with that of his colleagues. From this point of view, his initial successes might be read as exemplifying a wider prosperity, just as his claims to poverty at the end of his time in the Prefecture might be taken as representative of a wider decline. In this autobiography, the personal was explicitly to be informed by the departmental. Indeed, perhaps in his more academic moments John hoped that the successful inclusion of both these themes within a single work might be read (at least by those who appreciated such literary devices) as yet another demonstration of his claim to have reconciled his own achievements with the best interests of his colleagues.

A similar pattern of negotiation between the demands of individual officials and the interests of their departments is also evident in some imperial legislation which attempted to deal openly with the conflicting claims of ambition or ability, the exercise of personal influence, and the importance of family and kinship ties. Not all imperial laws unquestioningly recognized the priority of the principle of promotion by seniority or by long and worthy service. The *adiutores* of the *quaestor sacri palatii* were permitted to appoint their own successors, provided that the *quaestor* also consented.[54] An *agens in rebus* who had transferred to the *sacra scrinia* was, in case of incapacity, entitled to nominate a substitute, on condition that he was "suitable and possessed of the highest morals as well as having knowledge and experience of these matters."[55] High-ranking officials entitled to petition for the appointment of an *agens in rebus* were specifically listed.[56] Strikingly, others wishing "to shove themselves forward," even if they had imperial approval, had to secure the support of the majority of the department before they could be appointed. Promotion to a higher grade also required the "testimony and agreement" of the reliable members of that grade "given in the presence of the majority of the department."[57] In some cases, those promoted as the result of imperial influence might have to accept a reduction in seniority. In 396 Arcadius and Honorius ruled that an *agens in rebus* advanced by direct imperial command "shall be listed as last in that grade to which he has been promoted, and he shall not be placed before any other person who served with the same rank in the imperial administration before him."[58]

Similarly, among the *castrenses* (members of the domestic staff of the imperial household, and despite the title not necessarily eunuchs) an elegant, if complicated, system was devised to accommodate the conflicting interests of those in the department's three grades promoted by seniority and those more rapidly advanced by special imperial favor. Some of those enjoying preferment based on influence rather than seniority seem to have held posts additional to the department's official complement. As a result, as a law of 422 noted, when a vacancy occurred in an established post in the first grade it was occupied by one of the unestablished members of staff of the same rank, "thereby excluding the established members of the second and third grades from higher positions." To moderate this difficulty it was ordered

> that those unestablished members of staff who are placed in the first or second grades as a result of divine imperial favor, and those who are already in an established post in the second and third grades, shall be promoted by turns: that is, they shall alternate so that now one from the former and then one from the latter category shall advance to a higher position among the established staff if it should fall vacant.[59]

A concern that long-serving officials should not be passed over also seems to have been an important consideration in a law regulating *agentes in rebus* issued in 380 by Gratian, Valentinian II, and Theodosius I to the *magister officiorum*.

> If any *agens in rebus*, long after his retirement and his former imperial service, because of an unreasonable greed for enlistment, should attempt through the exercise of influence to return to a period of ser-

vice, he shall be offered the option of enrollment on the understanding that he shall serve in the last position in the most junior ranks.[60]

Equally intricate provisions also attempted to reconcile the demands of individuals or particular groups with more formal versions of a department's organization. In some instances, officials were permitted to occupy more than one position, allowed to move between departments, or to hold a post beyond its prescribed tenure. Other imperial laws acknowledged the competing pressures of family ties and obligations. In 396 Arcadius and Honorius permitted any senior *agens in rebus* seconded as *princeps officii* to head another department to nominate his son or brother to fill the consequential junior vacancy. Imperial assent was required before the appointment could be confirmed.[61] In 445 Theodosius II and Valentinian III allowed any member of the *sacra scrinia* who had a son serving in an unestablished post to advance him to an established position ahead of others more senior.[62] These advantages required careful monitoring. Those seeking appointment in the imperial bureaucracy were required to declare their place of origin, their family, and their parents.[63] Cliques based on provincial ties, like John's Philadelphian connections, could also be the subject of concern, especially for those who found themselves excluded.

In a rare moment, it is possible to follow (in this case through the bloody intrigues which characterized court politics in the 390s) something of the difficulties surrounding the promulgation of a specific imperial directive. In 392, on succeeding to office, the eastern praetorian prefect Rufinus had his immediate predecessor Flavius Eutolmius Tatianus exiled and Tatianus' son Proculus (urban prefect of Constantinople) executed.[64] Rufinus also secured an imperial edict stripping their fellow provincials from Lycia in southern Asia Minor of their positions in the imperial administration. In the towns of Myra and Sidyma (near the Lycian coast), in Aphrodisias (in Caria, to the east of Lycia), in Side (in Pamphylia, to the west), in Antinoopolis (in Egypt), and no doubt in other places, too, Tatianus' name was carefully chiseled out from inscriptions, some commemorating his dedications of statues to the imperial family. In Constantinople, Proculus' name was similarly skillfully excised from an inscription cut in 388 on the base of the Obelisk of Theodosius I celebrating its erection in the Hippodrome, where it still stands.[65]

Following Rufinus' assassination in 395, the ban on Lycians in the imperial administration was lifted. Proculus' name was neatly restored on the inscription in the Hippodrome. In an edict addressed in August 396 to the new eastern praetorian prefect Flavius Caesarius, Arcadius and Honorius decreed

> that the former reputation and worth of the province of Lycia, most loyal to us, shall be restored to its place among the other provinces . . . Its citizens shall retain the honors which they have gained as a result of their merits and labors . . . they shall have the high-ranking positions which they held before, and they shall hope for others to follow because of their loyalty. For the temporary hatred of a most shameful and hostile magistrate [Rufinus] for one man of illustrious rank, Tatianus, should not be reckoned so highly that the Lycians should still be dishonored by it, when that man himself has now been brought to nothing by the due absolution of time.[66]

Regrettably, the text of the law expelling the Lycians does not survive. But from the edict repealing it, something of the original's uncompromising tone may perhaps be guessed. No doubt those in the eastern Praetorian Prefecture who benefited from the breaking of the Lycian coterie were content to see the concerns of a greater number of staff preferred to those of a smaller group bound by a common provincial origin. It is interesting, in turn, to speculate how four years later the return of the Lycians to their former posts was managed and how they were greeted by their erstwhile colleagues. Under the circumstances, it is perhaps not surprising that it was thought necessary to instruct the prefect to ensure "by the posting of edicts" that "henceforth no person shall dare to injure a citizen of Lycia by using that name abusively as an insult."

The legislation so far cited is important precisely because it exposes something of the varied grounds of dispute, and of the broad range of responses both to specific instances of conflict and to the resolutions proposed by the parties involved. As suggested above, the laws preserved in the *Codes* isolated particular moments in a more complex series of trade-offs. Like a collection of prize specimens carefully displayed under glass, the *Codes* present one selection of examples culled from a much wider set of possibilities. The extent to which (as in all legal textbooks) extreme or unusual cases are overrepresented is difficult to determine. Under some circumstances, like the small number of contested matters in any society resolved through formal litigation, the very issuing of a law may indicate a disagreement irreconcilable by other means. In practice, most disputes are unlikely to have involved recourse to the emperor. Even so, for those hoping for a favorable imperial decision (given the variety of responses illustrated in the *Codes*) it must sometimes have been frustratingly difficult to predict the outcome of any particular adjudication.

Indeed, reading through the surviving legislation dealing with administrative affairs, it is easy to imagine aspiring or talented officials bitterly disappointed by the issuing of a long and detailed schedule which strictly enforced promotion by seniority or limited the number of posts available. One can only guess at what thwarted ambition might lie behind an early sixth-century ruling inscribed on the wall of the fort at Ptolemais in the Pentapolis (on the coast of modern Libya) and publicly displayed in the provincial capital Apollonia. In this decree, the emperor Anastasius confirmed that for the administrative staff serving the military commander stationed in the province, "the personnel register drawn up under the *dux* Daniel . . . shall remain in force."[67] Nor can an emphasis on the primacy of the formal aspects of a department's organization have always greatly pleased the sons, relatives, or fellow countrymen of those already in post. Whatever the expectations, such connections did not invariably guarantee more rapid advancement. But in any departmental dispute there were also winners. It is equally possible to imagine the pleasure of those holding unestablished posts allowed accelerated access to positions at the expense of established staff; or the satisfaction among a group of officials permitted to exercise some say in promotions and appointments; or the delight of those selected over their colleagues to assist or succeed high-ranking officeholders; or the importance to some fathers of securing a post in their department for their sons; or—perhaps most touching of all—the genuine and deeply felt relief of middle-ranking, long-serving (and perhaps not particularly talented) officials whose promotion by seniority within their department was, thanks to an imperial directive, no longer to be delayed or disrupted by the preferment of young high flyers with the right connections.

On the reconciliation of these potentially conflicting priorities, the prospects and prosperity of any department significantly depended. In striking that difficult balance, John emphasized the importance of collegiality. It helped to protect a department against its rivals; it gave some structure and predictability to officials' careers; and, in good times, it increased their chances of augmenting their areas of administrative responsibility. But John also openly recognized the claims of some individuals (himself included) to more rapid advancement. For his own part, he claimed in his autobiography to have managed his career in the Prefecture as well as could be expected, particularly given the sometimes difficult circumstances. He presented himself to his readers as a model bureaucrat, talented and well connected. At the same time, he repeatedly emphasized the importance of collegiality and the pride he took in its public display. In this regard, at least, John was perhaps pleased with *On the Magistracies of the Roman State*. Its account of his time in the Prefecture, read alongside the description of the judicial side, its duties, and its staff, mirrored the continual and often delicate process of negotiation between personal interest and corporate benefit which John believed of crucial importance both to a successful administrative career and to a prosperous department. Here was a work which celebrated the formal aspects of the judicial side, glorying in its camaraderie, asserting the superiority of its "customs, forms, and language" (*Pr.* 2.7), and detailing at length its regulations, "registers, titles, and duties" (2.22). Yet here, too, was a work warmly dedicated as a "thank offering" (1.15) to those praetorian prefects whose influence had been instrumental in helping John to advance his career.

Anatomies of Praise and Blame

In John's view, the fortunes of the staff on the judicial side of the eastern Praetorian Prefecture had always been heavily dependent on the men appointed by emperors to serve as praetorian prefects. At their best, prefects were able to maintain, or even expand, their department's jurisdiction; they fended off any attempt at disadvantageous reform; they held at bay other acquisitive departments. Moreover, these prefects were sensitive to the needs and ambitions of particular officials whom they might advance more rapidly. At the same time, they managed to hold their staff together and emphasize the importance of collegiality and mutual support. Under the careful guidance of these men, John had no doubt, the judicial side in its entirety had prospered.

But such advantageous virtue could not always be guaranteed. At their worst, some prefects might completely ignore the interests of their staff, using their office to pursue their own selfish ends. Under these men, a small number of handpicked individuals (perhaps with family or provincial ties) would be rapidly promoted, with no thought for either the careers of their colleagues or the consequences of such flagrant favoritism for the department as a whole. Significantly too, in John's view, the contrasting policies of "good" and "bad" prefects were reflected in their different characters. Good prefects were marked by generosity, moderation, decorum, piety, and a love of learning. Bad prefects dramatically rejected all such qualities. Their characters were manifestly unbalanced. They delighted in excess and brutality; they could control neither their desires nor their appetites; they were capricious, profligate, negligent, and untrustworthy. Unsuited to the task of running the department (and uncaring about the results), these prefects had, according to John, severely damaged the careers of those on the judicial side. At times they had even threatened to undermine the Prefecture itself.

John's short list of good prefects, perhaps unsurprisingly, coincided with those who had assisted him during his career: Zoticus, Sergius, Phocas, and Hephaestus. John himself was able to express something of his appreciation for all of Zoticus' valuable assistance in a brief verse panegyric in praise of the prefect's merits, character, and achievements. In his own autobiography, John noted (here recalling with evident pride the success of his literary *juvenilia*) that his poetic efforts were so well received that Zoticus had awarded him one gold coin for each line, the whole sum paid from public funds (3.27). Regrettably, the text of this panegyric does not survive. But it may be possible to recapture something of its tone and content (and perhaps a little of its style) from the verses written in praise of provincial officials by one of John's near contemporaries.

Dioscorus was born around 520 into a prosperous and well-respected family in the Egyptian town of Aphrodito (about 250 kilometers downstream from modern Luxor). He was educated in the law and classics, probably in Alexandria. A surviving archive of papyrus documents, written in both Greek and Coptic, show him to have been a prominent landowner, a successful lawyer, and a poet of some ability. Dioscorus' world and his concerns were decidedly provincial. Only on one occasion (in 551, just before John Lydus' retirement) did he journey to Constantinople to present Aphrodito's claim in a dispute over the right to collect taxes. In the 560s, in order to further his legal career, he moved to Antinoë, the seat of the local military commander, the *dux* of the Thebaid. Here, as he had done for most of the previous decade, he regularly wrote Greek verse panegyrics in praise of high officials. No doubt, alongside his legal talents, his literary efforts helped to get him noticed: to quote Leslie MacCoull, Dioscorus' modern editor, "he embodied the best qualities of local loyalty and of what a travelled and experienced person could bring to local culture." One of his most stylish pieces was dedicated to Romanos, probably *dux* in the mid-550s.

> O much-loved answer to the prayers of those who love divine wisdom, serving the Muses and the Graces as well as War; I have seen a second Homer, and Ares, and Love, Festivity's bridegroom, namesake of the sun. Soothe my illness, since I am not in my right senses, beholding the blessed descendant of most blessed ancestors, the wise ruler, who is close to the supreme sovereign himself . . . May your renowned glory continue to an innumerable time. Let me be bold: Where should I begin to sing of Adonis, famous for his beauty, or beloved Hyacinth?[68]

What John Lydus might have thought of Dioscorus' poetry, with its highly polished, often lavishly self-conscious turns of phrase, is difficult to say. Had he been in sympathetic mood he might have recognized and appreciated the cultural pretensions of one who, like himself, had come from a comfortable provincial background. After all, neither John nor Dioscorus could fairly be said to wear their learning lightly. Both were eager to parade before their readers their hard-won knowledge of the classical past. On the other hand, faced with these verses, John was equally capable of adopting the most brittle and rebarbative of metropolitan pretensions. He might well have regarded Dioscorus' poetry, for all its neatly turned compliments and endless literary allusions, as a pale, provincial reflection of how a high official could be praised by one in the imperial capital who really knew how.

However admirable and attractive John's panegyric on Zoticus might have been, it would have been exceeded by his praises of

Phocas.[69] In John's view, Phocas was to be considered the paragon of prefectural virtue. Here was a true gentleman: one who, though wealthy, practiced frugality and abstinence; a genuine connoisseur of the beautiful with no hint of empty pretension; a generous host whose first concern was the needs of his guests (3.72). Here, too, was a man who wept openly when told of prisoners of war and who used his own money to help pay for their return. The very model of moderation, the saintly Phocas had only virtue in excess: "since he overflowed with a love of humanity, he publicly sold his clothing, and, adding as much as he could, he sent off the proceeds to help pay their ransom" (3.75).

Phocas was appointed eastern praetorian prefect by Justinian in mid-January 532 during the so-called Nika riots in Constantinople. The precise causes of this disorder (as in many cases of crowd violence) are obscure. Following a complicated series of minor disputes, the long-standing rivalry between the factions in the Hippodrome rapidly escalated into a serious protest against the emperor, or at least provided an opportunity or pretext for open revolt. A week of rioting saw the near success of the usurper Hypatius and the destruction of many of the finest buildings in the capital, including the Chalke and Hagia Sophia. As John, probably an eyewitness to the events, recorded, "the city was a series of blackened, blasted hills, just like Lipari or Vesuvius, uninhabitable because of dust, smoke, and the foul stench of building materials reduced to ashes" (3.70). The sedition was suppressed after troops led by Belisarius butchered Hypatius' supporters, who had assembled in the Hippodrome to cheer his coronation. According to John, more than 50,000 people were killed. Justinian, in an unsuccessful attempt to quell the rising unrest in the city, and in the hope of publicly shifting the blame for any unpopular policies, had replaced three of his closest advisers: the praetorian prefect, John the Cappadocian (in office since April 531); Eudaemon, the urban prefect; and Tribonian, the *quaestor sacri palatii*. But this was only a temporary measure. Justinian recovered quickly from the riots, undoubtedly helped by the brutal advertisement their suppression offered to any further opposition. Within forty-five days of the massacre in the Hippodrome, the building of a new Hagia Sophia commenced. Reconstruction in other areas proceeded rapidly. Phocas was in office for only ten months before John the Cappadocian was reinstated with a renewed imperial mandate for his extensive program of administrative and financial reform.[70]

John made the most of Phocas' short prefecture. His inauguration ceremony was graced by the best of omens. An attempt at assassination failed, the marksman's arrow missing its target: "And as Phocas was unharmed, he was shown clearly to be a man of providence" (3.76). The crowd rejoiced at the sight "and, singing the praises of their most excellent emperor, began to live peaceably and put an end to rioting, having suddenly turned from the greatest troubles and fears to flutes and dances." All this good cheer and "an abundance of blessings" benefited the empire and, in particular, the judicial side of the Praetorian Prefecture.

> The staff shone brightly just as when a flame is about to go out one pours plenty of oil on it. The pressing demand for administrative services was pleasing . . . and rhetoricians became famous for their speeches, and books were produced, and the competition for glory returned over the whole face of government. The . . .   (3.76)

At this point the one surviving manuscript of John's work breaks off.[71] It is not known how he dealt with the snuffing of this brief efflorescence in the Prefecture's fortunes by the return of John the Cappadocian a few months later. No doubt similarly exaggerated language again deepened the contrast between the two prefects. Already by eliding any distinction between the reforms introduced by the Cappadocian in his first and second terms in office, and by placing his account of his prefecture and its policies (3.57–71) before any mention of Phocas (3.72–76), John had heavily weighted his account. In this version, Phocas appeared as the much-needed antidote following John the Cappadocian's maladministration and the bloodshed of the Nika riots.

With equal skill, John glided smoothly over any suggestion of friction between Phocas and emperor arising from such a brief term as praetorian prefect and the reinstatement of his predecessor. During the riots, Phocas was seen to accede graciously to Justinian's request that he take up office; he was closely associated in John's account with the emperor's eagerness to rebuild Hagia Sophia (3.76). Nor did John directly refer to Phocas' acquittal on charges of paganism in 529, or to his suicide in the mid-540s when the same charges were again leveled.[72] In John's account, the issue of the prefect's religious preferences was carefully blurred. Many of Phocas' qualities, his generosity, his frugality, and especially his concern to ransom prisoners, could be

read as Christian virtues.[73] John explicitly mentioned Phocas' dona-
tions to churches as well as his enthusiasm for Justinian's rebuilding of
"The Temple of the Great God" (3.76). His providential escape from
assassination was also offered as evidence of divine approval of his
appointment: "When God has thought it right to convince men, he
shows himself present at what is being done" (3.76).

It might, of course, be equally possible to find in Phocas' good
deeds a polytheist claim to virtue, or to read in John's highly stylized
classicizing circumlocutions (which avoided any direct mention of the
Christian God or even of Hagia Sophia) an invitation to discern some
deeper meaning. But John offered no encouragement. In this version
of Phocas, such ambiguities were important. They were part of a carefully constructed portrait of the ideal prefect in which certain admirable qualities and their beneficial consequences were to be sharply
foregrounded. Those features which might detract from such a clear-
cut image (or add to it an unwanted complexity) were delicately
veiled. The result was a powerful statement of the attributes of a model
prefect. And more than that. In John's view, to be fully convincing it
was also necessary to show that the empire at large had benefited from
such sudden prosperity, and that all had taken place (as it should) with
the blessing of God and the unstinting support of the emperor.

Above all, in this bureaucratic morality tale, Phocas was to be portrayed as the antithesis of John the Cappadocian.[74] Moreover, despite
overwhelming evidence to the contrary, John boldly claimed that the
Cappadocian did not enjoy Justinian's support. On this point, John's
argument was shamelessly sophistic. In part, it involved fulsome praise
of Justinian, whose many virtues paralleled those of good prefects.
Indeed, in many ways the emperor was himself to be seen as the ultimate administrator. Like the great prefects of old, he was said to work
through the night processing unfinished paperwork (2.15, 3.15).[75]
Such a ruler could have nothing in common with the Cappadocian. In
part, John's claim of a rift between praetorian prefect and emperor
rested on an explicitly circular argument from silence: since Justinian
was self-evidently an excellent emperor, had he known of his prefect's
actions, he would have moved to prevent them. Since he did not so
move, he could not have known (3.57, 3.61, 3.62, 3.69).[76]

But such reasoning was not without its problems. It might, for example, be thought that knowledge of such an important subordinate's ac-

tions and the ability to act quickly to correct them was a crucial part of what it was to be an excellent emperor. In an uncomfortable passage, John explained that in the year before the Nika riots, Justinian knew nothing of the Cappadocian's outrageous behavior: "For our most gentle emperor knew nothing of these things. And indeed everyone, although they were wrongfully treated, used to plead the cause of the worthless Cappadocian on account of his unbridled power and before the emperor all used to praise him in superlative terms" (3.69). Only the empress Theodora dared speak out. She "went to the emperor and informed him of all the things which up until then had escaped his notice." But still Justinian did not act. John offered further explanation.

> Naturally, then, the emperor, being good, though slow in requiting the wicked, was in an impossibly difficult situation and was unable to find a way to dislodge this subverter of the state. The latter had badly disrupted the business of government . . . in such a way that there might never be an end to his magistracy . . . Even so, the emperor assisted his subjects so far as was humanly possible.   (3.69)

Of course, it is impossible to know what John really thought of Justinian's relationship with John the Cappadocian. Perhaps he accepted that any attempt to distinguish between them would inevitably result in some distortions and inconsistencies. Perhaps, too, he later strengthened his case by including (in the now-lost portion of his final book) a lurid account of the Cappadocian's disgrace in 541 following his alleged implication in a plot to overthrow the emperor, a conspiracy again apparently uncovered by Theodora.[77] But what mattered most to John was that he had cast some doubt on the strength of the bond between emperor and prefect. For John, that impression of distance was crucial. It allowed him to dissociate Justinian from the reforms promoted by John the Cappadocian. And, above all, it enabled him to assert that the emperor was merely waiting for the appropriate moment to restore the Prefecture to its former glory (2.5, 3.1, 3.39).

In John's long litany of blame for the judicial side's declining fortunes, others, too, were strongly criticized. John was particularly unimpressed with Cyrus of Panopolis, who in the mid-fifth century had permitted decrees and legal judgments to be issued by the Prefecture in Greek rather than Latin. He condemned Rufinus, in office 392–395, as the cause of the emperor Arcadius' decision to transfer to the *magister officiorum* the Prefecture's responsibility for the palace guard *(scholae palatinae),* the state arms factories *(fabricae),* and the public post *(cursus publicus)* (2.10 = 3.40).[78] His judgment on a man he regarded as having "wrecked the Prefecture by his despotic rule" (3.7, 3.23) was curt and uncompromising. "Rufinus, called 'the insatiate' (who was then prefect) because he intended to usurp the throne, ceased to have as his objective the public good and hurled the magistracy down into a deep pit" (2.10 = 3.40). Two of John's contemporaries were similarly to be despised. Demosthenes (in office 521–522 and again in 529) for refusing to grant taxation remissions and presiding over a decline in the number of cases heard on appeal in the prefect's court (3.42); and Marinus (Zoticus' successor, in office 512–515 and again in 519), "a Syrian, and worthless, as is usually the case," for establishing a new set of financial officials in the provinces *(uindices)* and thereby reducing the flow of fiscal matters dealt with by the Praetorian Prefecture. Those on the department's judicial side who saw their career prospects decline with this loss of administrative responsibility were said, according to John, to be suffering from a bad case of "Marinusitis" (3.49).[79]

But next to John the Cappadocian's neglect of the interests of the judicial side of the department, these prefects' lack of care either for their staff or for the administrative competence of their department was insignificant.[80] The poison-pen portrait which John Lydus presented to his readers was a splendidly vituperative tour de force: "for rage both impels and compels me to recollect countless evils" (3.57). As in the very best of eighteenth-century political cartoons, no weakness was left unexploited, no character trait undistorted, no action unexaggerated. John's images for his most hated superior were of uncontrollable avarice, extraordinary luxury, gluttony, gross sexual depravity, physical deformity, surpassing cruelty, and a cavalier disregard for the hallowed traditions of the Prefecture.

> When the Cappadocian had fallen upon the magistracy, he turned over the prefect's old and impressive quarters to his battalions of servants. He himself made his lair in the upper story. Urine and excrement covered the walls of his bedchamber. Naked he used to lie sprawled on his bed, and ordering all the members of his office staff, as if they were base household slaves, to keep watch outside his bedchamber, he singled out those whom it pleased him so to do and handed them over to the most brutal of his domestic staff. (2.21)[81]

This was an administrative world turned upside down. The staff of the Prefecture was judged and punished by household servants; the prefect lay naked in bed instead of presiding, magnificently robed, in his court. When the Cappadocian consented to dress, he would tie up his hair in a large scarf and, looking more like a pimp than a prefect—"like Pompey's pretty boy as described in Plutarch"—would venture out.[82] But not to perform his duties in the city. Instead he had "himself carried to the country houses which he had built for himself" (2.21). Decency and good order were inverted. On the rare occasions when the prefect appeared in public, he was not escorted by the ordered ranks of his uniformed staff but by troops of scantily clad women "clearly revealing that which they 'ought to have concealed from the eyes of men'" (3.64).[83] The bathroom of the prefectural residence was turned into a stable (2.21); the prefect's court, once renowned for the splendor of its forms and "its august and worthy procedures" (2.17), was converted into a torture chamber (3.57); and, more offensive still, the Cappadocian promoted only his close friends, showering wealth on all his associates and his household staff, including his cooks (3.62). Under this regime, even nature itself was diverted from its proper course. In pursuit of ever-greater luxury, an outdoor bathing pool was constructed and "the normal flow of the water forced up to an unnatural height" (2.21). The Cappadocian himself was out of all (administrative, ceremonial, and moral) order. Although, like many of his worthy predecessors, he often remained active throughout the night, he was available only to perform "countless and indiscriminate" sexual feats rather than to discharge the responsibilities of office (3.65, 2.21, 3.62).

Nor were these legendary perversions confined to the capital. "But, just as Briareus, who in stories is said by the poets to have had countless hands, so that fiend also had innumerable minions for his evil deeds" (3.58).[84] From the many tales of woe John claimed he could relate—"they are numberless, so that they alone could fill up many large volumes with grief" (3.59)—he concentrated on the brutal operations of a fellow Cappadocian sent out by the prefect to collect taxes in John's own home province of Lydia.

Out of all his [John the Cappadocian's] minions, I shall recall one to demonstrate the loathsomeness of the rest. There was a namesake of his, a close relation, a man of demon-inspired viciousness beyond all imagining, who himself was also a Cappadocian. And the shape of his body alone revealed the deformity of his character. For in addition to being very corpulent, he was also strange in appearance as his jaws were swollen due to their disfiguring width and an excess of flesh, and, because of the weight of the flesh, it hung down in folds from his face just like a cloak. The people nicknamed him *Maxilloplumacius:* "Leaden Chops." (3.58)[85]

In Lydia, in his search for hidden taxable funds with the aid of an "army of demon despoilers and hordes of Cappadocians" (3.61), John Maxilloplumacius systematically raped, murdered, and pillaged his way through the population, leaving "no wife, no maiden, no youth unharmed and undefiled" (3.58). But none of his subordinates ever surpassed their prefect in the extent or variety of their excesses. The Cappadocian was untiring in his pursuit of pleasure and luxury. His private building programs could be compared only with the architectural follies of the Mausoleum at Halicarnassus or the pyramids of the pharaohs (2.21). His desires were gross and indiscriminate. "He used to gulp down the products of air, land, and sea, all with wines from everywhere" (2.21). His appetite was so vast that it depleted the Hellespont and then the Black Sea of fish; even scallops (in one of John's less successful images) to avoid his gluttony attempted to take flight, "using their shells as if they were wings" (3.62). Memorably, too, amid this grand display of rhetorical venom, John reproduced a dirty ditty lampooning the predictably unwholesome habits of Cappadocians. Perhaps, in an idle moment, such a pasquinade had once been circulated among his disgruntled colleagues?

> Cappadocians are always foul. When they have put on the belt
> of office
> they are fouler, and for the sake of gain they are foulest.
> But if they then get their hands on the [prefect's] grand carriage
> twice or thrice,
> then straightway hour by hour they are the foulest of the most
> foul. (3.57)[86]

Morality and Bureaucracy

John's starkly drawn diptych of virtue and depravity had an undisguised personal edge. It was part of a justification (to himself, to his colleagues, and to his readers) for his decision, at what should have been the midpoint in a successful bureaucratic career, to concentrate instead on teaching and research. It serves as a reminder that, for all the impressive information John provided on the formal workings of the department, its history, and the attitudes of its staff, his was also a highly charged autobiography written by a bureaucrat struggling to come to terms with his own failure to realize his ambitions. In John's view, the Cappadocian was undoubtedly a godless man, an evil spirit (3.12), and the proper subject of divine vengeance (3.69). He had been directly responsible for a series of reforms which had undermined John's position and those of his colleagues. In contrast to the praiseworthy Phocas, the Cappadocian was a prefect who, far from looking after the interests of the judicial side of his department, had "lacerated and robbed us of every excellence" (3.12).

That judgment is revelatory, and must be respected. But it is only one possible version. For the emperor Justinian, John the Cappadocian, in office for nearly a decade, was clearly an effective and successful administrator. The *scriniarii*, on the increasingly more powerful financial side of the Prefecture, would no doubt also have wished to celebrate his achievements. Perhaps they might even have commissioned a panegyric in the Cappadocian's honor. Indeed, from that point of view, it is interesting (and necessary) to imagine how *On the Magistracies of the Roman State* might have been written, and how the characters and actions of the various prefects and their supporters might have been depicted, if (as he originally intended) John had joined the *sacra scrinia* and followed a career largely unaffected by major administrative reform. Or, better still, if, with the Cappadocian's personal backing, John had entered the Prefecture as a *scriniarius* and had eventually realized his bureaucratic dream, securing in the end not a poorly paid professorship in the University of Constantinople, but an official post which guaranteed him "preeminent honor coupled with effective power" (3.10).

John's passionate tales of prefectural paragons and perverts can also be seen as part of a coherent series of responses by one long-serving official to his experiences in an often-hostile and unremittingly competitive environment. The harsh realities of an introverted administrative world imposed their own restrictive set of priorities and a complementary small-minded morality. A secure position and a reasonable prospect of advancement were what mattered most. Officials (individually and collectively) were forced to weigh the relative advantages of promotion by seniority, influence, merit, or connections. They had to reconcile individual demands against the collective need to share among loyal colleagues the rewards of success and the opportunities to secure a more senior post. Above all, they had to balance a set of competing—and sometimes contradictory—concerns in often uncertain and unstable circumstances unpredictably crosscut by imperial legislation and its insistent demands.

Alongside the obvious benefits enjoyed by the successful, later Roman officials had to reckon with the risks and limitations which went with being a member of the imperial bureaucracy. Their prospects were intimately bound up with their department, in which they might expect to spend the whole of their working lives. In the good times, that close connection undoubtedly worked to their benefit. But no matter how successful a department appeared or how certain its future might seem, there was an ever-present possibility—often unpredictable, often unavoidable—that departmental rivalries or an unsympathetic prefect would result in a change of fortune. Officials might find, as a result of reforms which they had failed either to foresee or to prevent, or of opportunities for advancement which they had neglected to exploit, that their careers took a different and unwelcome turn. Only then might they remember, perhaps with the bitter benefit of hindsight, a seemingly more golden time. Back then, as enthusiastic new recruits in a large and influential department, they had felt secure in their smug expectations of a long and rewarding career. Back then, like John, they had looked forward to continued success and to the unruffled enjoyment of "preeminent honor coupled with effective power."

As it stands, John's autobiography presents its readers with a different set of career choices and thwarted ambitions. It is, in its own way, a memorable and moving story. Nor should John's orotund rhetoric, his all-too-obvious exaggerations, or his highly emotional and sometimes harshly uncompromising judgments be too hastily dismissed. His repellent (yet fascinating) picture of John the Cappadocian, so carefully contrived, should be taken seriously as a memorable lesson in abuse; just as his attractive portrait of Phocas should be admired as an artfully executed exercise in praise. These strongly contrasting images helped to buttress the narrow confines of John's bureaucratic world. They

gave greater force to his near-obsessional insistence on the maintenance of the Prefecture's powers and perquisites. They offered clear
reference points for judging the actions of those who failed to advance
a department's best interests and, where necessary, for distinguishing
between an emperor and his closest advisers. Above all, they provided
a moral basis for interpreting administrative change and for understanding the strategies of winners and losers (among both rivals and
friends). In reinforcing his colleagues' separate and superior sense of
their own identity, these stereotyped studies of "good" and "bad" prefects were as important as the ceremonial moments captured on the
Missorium of Theodosius, in Corippus' brilliant description of the
consistorium in the Great Palace at Constantinople, and in John's own
account of the magnificent parades on the day of his retirement.

For John, strong language—like strikingly memorable images—mattered. In modern accounts of later Roman bureaucracy, such strident
rhetoric should not be effaced or politely downplayed in favor of more
comfortable (and often less enjoyable) descriptions of the internal organization of departments and their personnel. In establishing and
policing their own code of acceptable practice, and supporting it with
a series of explicit moral judgments, bureaucrats' own colorful terms
of praise and abuse were as important as the often more monochrome
tones of imperial legislation, with its more dispassionate regulation of
appointment and promotion. In John's own account of the Prefecture,
insiders' jokes, crude pornographic fantasies, and the unsubtle moralizing of his fellow bureaucrats (whatever they claimed to despise, whatever they affected to admire) also played a significant part in creating
and reinforcing a distinctive sense of order and collegiality. Like splendid uniforms, specialist jargon, and arcane expertise, they marked
out and defended what it was to be a bureaucrat in the later Roman
Empire.

CHAPTER 2

The Competition for Spoils

This is perhaps the most fundamental thing of all that you should remember—that as a civil servant you are a public servant. You must be scrupulously fair in your dealings with the public, showing favour to no sectional interest whatever your own views may be; you must be quick, accurate and efficient; you must be courteous to the members of the public with whom you have to deal, and within the limit of your department's powers . . . you must be as understanding and helpful as possible. That is your job.

—*Handbook for the New Civil Servant*

Costs and Charges

That money counted in administrative transactions in the later Roman Empire is a simple matter of fact. Bureaucrats expected that they would be paid by those who benefited from the tasks they performed. For John Lydus (like a modern doctor or lawyer) the charging of fees was, for the most part, a straightforward business proposition. Indeed, the establishment of a relationship between bureaucrats and those who sought or needed the services they could provide can profitably be compared to the settling of a deal between sellers and buyers in a marketplace. The allocation of priority among those demanding administrative action was to a great extent determined by a process of negotiation. In play was a range of interrelated factors including personal standing, family and other connections, future advantage, past favors, and their infinitely variable combinations. That the payment of money might also be a factor in this complex equation was something expected both by bureaucrats and by those requiring or demanding access to government services. For John, as no doubt for the majority of his colleagues, the charging of fees was a routine part of a system within which both parties in any administrative transaction openly operated. Importantly, too, it was a subject which he felt able to discuss without any sense of shame or discomfort. In John's opinion, the fee-income a bureaucrat earned from his official activities could be regarded as "both reasonable and acceptable to the law" (3.76).

In 511, in his first year as an official *(exceptor)* on the judicial side of the eastern Praetorian Prefecture, John, as a result of the special favor of the prefect Zoticus, earned 1,000 *solidi* in fees, the equivalent in weight of about 14 (Roman) pounds of gold (3.27).[1] For a new recruit, such a sum was exceptional. It undoubtedly reflected the wide-ranging opportunities for additional lucrative work provided by Zoticus' support.[2] Roughly speaking, on John's reckoning, his earnings equaled the fee-income of a reasonably successful middle-ranking *exceptor* who, perhaps after ten to fifteen years in post, had been selected to serve as one of the principal assistants *(adiutores)* to the department's senior officials (2.18). A detailed schedule issued in 534 by the emperor Justinian for the establishment of the Praetorian Prefecture of Africa (recently regained from the Vandals) provides some further sense of scale: a newly appointed *exceptor* was entitled to receive an annual salary of 9 *solidi,* his middle-ranking colleagues 16.[3] Under a series of laws issued in 535–36, even provincial governors, depending on their rank, military responsibilities, and other duties, could expect to receive an official stipend of only between 720 and 1,440 *solidi* a year (that is, between 10 and 20 pounds of gold).[4]

These figures belong to an extensive restructuring of the imperial administration. In his legislation, Justinian claimed to have raised salaries substantially, and to have reduced the sums bureaucrats were permitted to charge for their services.[5] The salaries prescribed in these laws can therefore reasonably be taken to represent *maxima.* Before the reforms of the 530s, bureaucrats were paid even less. It was no doubt the 1,000 *solidi* in fee-income earned in his first year which John felt more than justified his decision to accept a position as an *exceptor.* It also underscored the value of Zoticus' continued goodwill. But importantly, even without such close and advantageous connections, most bureaucrats on the staff of the eastern Praetorian Prefecture assumed as a matter of course that they would derive a significant part of their income from fees. The *cornicularius* (the most senior officer on the judicial side) regularly earned a minimum of 1,864 *solidi* a year, just under 26 pounds of gold (3.24). Under Justinian's schedule of 534, the equivalent official in the African Prefecture was entitled to an annual salary of 23 *solidi.*[6]

This difference between stipend and fee-income neatly exposes the extent to which officials depended for their financial security on a steady flow of payments from "contributors," as John called those who paid him for his services (3.11). Salaries were modest, even at the increased rate of 9 *solidi* for junior *exceptores* in the African Prefecture. In the sixth century, a builder's laborer in full employment might hope to earn around 7 *solidi* a year; a poor family in a provincial town could perhaps live on somewhere around half that amount; a subsistence farming family on even less.[7] But as John made clear, his colleagues—the majority from prosperous provincial backgrounds—expected a much better standard of living than their salaries alone would permit. They also had to afford the metropolitan costs of Constantinople.

Money earned from fees was also an important means of recouping the outlays necessary both for securing a post in the administration and for ensuring that promotion followed. In neither case does John give any indication of the sums which might have been involved. Some sense of scale may tentatively be gained from two fifth-century laws which aimed to regulate appointment and promotion practices in the *sacra scrinia* (the palace secretariats responsible for judicial and administrative matters directly involving the emperor). A new recruit, occupying the most junior position on the staff, had to pay 250 *solidi* to the head of the *scrinium (proximus)*, if his retirement had caused the vacancy. If the vacancy arose because of a death in post, the same amount was to be paid to the deceased's heirs, assignees, or creditors. In addition, 15 or 20 *solidi*, depending on the custom of the different *scrinia*, was payable to the deputy head *(melloproximus)*. In all, the fees levied by his colleagues would cost a newly appointed official around 270 *solidi*, or nearly 4 pounds of gold.[8]

Under such circumstances, it is again not surprising that, for bureaucrats, the payment of money in exchange for administrative action was regarded as a standard and necessary practice. Moreover, in the absence of any system of state-funded pension or superannuation, fee-income also contributed toward a "lump sum" which an official, following his retirement, hoped would see him through old age.[9] Equally, from an emperor's point of view, allowing bureaucrats to charge fees, which both raised money from those requiring their services and redistributed income across departments, substantially shifted the cost of the empire's administration away from the imperial exchequer. That salaries were regarded as only a basic component of bureaucrats' income is perhaps most clearly seen in the laws regulating absentees. They remained on the register of the department concerned and continued to receive a stipend. But nothing more. Only those in active service could benefit from fees earned in the course of their duties.[10]

In some cases, the amounts officials were permitted to levy were specifically prescribed in imperial legislation. A set of mostly late fifth-century laws laid down the sums certain designated groups were to pay for litigating before the *magister officiorum,* who as head of the palatine bureaucracy had both criminal and civil jurisdiction over a wide range of administrative personnel.[11] Officials staffing the *magister*'s court (and responsible for the conduct of cases and the drawing up of all the necessary legal documentation) received 6 or 7 *solidi* from those who could claim privileged status. Discounts were typically granted to those connected with the palace, as bureaucrats, guards, or servants. And the laws made clear that these sums represented substantially less than litigants not falling into one of these special categories might expect to pay.[12]

Reductions in fees were also prescribed for the praetorian prefect's court. In 456 the emperor Marcian ruled that members of the clergy in Constantinople, if required to defend a case, should have to pay no more than 2 *solidi* to the *executores* (the officials responsible for carrying out the orders of the court from summoning the defendant to enforcing the final judgment). He further instructed the prefect to keep the other administrative charges, regrettably not cited, well below those normally levied.[13] Some idea of the scale of these discounts can be gained from John's claim that in the heyday of his career (probably in the 520s) a plaintiff in the prefect's court might expect to pay 37 *solidi* just for a *postulatio simplex,* the pleading necessary to initiate an action (3.25).[14] At first sight, this amount seems high; but it is in line with the claim made in some of Justinian's other legislation that in matters worth less than 720 *solidi* some in the provinces might find bringing an action to court in Constantinople simply too expensive. In some circumstances, the fees and other costs (travel, board, lodging, and so on) associated with litigating in the imperial capital could be disproportionate to the value of the case itself.[15]

These detailed and sometimes tedious laws (like the legislation regulating the distribution of funds among bureaucrats following appointment, promotion, or retirement) emphasize the significant lack of imperial embarrassment about the payment of money in return for administrative services. Provincial governors, high-ranking officials, the staff of the palatine departments, even priests were expected to pay. Similarly, bureaucrats expected to be paid. Of course, the rate at which these services should be charged was endlessly disputed and frequently regulated. Yet even on the reduced rates payable by certain privileged groups, the amounts involved were considerable, particularly in the light of the salaries prescribed in 534 for the staff of the Praetorian Prefecture of Africa. All the more so when these salaries are, in turn, compared with the standard costs of litigation in the prefect's court, the charges for appointment or promotion levied on those working in the imperial capital, and the sums quoted by John for the fee-income of officials on the Prefecture's judicial side. Most important, this scatter of figures again underwrites John's tacit—and to his mind entirely uncontroversial—assumption that payment for administrative transactions would provide his colleagues with the bulk of their annual earnings. Indeed, on such a scale, even an unambitious bureaucrat who scrupulously followed imperial directives must comfortably and honestly have expected to enjoy an income substantially in excess of his official stipend.

The Survival of the Fittest

Given the importance of fees to their livelihood, their promotion prospects, and their retirement plans, bureaucrats were particularly concerned that they should continue to be able to secure a sufficient workload to maintain their income. In John's view, a flourishing department was marked by a high number of administrative transactions and a correspondingly large number of officials. John had treasured memories of his early years in the Prefecture. He presented himself as a successful young man with every expectation of steady advancement (3.26–27). He recalled with pride those prosperous times when both the prefect and his staff had worked "from the dead of night to the break of day" (3.15). Then, too, the *adiutores*, though appointed for only one year, had continued to earn fees for some time after their term in office. A special place was set aside for them in the building which housed the prefect's tribunal.

They had an area allocated to them at the main entrance of the prefect's court . . . where they assembled and finished the business which
had been transacted during their time in post. And those who had recently come to the end of their terms as *adiutores* in the secretariats on
the judicial side paid close attention to these matters, culling for themselves no small consolation in earnings; while those former *adiutores*,
who had retired before them, gathered there and were entrusted with
the Prefecture's most important and prestigious administrative work
and with anything some other official had been unable to complete.
(3.13)

The advantages were clear to all. New recruits were plentiful. Before
the reforms of John the Cappadocian, it seems that the eastern Praetorian Prefecture supported around one thousand bureaucrats on its judicial side (3.66).[16] If the relative sizes of the staff in the African Prefecture (as set out in Justinian's legislation of 534) can be taken as a
rough guide—98 *exceptores* (on the judicial side), 130 *scriniarii* (on the
financial side), and 168 nonadministrative staff—the total number
may have been as large as 4,000.[17] Among the *exceptores* (and perhaps
too the *scriniarii*), this figure probably also included a large number
of *supernumerarii*, officials who (as their rank suggests) were not yet
formally included on the department's personnel register, but who
processed surplus work and competed for established posts as they
arose. Their annual income consisted entirely of fees. The number of
supernumerarii a department could support was a crude and highly visible index of its success in generating income by charging for its services. At the height of its prosperity, the prefect's court (at least as John
chose to remember it) was thronged with *supernumerarii* who had "no
small opportunity for the gainful pursuit of earnings" (3.6).[18]

For John, social standing, income, and the volume of administrative
transactions were all intimately related. A steady and predictable flow
of work ensured that all members of a department benefited from "the
limitless influx of earnings coming from the documents which were
being processed" (3.15). Moreover, their status and reputation were
secure. The most experienced officials on the Prefecture's judicial side
came to be respected for their literary and legal abilities as well as for
their scholarly erudition and impressive learning. Indeed, at that time,
claimed John (perhaps reacting against the annoying pretensions of
some of his professorial colleagues at the State University of Constan-

tinople), it was not uncommon for distinguished bureaucrats to be sought out by academics who hoped for enlightened discussion "on matters of which they were ignorant" (3.13, 3.11).

The highest officials in the Prefecture occupied an enviable position. The *commentariensis* (who held the third most-senior post on the judicial side) was a personage of some considerable eminence. Again recalling the golden years of his early career, John claimed that when he first joined the Prefecture, "anyone who had met a *commentariensis* as he was passing by, was himself thought worthy of conversation" (3.17). Importantly, too, those requiring administrative services were (at least in John's opinion) happy to pay. Almost, it seems, like wise bureaucrats, they realized that a continual supply of official business meant that the prefect with the help of his hard-working staff could fulfill "every desire of those involved in the provision of justice, those who had matters to be dealt with, and those who had completed their litigation" (3.15). For John, the perfect administrative world was defined by a stable and predictable balance between those controlling and those demanding access to government. Ideally, an official would have a sufficient "market share" to satisfy his own financial needs, while neither overpricing his services (and so risking unremunerative inaccessibility) nor continuing to offer those no longer required.

John's charmingly soft-focus picture is in large part wishful thinking. That delicate and mutually profitable relationship between officials and those requiring their services was difficult to maintain. The security of such an arrangement was ever-threatened by the predatory activities of rival departments seeking to arrogate to themselves control over profitable areas of responsibility. It was also dangerously subject to imperially sponsored reforms, which might redistribute some of a department's core activities or demand reductions in the levels of fees charged. From an emperor's point of view, low salaries (and a large number of *supernumerarii* dependent on fee-income alone) offered some protection against the adverse consequences of administrative reform. The expectation that the greater part of even a junior official's income would be derived from fees meant that a substantial proportion of the cost of any reorganization, and in particular the redundancy or underemployment of individuals, fell neither on the government nor on those seeking its services (who could redirect their resources), but on bureaucrats themselves.

Individuals carried the greatest risks. Officials might benefit from advantageous shifts in jurisdiction, but at the same time they personally bore the costs of their department's loss of control over a particular set of transactions or of any reduction in the amounts paid for their services. The risk of a sudden contraction in workload and the unpredictable fluctuations in fee-income were undoubtedly also factors taken into account by officials in setting the level of charges. For bureaucrats, current earnings (like John's initial fee-income of 1,000 *solidi*) had always to be seen as insurance against the possibility of future losses.

In midcareer John himself paid the price of a series of administrative reforms. In the 530s the system of provincial government was restructured, and correspondingly the appellate jurisdiction of the empire's superior courts. The basic principle behind these reforms was the devolution of greater administrative, judicial, and in some cases military responsibility to governors both sufficiently senior and sufficiently powerful to deal effectively with local issues without appeal either to the emperor or to courts in Constantinople. This decentralization of authority had the direct effect of reducing the number of matters dealt with by the Prefecture's judicial side. John's account was predictably hostile. He closely linked these reforms with a dramatic drop in his own fee-income, with a decline in the importance of the prefect's court, and ultimately with his own and his colleagues' financial ruin. For John, this was just cause for a judicious mixture of explanation, lamentation, and philosophical reflection. Execration would follow in its proper place.

> Time, being destructive by nature, has either totally extinguished the many useful and well-ordered features of the staff serving the Prefecture or has altered those features so much as to preserve for the future only a faint trace of what was once admired . . . It is now therefore the appropriate moment to advance my narrative further and to state the reasons why the staff's circumstances were reduced to the point of such great change.   (3.39)

Before Justinian's reorganization, the system of appeals from provincial governors to high-ranking courts in Constantinople followed in its basic outline the administrative structure of the eastern Praetorian Prefecture.[19] The Prefecture was divided into five dioceses, or groups of provinces. In turn, each diocese was headed by a direct deputy of the prefect *(uicarius),* whose precise title varied: Pontica and Asiana were both the responsibility of *uicarii,* Oriens of the *comes Orientis,* Egypt of the *praefectus Augustalis,* and Thrace of the *uicarius longi muri.* All five *uicarii* held the formal honorific rank of *spectabilis* along with a small minority of provincial governors. The rest held the lower rank of *clarissimus.*[20] On the basis of these divisions in responsibility and status, John distinguished two types of cases. First, *causae temporales:* appeals from governors of the rank of *clarissimus,* which went either to *uicarii* or directly to the prefect himself.[21] Secondly, *causae sacrae.* As set out in a law promulgated by Theodosius II and Valentinian III in 440, appeals from the courts of *uicarii* and the more senior governors of the rank of *spectabilis* went to a tribunal in Constantinople under the joint control of the praetorian prefect and the emperor's chief legal officer, the *quaestor sacri palatii.*[22] *Causae sacrae* ("sacred cases") were so called, as John explained, because they had originally been heard by the emperor himself (2.15–16). As a result, hearings before the prefect and *quaestor* (at least until altered by a law of Justinian in 546) still incorporated much of the grandeur and formality appropriate to proceedings in the imperial presence.[23] Matters brought before either the prefect's court or the joint tribunal were also subject to strict time limits. Hence, as John patiently explained—to a perhaps now understandably confused readership—the original designation of the first category of appeals as *causae temporales,* or "timed cases" (2.15).[24]

These administrative arrangements were significantly altered during John the Cappadocian's second term in office (October 532 to May 541). In April 535 the vicarates of Asiana and Pontica were made redundant and replaced by two provincial governorships (Phrygia Pacatiana and Galatia Prima respectively), whose holders had their remits greatly expanded and both of whom now ranked as *spectabiles.* At the same time, the *comes Orientis* was amalgamated with the governorship of Syria Prima, also promoted to *spectabilis* rank.[25] Over the next eighteen months, eleven governors in these three dioceses (Asiana, Pontica, and Oriens) had their provinces reorganized, their authority augmented, and their rank raised from *clarissimus* to *spectabilis.*

This extensive restructuring of provincial government affected the flow of cases to the prefect's court. In their own provinces, governors of *spectabilis* rank now heard, at first instance or on appeal, all cases

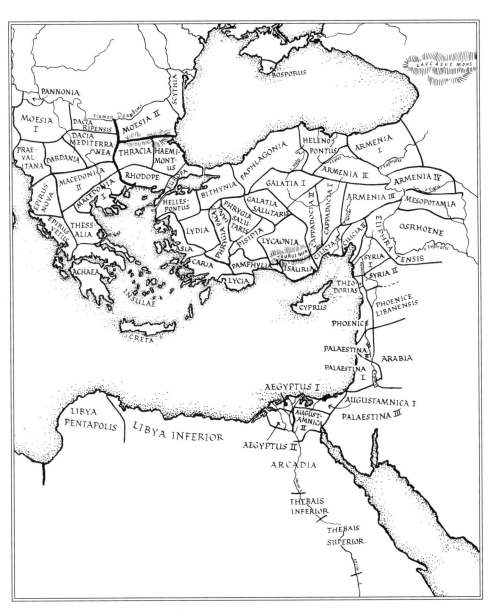

The eastern Roman Empire in the last years of Justinian

worth up to 500 *solidi* (a threshold raised to 720 *solidi* by July 536).[26] In addition to these reforms, the Prefecture's responsibilities were eroded in the diocese of Thrace in May 535 by the abolition of the *uicarius longi muri* and the creation of a more powerful governor with civil and military authority and the rank of *spectabilis;* in the diocese of Egypt in 539 by the abolition of the *praefectus Augustalis,* who was replaced by a number of higher ranking governors with both civil and military powers; and in May 536 by the institution of the *quaestor exercitus* or prefect of Scythia, who had control over five provinces detached from the eastern Praetorian Prefecture.[27] Not all of these changes were lasting. The gradual reestablishment of an intermediate tier of government acknowledged that, whatever the advantages of greater autonomy, some provinces had been unable to deal effectively with larger, regional problems such as border defense and brigandage.[28] Even so, these later adjustments did not significantly alter the basic pattern of decentralization which under John the Cappadocian had so effectively devolved power away from the great departments of state in Constantinople.

The administrative reforms of the 530s had a cumulative impact on the eastern Praetorian Prefecture. First, as a result of the creation of the *quaestor exercitus,* it lost all jurisdiction over a large and prosperous area once under its control. Second, the categorization of cases according to value acted to ensure that more legal disputes were settled in the provinces than before superior courts in Constantinople. Third, the promotion of a number of governors from *clarissimus* to *spectabilis* rank meant that a much greater proportion of cases which did go on appeal to the imperial capital were heard by the joint tribunal of the prefect and *quaestor sacri palatii* rather than by the prefect sitting alone. For those on the judicial side, the inevitable result was a drop in fee-income. And worse was to follow. In parallel with this reorganization of the empire's provincial administration and its judicial system, Justinian and his advisers sought to reduce the fees bureaucrats received from those requiring or demanding their services. A schedule of charges annexed to a law issued in April 535 set out the amounts provincial governors were to pay various officials both for helping to secure an appointment (perhaps by presenting the candidate's name to the emperor himself) and for processing the necessary paperwork. Probably in return for issuing a warrant authorizing the new post-holder to draw his official salary, the staff of the eastern Praetorian Prefecture received en bloc from the *comes Orientis* and the governor of Asia 80 *solidi*, from the governors of Phrygia Pacatiana and Galatia Prima 50, from other governors of *spectabilis* rank 40, and from *clarissimi* 36.[29] For providing similar services to newly appointed governors, the staff of the African Prefecture was to receive 12 *solidi*.[30] How these charges were divided up among officials in the Prefectures (or between *exceptores* and *scriniarii*) is not known. No doubt little filtered down to the junior ranks.

Justinian's reforms were also aimed at reducing the fees paid to individual bureaucrats (or to small groups of officials) for specific administrative tasks. According to a contemporary of John's, the historian John Malalas, in 530, "The emperor dispatched to all the cities laws for litigants dealing with the permitted costs involved in taking a matter to court. Similarly, in regulating the fees to be charged, he decreed that no one should dare to take more than the sum specified by him."[31] Regrettably, this law does not survive.[32] Nor is it known how generally successful such prescriptions were in cutting the cost of litigation. The carefully tabulated schedules of charges in Justinian's laws have an air of confident administrative efficiency which may in itself be misleading. As with much imperial legislation, the likelihood of its enforcement or the effectiveness of its policing is difficult to judge. Yet even if there was a considerable degree of latitude, Justinian's legislation cannot have passed unnoticed. Like the laws of 534 and April 535, which reduced the amounts payable by newly appointed governors and threatened fines for noncompliance,[33] scattered references in subsequent legislation indicate that the schedule of charges issued in 530 was another memorable and forcefully phrased advertisement of imperial policy.[34] And, at the very least, in setting their fees officials must have had to take that declaration into account.

The impact of these measures was greatest on departments which already faced cutbacks in their workload. Alongside the reorganization of the Empire's courts, which reduced the number of cases that were solely the administrative responsibility of the Prefecture's judicial side, Justinian's earlier legislation must have inhibited any move by the *exceptores* to increase their charges in order to compensate for an inevitable decline in fee-income. Indeed, it is likely to have forced some overall lowering of the amounts it was thought possible or prudent to levy. Moreover, the most far-reaching of these changes was implemented within the short space of three to five years around 535, although many of the consequences no doubt took some time to become fully apparent. It was not, after all, until 546 that the procedures to be followed in cases before the joint tribunal were revised and the prefect and *quaestor* ordered to abandon many of the solemnities of language, dress, and etiquette thought appropriate only to the imperial court itself. That said, for many on the judicial side of the Prefecture the long-term effects of these reforms must have been only too immediately obvious. Those already fully committed to service in the department and financially dependent on the opportunities it offered for charging fees clearly had the most to lose.

For John, any reduction in the Prefecture's responsibilities was a matter of deep personal concern. In his self-centered version of events, he was not particularly interested in discussing the reasons for the devolution of power to provincial governors, for the strengthening of their authority by the combination of civil and military authority, or for the reforms which claimed to reduce the delays and expense of litigation. He made little attempt to explain the policies pursued by Justinian or his advisers or to appreciate the wider strategic advantages of any reorganization. He offered his readers no analysis of either the financial pressures or the structural problems faced by an imperial government attempting to recover Italy and North Africa, to secure its northern frontiers, and to fend off (or buy off) the persistent threat of a serious Persian invasion. Rather, John's anxieties were much closer to home. In midcareer, what worried him were the continued opportunities to earn fee-income. For John, the restrictions on the Prefecture's administrative and judicial competence and on its ability to set the amounts charged for its services were to be seen almost entirely in terms of the constriction of funds. As litigants sought access to other courts, as those requiring administrative action transferred their business to officials in other departments, and as the level of fees paid was reduced, John fretted about the consequent impact on his prospects, his earnings, and the morale of his colleagues on the Prefecture's judicial side. "And so the staff perished; and as there was no business to transact, a dreary desolation defiled the court, and those who were nearing the end of their time in the department lamented and wept, sinking as they were into an old age of poverty" (3.66).

Nor was John exceptional in his obsessive financial concerns. The elevation of a governorship from *clarissimus* to *spectabilis* rank and the consequent recategorization of appeals from the governor's court in matters worth more than 720 *solidi* (now to be heard by the joint tribunal of praetorian prefect and *quaestor sacri palatii*) had a direct effect on the officials involved in the administration of the case. Under the law of 440 issued by Theodosius II and Valentinian III, the joint tribunal was served both by *epistulares* (members of the *scrinium epistularum,* one of the *sacra scrinia,* chiefly responsible for processing the paperwork of cases on appeal) and by officials from the judicial side of the Prefecture (chiefly responsible for providing the staff for court hearings).[35] Thus when a provincial governor's post was raised in rank, the judicial side of the Prefecture significantly lost out. Prior to the change, appeals had been heard by the prefect sitting alone, and all the necessary legal and administrative services had been provided by his department. A change in the status of a province gave the *epistulares* an opportunity to expand their functions and to increase their fee-income. Any gains were made at the direct expense of the Prefecture's judicial side.

Following the initial upgrading of a series of governorships to *spectabilis* rank, the Prefecture's officials moved quickly to prevent the sudden losses in services and fees which would result if the same disadvantageous division of duties were also held to apply to cases on appeal from these provinces. Through their prefect John the Cappadocian, the judicial staff entered into negotiations with the *epistulares.* Both parties subsequently sought imperial ratification of the ensuing agreement. The resulting law of March 536 addressed "to our most glorious prefect John" clearly set out the basic conflict of interest between the *epistulares* (pressing to expand their activities) and the Prefecture's judicial side (fighting hard to maintain its current level of earnings). The preamble to the law summarized the problem, albeit in rather prolix terms.

It is certainly the case that very many doubts have arisen concerning the discharge of these functions, since those from the *sacrum scrinium* of the *epistulares* claim for themselves the administration of appeals from governors of *spectabilis* rank, while those from your highness' department state that they will be greatly affected if, as a result of a change, they no longer solely administer those appeals (which came from governors of *clarissimus* rank to your court alone) just as before, when you yourself heard these cases in your own court, and your department was in charge of the administration. But because of the elevation of those governors to the rank of *spectabilis,* the business before your court has moved, and is now heard jointly by your highness and our most glorious *quaestor.* In consequence, those from your department ask that all the business which comes before both these judges be their responsibility alone, whereas up until now at the joint tribunal of your highness and our most glorious *quaestor* it was shared with those from the *sacra scrinia* who administered appeals.[36]

The compromise approved in this law was that cases on appeal to the joint tribunal from the courts of governors recently raised to the rank of *spectabilis* should—clearly contrary to the law of 440—be the sole responsibility of the staff on the judicial side of the Prefecture.[37] For the *exceptores,* this was a victory of sorts. By soliciting imperial approval for their claim to be the only officials concerned with the conduct of these appeals they had prevented any contraction in the range of their administrative duties—and at the direct expense of a rival department. Regrettably, it is impossible to estimate what difference this may have made to the judicial side's fee-income. Undoubtedly for those *exceptores* serving the tribunal the successful assertion of their claim was a worthwhile demonstration of the Prefecture's continued importance, even more so against a background of an overall reduction in charges for administrative services. But, for all that, the financial gains were limited. There was no change to previous prescriptions on time limits or to the value of cases which could be litigated before the joint tribunal. Nor seemingly were the provisions of this law extended to cover the reorganization of the Thracian diocese (carried out a year earlier, in May 535), or the institution of the *quaestor exercitus* in May 536, or the further administrative reforms in Oriens (with the creation of three more governorships of *spectabilis* rank for Arabia, Palaestina, and Phoenice Libanensis), or the changes made in Egypt following the abolition of the *praefectus Augustalis* in 539. The *exceptores* may initially have improved their position, but as the restructuring of the empire's provincial administration continued, the *epistulares* perhaps felt that they had conceded enough. At least, they seem successfully to have resisted any further erosion of their duties.

The agreement between the *epistulares* and the *exceptores* and its imperial ratification is again important evidence for a wider recognition (among bureaucrats, high officers of state, and perhaps even the emperor himself) that administrative and judicial reform could have a direct impact on the earning capacity of officials serving in the various departments of government. It also underlines the point that the main cost of any reorganization would be borne, not by the imperial exchequer, nor by those seeking to litigate, but by those officials who lost out. For *exceptores,* as the various reforms began to take effect, that consequence must have been their overwhelming concern. Imperial ratification of the agreement with the *epistulares,* no matter how welcome, could have offered only slight compensation for the steady contraction in the Prefecture's remit and the concomitant reduction in the judicial staff's opportunities to earn fee-income. Among his colleagues, John cannot have been alone in his worries about the future.

The concession won from the *epistulares* in March 536 (perhaps, in part, because it showed the Cappadocian acting in the department's interests) did not rate a mention in John's intensely personal account of the decline and fall of the eastern Praetorian Prefecture. For him, it was only a minor interruption in an epic story of degeneration. The decay of the judicial side following the reforms of the 530s was, in John's view, nothing less than a tragedy in the grandest manner (3.67). "'What follows no longer would I be able to express in words without weeping,' to quote Euripides' *Peleus*" (3.25). This was a tale worthy of the finest dramatic exaggeration. On four more occasions, John confessed himself close to tears (3.11, 3.12, 3.20, 3.43). It did not matter that this literary effect was, in part, achieved by some economy with the truth. In all his discussions of *causae sacrae* John, no doubt to stress the effect of the reforms on the Praetorian Prefecture alone, never mentioned that the prefect had since 440 exercised his jurisdiction jointly with the *quaestor sacri palatii.* Nor did he ever let on that his account of the magnificence of the prefect's court (2.16) actually described the procedure followed by the joint tribunal.[38] Moreover, John did not hesitate to telescope events to lend his account a greater urgency. His insistence that the decline happened under John the Cappadocian would strictly exclude both the legislation of 530, which aimed to restrict the charging of administrative fees by bureaucrats, and that of 546, which altered the form of proceedings in the joint tribunal, sweeping away many of its most impressive formalities. Given its date, this second law might also indicate a more gradual decline in the fortunes of the judicial side than John suggests in his compressed account of sudden collapse.[39]

But these technical niceties, the business only of an academic historian overly concerned with the cold facts of the matter, were of little importance against the flow of a finely constructed narrative which might make a more sympathetic reader weep. Under the Cappadocian (John's lamentations continued), in the prefect's court "not even a trace of solemnity remained." Cases were conducted "accompanied by the laughter of bystanders just as though they were watching cheap entertainment" (2.16). The once-famous standard of advocacy declined. Among the staff, callow youth usurped the dignity of age (2.18). Juniors ignored the wisdom and experience of their superiors (3.14). The forms and "the august and worthily decorous" procedures, the responsibility of the Prefecture, which staffed the court, were done away with (2.17). Among the "tokens of an antique dignity which has utterly perished" (3.14) John particularly regretted the abandonment of the splendidly ritualized method of timekeeping. Its importance was reflected in the fact that it was the responsibility of the *primiscrinius,* the second-highest-ranking officer on the judicial side. "For he . . . in a dignified manner without warning let fall to the ground certain small spheres. Nor were these worthless, as they were made of silver and they had markings, in Latin numbers and letters, to show the hours of the day. And each made a solemn sound, the sphere which was cast upon the marble floor thereby indicating the hour of the day" (2.16).

The judicial staff of the eastern Praetorian Prefecture could do little to reverse the decline in their fortunes. Whereas once a litigant might have expected to pay 37 *solidi* for a writ to initiate a legal action in the prefect's court, subsequently only "a very modest copper (not even a gold coin) was given out of pity, by way of charity, and not always even that" (3.25). The staff were no longer able to afford the parchment on which to draw up the legal documents required even by the greatly reduced number of cases which they were permitted to administer. Once, only the finest parchment had been used. For it was necessary, explained John, to have materials of the highest quality to match the impressive magnificence of those who wrote on them (3.14). But with John the Cappadocian's reforms, all that had been swept away. Now "the remaining staff demand even paper from those who transact business . . . and they issue grass instead of parchment, covered with in-ferior writing and redolent of poverty" (3.14).[40] In the face of these pitiable instances of degeneration, John again recalled the once-impressive number of his senior colleagues and their seemingly endless workload. He appealed to his readers to remember the lost glories of former times. "For who indeed, when considering the large number of *adiutores*, could not surmise the greatness of the court of justice and the vast amount of business which was once transacted in it?" (3.9).

Insurance Policies

For later Roman bureaucrats, the expansion of rival departments and the schemes of reorganizing emperors and their advisers posed a con-stant, if unpredictable, threat. For all his exaggeration and tragic hy-perbole, John's strident reactions to administrative change amply illus-trate the ever-pressing importance of these concerns. As far as they were able, some officials (like any prudent long-term employees) tried to protect themselves against shifts in their responsibilities and in any consequent downturn in their earnings. As suggested above, the amounts charged for administrative services reflected in some mea-sure the recognition, both by the department as a whole and by its individual members, that fee-income might vary considerably across time. Other tactics were also deployed. At one extreme, a bureaucrat though a full member of a department (and drawing an official salary) might have another occupation from which he derived a good propor-tion of his income. Regrettably, it is difficult to tell how widespread this practice was. But for those who devoted most of their time to other ac-tivities there were penalties attached. In 379 Gratian, Valentinian I, and Theodosius I ruled that certain staff (including members of the *sacra scrinia*) who were absent from their posts for six months would lose five places in seniority; for twelve months, ten places; for four years, forty places; and after four years' absence an official could ex-pect to lose his job.[41]

In the face of such legislation and the other risks of holding office, absentees had to balance a series of competing factors. First, the in-come derived from their alternative occupation had to be set against the fees they would earn if they spent time working for their depart-ment. Second, the possibility of promotion to more remunerative higher grades, and the rewards of being in a more senior post if a department were to expand the scope of its duties, had to be weighed against the penalties imposed as a result of absence. And third, the advantages of having an alternative source of income in case of a sudden (and unpredictable) restriction in a department's administrative responsibilities, and a consequent downturn in fees, had to be judged against the possibility of being deprived of a post altogether.

In 528 or 529, at the beginning of Justinian's reign, an imperial law aimed to force those officials still pursuing interests outside their departments into making a final decision. All those engaged in commercial ventures *(negotiatores)*, except those involved in the state monopoly on arms manufacture, were banned from holding a position in the imperial bureaucracy. Those in post were to decide between their department and their business. They could no longer continue to keep their options open.[42] It was clearly the intention of Justinian's legislation (as with the graded penalties imposed by Gratian in the late fourth century) to ensure that, as far as possible, bureaucrats depended on their official activities for the bulk of their income; or that, at the very least, they should be prepared to shoulder the risks that doing so entailed. No doubt, too, many bureaucrats like John, who had few alternative sources of income and relied for their livelihood principally on their administrative work, felt strongly that their colleagues should be in the same position. Certainly John had no doubt that conspicuous devotion to duty should always be amply rewarded.

Officials in active service might hope to spread the risk of being deprived of any particular responsibility by undertaking to process as wide a range of work as time and competence allowed. At the very beginning of his career, John was selected as a *chartularius* (chief administrative officer) to the *adiutores* of the *ab actis*. In that post, tenable for only one year, his duties included the compilation of the *regesta* or *cottidiana*, the daily register which recorded a summary of business transacted in the prefect's court, and the *personalia*, the digest in Latin of cases on which judgment had been entered (3.27, 3.20). In addition he wrote the briefs *(suggestiones)* setting out the reasons for judgment in cases taken on appeal from the prefect to the imperial court *(consistorium)*. John also spent some time helping his fellow *exceptores*, particularly those staffing the prefect's court (3.27).[43] As well as all this—"with the help of God and spurred on by the fee-income which fell to me and made me unaware of my toil" (3.27)—he took on work for the *a secretis,* a corps of confidential imperial secretaries, entirely separate from the Prefecture, who acted as officials for judicial proceedings before the *consistorium.*[44]

How long John intended to work for both the judicial side of the Prefecture and the *a secretis* is unclear. At some stage in this early part of his career, he decided to concentrate his efforts on the Prefecture alone. Perhaps he felt that his earnings were sufficiently high. He had, after all, netted 1,000 *solidi* in his first year in post. Perhaps, too, he reckoned that his career prospects were sufficiently good. He had, thanks to the favor of the praetorian prefect Zoticus, been enrolled immediately as an *exceptor* (rather than a *supernumerarius*) and had served as a *chartularius.* In addition, John may have calculated that the wide range of his activities on the judicial side was sufficient insurance against any shift in the Prefecture's responsibilities. It also meant that he was well placed to benefit from any expansion in the department's competence. Lastly, the advantageous marriage John had contracted soon after joining the staff, which brought him a dowry of 100 pounds of gold (3.28), gave him some additional financial security and was yet another expression of confidence (this time from his father-in-law) in his prospects. "Since I was expecting much better things to come to me as time went on, I curbed my enthusiasm for the court and gave my whole life over to service in the department" (3.28).

Depending on when his decision to devote himself to the Prefecture was made, John's curtailment of his work for the *a secretis* may also have been caused by the successful maneuvering of officials in other departments. A law issued in 524 by the emperor Justin I (and forcefully reiterated by his successor Justinian in the early 530s) banned the holding of more than one post: "no one hereafter shall have the right to belong to more than one department at the same time; and all persons are forbidden to hold two or more posts." Only *memoriales* (who staffed the *sacra scrinia*) and *agentes in rebus* were allowed to hold certain joint appointments. One permitted combination was a post in the *a secretis.*[45] Double service of the sort John seems at one time to have contemplated, on the judicial side of the Praetorian Prefecture and in another department, was henceforth prohibited.

Some of John's colleagues (and perhaps even John himself) may have found themselves disadvantaged by this legislation. Regrettably, as with absenteeism, it is difficult to know how widespread the practice of holding more than one position was.[46] But such restrictions on the range of their activities undoubtedly made officials even more vulnerable to any constriction in their own department's responsibilities. As with the prohibition on bureaucrats' involvement in outside business interests, imperial proscription of the doubling-up of posts cut off (or at least made more hazardous) yet another escape route which could be carefully prepared in advance. But in a flourishing department with a high fee-income and a steady supply of administrative transactions, the need to look for outside work cannot have seemed so pressing. Indeed, if John's account of the *adiutores* still completing their tasks long after their annual term of appointment (3.13) gives any reliable indication of workload, it may have been difficult for any official in a successful department to find the time to fulfill the duties required by a second post.

In such circumstances, with the additional bar of imperial legislation, officials had little option but to trade present advantage against future risk, no matter how imprudent that decision might appear in retrospect. Indeed, for the majority of John's colleagues, and certainly it seems for John himself, the scale of the reforms in the 530s and the pace at which their consequences took effect seem to have come as an unwelcome surprise. No doubt (and perhaps understandably) many had assumed that the Prefecture would continue to maintain its advantageous position and its capacity to command high levels of fees for its services. Like John, they expected "much better things to come . . . as time went on." Few—perhaps only an unlikely coalition of the most pessimistic, the most risk averse, and the most politically farsighted— could have made adequate advance provision against any such long-term loss of fee-income.

Following the reforms of the 530s, many officials on the judicial side, and especially those in midcareer, may have found themselves trapped in unremunerative posts with little better in prospect. (Given only John's version of events, it is difficult accurately to assess the severity or extent of the problem.) At worst, some perhaps abandoned their careers. With a decreased workload combined with the pressure to reduce the fees charged for their services, they may have been unable to afford either the cost of living in Constantinople or the price of further promotion. Nor, except for the most junior, was transferring to another department a viable alternative. As a result of the legislation prohibiting joint appointments, bureaucrats could move only if they were willing to accept a low-ranking position, perhaps even as a *supernumerarius*. For an official on the judicial side in midcareer, perhaps one who had served as an *adiutor* and had once been accustomed to an annual income of 1,000 *solidi,* moving to a junior job elsewhere must have looked more unattractive than trying to stay in post, even in a department where the opportunities for fee-income risked yet further restriction.

John himself, despite his many well-phrased lamentations, was considerably better placed than many of his colleagues. Around 543, on the emperor's recommendation, he was appointed to a professorship in Latin language and literature at the State University of Constantinople. The establishment provided for thirty-one chairs: three in Latin rhetoric, ten in Latin language and literature, five in Greek rhetoric, ten in Greek language and literature, one in philosophy, and two in law. Lectures were held in a public building known as the Auditorium Capitolii in the middle of the city. The running of the university, the regulation and control of students, and the payment of professors' salaries was the responsibility of the urban prefect.[47] But John's chair was by specific imperial permission to be held jointly with his position in the Prefecture. Perhaps because, strictly speaking, it contravened his own and his predecessor's legislation on holding more than one official post, Justinian's notice of appointment confirming this arrangement was issued to both the urban and the praetorian prefects.[48] In his new position John also received an additional salary, in this case, it seems, paid by the Praetorian Prefecture, again perhaps reflecting something of the exceptional arrangements his appointment entailed. John is charmingly coy about the amount he received. In his lengthy quotation of Justinian's confirmation of his new post (complete with its fulsome praise of his literary and linguistic abilities) he deliberately omitted the precise figure.

We are aware of the extent of the most learned John's education in literature, his precision in matters of language, his grace among the poets, and the rest of his erudition; and in order that through his own efforts he might make the language of the Romans more revered (although strictly speaking he is serving in your eminence's [the praetorian prefect] courts of justice) we are aware that he has chosen along with that to spend his life among books and to devote his whole self to scholarship. Therefore, since we judge it unworthy of our times to pass over unrewarded one who has reached such heights of excellence, we instruct your eminence to present him with such-and-such a sum from the treasury.   (3.29)

But John's earnings in academe are unlikely ever to have matched his previous income. Justinian's schedule for the annual salaries to be paid officials in the Praetorian Prefecture of Africa also included amounts to be paid to senior teaching staff in Carthage. The *grammaticus* was paid the equivalent of 35 *solidi*, and with pupils' fees might perhaps hope to earn 100 *solidi* a year.[49] No doubt, as for bureaucrats and those paying for their services, the salaries and fees received by teachers benefiting from the metropolitan prestige of Constantinople were far greater. After twenty years' service, professors at the State University received the honorary title of *comes primi ordinis*, the same as a retiring *cornicularius*, the most senior official on the judicial side of the eastern Praetorian Prefecture.[50] Moreover in the capital there was always the possibility of being commissioned by the emperor to deliver a public oration in his praise or to write an official history of his military campaigns. In addition, John had whatever fee-income he was able to earn by his continued service in the Prefecture, even if by comparison with his early career it seemed to him that at the end of a lifetime's devoted service to his department he had "obtained nothing from it by way of consolation" (3.25). Yet in the decade following the reforms to the Prefecture, however much John objected to his change in fortune, to the drop in his earnings, and to his dependence on a teaching post, he must have fared much better than many of his colleagues who had no alternative sources of income.

Indeed, it may be one of the great ironies of John's career that the reforms carried out under John the Cappadocian actually increased his chances of advancement. As those with alternative and preferable sources of income left the department, and as others could not afford either to remain in the imperial capital or to pay the costs of promotion, John may well have benefited from an increased number of vacancies among those senior to him. Able to stay in post, partly as the result of the financial cushion provided by both his previous earnings and his advantageous marriage, and partly because of his imperially sanctioned combination of positions, John perhaps progressed through the middle ranks of the Prefecture's judicial side more rapidly than he might otherwise have expected.[51] Perhaps something of the difficult and somewhat embarrassing circumstances surrounding an accelerated promotion to the judicial side's most senior post lay behind John's revealing reflection that despite the losses in fee-income (which he continued bitterly to resent) he had gained from his time in the Prefecture an "honor as good as a large sum of money" (3.30).

For officials who found themselves committed to a department faced with a declining workload, a range of defensive tactics were available. It was possible to lobby for the passage of an imperial law which might go some way to mitigating collectively (as in the case of the compromise reached between the judicial staff of the Prefecture and the *epistulares* in March 536) or individually (as with John's appointment to a chair) some of the effects of a wider program of reorganization or of the reallocation of tasks between departments. More crudely, in the face of declining fee-income and a drop in demand for their services, officials might raise the charge they levied for each transaction. In part, the effectiveness of this strategy depended on the restrictions imposed by imperial legislation. In part, too, the possibility of increasing fees depended on both the willingness and ability of those demanding or requiring a particular administrative service to pay more for it.

The parameters are neatly delineated by a second clash between the judicial side of the Prefecture and the *epistulares* over the distribution of fee-income. Following the reforms of the 530s, in the face of falling recruitment to the Prefecture, John claimed that the *epistulares* quadrupled their charges for issuing a certificate of appointment *(probatoria)* to a newly appointed *exceptor* from 5 to 20 *solidi*. Perhaps predictably, the reaction of new appointees was to attempt to avoid payment by failing to obtain *probatoriae* and taking up their posts on the authority of the praetorian prefect alone. The legality of such a cost-saving measure was open to dispute. A series of imperial laws (the earliest surviving dating from 356) clearly required *exceptores* to apply for a *probatoria* as a necessary part of an appointment to an established position on the prefect's staff.[52] Against these imperial rulings, those on the judicial side asserted that "the law had originally given the Prefecture the right through its own decisions to enroll among the *exceptores* serving its court of justice whomsoever it wished" (3.67). John himself claimed to know many colleagues who had joined the service on the prefect's authority alone and had gone on to render distinguished service. As a counter to the judicial side's attempts to avoid payment, and their seemingly specious justifications, the *epistulares*' response was both well judged and to the point. "When, however, they realized that no one ventured, or rather was not able, to procure a *probatoria* for such a sum, they extorted for themselves a ruling [from the emperor] in which it was conceded that no one without an imperial letter of appointment should enter service under the prefects" (3.67).

The effect of this imperial decision was to force those appointed to established posts to apply for *probatoriae* and to pay the *epistulares* at the higher rate. In a department whose opportunities for earning fee-income had recently been restricted, and which was already experiencing a reduction in the number of those willing to join, an increase in the cost of appointment was a further setback. Moreover, the payment of these fees to bureaucrats outside the Prefecture made the imperial decision a double loss. Senior *exceptores* nearing retirement, who expected to benefit from the fees ordinarily levied on new recruits, might find that in a shrinking market there was no one willing to fill the vacancy their retirement would create. All the more so if they insisted on holding to their accustomed level of charges, or even raising them as the number of appointees dropped. The *matricularius* faced a similar dilemma. As the senior official in charge of personnel and their promotion, he also expected to derive fee-income from new appointees.[53] It seems likely that, like those wishing to retire, the *matricularius* had to reduce his charges to compensate both for the increased cost of a *probatoria* and for the drop in the number of recruits.

As a result of losing this dispute with the *epistulares*, senior officials on the judicial side faced the unpalatable combination of a diminished demand for their administrative services, a reduction in the fees which they might expect to charge, and a decline in the number of new recruits willing or able to pay the costs of joining the department. In John's ever-overdramatic version of events, "the staff's circumstances were stricken by utter misfortune, and the office of the *matricularii*, as it was called, perished because it had been torn up by the roots" (3.67). By contrast, in this hard-fought competition for spoils, the *epistulares* scored a threefold victory. First, they reasserted that a *probatoria* was required to effect an appointment in the Prefecture. Second, they had a higher rate imperially approved. Third, by increasing their charges, they reduced the deficit in their own fee-income, caused by a drop in numbers seeking posts on the judicial side of the Prefecture, by transferring that loss to the *matricularius* and to senior *exceptores* nearing retirement. For the *epistulares,* equally concerned to preserve their level of earnings, this was an advantageous resolution of the problem of a possible downturn in their own fee-income. Their strategy helped to insulate them against the judicial side's reduced ability to pay. Against a rival department, the *epistulares* had (at least in the short term) maintained their share in a contracting and less lucrative market.

Pay Scales and Promotion

John viewed the administrative history of the Prefecture in similar stark financial terms: the shifts in its administrative competence, the variations in the distribution of tasks among its senior officers, and the changes to its internal organization and system of promotion. In John's account, the career of an *exceptor* was dominated by financial concerns, from a new recruit's first post, through the long series of middle-ranking grades, and finally—for the successful few—the senior administrative offices. In the early sixth century there were nine senior posts on the judicial side of the Prefecture. In ascending order these were: the *cura epistularum* for each of the Prefecture's four dioceses (Thrace, Asiana, Pontica, and Oriens, which, for this administrative purpose, included Egypt), in charge of the paperwork associated with official reports and correspondence with *uicarii* and provincial governors on matters of finance and taxation (3.21); the *regendarius,* responsible for the infrastructure and operation of the public post *(cursus publicus)* and for issuing warrants *(euectiones)* for its use (3.21); the *ab actis,* dealing with civil cases and judicial records (3.20); the *commentariensis,* mainly concerned with criminal trials (3.16–19); the *primiscrinius,* responsible for the enforcement of judgments and court orders (3.11–15); and the *cornicularius,* who headed the judicial side (3.3, 3.22–25).

Each of these officials had a secretariat *(scrinium)* staffed by *exceptores.* The business of each *scrinium* was supervised by three principal assistants *(adiutores)*, who in turn were supported by chief administrative officers *(chartularii)*. An *exceptor* joined the department as a *supernumerarius* (an unestablished and unsalaried post whose earnings were derived entirely from fee-income) and, as vacancies arose, was enrolled as a member of the established staff in one of the fifteen sections *(scholae)* into which the judicial side was divided. An *exceptor* on the established staff was eligible to be selected as a *chartularius* and, after serving nine years, as an *adiutor.* In the course of his career, an *exceptor* might hope to serve a number of stints as a *chartularius* or *adiutor.* These posts lasted only one year. On completion, their holders returned to their *scholae.* Advancement through a *schola* was by seniority. The longest-serving head of the fifteen *scholae* might expect to be raised to *cura epistularum* of the most junior diocese and work his way steadily by annual promotion up through the department's most senior posts.[54]

As in any large and complex organization with a steeply hierarchical structure, the vast majority of personnel, even after a lifetime's service, rarely went further than the middle ranks. But even for those who served as *exceptores* for all of their career (with perhaps, for the best placed, occasional selection for a term as *chartularius* or *adiutor*), reforms, even at a fairly senior level, had an impact on their career structure, their prospects of promotion, and their earnings. An important series of changes, which John dated to the reign of the emperor Arcadius at the very end of the fourth century, both increased promotion rates on the judicial side and altered the distribution of fee-income among the staff. According to John:

> Since formerly in peacetime the *adiutores* of the abovementioned *scrinia* [the *primiscrinius, commentariensis,* and *ab actis*] were enjoying a not insubstantial income, and preeminent honor coupled with effective power, it was reasonable, since they were getting their fill, for them to regard it as beneath them to return again to their position on the register [of the established staff] and to the modesty of a greatly reduced income. Hence, as a result of their petition, a law was promulgated by Arcadius, who decreed that the Prefecture should set up a special and altogether separate corps of men thirty in number (who had already previously distinguished themselves as *adiutores*) to serve it . . . And the law prescribed for that corps of the aforementioned thirty men the name of *Augustales.* (3.10)

At the same time, a second career path was opened up with the doubling of all the senior posts except that of *cornicularius.*

> I have stated above that the body of *exceptores* was originally one, but that it has been split into two branches and two sets of final posts. For some of them spend their time remaining on the register [of the established staff] and are promoted to the final post of *primiscrinius,* whereas others, because they are transferred to the rank of *Augustales,* both complete their service more quickly than the other *exceptores* and reach in the end the office of *cornicularius.* (3.9)[55]

The institution of a corps of thirty *Augustales,* along with the duplication of the judicial side's senior offices from the most junior of the *curae epistularum* to *primiscrinius,* changed the career patterns of *exceptores* holding established posts. For the most successful, joining the *Augustales* offered significantly greater financial security and markedly enhanced promotion prospects. After nine years in post, an *exceptor* was eligible to be selected as one of the three *adiutores* assisting one of the less senior administrative officers (the *regendarius* and the four *curae epistularum*). The duplication of these five posts meant that thirty *adiutores* were required annually. An *exceptor* who had served as an *adiutor* then qualified to join the *Augustales,* competition and vacancies permitting. There were two automatic vacancies per year. One resulted from the promotion of the most senior *Augustalis* to *cura epistularum* of the most junior diocese; the other from the annual appointment of the *cancellarius,* a personal assistant to the prefect, regulating access to his court and responsible for the presentation of documents requiring his signature (3.36–37).[56] *Augustales* also had the protected advantage of the duplication of the Prefecture's most senior positions. Access to one set of these offices and to the most senior post of *cornicularius* was open to them alone.

Some sense of the length of career necessary to reach the department's most senior offices is provided by John's own *curriculum vitae.* It took John forty years and four months from his initial appointment as *exceptor* to reach the end of his career and the post of *cornicularius,* which he held probably in his early sixties, retiring on April 1, 552. But John, at least at the time of his appointment, had the strong backing of his fellow Philadelphian the prefect Zoticus. He was never a *supernumerarius* and was enrolled straight into one of the *scholae.* Moreover, that John was selected to serve as a *chartularius* at the very beginning of his career—no doubt thanks again to the prefect's support—would suggest that, in time, he had a good chance of an appointment as an *Augustalis* (following, as a minimum, nine years' service as an *exceptor* and a year as an *adiutor* assisting one of the two *regendarii* or eight *curae epistularum*). His evident competence in Latin, publicly acknowledged by his appointment to the State University of Constantinople, no doubt also aided his advancement.

Longevity mattered, too. John noted that when he was only in his early twenties, those who served with him as *chartularii* to the *adiutores* in the *scrinium* of the *ab actis* were already old men (3.27). Likewise, he accepted that the most senior officeholders would, as a matter of course, be old—"they are weary with old age, which is utterly useless for toil" (3.9)—and therefore have need of *adiutores* and *chartularii* to help them transact business.[57] This was only to be expected. Compared to modern Western societies, death rates in the Roman world (even for those who survived the perils of birth and infancy) were high. In crude terms, of those who joined the Prefecture in their early twenties with John, one-quarter may have been dead by forty, and only half of those remaining may have survived into their sixties, the age at which John retired. In other words, at a rough maximum, two-thirds of John's peers may have died across the forty years it took him to rise from a newly appointed *exceptor* to *cornicularius*.[58]

The death of superiors was another factor in speeding the advancement of juniors. At the same time, it reduced the numbers of those eligible to be appointed to senior positions. Even so, the rate of promotion must have been painfully slow and often highly erratic. Indeed, if he followed the statutory career path, it must have taken John sixteen years to secure a position in the *Augustales*: the forty years of his career, less fifteen for a maximum term to work his way up to the most senior of the thirty *Augustales* (two were automatically promoted annually), and nine for his progression from the most junior *cura epistularum* to the completion of his year-long stint as *cornicularius*. That this represents an accelerated career should give pause for thought. It again underlines the number of officials who must never have made it very far up the ladder of promotion. A large number of *exceptores* can never have advanced beyond their *scholae*. Indeed, many can never have been more than *supernumerarii*. That said, as John's complaints make insistently clear, even these most junior of his colleagues, however they calculated their own chances of promotion, must have reckoned (as John certainly did) that there was every chance that the administrative responsibilities of the judicial side of the Prefecture would continue to provide them with a steady income from fees for the whole of their working lives.

For a fortunate few, selection as an *Augustalis* must have been the "midcareer break" which distinguished success from long service in the anonymous middle and lower ranks of the department. First, as John indicated, the creation of the *Augustales* created a "fast track" for promotion out of the *scholae*. Its establishment openly recognized that factors other than seniority should explicitly be taken into account in determining promotion. As John remarked, it was only those who had displayed their administrative experience and competence who were selected as *Augustales* (3.6, 3.10, 3.50). (Only an *exceptor* already far advanced in his career might calculate that he would become the longest-serving head of a *scholae*, and in line for promotion to *cura epistularum* of the junior diocese, sooner than if he joined the *Augustales* and had to work his way up an additional thirty positions.) Second, the doubling of the Prefecture's senior offices resulted in a dedicated career track open only to *Augustales*, greatly increasing their chances of further promotion to even more lucrative senior administrative offices. Third, senior *Augustales* were also allowed to perform administrative services for judicial proceedings in the imperial court. In other words, the *deputati*, as these officials were known, were specifically authorized to process work strictly falling outside the responsibility of their department. The number of *deputati* was limited to fifteen, since, as John euphemistically remarked, "it was not easy for the best to do everything" (3.10).[59] Fourth, and most important, membership in the *Augustales* offered exclusive access to an appointment as one of three *adiutores* serving each of the seven most senior officers (the *ab actis, commentariensis,* and *primiscrinius* all doubled, plus the *cornicularius*). Twenty-one positions were now open to only thirty officers, rather than to any established member of staff. Most *Augustales* must have been able to rely on holding several such posts in succession, maintaining, as a result, a more predictable (and greatly enhanced) annual income. It was this financial advantage which, at least in John's account, was the main motivation for the reform.

In a large and prosperous department, these reforms to its internal structure had both a financial and an organizational logic. The doubling of administrative posts increased the chances of promotion for the most successful *exceptores* and widened the distribution of fee-income at the most senior levels of the department. The establishment of the *Augustales,* while it restricted access to some posts, also increased the number of vacancies in the *scholae,* accelerating the promotion through seniority of established *exceptores* and opening more vacancies to be filled by *supernumerarii.* Similarly, while only the thirty *Augustales* were entitled to serve as an *adiutor* to one of the judicial side's seven most senior officers, the duplication of the five less senior posts (and the consequent increase in the number of *adiutores* and *chartularii* appointed from the established staff) widened the opportunities for many in the department's junior ranks to increase their fee-income, if only for a year at a time. On balance, these reforms gave greater security of income to the more senior *exceptores,* while ensuring through the doubling of senior posts and their ancillary staff a wider distribution of fee-income across the department as a whole.

On paper, at any rate, the organization of the judicial side of the Prefecture as presented by John seems both impressive and well designed. In formal terms it certainly seems superior to what is known of some aspects of the internal structure of the *sacra scrinia.* Here, according to repeated imperial prescription, the number of *adiutores* drawn from the *memoriales* (the basic established grade) to assist the *quaestor sacri palatii* was fixed at twenty-six: twelve from the staff of sixty-two in the *scrinium memoriae* and seven each from the staff of thirty-four in both the *scrinium epistularum* and the *scrinium libellorum.*[60] But it seems that this number was frequently exceeded. Twice in the 520s under the emperor Justin I (who claimed that expansion had been so great there was now "very little difference in the number of *memoriales* and those who are *adiutores*") and again under Justinian new appointments were prohibited until the established number was restored.[61] But the seeming disorganization of the *sacra scrinia,* its cycle of expansion and imperially enforced contraction, had some advantages. For any department, allowing the number of appointments to exceed imperially prescribed numbers was one means of responding immediately to demands by its staff for more rapid promotion and greater access to fee-income, perhaps as a result of a growth in its administrative activities. Equally, under imperial pressure or in response to a decline in fee-income, as a first reaction, these "unestablished posts" could be shed without any great change in the department's internal structure. And again those who had their promotions delayed or who were unable to sell the vacancy resulting from their retirement personally bore the costs of any contraction in their department's size or responsibilities.

By contrast, the judicial side of the Prefecture lacked this first line of defense. In the face of a decreased demand for its services, it did not have in its senior ranks a set of informally appointed officials whose removal might increase the chances of a smaller core maintaining its fee-income without the need for the reallocation of duties or the loss of formally designated positions. Rather, the doubling of senior posts and the creation of the *Augustales* committed the Prefecture to an enlarged establishment. From that point of view, the internal organization of the judicial side was one which was founded both on the assumption of a certain level of fee-income and on a high degree of security about the future. Broadly speaking, the staff, even at junior levels, benefited from a career path which, in comparison with the *sacra scrinia,* offered them better chances of predictable, formally approved promotion and a resulting share of the department's earnings. Against these advantages, the expanded and more complex structure of the Prefecture was much less able to respond flexibly either to any changes in its remit or to any significant drop in fee-income. It could not shed redundant staff so easily. Nor was there any obviously predetermined core of officials among whom reduced fee-income might be shared. But then, as John strongly emphasized, this inflexibility was hardly surprising: after all, no *exceptor* ever really thought that the judicial side of the Prefecture—"the greatest staff of the foremost of the magistracies" (3.1)—would be forced to deal with a sudden contraction in its administrative responsibilities.

Profit and Loss

The pressing need of the judicial side of the Prefecture to maintain its levels of fee-income (in part driven by the very way in which the department was organized) was clearly reflected in John's account of the various changes in its duties in the two centuries before the reign of Justinian. In John's version, the Cappadocian's reforms of the 530s cast a baleful light over any previous restrictions of the judicial staff's competence. Even the reallocation to other departments of functions which perhaps had once seemed peripheral to the judicial staff's main and most remunerative activities was to be regretted. Had control over these areas been retained, they might now have yielded valuable and much needed revenue. For John, no reduction in the scope of the Prefecture's activities was defensible, no argument in terms of efficiency or the more coherent distribution of tasks persuasive.

For a department in decline, the loss of any fee-income was to be viewed in reproachful retrospect, no matter how long ago the opportunity had been lost. John particularly objected to the subordination of the *cornicularius* to the *princeps officii* (the highest-ranking officer in the eastern Praetorian Prefecture in charge of all administrative staff). The secondment of the *princeps* from the *agentes in rebus* was clearly intended to prevent the most senior post on the prefect's staff being held by one of its own internally promoted members (3.12, 3.23–24, 2.10 = 3.40). For John, the intrusion of an official whose loyalties lay with another department was greatly to be regretted, "for he himself is not part of the staff, but he gradually came from the *magistriani* into the once great courts of justice" (3.12). Moreover, the *princeps* demanded control of the fee-income which had previously been the *cornicularius*' alone. The *cornicularius* was to be paid one pound of gold per month and, in addition, was permitted to earn further income from the paperwork which he personally processed (mainly *completiones*, the final "signing off" of a file marking the conclusion of a judicial action). These transactions alone yielded, on John's estimate, just under 14 pounds of gold annually (3.24). Even with his fee-income reduced, the *cornicularius*' annual earnings were still impressive. But that was not John's point: an outsider, an untrustworthy *arriviste* from a rival department, had been allowed into the Prefecture and had taken what properly belonged to the *cornicularius*. It mattered not that this had all happened two centuries ago. After all, as John recalled with pride, the *cornicularius* had been "head of the staff for more than 1,300 years, and appeared conducting public business with the very founding of sacred Rome" (3.22).[62]

With equal grimness, John carefully catalogued a series of other, some more recent, shifts in the judicial side's responsibilities. The rise of the *a secretis,* a corps of imperial secretaries attached to the *consis-*

torium, gradually deprived the *deputati* of their administrative functions at court (3.10). Indeed, by the mid-sixth century, their titles may have been merely a reminder of the functions they had once performed.[63] Similar changes (some as early as the fourth century) removed the Prefecture's control over the palace guard (*scholae palatinae*) and the imperial arms manufactories (*fabricae*), and split some of the responsibility for the public post between the Prefecture and the *magister officiorum* (2.10 = 3.40). By the early sixth century, when John started his career, the *regendarius,* the senior official on the judicial side responsible for the infrastructure and operation of the imperial post and for issuing warrants (*euectiones*) for its use, had only limited authority. According to John, any warrants issued had first to be checked by the *princeps officii,* who was authorized "to investigate closely and inquire into the reasons why many obtain from the Prefecture the travel warrants, as they are known, and have the use of the public post," and then countersigned by the *magister officiorum* (3.40 = 2.10, 3.21).[64]

Within the Prefecture too, the judicial side was gradually losing its control over certain financial matters. By the early sixth century, some of the functions of both the *curae epistularum* and the *regendarii* had been taken over by the *scriniarii,* the Prefecture's financial staff (3.21).[65] More damaging, Zoticus' successor Marinus established a new set of financial officials (*uindices*) empowered both to supervise the collection of land tax in the provinces and to oversee municipal finances.[66] As a result, John alleged, the number of fiscal disputes litigated in the Prefect's court was substantially reduced. The dismal consequences for those on the judicial side were all too predictable. "The staff lapsed and began to experience poverty. For what was left to it when it was providing administrative services only for the court cases of private litigants?" (3.49).[67]

Given this gradual loss of responsibility, it is unsurprising that in establishing the Praetorian Prefecture of Africa Justinian's law of 534 took the opportunity to eliminate some senior posts. No mention was made of a *princeps officii,* a *cornicularius,* a *regendarius,* or a *cura epistularum.* The three *scrinia* serving the *primiscrinius,* the *commentariensis,* and the *ab actis* were retained, but the remaining business was now thought sufficient to justify only one secretariat, known as the *scrinium libellorum,* the smallest on the new African Prefecture's judicial side.[68] For John, such an efficient streamlining of a department's internal structure could only be the result of a culpable decline in its competence. It signaled the collapse of a sometimes complacent corps of officials (3.39) unable, often through a mixture of stupidity and bad luck (3.20), to hold its own in an unremitting contest for lucrative administrative duties.

Of course, officials in a flourishing department blessed with a steady and predictable flow of fee-income could afford some reduction in the scope of their duties. Across a long career, they might be prepared to carry a set of relatively unrewarding posts, perhaps particularly in areas where they hoped at some stage they might regain or expand their administrative responsibilities. A network of internal transactions also ensured the redistribution of some proportion of the total income earned by a department. On retirement, officials received a fee from those appointed to fill the resulting vacancy in the junior ranks. They also seem to have contributed to, and received payments from, some sort of central departmental fund. Regrettably, little is known of its operation. In describing the financial arrangements made between the *princeps officii* and the *cornicularius,* John noted that the *cornicularius* was allocated one pound of gold each month "after every member of staff had received, as was standard practice, a certain share of the revenue given without demur as part of their customary remuneration" (3.24). A similar fund in the Urban Prefecture of Rome seems in some way to have been under the collective control of the department. In 382 an imperial law directed that certain payments be continued: "We decree that the benefits and other perquisites which support the office staff of your magnitude [the urban prefect] are not to be taken away from those upon whom they have been conferred through the generosity of the said department."[69] The same fund may also have been used to distribute fees and salaries (which were customarily allocated to a department en bloc) and to pay the fines which some imperial laws threatened, in case of breach, to levy on the staff as a whole. In some departments, it was probably also used to pay retiring officials an additional "lump sum" and to compensate the relatives or heirs of a serving official who had died in post by awarding them an amount equivalent to the income the deceased might have been expected to earn during the remainder of his term in the office he held at his death.[70]

In performing these functions, a central fund helped neatly to negotiate individual and corporate interests. For an official (no matter how senior), any contributions deducted from his fee-income could be seen, first and most importantly, as a way of protecting himself against often unpredictable fluctuations in earnings, or the risk of holding a potentially profitable post in a lean year. Second, it spread the loss, which might otherwise be borne by those officials most directly concerned or their successors, resulting from the imposition of any punitive fines. Third, in the case of an official's death in post, it also meant (like a form of life insurance) that his family was not, at least immediately, deprived of anticipated income. For a department, the provision of such financial protection once again underlined the advantages of solidarity. It was yet another way of reducing the risk of any individual acting contrary to the best interests of his colleagues. At the same time, disbursements from a centrally organized fund helped ensure that a department's fee-income benefited more than just a few high-ranking officeholders.

Under the right conditions, both for individuals and for the department as a whole, gains and losses could be made to balance out over time. In the eastern Praetorian Prefecture, successful *exceptores* were no doubt prepared to serve as *cura epistularum* or *regendarius,* since these posts, by automatic annual promotion, led directly to the most senior and most remunerative positions on the judicial side. But, as with the establishment of the *Augustales* and the duplication of the judicial side's senior career track, the maintenance of this system was crucially dependent on a continual and predictable level of administrative work and the fee-income it earned. Following the reforms of John the Cappadocian, such an advantageous stability could no longer be guaranteed. Unremunerative posts were immediately threatened. The weaknesses resulting from previous losses in administrative responsibility were unavoidably exposed. Even the most secure posts on the judicial side had their workloads and fee-income reduced. John (perhaps now all too predictably) emphasized his opposition to these changes and their consequences by offering his readers yet another set of forcefully overdrawn contrasts. The specially designated area near the entrance to the prefect's court, where *adiutores* had once gathered to complete the business transacted during their term of office, was deserted (3.13). The vaulted chambers in the substructure of the Hippodrome (next to the imperial palace in Constantinople), where the records of the Prefecture had been carefully filed, now lay empty and abandoned. The *instrumentarius,* the officer in charge of these archives, had been made redundant (3.19).[71] The number of new recruits dropped rapidly as they faced both "a dearth of transactions" and a quadrupling in the cost of a *probatoria* (3.66, 2.17).

In a contracting market, this was a vicious downward spiral. Insufficient income meant that many positions remained unfilled and unfillable. The hitherto strict selection requirements for *adiutores* were abandoned (2.18, 3.9). According to John, the Prefecture now promoted the inexperienced, the unqualified, and, worst of all, the young, who "in puerile acts of arrogance crack the reins of the first honors" (3.14, 3.2). "For no one of any note any longer joined the staff, because it had been so demeaned and brought disgrace rather than any honor to anyone who belonged to it" (2.17). Even then, many could not afford to remain in office for the full term of their appointment. John, in a rare moment keen to dispel any suspicion of exaggeration, claimed, "as truth bears witness to me," not to know of "any *exceptor* who has served a whole year in his post" (3.66). Those nearing retirement were hardest hit. Deprived—at the very least—of the possibility of benefiting from the fees paid by a new recruit and (if successful) of the substantial income formally enjoyed by the Prefecture's senior officers, they "lamented and wept, sinking as they were into an old age of poverty" (3.66). John was particularly angry at the fate of his former colleagues who had joined the Prefecture with him and had had their careers blocked or ruined by the reforms of the 530s. Choked by a mixture of resentment and frustration, John at long last professed himself lost for words. "What should I say when, after the completion of their service in the department, all of them, without exception, drag out the rest of their life distressingly in shameful poverty?" (3.67).

Paying Your Way

The reforms of John the Cappadocian and their impact on the judicial side of the eastern Praetorian Prefecture starkly underscored John's views on how a bureaucrat might best secure his position within his department, earn a good income, and advance his career. Fundamental to John's version of later Roman bureaucracy was a recognition that an official would derive a significant part of his income not from his salary, but from fees paid by those who demanded or required the services he could perform. In addition, a bureaucrat expected to pay fees to his colleagues (and perhaps to officials in other departments) in order to secure promotion. In turn, on retirement he expected to receive fees from those promoted in consequence of the vacancy so created. In an ideal world, an official's post would be one which offered more work than could be processed. A well-run department would maintain its monopoly over a set of administrative transactions, defending it (perhaps by securing a favorable imperial ruling) against the pressure of acquisitive rivals. As a result, it would best be able to provide its members across what might be a long career with a series of rewarding positions and the security both of promotion to senior offices (whose number might be increased in proportion to a department's resources) and of a steadily increasing income from fees. Better still, a successful department might manage to enlarge its competence, offering even greater opportunities for its staff.

The possibility of a post in Constantinople and the chance of a career which might bring both advancement and enrichment no doubt made a position in the imperial bureaucracy attractive, particularly to well-educated and ambitious young men from the provinces. But these substantial advantages carried significant risks. Officials who benefited directly from the charging of fees immediately suffered when reforms (perhaps motivated by rival bureaucrats in another department) removed or reallocated their duties, or sought to reduce the sums paid for their services. Moreover, imperially imposed restrictions on alternative employment, absenteeism, and the joint holding of posts limited the degree to which bureaucrats could protect themselves against losses resulting from their own department's failure to retain its control over a sufficiently profitable share of official business. Nor could salaries ever offer much compensation for any substantial reduction in fee-income. Rather, by keeping salaries low and permitting officials to charge for their services, the state supported a system which shifted the cost of any administrative reorganization directly onto individual bureaucrats themselves.

The vulnerability of officials disadvantaged by a reduction in their responsibilities was the central, and often acrimonious, theme of John's autobiography. In his account, he explicitly linked the fading of his once-bright hopes as a new recruit with the breakup of a department in which he had hoped he would prosper until his retirement. John—despite his academic appointment and his eventual promotion to the senior post of *cornicularius*—was ever eager to stress that he had "shared in the misfortunes" following John the Cappadocian's reforms of the 530s (3.25). As the number of new recruits declined and the cost of *probatoriae* rose, and as many on the judicial side could no longer afford the costs of promotion, John emphasized that when serving as *matricularius* (in charge of the department's personnel registers) his fee-income, too, had been directly and severely affected. "I also partook of this ill fortune, because while discharging that post I was not even recompensed for my daily expenses" (3.66).

Worse followed. As *cornicularius,* at what should have been the rewarding apogee of a successful career, John complained that his earnings from fees were negligible, "as though I were not even in post" (3.30). He claimed to have received nothing from *completiones,* "signing off" files at the completion of judicial proceedings in the prefect's court. Nor (as the judicial side's fee-income declined yet further) could the *princeps officii* be compelled to keep his side of the long-established "agreement" to pay the *cornicularius* one pound of gold a month. As John unhappily recalled, "Not so much as one small coin am I aware of having received either from the *princeps* or from the *completiones* as they are known" (3.25). In John's view, his own career, like the Praetorian Prefecture itself, had steadily been ruined. Marooned in the State University of Constantinople, where he found his academic colleagues fractious and uncongenial (3.47), John was left only with fond memories of a time in the Prefecture when "the golden age was at its brightest" (3.67) and with his painful regrets at its subsequent eclipse. "I repent as I reflect so late in the day for what return I devoted myself to the court of justice for such a long time having gained nothing from it by way of consolation. (3.25) . . . I laid aside the service having persisted in it for forty years and gained no reward save the rank I reached on retirement" (3.67).

Disappointed bureaucrats are rarely objects of sympathy, no matter how unsuccessful they claim their careers to have been, nor how poverty-stricken their retirement. But despite all his undoubted exaggerations, his often-tiresome pomposity, and his paraded self-importance, it is worth pausing a moment to take John on his own terms. Whatever judgment should be passed on his own career choices, John's autobiography makes starkly clear that the striking of an advantageous balance between the range of competing concerns which confronted later Roman bureaucrats was not always easy, and, even if achieved, not always possible to maintain. At times personal, family, or financial ties or promotion on the basis of criteria other than strict seniority helped to strengthen the bonds between some members of a department. It heightened their sense of belonging to the same organization; it lessened their frustrations at a rigid policy of promotion by seniority alone. Yet, taken too far, as John's autobiography also neatly exemplifies, a marked preference for certain members of staff over their colleagues risked a department's fragmentation into self-interested coteries of uncooperative officials more vulnerable both to the expansionary claims of other groups of bureaucrats and to imperially sponsored administrative reform. Similarly, the role of complex forms and procedures (undoubted impediments to clarity and communication) in staking out and defending a department's administrative responsibilities had always to be set against a need to offer a range of services at a cost which would ensure a steady flow of fee-income from transactions. (Of course, the closer any department came to establishing a secure monopoly over the services it offered, the less concerned it had to be about incomprehensibility, alienation, or overcharging.) Importantly, too, bureaucrats had carefully to balance the desirability of approving or condemning the policies of a prefect—and perhaps behind him an emperor—with the protection of their own best interests.

Continual negotiation—sometimes bitter, disputed, unresolved—between individual interest and collective advantage was fundamental to the institutional shape of later Roman bureaucracy. These pressures resulted in a set of work practices, administrative arrangements, and sharp moral judgments which can profitably be seen as resulting from an often-uncomfortable compromise between the more impersonal, hierarchical structures which gave shape, order, and predictability to a department and the more informal networks of personal, provincial, and financial ties which were important in promoting the interests of individuals or particular groups. The former, if imposed too rigidly, threatened to alienate talented and ambitious officials. The latter, if taken too far, threatened to weaken any sense of mutuality or collective purpose. As John's autobiography so amply illustrates, the negotiation of these often-incompatible concerns were key to the success or failure of any department or group of officials. In its operation, later Roman bureaucracy represented a remarkable trade-off between these potentially conflicting patterns of power. It was a curious hybrid. It supervised its members and regulated their actions much more closely than any loose network of informal contacts and favors; yet it remained significantly less rationally or coherently organized than any modern publicly funded administration.

PART II

Rulers and Ruled

Passages from the Principate to Late Antiquity

It is easy to score points over a dead society, more difficult and more rewarding to examine what they were trying to do, how they went about it, the extent to which they succeeded or failed, and why.

—Moses Finley

One afternoon in late A.D. 362 or early 363, local workmen in the North African town of Timgad (modern Thamugadi in Algeria) fixed an inscribed limestone slab to a shady wall sheltered by a colonnade running along the northern side of the town hall *(curia)*. The *curia* was one of the most imposing structures in the western part of the forum; like many of the finest buildings in Timgad it dated from the town's foundation by the emperor Trajan at the very beginning of the second century A.D. The carefully lettered stone, over a meter high and about 50 centimeters wide, was a copy of a bronze original which had been set up in Cirta, the provincial capital 130 kilometers to the north toward the coast.

Had any of the laborers who erected the inscription been able to read, they would have discovered that it promulgated a decree issued by the local provincial governor, Ulpius Mariscianus. The proclamation was an important one; hence its careful copying and public display. In the preamble the governor proudly advertised his appointment "by our lord the unconquered emperor Julian," whose statue had been erected the previous year in front of the *curia*. The main text of the decree dealt with matters of disputed municipal concern (such as regulating the rank order of notables and officials for admission to the governor's levees). It also laid down the cost of administrative and legal services for those wishing to litigate in the governor's court. The sums payable to officials on the governor's staff for the performance of various of their duties were carefully graded. Charges were specified for the completion of the necessary paperwork at each stage of the litigation (for both plaintiff and defendant) and for the service of any official documentation relating to the trial.

> The payment which must be made to the head of the governor's staff for appointing an official [to serve a summons on a defendant]: within the town, five *modii* (bushels) of wheat or the price thereof; within one mile of the town, seven *modii* of wheat or the price thereof; for every additional ten miles, two *modii* of wheat or the price thereof; if the official is required to travel overseas, then one hundred *modii* of wheat or the price thereof is required.[1]

This inscription is significant. The proclamation of a carefully graded schedule of fees for administrative services represents a shift in the pattern of power within an ancient Mediterranean society in which access to government and its advantages was traditionally determined by the personal influence exercised by friends, family, and their connections. The Timgad inscription is evidence both of the operation of a new currency of power and of its imposition and careful control by centrally issued regulation. Against conventional ways of "working the system" and the long-held expectation that these would generally be successful, the payment of money introduced new opportunities to be negotiated by those demanding or requiring access to government services. The posting of a detailed schedule of fees—issued by the imperial authorities and openly (and seemingly legitimately) displayed in a public place in the middle of a town—is in itself an important index of a pronounced change in the way the Roman Empire was ruled.

The traditional system of Roman rule was founded on an intricate set of patronage networks fueled by a continual exchange of goods, services, and obligations. Early imperial government, in the two centuries after the emperor Augustus, strengthened this pattern of power. Centralized bureaucracy was kept to a minimum as the detailed business of imperial government devolved on local notables. These men acted as mediators between central government and provincial populations. They retained much of their autonomy, and a more easily assured superiority over their social inferiors, in return for their cooperation in keeping the peace, drafting recruits for the army, and collecting taxes.[2] This complex and sophisticated relationship between central government and local elites was, in part, expressed in the impressive civic rituals of the imperial cult and the well-funded festivals held in honor of less far-distant deities; in part, buttressed by an ever-present fear of bloody imperial intervention; and, in part, softened by an often highly emotional rhetoric of honor which could explain and justify individuals' positions (from the emperor down) and affect their actions as both rulers and ruled.[3] This "minimalist system" of government was remarkably successful, representing as it did (at least from the imperial authorities' point of view) a "magnificent economy of effort."[4]

Yet this was a success for which central government also paid a high price. "When official and local strength clashed, local strength often won. In the empire the power to collect taxes might well presuppose, also, the power to resist taxes."[5] Central government might sometimes find its peremptory authority becalmed (in Peter Brown's elegant phrase) "on a Sargasso Sea" of silent protest and provincial noncooperation.[6] No doubt, too, the ability of local notables to muffle the demands of central government both deepened their own sense of self-importance and reinforced their loyalty to a system of rule which (at least within the limits imposed by the possibility of armed intervention or the moralizing restraints of honor) also clearly operated to their advantage. For central government, whose capacity closely to control the empire's inhabitants or greatly to increase a low overall tax take was strictly limited, cooperation with the locally powerful was an expensive way to rule. Yet in the absence of any persistent external threat, or of any other medium-term cause requiring significantly increased government expenditure or the organized deployment of large resources, it was an affordable cost, and one well worth paying.

The web of mutual advantage which had both encircled and enabled (in J. E. Lendon's homely phrase) the "cosy relationship" between imperial authorities and local elites in the two hundred years after Augustus was strained (sometimes to breaking point) in the middle of the third century A.D., during the so-called Third-Century Crisis.[7] Regrettably, the lack of reliable sources prevents any detailed reconstruction of the events from about 240 to 280. Only the roughest of sketches is possible. One of the better-delineated features is the difficulty imperial government faced in responding to any need which involved sudden extraordinary expenditure. In an empire accustomed to a relatively low overall tax rate, and lacking the administrative apparatus either to regulate or to redistribute any unexpected fiscal demand, central government's inability to accumulate significant strategic reserves or to fund more than the ordinary ongoing expenses of empire was clearly exposed. War had always strained the imperial treasury. Against continued military pressure on the northern and eastern frontiers, successive emperors failed for nearly a generation to maintain either the unity or the integrity of the empire. Random imposts, the confiscation of property, and the debasement of the silver currency were all desperate attempts to cover or to delay the rapidly escalating costs of defense. In the face of these ever-increasing demands for revenue, local notables protested loudly (and in some cases simply refused to collect) the war taxes which central government attempted to impose on the provinces of empire.[8]

The success of a series of emperors at the close of the third century depended in great part on their ability both to ignore and to override those protests. Reforming measures (military, economic, administrative, ideological) were introduced with the aim of more tightly unifying the empire and of exerting a greater degree of central control over its human and economic resources. The process of change was slow and difficult, and not infrequently imposed by undisguised force and the cruel exigencies of civil war. But it was cost effective. Despite obvious shortcomings and some inevitable haphazard inefficiencies (on which many historians and many contemporaries have understandably concentrated), it is worth bearing in mind that in the fourth century alone the Roman state raised enough revenue to enable it (among many other expenses and obligations) to pay for a professional standing army larger than that maintained in the first two centuries A.D., to finance a new religion, and to found a second imperial capital at Constantinople. For a preindustrial empire, these achievements should not be underrated. Such a degree of centralized government control was not reached again in Europe until the eighteenth-century absolutisms of France and Prussia.

The creation of a comparatively sophisticated and centralized bureaucracy (dedicated primarily to the maintenance of imperial authority through the collection of taxes and the administration of justice) was an important element in the establishment of this new pattern of power. It was one of the significant factors separating the nature of imperial rule in the early and later Roman Empire. Indeed, without some increase in the number and effectiveness of its officials, it is difficult to understand how later Roman government could have operated in so many new areas or have hoped to pay for so many new obligations. In the first two centuries A.D., there were a few hundred salaried imperial officials with perhaps up to 10,000 slaves and seconded soldiers performing administrative duties throughout the empire.[9] By the beginning of the sixth century, at a fairly conservative estimate, there were perhaps 30,000 to 35,000 bureaucrats on the imperial payroll.[10] These commonly quoted figures have no great pretensions to accuracy. But they do give a rough sense of the shift in scale (somewhere between two- and threefold) in the numbers of personnel involved in the administration of the empire.[11]

Moreover, as John Lydus' autobiography amply illustrates, the steady development within the imperial bureaucracy of well-defined hierarchies and career paths helped to promote a sense of solidarity and corporate identity. Bureaucrats (particularly the highly skilled, more senior personnel primarily dedicated to administrative duties) regarded themselves as separate from those over whom they ruled. Theirs was a strong sense of difference and of a collective self-interest fostered by a deep love of formality and administrative arcana, by the unstinting use of impenetrable technical jargon, and by splendid official uniforms which set bureaucrats apart as servants of the state. These factors are significant. They not only contributed to the formation of an effective and recognizable permanent corps of imperial officials (as opposed to slaves, freedmen, or soldiers), they also helped insulate that organization from the competing and often-conflicting claims exercised by those operating outside this "elaborate centralised machine."[12]

It is within this broader context that the charging of fees for administrative services can most profitably be understood. Like the other factors which made later Roman officialdom more formally structured, more rationally organized, and more institutionally distinctive, the payment of money for access to administrative services or for the purchase of office can also be seen as part supplement, part replacement, and part antidote to traditional methods of controlling the allocation of government resources through patronage. Against or alongside clout and connections, the payment of money established an alternative method of determining priority and order in the long queue of those seeking access to later Roman government. Fees were carefully set. A number of publicly displayed inscriptions (discussed in detail in Chapter 4) shows that the charges levied by central government were neither extortionate nor inconsistent. The line was carefully drawn to exclude small landholders and the urban poor, but to include those wealthy enough to voice their discontent if their concerns went unheard. Most important, access to Roman government was made possible without the necessity of entanglement in a web of endless reciprocal obligations. Impersonal monetary transactions enabled those not enmeshed in traditional patronage networks to purchase power.

The extent of these changes should not be exaggerated. The passage from the Principate to late antiquity was slow and intricate. For all its formalities and institutional features, later Roman bureaucracy still preserved a range of practices (such as accelerated preferment for officials' sons or, more generally, the more rapid advancement of those connected to senior officeholders) which would be judged unacceptable in more formally structured administrations.[13] The difference between the government of the early and later Empire lies principally in a shift in the way power was organized and exercised, rather than in any great change in the social backgrounds of those involved in the business of government. In an acute study of the composition of the new Senate created in Constantinople by Constantine and his imperial successors, Peter Heather has observed that the overwhelming majority of its members was drawn from existing urban elite groups in the eastern Mediterranean. "The evidence suggests that the senate recruited from the already rich: the curial classes who had exercised power in the eastern Mediterranean. Bureaucratic expansion, likewise, drew on this group."[14]

Aside from a handful of spectacular exceptions, whose prominence attracted both attention and abuse, the imperial bureaucracy in late antiquity was not a significant route for social mobility. As John Matthews has rightly noted, "The dust-storms raised by the achievements of such men must not be allowed to obscure the sheer traditionalism of the provincial backgrounds from which they came."[15] For the most part, central government was staffed by well-educated, reasonably well-off men from the provinces who secured their future (and their place within the empire) by looking to hold an official position in Constantinople, rather than choosing to rely solely on their locally based social superiority. And, as in the early Empire, the continued cooperation of these notables (both in official service and in their hometowns) was vital to the success of imperial government.

Under such conditions, the old system of rule could not simply be swept aside. As Peter Brown has observed, "Despite the more drastic assertion of state power that characterized the fourth century, a system of government based upon collusion with the upper classes had continued to idle under a centuries-old momentum."[16] The countervailing strengths of the traditional networks of influence, which for nearly three centuries had becalmed central government's attempts to assert its own authority, prevented the easy emplacement of any new pattern of power. Old (and still advantageous) loyalties died hard. New ways of organizing power and influence jostled against deeply entrenched networks of remarkably resilient relationships. Many of those seeking access to government learned to manipulate and combine a variety of tactics in order to ensure success. The payment of money for services or office—as supplement or alternative to more-traditional methods based on clout and connections—offered an acceptable and effective currency of power. From that point of view, in an increasingly centralized state, the charging of fees as a way of regulating bureaucratic transactions can be seen as representative of the shift in the pattern of power away from the "cosy relationships" which had shaped the possibilities for rule under the Principate. In late antiquity, the payment of money rendered much less certain the more comfortable sureties on which those seeking to influence government in the first two centuries A.D. might have expected to rely.

CHAPTER 3

Standing in Line

Mr Harry Barnes MP (Derbyshire North-East): To ask the Prime Minister what is her policy as to whose signature appears on replies to letters she receives from members of the public? Mr George Flynn of 24 Amber Place, Holingate, sent a letter to the Prime Minister about his loss of £6.20 a week housing benefit. The reply did not come from the Prime Minister's Office . . . but from the transitional payments unit in Glasgow.

The Prime Minister (The Rt. Hon. Margaret Thatcher MP): The Hon. gentleman is being totally unreasonable. I receive several thousands of letters each week from members of the public. It is not possible for me to deal with all those personally . . . He knows full well that I should never even be able to come to the House to answer his questions if I spent all day opening letters.

—Prime Minister's Question Time, Thursday, January 12, 1989

Access and Accessibility

Once (upon a time) in the early second century, the emperor Hadrian, on tour somewhere in the eastern provinces of the empire, found himself harassed by a woman who persistently demanded that she be given a hearing. In frustration, Hadrian rounded on her. Loudly explaining that he simply could not be expected to deal personally with every petitioner, he refused to listen to her complaint. οὐ σχολάζω, snapped the emperor; "I haven't the time." The women retorted: "Then do not be king."[1] The delight of this story, like so many surrounding the exercise of imperial power, lies in its subversive juxtaposition of ideal and reality. The limits of imperial power are here brutally revealed. It is ironic, too, that such a story could be told of an emperor who took some considerable trouble to be seen in the provinces. Faced with a greater administrative burden as a result of his travels, Hadrian might perhaps have sympathized with his imperial predecessor Tiberius, who was allegedly deliberately dilatory in receiving embassies, in the hope of discouraging others; or with the early third-century B.C. Macedonian king Demetrius Poliorcetes, who, as he rode through villages, is said to have received petitions in the fold of his cloak and then, once safely out of sight, to have thrown them off the nearest convenient bridge.[2]

An obvious problem confronts any government: How can it hope to satisfy all the claims made upon its services? How does it regulate demand? How does it decide which claims to process and which to ignore? The problem was acute in the Roman Empire. Even at its most developed, the number of salaried officials involved in administration numbered only about 30,000 to 35,000 for a population of somewhere between fifty and sixty million, in a superstate which stretched from Hadrian's Wall in northern Britain to the river Euphrates in eastern Syria. Roughly speaking, there were fewer bureaucrats in the whole Roman Empire than in a large modern British government department.[3]

That is only one measure of scale. But it does highlight some of the limitations imposed on later Roman bureaucracy simply by virtue of its size in relation to the population and area it attempted to govern. Of course, modern Western governments are much more ambitious in the scale and scope of their regulation. The Roman Empire never attempted (or even thought it necessary or desirable) to provide mass education, housing, health, or social security. As Sam Barnish, Doug Lee, and Michael Whitby have rightly emphasized, "The fundamental purpose of the administrative system remained the delivery of the resources upon which the empire's existence depended."[4] But even in carrying out much more limited aims, in addition to the small number of bureaucrats it employed Roman government was hampered in its operation by unreliable communications and a limited ability (especially over long periods) either systematically to store or reliably to retrieve the information necessary for the administration of the Mediterranean world.

The empire's greatest tyranny was distance. Against modern expectations, the communication time, even for the most urgent news, seems painfully slow: overland, Rome to Ravenna in five days, Antioch to Constantinople in five and a half; by river, from near Ulm (in southern Germany) down the Danube to near Sirmium (now Mitrovica, west of Belgrade) in eleven. And these are among the swiftest recorded times.[5] For the most part, official information traveled at a considerably slower pace. In the fourth century it might take between twelve and sixty-six days for an imperial ruling given in Milan to be received in Rome.[6] An edict issued by Valentinian III at Ravenna in June 449 was posted in Trajan's Forum thirty-three days later.[7] Communication by sea was comparatively quick. In the most favorable conditions, it might be possible to sail from Rome's port at Ostia to Carthage in two or three days, or from Puteoli (just up the coast from Naples) to Alexandria on the Nile delta in nine.[8] Some information no doubt traveled at this speed; but, as on land, official communications (always more cumbersome to transmit than verbal reports or rumor) generally took much longer.[9] As Richard Duncan-Jones observes, "Even the best transit-times for news are normally a generous multiple of the sailing-time under optimum conditions."[10]

Most striking is the variability in transit times. It could take somewhere between 25 and 135 days after an emperor's death in Italy for officials in Egypt to start dating documents in his successor's name. In great part, this variation is attributable to strong seasonality. Seaborne news traveled fastest in the early spring and summer, and slowest in the winter, when Mediterranean navigation was often hazardous and sometimes impossible.[11] But differences could also be great over the same route at roughly the same time. The last letter from the emperor Caligula to Publius Petronius, the governor of Syria, took three months to arrive. It reached Petronius twenty-seven days after he had learned by a later ship that the emperor had been assassinated. No doubt with some satisfaction, Petronius was able to ignore the emperor's order to commit suicide.[12]

Marked differences in transit times might also characterize official communication over comparatively short distances. The variation is neatly illustrated by a surviving set of documents from the archive of Apolinarius, the chief official (strategos) in charge of one of the administrative districts (nomes) in the subprovince of the Lower Thebaid (downstream from Luxor in Egypt). Between late January and the beginning of March 300, Apolinarius received forty-nine letters from his superior the procurator Aurelius Isidorus, the most senior administrator in the subprovince. The distance between the two officials, Isidorus in Hermopolis and Apolinarius upstream in Panopolis, was about 180 kilometers. At times communication could be impressively rapid. Three letters dispatched by Isidorus reached Apolinarius on the same day.[13] But there was little regularity. Others in the same five-week period took one to two days, some eight to ten, some—the slowest—nearly a month.[14] Again, what seems most significant is the variability in communication time. On some occasions, news could travel swiftly. Yet for the most part, Roman government, even at a local level, seems (again to quote Richard Duncan-Jones) "to have acted within the constraints of a slow communication-system made slower by seasonal delays" and dogged by unpredictability.[15]

Administrative difficulties arising from the unreliability of communication were compounded by the absence of any sophisticated methods of information storage or retrieval. Data, in some cases assiduously collected, often could be put to only limited use. Archives worked best at the local level.[16] The Roman administrative ability to record information with meticulous care is impressively exemplified by the surviving paperwork associated with tax assessment and collection (daybooks, ledgers, registers, receipts, reports, accounts). Fundamental to the determination of tax liability was the ownership of land. Fragments of two surviving mid-fourth-century registers record the names of those who owned property in the Hermopolite nome. Both registers carefully distinguish between those resident in the West Citadel quarter of Hermopolis and in nearby Antinoopolis (both towns about 100 kilometers upstream from Oxyrhynchus). The earlier of the two registers, the work of three separate scribes, lists the landowners' names in alphabetical order. Each entry also includes a detailed description of the holdings themselves, noting for each individual plot its size and location, and its classification for taxation purposes as "public" or "private" land. The register was written on papyrus made up as a book (rather than as a roll). Each page held two columns of text and was numbered. Originally forty-four pages long, pages seven through thirty-eight (ζ to $\lambda\eta$) listing the details of 320 landholders survive. The second register (compiled perhaps five to ten years later) takes roughly the same form.[17] Some entries have marginal notes; many are also highlighted with check marks: a capital zeta (Z), perhaps indicating that an entry needed further work; and two oblique strokes (//), perhaps recording that individual entries had been checked against another list, or had been transferred from this "working book" to a more comprehensive register, or had been extracted to compile a separate ledger dealing with a different set of tax liabilities.[18]

The detailed information contained in documents of this kind allowed officials to undertake basic administrative cross-checks. The instructions sent to the *strategos* Apolinarius by Aurelius Isidorus give some indication of how one bureaucrat attempted to make use of the available data. For the most part, Isidorus' communications dealt with the provisioning of troops, the transport of various goods, the prompt receipt of official monthly reports on revenue collection, and the elimination of tax avoidance. Confronted by landholders in the Lycopolite nome who had cultivated plots designated as wasteland (and, in so doing, hoped to avoid paying the taxes imposed on cultivated land), Isidorus instructed the *strategoi* that "the revenues for the previous years should be recovered for the treasury from the proprietors and a similar procedure should be followed in the other nomes." A list of those liable was to be compiled by checking census returns. "See that each of you as accurately as possible picks out from the census returns the names of the holders of cultivated land reclaimed from that designated as wasteland and reports them to me in writing."[19]

A similar exercise was undertaken to reveal those who had attempted to defraud the state by underreporting their tax liability. The failure of certain individuals to include taxable land (in this case vineyards) in their own sworn declarations of property which they owned or cultivated was exposed by checking their tax returns against a recently completed official census. "I command you to make a comparison of all the returns, under each nome and each locality, with the records compiled by the census, in order that those who neglected to make returns, either in whole or in part, may be detected."[20] Isidorus was also requested to supply information to his superior in Alexandria listing the amounts of persea and acacia wood sent to shipyards both in the provincial capital and at Nikiou in the delta: "specifying how much of each kind of wood was sent down, and of what dimensions, and by what overseer or conductor, by what ship-captains, and on what day." The information, "to be sent immediately," was necessary (explained Isidorus) in order to check and compare production figures submitted by those who managed the yards. The data could not only act as a check against fraud; they could also be used to measure comparative output and efficiency.[21]

But on some occasions, no matter how insistent the official requests, the information may not have been available. Isidorus frequently had to demand the "immediate" provision of reports, and in one case upbraided and fined Apolinarius for his failure to provide important data: "You should now take care both to pay the prescribed fine yourself, and to exact the same amount from the assistant to your office . . . and also to send in the accounts immediately, so that the entire public accounts may not be held up any further through your slackness."[22] Even in the great departments of state, documents might go astray. In the mid-sixth century, John Lydus, a staunch defender of the excellence of his colleagues' administrative practices, had (protestingly) to admit that during his time on the staff of the eastern Praetorian Prefecture in Constantinople there were embarrassing occasions when the relevant case files simply could not be found. "For the most learned of the principal assistants [*adiutores*] summarized the judicial proceedings in Latin with such detail that, if by chance it ever happened that the record of proceedings was lost, from the summary alone, even in outline, the record could immediately be restored. And I myself distinctly remember such an occurrence."[23]

More problematic than these local administrative difficulties was the regular compilation and collation of information from a number of different sources or over a long period. There was, for example, no official large-scale consolidated collection of imperial edicts until the promulgation of the *Theodosian Code* in late 437. The emperor Theodosius II praised the *Code*'s editors for their achievement in sorting through "that mass of imperial constitutions, which, sunk in a thick fog, has, by a bank of obscurity, cut off knowledge of itself from human minds."[24] Their task had been made all the more difficult by the seeming failure of central administrative departments to retain copies of all the laws they themselves had issued. The problem was exacerbated for earlier imperial legislation. As John Matthews has demonstrated, the *Code* was patched together from a set of miscellaneous sources including (where available) the central imperial archives, the archives of provincial governors, the libraries of the major law schools, the private collections of academic or practicing lawyers, and perhaps even the family papers of former high-ranking imperial officeholders.[25]

The problems encountered by those commissioned to compile the *Theodosian Code* stand as a useful warning against a too-regularized view of Roman government. It would be wrong to think of imperial administration at any time in the later Empire as operating systematically across the Mediterranean world with the same exacting attention to detail displayed in the archive rolls of Apolinarius in Panopolis or in the surviving land registers from the Hermopolite nome.[26] On occasions, too, Roman bureaucracy must have been completely paralyzed by ever-mounting piles of *paperasserie,* or, in A. H. M. Jones's wryly pleasing term, *papyrasserie.*[27] (No doubt only some of Aurelius Isidorus' insistent requests for information were met, only some of the data he demanded used to detect tax fraud, only some of those taxpayers he caught out ever successfully forced to pay arrears.) Like the speed of communication, both the efficiency and the effectiveness of Roman administration were highly variable. But against its manifest inadequacies must be set those occasions on which its officials were successfully able to collect, collate, and interrogate a mass of carefully compiled items of information. At the very least, the risk that archives could be put to good bureaucratic use, or that a persistent official might take the time to unravel a complex case or to cross-check registers, must have affected the calculations of those who decided to ignore or to resist government directives, or chose not to pay their taxes or to transmit them once collected. The possibility of effective and meticulous administrative action remained ever-threatening—even if its frequency, duration, and outcome were often unpredictable.

Yet, for all these too obvious operational difficulties, in broad terms Roman bureaucracy following its expansion in the fourth century could be argued to have been surprisingly effective. Despite limited information storage and retrieval systems, the relatively small number of staff, and the unreliability of communications, government officials managed consistently to perform a wide range of basic tasks. A. H. M. Jones neatly summarizes the chief administrative achievements of Roman government in the later Empire.

> Though the collection was often slow and incomplete, and arrears had periodically to be written off, the bulk of the revenue came in. Recruits were levied, and the armies were fed and clothed and armed and paid. Order was on the whole maintained, and the judgements of the courts were executed. Overt defiance of the government was rare, and was usually repressed without difficulty, if the government acted firmly. Military commanders very rarely rebelled, and were even more rarely successful in the end.[28]

Such a level of control, though no doubt to the advantage of central government, also had its costs, especially for those requiring or demanding access to administrative or judicial services. Precisely because of its restricted capacity to process information and its inability (or unwillingness) to perform more than a limited range of tasks, Roman government could never hope to accommodate all the claims made on its time and personnel. It could never deal with all those in the empire who demanded some official adjudication of their disputes. Even in the first century B.C., Cicero had remarked, "So great is the amount of business transacted at Rome that it is scarcely possible to pay attention to what happens in the provinces."[29] A similar sentiment was echoed four centuries later in a law issued "to those in the provinces" in which the emperors Gratian, Valentinian II, and Theodosius I sought to restrict the number of embassies traveling to the capital. "Just as we wish those who are oppressed to be allowed to lament their sufferings, so our provincials shall know . . . that they should convey to our sacred ears those matters which are most suitably brought before emperors, and they should not assume that our everlastingness should be taken up with superfluous matters."[30]

Access to central government was never an easy matter, even at the best of times. For those with petitions, the chances of successful contact were further reduced by the requirement that they be handed to the emperor by the litigant himself or by an agent closely connected with the case.[31] Despite these obstacles, those who decided to follow doggedly (to quote one second-century petitioner) "in the footsteps of our masters, the all-conquering emperors," had to be prepared to face considerable costs, delays, and difficulties.[32] When, in the early sixth century, the emperor Justinian attempted to limit the time for appeals, litigants whose cases were struck out protested that they had not been able to obtain a hearing because of "the inevitable amount of business" dealt with by the courts, nor had they been "able to sail from the provinces because the winds had been contrary, nor could they come overland because they were too poor, or indeed living on islands, had no other way of traveling except by sea."[33] Emperors were not always sympathetic to such complaints. In the early first century an embassy from Troy, seeking to express its condolences on the death of Tiberius' son Drusus, arrived at court some considerable time after the funeral. Receiving the belated Trojan envoys, the emperor cuttingly quipped: "And may I sympathize with you on the death of your eminent fellow citizen Hector?"[34]

For ambassadors or litigants, even winning access to the emperor did not always bring immediate or favorable results. In A.D. 40 an embassy from the Jewish community in Alexandria, led by Philo, a philosopher and prominent local worthy, came to Rome to present to Caligula its complaints against Avillius Flaccus, the previous prefect (provincial governor) of Egypt. After several false starts, the embassy— now a little out of breath—caught up with the emperor and his entourage near an elaborate gazebo in the Gardens of Lamia and Maecenas on the Esquiline Hill. The Jewish envoys did not, however, have Caligula's undivided attention. According to Philo's version of events (in part written to explain the failure of his attempts to secure imperial support for his cause):

> We started to speak and offer our explanations . . . but the emperor cut short our initial points before we could follow them up with stronger ones, and running dashed into a large pavilion and walked around it and ordered the windows on all sides to be restored with clear glass . . . Then he advanced in an unhurried manner and asked in a more reasonable tone, "What is it you are saying?" But when we began on the points which came next in our argument, he ran into another building, where he ordered paintings (all of them originals) to be hung.[35]

Others might be luckier. They might find a more attentive emperor or a better moment at which to present their cause. According to the early third-century historian Cassius Dio, the emperor Marcus Aurelius, even during the early 170s when he was commanding armies along the Danube frontier, was scrupulous in the exercise of his judicial functions. "But the emperor, as often as he had time away from the war, gave judgment. He ordered that ample time on the water clock be allocated to the advocates, and undertook the most exhaustive enquiries and interrogations, so that a just result could be reached by all possible means. In this way he often spent eleven and even twelve days deciding a case, sometimes even holding sessions at night."[36] No doubt some litigants (at least the successful parties) were impressed by the care which Marcus Aurelius took to ensure that those who appeared before him received a full hearing. All those whose cases were further delayed or even dismissed as a result of the emperor's spending nearly two weeks dealing with one issue may have taken a different and less sympathetic attitude toward his attention to detail. From their point of view, Marcus Aurelius' judicial enthusiasm for other litigants' cases was no less damaging to their own chances of success than Caligula's ostentatious indifference had been to Philo's embassy.

Most who attempted to gain access to the imperial court were probably well aware of the risks involved. Many perhaps never even expected to be heard. They may instead have hoped that the threatening possibility of presenting their case before an emperor might force their opponents either to capitulate or to seek a settlement out of court. Similar difficulties, chances, hopes, and expectations also surrounded litigation at a local level. Again for some, the problems of gaining access to the courts or to government officials may not have been of overwhelming concern. They may have preferred self-help (sometimes violent) or less formal arbitration, mediation, or negotiation of their disagreements. In other cases, as with those seeking imperial adjudication, the submission of a formal petition requesting a judicial hearing might have had less to do with any pressing desire to litigate than with a series of threats or bargaining positions in the face of what one party (at least) wished to present as the unwelcome risks of going to law.[37]

Sometimes, too, the opposing parties may also have sought to improve their chances of success by appealing to (what they hoped were) propitious deities. These otherworldly powers were notified of the details of a dispute on lead tablets deposited in wells, streams, or graves or publicly displayed in the precincts of the local temple, perhaps as a deliberate tactic to frighten an alleged wrongdoer by advertising a case both to the community and to its gods.[38] Sometime between the late second and mid-third centuries, Alexandros, a defendant in the town of Amathous, on the southern coast of Cyprus, invoked the gods on a lead tablet buried in a grave. Alexandros was concerned at the activities both of one Timon and particularly of Theodoros. The latter was probably the governor of Cyprus, perhaps a powerful backer of Timon, and most likely the judge if the case were to come to court. The efficacy of Alexandros' appeal was strengthened by the inclusion of magical words which might further persuade the spirits of the dead to take his side in this dispute.

> Spirits under the earth and spirits wherever you may be; fathers of fathers and mothers [who are] a match [for men], whether male or female, spirits whoever you may be and who lie here, having left grievous

life, whether violently slain or foreign or local or unburied . . . take over the voices of my opponents . . . namely Theodorus the governor and Timon to whom Markia gave birth . . . NETHIMAZ . . . MASOLABEO MAMAXOMAXO ENKOPTODIT . . . ENOUOUMAR AKNEU MELOPH-THELAR AKN . . . And give a muzzle to Theodorus the governor . . . and to Timon, so that they will be unable to do anything against me, Alexandros . . . But just as you are . . . wordless and speechless . . . so also let my opponents be speechless and voiceless, Theodorus the governor and Timon.[39]

But in some disputes, an appeal to powers in this world may have been regarded by one or both parties as the most advantageous course of action. Here again, litigants faced considerable problems in bringing a case to the authorities' attention. Governors' judicial activities—like emperors'—were (in Graham Burton's phrase) "unevenly spread geographically, and sporadic in their frequency."[40] Assizes could be canceled without warning.[41] Conversely, governors might insist on holding court even if the parties preferred an adjournment.[42] Nor was there any fixed order for hearing cases; no guarantee that those who had submitted their petitions first would be heard first; no assurance that litigants who (at their own expense) had assembled for an assize would in the end obtain a hearing.[43]

Proximity—as with emperors—was always a significant factor in successfully prosecuting any cause. In the late third century, Septimius Heracleides, one of the wealthier residents of Oxyrhynchus, acting through his agent Nemesianus, petitioned the prefect Caius Valerius Pompeianus. The reply instructed Nemesianus to present the case in person. His first attempt was unsuccessful. He was instructed to return on a day set aside for hearing cases. On his second attempt, he found the prefect was unavailable because at the time he was celebrating a festival in honor of Zeus. The next day, on the third try, Nemesianus succeeded in gaining entry to the prefect's court, only to be told (no doubt as he was hastily dismissed) that other business, including receiving ambassadors, would take priority on that day. On his fourth attempt, Nemesianus finally managed to speak to Pompeianus as the latter was walking in a laurel grove (perhaps in the grounds of his official residence in Alexandria). But hopes of an immediate decision were again thwarted. Perhaps disinterested, or pressed for time, or merely wishing to enjoy an uninterrupted afternoon stroll, the prefect instructed him to submit another formal petition, again setting out the case in writing.[44] Similar frustrations, and a similar persistence, characterized the attempts of Cephalion in Alexandria to present a petition on behalf of his friend Heraclas (also from Oxyrhynchus): "I have presented applications to our lord the prefect, and no decision has been handed down for me so far. Your opponent is tireless in making petitions, and so am I in making counterpetitions; so that I have heeded your instruction: 'Stay close to the prefect's office, and whenever you are cited, enter an objection.'"[45]

Nor—as with emperors—did gaining access to an official necessarily ensure a successful outcome. Some petitions were simply referred back to the local authorities or to subordinates.[46] Some merely received brief, formulaic responses (although the knowledge that a higher authority had noted the presence of a dispute might have been of benefit in forcing a hearing or a settlement).[47] Some petitions were never received at all. They were delayed, lost, mislaid, or deliberately blocked by those supposed to hand them on.[48] Among his many charges against Avillius Flaccus, Philo alleged that as prefect of Egypt in the mid-30s he had deliberately refused to send on a decree passed by the Jewish community of Alexandria in honor of the accession of Caligula.[49] Not all losses or delays necessarily had a malicious intent. In the late 360s an anonymous author submitted a short pamphlet (now known under the title *de rebus bellicis*) which outlined various military, administrative, and financial reforms, including plans for ingenious cost-saving devices such as a scythed chariot with automatic whips to control the horses and a warship with paddle wheels powered by oxen. These proposals probably never reached their intended readers, the emperors Valentinian I and Valens. In the view of its modern editor, E. A. Thompson, on its way through the imperial bureaucracy the dossier was probably just "intercepted by a civil servant and pigeonholed."[50]

Achieving access to government and obtaining the desired result, either for an individual or a community, was always a cause for celebration. Extravagant thanks were offered to local magnates who managed to secure favorable rulings from the imperial authorities. In the late fifth century the town of Aphrodisias (in western Asia Minor) put up a grandiloquent inscription and a statue in honor of Asclepiodotus.

Along with many other benefactions, including the funding of some impressive public buildings, he had secured privileges (probably financial or legal) for his city. That achievement alone deserved perpetual commemoration by his fellow citizens. "The light of virtue shines even for dead men, who, undertaking many labours for their country, established general benefits. The saying fits Asclepiodotus, for whom this city has dedicated this statue as for a founder. Long time wears away even stone, but the fame of Asclepiodotus' virtues is immortal, as is the number and kind of privileges which he obtained for his country."[51]

A century earlier, in the 380s, three towns in Tripolitania, on the North African coast (Gigthis, Sabratha, and Lepcis Magna), each put up statues of the local worthy L. Aemilius Quintus in order to display their thanks for his diplomatic success on a mission to the emperor himself. (Quintus had, in all probability, secured the assurance of military help against desert raiders from the Sahara, or perhaps the grant of subsidies or taxation relief to aid the towns' recovery following recent incursions.) Here was a man whose statues deserved to stand in prominent public places. These were notable monuments to a powerful provincial grandee erected, as the beautifully carved inscriptions on the statue bases proudly proclaimed, "in recompense for his hard work and the success of his embassy." Open celebrations were amply justified, "because he brought our shared troubles to the sacred [imperial] ears and obtained a cure for them."[52]

Such achievements deserved permanent record and public display. Those who won their cases or had their petitions granted seem to have regarded expensive commemorations of their success as appropriate and worthwhile advertisements of their status. These were fitting (and no doubt much sought after) expressions by their fellow citizens of well-deserved thanks. That gratitude in itself might be taken as an index of the difficulty faced, even by influential provincials, in gaining access to Roman government. No doubt, too, those successful outcomes noisily celebrated on stone or bronze represent only a small proportion of cases dealt with by Roman government, even by the emperor himself. But their exultant tones should not be allowed to obscure what must have been the significantly greater number of embassies or petitions which were never heard, nor perhaps (given the difficulties involved) ever sent or written. Regrettably, little trace remains either of these issues or of those to whom they mattered. Unsurprisingly, they have left no self-congratulatory epigraphic record.[53] Yet without a high proportion of silent, uncommemorated failures, the loudly jubilant inscriptions of the successful would have lost much of their impressive point.

The growth of bureaucracy in the later Empire did not make access to government any easier. Often it created additional obstacles for would-be petitioners. For most ordinary people, the very confusing complexity of the system made it impenetrable. Many found themselves disadvantaged by an endless maze of seemingly incomprehensible formalities and obscure technical language. In 450 the emperor Valentinian III issued a law with a splendidly elaborated description of the arrival of a tax collector in a province: "The first beginnings of his coming are that he produces and unrolls terrifying orders about various and numerous tax accounts. He presents a miasma of detailed computations confused with inexplicable obscurity, which among men ignorant of such subtleties has, to an even greater extent, the result that they understand less."[54] In practice, little was done to alleviate these difficulties. (Indeed, it is hard to tell whether Valentinian's law should properly be read as parodying the complexities of which it complained or, in its grandly convoluted style, merely adding to them.) In judicial matters, most imperial effort was directed toward the elimination of whole classes of action on appeal, or the imposition of statutes of limitation laying down maximum times for litigation. In 313 Constantine instructed a provincial governor to restrict the flow of cases sent on appeal to the imperial court: "you must consult our majesty only concerning those few matters which cannot be decided by previous judicial rulings, so that you may not interrupt our usual business."[55] In 331 the same emperor ruled that an unsuccessful appellant to the court of the praetorian prefect "shall be punished by exile to an island for two years and one half share of his goods shall be sequestrated and surrendered to the benefit of the imperial treasury."[56] Such laws are conventionally interpreted as honest attempts to eliminate vexatious or unnecessary litigation in order to ensure a more expeditious hearing for those seeking justice.[57] But in reality, when an administration has a greater caseload than it can possibly manage, statutes of limitation place more pressure on litigants than on officials. Only a certain (or reckless) appellant would risk further legal action when the penalties for failure were so severe.

Despite continual attempts to stem the flow, officials seem to have been inundated with ever more requests and petitions. At the beginning of the third century the prefect of Egypt, Subatianus Aquila, posted formal responses to the 1,804 petitions which had been submitted to him in two and a half days (March 22, 23, and part of 24, 210). In other words, on this occasion, assuming a ten-hour working day, these petitions were received at the rate of more than one a minute.[58] In the early sixth century in the eastern Praetorian Prefecture (before the reforms of John the Cappadocian), John Lydus claimed a similar administrative overload: "So many were the transactions of that time that (even summarized) they could hardly be included in ten volumes . . . So great was the number of transactions that the entire year was not long enough for the *adiutores* (as they were called) to complete them."[59] Roman administration in both the early and later Empire undoubtedly managed to process an impressive number of documents. Most bureaucrats must have found themselves overwhelmed by the paperwork they were called upon to complete. Many emperors, too, faced heavy administrative burdens. Confronted with "the innumerable crowds of people who arrive not only from neighboring provinces but also from the most distant frontiers of the Roman world, congregating and bringing complaints against their enemies," emperors could (if they were so inclined) read, write, and deal with a considerable amount of business.[60] Fergus Millar is surely right to observe that "those who were conscientious did indeed work very hard."[61]

But there were strict limits. Marcus Aurelius confessed himself exhausted after an administrative stint in which he had dictated "almost thirty letters."[62] Such restrictions (endlessly multiplied) were an inescapable part of imperial rule. Despite the enthusiastic encomiums of those provincials who actually made it, or the laws which sweepingly proclaimed that "the ears of the governor shall be open equally to the poorest as well as to the wealthiest," or the well-turned praises of panegyrists for those emperors who allegedly gave justice to all comers, easy access to government in the Roman Empire remained a grand ideal rather than an administrative reality.[63] Many, confronted with the resulting difficulties and legally imposed impediments, sought arbitration or mediation; others relied on self-help, threateningly phrased appeals to the gods, or direct action. Some, with widely varying degrees of skill and success, combined or shifted between these various strategies according to their own best estimate of advantage. Importantly, too, as is still the case in many modern societies, a large number faced with the costs and time-consuming difficulties of litigation simply learned to live with their grievances.

These manifest "inefficiencies" and "inadequacies" were to a great degree systemic. Roman government's ability to deliver administrative and judicial services was not maintained for the benefit of the ordinary inhabitants of empire. Rather, it was part of a pattern of imperial domination. It both underwrote the successful exploitation of the resources of the Mediterranean world and, at the same time, contributed to the more secure emplacement of the conquering power. For the most part, the chance of intervention in the everyday concerns of provincials remained an unpredictable (if threateningly ever-present) possibility. Emperors' interest or willingness to arbitrate—like their officials' ability to collect, collate, or manipulate data—could neither always be guaranteed nor ever entirely dismissed. Unsurprisingly, in practice the disputes which mattered most, and which always had the best chance of being heard, were those which threatened the security of a city, its financial stability, or the social and economic dominance of those upon whom central government depended for the continued collection of taxes and the maintenance of good order. Yet even here, given the obvious discrepancy between the total potential service which the bureaucracy could possibly deliver and the total demand for those services, it was necessary to establish some mechanism for the allocation of scarce resources and the effective deployment of a proportionately small number of personnel. The results of such a system were unavoidable: no matter how favorably they might have regarded the prospects of obtaining justice, no matter how enthusiastically they may have celebrated the benefits of imperial rule, the vast majority of those who sought access to Roman officials or courts had little option but to compete against each other for limited administrative time. Even for those prepared to risk the attempt, both queuing and queue jumping were inevitable.

Clout and Connections: The Early Roman Empire

In the early Roman Empire, order in the queue of those demanding access to government services was (to quote Ramsay MacMullen) determined largely by the operation of elite networks "of kin and correspondence, debts and favors."[64] The early third-century jurist Ulpian regarded governors' failure systematically to allocate time to those seeking to litigate before them as a significant factor in permitting those with social advantage to gain preferential treatment and in discouraging the less fortunate from going to law.[65] Access to the courts or to administrative services was more easily available to those possessing *potentia* and *gratia*, clout and connections. These were the commonest and most effective currencies of power. They were part of a system closely policed by an openly nonegalitarian vocabulary of privilege which gave unashamed precedence to those with suitable character, birth, wealth, education, and moral values. Those who qualified enjoyed a range of commercial, trade, taxation, legal, and administrative advantages. Those who failed to come up to the mark were (as far as possible) excluded, denied access to government by violence and intimidation if need be. In practice, the poor or friendless had little hope of redress against a powerful defendant. They rarely even bothered to litigate.[66]

The appointment of candidates to office displayed a similar bias. There is little evidence that selection or promotion was primarily dependent on a set system of seniority or on specialized skills, experience, or expertise. Rather, for the most part, "personal criteria"—*constantia, rectitudo, integritas,* and *industria*—weighed more heavily.[67] It was the task of letters of recommendation *(commendationes)* to stress a candidate's suitability and to indicate his advantageous connections. The rank-order of desirable qualifications is clearly on display in the *commendatio,* addressed by the middle-ranking senator Pliny the Younger to Lucius Javolenus Priscus (governor of Syria at the turn of the first century), seeking an army commission on behalf of Voconius Romanus:

His father was distinguished . . . His mother comes from a prominent family . . . I have valued him as a close friend ever since our student days together . . . In his conversation, and even in his voice and countenance, there is an extraordinary charm. Besides, he is possessed of a powerful, subtle, charming, quick intellect, well-versed in legal matters; moreover his letters are such that you would believe that the Muses themselves speak Latin . . . [etc., etc.] . . . So I have given you a faithful account . . . Let me ask you to honor him as your generosity and position best allow. And, of course, what really matters is that you should like the man.[68]

Such references were an important means of both creating and discharging obligations. They are the best (and the most unabashed) evidence of the workings of power in the early Empire, and of the language in which those transactions were conducted. In turn, central government's "cosy relationship" with the great and good—*homines nobilissimi ac potentissimi*—restricted its ability (or willingness) to deploy alternative strategies for the selection of its senior staff.[69]

But these comfortable strategies for regulating access to administrative services or office did not always enjoy an unchallenged monopoly. Money, too, sometimes changed hands. In this context, the ability to pay, like the possession and exercise of *gratia* or *potentia,* can usefully be seen as an alternative or supplementary way of creating order and priority within a queue of potential consumers competing for limited government resources. At worst, the purchase of office or influence might cut across existing priorities established by carefully constructed, long-term networks of exchange. Set against the delicate balance of reciprocity and dependency, upon which those emphatically personal relationships depended, the payment of money was comparatively cut and dried. It involved no lasting social ties, no emotional links, no subordinating or continuing relationships. Simply put, it offered the possibility of access to those with the ability to pay.

The potentially corrosive effects of money payments upon traditional methods of organizing access to government was clearly recognized. Those members of the elite involved in such transactions sought to incorporate them within their own pattern of social prejudices and moral justifications. Properly regarded (or at least so it was argued), payments of money or "gift giving" were to be seen as strengthening, rather than replacing, personal relationships. On the so-called Thorigny Marble, erected in 238 in the provincial town of Aregenoua (modern Vieux-la-Romaine, near Caen in northern France), a local notable, Titus Sennius Sollemnis, publicly advertised his relationship with the ex-governor of Gallia Lugdunensis, Claudius Paulinus, and his successor, Aedinius Julianus. In 220 Sollemnis had been responsible for blocking an indictment of Paulinus by delegates to the provincial Gallic Assembly. On one side, Sollemnis' monument displayed a letter from Julianus praising his actions, "his upright conduct, and his honorable ways." On the other was a copy of a letter from Paulinus in which he recorded his thanks and listed the presents he had sent, both as a material indication of his gratitude to Sollemnis and (he stressed) as an expression of his desire for a closer, more mutually beneficial relationship.[70]

Some combination of money, gifts, honor, praise, and favors was not uncommon in the formation and maintenance of such networks. The early Roman Empire (as Ramsay MacMullen has rightly observed) was an "oily, present-giving world."[71] Those swapping or securing obligations might ease the passage of their requests by offering a tangible "sweetener" as a token of good faith. But the order of priorities, as publicly displayed on the Thorigny Marble, was significant. As far as possible, those involved attempted to ensure that offers of gifts or money remained subordinate to any ties of reciprocal obligation. Any immediate benefit which such offers might confer was (on this view) to be directed toward securing the advantages offered by a long-term commitment to further exchanges. Both the payment of money and the giving of gifts were to be presented as congenial contributions to the development of a proper, lasting personal relationship, not as substitutes for it.

The subordination of gift giving to traditional patterns of power was not always secure. It was, after all, often a disputable question of perception. The difficulties involved were clearly exposed in 103 in the trial of Junius Bassus, ex-governor of Bithynia (on the Black Sea shore of modern Turkey) on charges of extortion. That Bassus had received gifts and money was not in doubt. What was at issue was how this act should be interpreted and judged. Pliny (Bassus' defense attorney) summed up the opposing views: *haec accusatores furta ac rapinas, ipse munera uocabat*—"these things which his accusers called illicit thefts and plunder, he called presents."[72] The terms of debate are revealing. Pliny's speech before the Senate concentrated on presenting his client as an exemplar of commonly held standards of virtue, one whose error was committed in innocent and understandable confusion. His arraignment was the result of dubious information provided by informers. By contrast, three years previously, in supporting the condemnation of Hostilius Firminus, also on extortion charges, Pliny portrayed him as transgressing accepted standards of behavior. Here was a man who in his accounts allegedly had disguised his ill-gotten gains as *unguentarii*—"perfume money" (or, perhaps, *douceurs*). "An entry," bitched Pliny in a letter to a friend, "quite in keeping with his over-groomed and effeminate personal habits."[73]

Not everyone was convinced. For some members of the Senate, their moral code was to be upheld at all costs and publicly affirmed. They remained unpersuaded by Pliny's claims that Bassus' receipt of gifts posed no threat to traditional ways of exercising power and influence. A substantial minority was not openly prepared to admit any accommodation between these two rival currencies of power. On this view, Bassus was to be condemned outright as "one who had accepted presents illegally." Others were more circumspect. They preferred to "grant indulgence to a course of action which, though prohibited, was not uncommon."[74] Some level of "rapacity," though far from ideal, might, in practice, be countenanced. In the end, the case was only partially resolved. Bassus was convicted and fined, but he was not expelled from the Senate.

The relationship between these two currencies of power remained uncomfortable and difficult. Only at extremes were members of the Roman elite prepared unequivocally to condemn the receipt of money by one of their own. For the most part (while recognizing the threat which money payments posed to the security and stability of traditionally constructed networks), their attitudes remained studiously ambiguous. According to the jurist Ulpian, a governor "should aim for a balance, neither sulkily refraining altogether nor greedily exceeding a reasonable level for gifts." He further recommended, as a rough guide, the rule laid down by the late second-century emperors Septimius Severus and Caracalla. They advised (quoting an old proverb) that governors should, in demanding gifts in return for their services, be careful to take οὔτε πάντα, οὔτε πάντοτε, οὔτε παρὰ πάντων— "neither everything, nor every time, nor from everyone."[75]

But from the point of view of the imperial authorities, the potentially disruptive effect of money payments offered one means of promoting their interests against the limitations imposed by the prevailing pattern of rule. Above all, it was an important tactic in insulating those involved in government from the competing demands of those with clout and connections. It is notable that, in the early Empire, three groups most commonly associated with the payment of money in return for administrative advantage were also closely connected with the advancement and enforcement of imperial interests: *apparitores* (salaried civilian administrators, including scribes, messengers, heralds, lictors, and porters, attached to the staff of magistrates in Rome and in the provinces); *frumentarii* (a corps under the direct control of the praetorian prefect formed from legionaries on secondment who acted as imperial messengers between provincial governors and Rome); and the emperors' freedmen (who carried out a wide range of administrative and domestic tasks at court and in the imperial household). These groups' sense of internal solidarity, their more formal organizational structures, and their greater permanence helped distance them from the more diffuse and highly personal networks of exchange and obligation.[76] Among the *apparitores* in particular, these boundaries, important to the development of a distinct (and distinguishing) corporate identity, were further reinforced through the development of a well-regulated hierarchy of posts which allowed a greater security of tenure, a more reliable allocation of specific tasks, and the possibility of some specialization.[77]

Money payments both complemented and reinforced that sense of separation. They provided a means of transacting government business which did not involve participation in an endless round of reciprocal obligation. The possibility of securing appointment or promotion through purchase provided an alternative method for advancement less dependent on the need either to rely on traditional networks of support or to subscribe to conventional criteria of excellence. Among *apparitores,* the sale of office seems to have been (to quote Nicholas Purcell) "entirely regular and above board": the most famous purchaser was the first-century poet Horace.[78] By the early second century, jurists, similarly without any sign of embarrassment, discussed the legal problems arising from the sale or bequest of a *militia* (a term covering both administrative and military posts).[79] Some emperors, too, with equal unabashed openness, were alleged to have permitted the sale of offices, favors, and influence. Claudius was accused by the historian Cassius Dio of allowing his freedmen to sell "military commands, procuratorships, and provincial governorships."[80] Dark tales were told of money changing hands at court. According to the early second-century imperial biographer Suetonius, Vespasian was once approached by one of his favorite subordinates seeking preferment for a man whom he spuriously claimed to be his brother, but who had in fact agreed to pay to have his case brought before the emperor. Vespasian delayed his decision. Meanwhile he summoned "the brother." When the truth was revealed, Vespasian compelled the man to pay him as much money as he had previously agreed to pay his supposedly fraternal intermediary. When the same subordinate (no doubt wondering what had happened) again raised the matter of his "brother's" advancement, the emperor acidly quipped, "Find yourself another brother; the one whom you thought was yours, is mine."[81]

But for many involved in the government of empire, these practices went beyond a joke. *Apparitores* could be portrayed as dangerous social upstarts. These were the kind of men (at least in Cicero's damning version) who might be expected to surround a vicious self-seeking provincial governor such as Verres. "Men who in order to purchase their positions scrape together the cash from the gifts of playboys and from the gratuities of the theater audience and then claim to have come from the front row in the cheer squad to the second rank in the state."[82] Only clout and connections, *potentia* and *gratia*, exercised in the right way, by the right sort of people, were proper subjects for legitimate praise. To deviate too far from these precepts was to risk jeopardizing the stability of a desirable social order. Pliny, in congratulating his friend Calestrius Tiro for preserving the correct distinctions of class and rank in the administration of his province, ominously remarked that "if these are confused, thrown into disorder, mixed up, then nothing is more unequal than that equality."[83] Emperors who acted to preserve an advantageous social order (at any rate from the point of view of men like Pliny) were also warmly commended. In the early third century Alexander Severus was said to have found one of his close associates receiving money in return for his (allegedly illusory) influence at court, a practice known colloquially as *fumum uendere*—"selling smoke." In another blunt and less immediately amusing example of imperial humor, Severus ordered the offender to be burned alive on a pyre of straw and wet logs. As he suffocated to death, a herald wittily proclaimed: *Fumo punitur qui uendidit fumum*—"The smoke seller is punished by smoke."[84]

Such stories helped to reinforce the view that the open use of money as a means of regulating access to government services was part of an unnatural and menacing *interior potentia*—a clear sign of troubled times.[85] These transactions belonged to that concealed backstairs influence which could make *apparitores,* imperial freedmcn, or *frumentarii* sinister figures of hate. They were regularly accused of moral perversion, sexual depravity, extravagance beyond measure, cowardice, and cruelty.[86] "Like scum" (remarked Cassius Dio), "these men rise to the surface of a lake."[87] They were, echoed the *Historia Augusta,* the "filth of tyranny."[88] Pliny would have agreed. While traveling along the Via Tiburtina outside Rome, he came across the grand tomb of the emperor Claudius' influential freedman Pallas (notorious for his wealth and sale of favors) with its impressive inscription celebrating the honors voted him by the Senate. Affronted by the very sight of this monument, Pliny fulminated (for two whole letters) on the "absurd farce" of these accolades' being "thrown away on such dregs and filth"—"How pleased I am that I did not chance to live in those times; yet I blush on their account as if I had lived in them."[89]

This black-and-white world of elite moral fantasy exaggerated the degree to which traditional methods of exercising influence were in practice disrupted by such factors as the payment of money or the purchase of office. As Fergus Millar has rightly noted, any incident involving such transactions inevitably "aroused attention and resentment."[90] These were cues for warnings about the dangers of such practices and the immorality of those who followed them. They should not be taken as indicating the norm. The level of sheer partisan invective in the surviving accounts of the Principate makes it easy to magnify the extent to which traditional interests were ever successfully deflected. As always, it is largely a question of perspective. The prominence of the much-repeated stories of a few wealthy and highly influential imperial freedmen should not be allowed to obscure the experience of the majority in the imperial household who (again in Millar's phrase) "were no closer to the emperor than the rest of the population."[91] Equally, the possibility that *apparitores* might legitimately purchase or bequeath their positions should not be permitted to overshadow the strong impression that, for the most part, successful appointment and advancement depended on influence and connections.[92] Nor does the extreme vilification of the *frumentarii—pestilens frumentariorum genus—* justify their subsequent description in modern scholarship as an "imperial secret service."[93] It sits uncomfortably with the other known evidence of their activities, and with the impact such a corps could possibly have made. There were, after all, at any one time no more than a few hundred *frumentarii* in the whole Empire.[94]

In the first two centuries A.D., the payment of money must always be seen against the background of the dominant pattern of rule. Attempts to purchase access to government inevitably met with only limited success. In the end, it was personal connections which counted most, no doubt supplemented and strengthened in the short term by the regular exchange of gifts and in the long term across the generations by the giving and receiving of legacies. Equally, for those seeking office, *commendationes* remained the most effective way of securing an advantageous position in the queue of those desiring preferment. For most people in the early Empire, that open preference for personal contact, for participation in a traditional network of long-term reciprocal exchange, can be matched again and again. In 103 an officer at the frontier post of Vindolanda, on Hadrian's Wall in the north of England, wrote to a newly appointed member of the governor's staff. The draft of his letter survives. It is the banal typicality of its expectations which is important. "With the governor's permission I know that very many of those whom you help have just what you promise them. Please repay my faith in you and . . . so furnish me with friends that thanks to you I may be able to enjoy a pleasant period of military service."[95]

CHAPTER 4

Purchasing Power

Mouth smile—but money smile better.

—Ghanaian proverb

In point of fact, the promotion of the Officers of the Army by purchase is a saving of expense to the Public, and highly beneficial to the Service, although it falls severely upon individuals . . . It is the promotion by purchase which brings into the Service men of fortune and education; men who have some connexion with the interests and fortunes of the Country.

—Duke of Wellington

The Uses of Money

In the later Roman Empire, the relationship between influence and money (as competing means of ordering the queue of those demanding government services) perceptibly shifted.[1] Money became a more important currency of access. Charging by bureaucrats, who had themselves sometimes purchased their offices, or on appointment or promotion had paid fees to their superiors, was commonplace: from taxation rake-offs, through charges on the locals by the military commander of the Euphrates frontier for wood to heat the officers' baths, to fees for "wheel wearage" (*pro rotarum tritura*), and standard payments for the processing of documents.[2] The last is appropriately called in some modern African countries "speed money" or "dash," a colloquialism which finds its parallel in an early sixth-century tax roll (from the Egyptian village of Aphrodito) recording a sum paid ὑπὲρ σπουδῆς—"for expediting."[3]

More significantly, in the later Empire, payment for services was promoted, institutionalized, and regulated. Central government issued "charge-sheets" which listed, in often complex and knowingly opaque legalistic detail, fixed prices for specified bureaucratic actions. One of the most comprehensive surviving examples (quoted above at the opening of Part II) is the mid-fourth-century schedule of legal and administrative fees inscribed on a limestone slab and displayed on the colonnaded north wall of the *curia* in the center of Timgad, modern Thamugadi in Algeria. This charge-sheet (known as the *ordo salutationis*) was a copy of a bronze original which had been posted in the provincial capital, Cirta, by the governor of Numidia, Ulpius Mariscianus, and perhaps originally displayed near his tribunal.[4]

The cost of litigation (expressed as so many bushels of wheat or its cash equivalent) was specified for each stage of the judicial process and the distance to be traveled in serving the writs. To commence an action, the plaintiff paid 5 *modii* to the *exceptores* (the officials who staffed the governor's court) for the registration of a *postulatio simplex* (the initial pleading which detailed the complaint) and 5 to the *scholastici* (attorneys) for its presentation in court. If the *postulatio* was successful, the plaintiff would receive an interlocutory judgment entitling him to summon the defendant to a public hearing in front of the governor. To then issue a summons, the plaintiff paid 5 *modii* to the *princeps officii,* the head of the governor's staff, and 2½ each to his two senior subordinates, the *cornicularius* and *commentariensis*.[5] The *executor,* the official appointed by the *princeps* to carry out the orders of the court from serving the summons to executing the judgment, received a fee of 2 *modii*. If the case involved a defendant outside the city, a system of carefully prescribed surcharges detailed the extra sums payable. Again, the *princeps* received the full amount, and both his subordinates half each. (In turn, these senior officials may have redistributed some of the fees among their junior colleagues.) It is likely, too, that in such cases the *executor* received an additional fee. In the event of a defendant's electing to contest the action, both he and the plaintiff paid 12 *modii* to the *exceptores* and 10 to the attorneys. At the conclusion of litigation, the *exceptores* received (in all likelihood from both parties) 20 *modii* and likewise the attorneys 15. The *libellensis,* responsible for drawing up the *postulatio simplex* and any necessary documents for the hearing, and for drafting the final judgment, received 2 *modii*.[6] Finally, at all stages of the case, litigants (depending on how a confusing and damaged passage in the inscription is understood) either had to pay for the papyrus used in drawing up the necessary legal documents or, more probably, were charged the comparatively trivial sums levied as an imperial tax on papyrus.[7]

On this reading of the *ordo salutationis,* for a plaintiff the cheapest possible total in administrative and legal fees for litigation, through all its stages and not including any payment for papyrus, in the provincial capital of Numidia was 81 *modii*. For a defendant, the cost of deciding to join an action was 59 *modii*.[8] Distance imposed still greater charges. Anyone in Timgad weighing up the cost of going to law in the provincial capital seventy (Roman) miles away would, from the outset, have to allow a surcharge of 7 *modii* (for service more than one mile from Cirta) and a further tariff at 2 *modii* per ten miles after that: a total of 20 *modii* payable to the *princeps* and 10 to each of his two senior subordinates. These additional costs raised the fees payable by a plaintiff to 121 *modii*.[9] These figures represent important cutoff points. In practical terms, these were the thresholds to litigation which through the imposition of fees helped to establish some order in the queue of those wishing to go to law in a provincial governor's court.

What did these thresholds mean? A peasant landholder—in Timgad perhaps to sell his produce, to attend a festival, or to enjoy some entertainment at the theater just next to the forum—when he cast his eye down the charge-sheet displayed on the northern wall of the *curia* (or had the inscription read or explained to him by a friend), did he feel included or excluded? Did he feel inclined to contemplate litigation, or was he, right from the start, elbowed out of the queue: forced to bear his grievance in silence, to band together (if at all possible) with others with similar problems, or to find a solution outside the official legal system? These charges for litigation can be thought of in the most basic terms. At 121 *modii*, the cost of a case brought by a plaintiff in or near Timgad represented roughly four-fifths of the amount of wheat required to meet the minimum needs of a family of four at subsistence level for a year.[10] Faced with such a charge in fees alone, it is easy to imagine some smallholder, already struggling to provide for his household, simply turning and walking away. Perhaps the *ordo salutationis* merely confirmed his views on the inaccessibility of Roman justice, even at a local level. Perhaps, too, he had other, more immediate financial concerns: the payment of taxes and rents, and the need to ensure some small surplus against the ever-present uncertainty of a poor harvest. Perhaps, amid other pressing priorities and the pleasurable diversions of a visit to the local town, he may not even have bothered to waste his time trying to puzzle out the possible consequences of a deliberately complex inscription.

A (similarly crude) sense of scale can also be gauged by converting the fees for litigation expressed in *modii* of wheat into equivalent money values. (As before, these figures should not be understood as having any great pretensions to accuracy; but they do again offer a usefully broad impression of how the fees for litigation as listed on the Timgad charge-sheet might have appeared to a small landholder or his family.) On the contemporary mid-fourth-century North African market, one *modius* of wheat was probably worth somewhere between one-thirtieth and one-fortieth of a *solidus*.[11] At such a rate, the cost of litigation (at Timgad prices) works out at around 3 to 4 *solidi*.

Even one *solidus* was no mean amount. A single working person could live for several months on such a sum; the poorest could perhaps live for a whole year on only a little more. Upon enrollment in the late fourth century, an army recruit received 6 *solidi* to cover his uniform, equipment, and other initial expenses.[12] In late sixth-century Palestine, in the village of Nessana (modern Hafir el-Auja in the central Negev), one *solidus* purchased a donkey, 2 *solidi* a colt, 3 a slave girl, 6 a slave boy, and 5 *solidi* a camel.[13] Moreover, the money required to pay just the administrative and legal costs of litigation (in which a successful outcome was by no means ever certain) might for many mean risking too great a proportion of their hard-won savings. In the late third century the jurist Hermogenian, in this case like the *ordo salutationis* using money as a means of regulating access to the empire's courts, suggested some restriction on the legal rights of the "poor," whom he defined as "those possessing less than 50 *aurei*" (roughly equivalent to 50 *solidi*).[14] For many smallholders, this was a significant sum. In mid-sixth-century Nessana, the daughters of two army veterans living in the village both received dowries worth around 40 *solidi;* a divorce settlement provided for the return of marriage gifts and property belonging to the bride worth 30 *solidi*. Even these amounts might be considered beyond the means of many. A soldier serving in contemporary Antinoopolis, in Egypt, agreed to pay a local girl 4½ *solidi* as his marriage gift.[15] Nor could such sums, particularly in cash, always readily be found. In the 530s, in John Lydus' hometown of Philadelphia, John Maxilloplumacius ("Leaden-Chops"), sent out to Lydia by John the Cappadocian to supervise the collection of taxes, demanded 20 *solidi* from the veteran Proclus. This was an apparently impossible impost, which he was unable to meet despite the efforts of Maxilloplumacius' agents, who (at least according to John Lydus' openly partisan account) "blunted all the instruments of torture on the sinews of the wretched pauper."[16]

The scatter of isolated figures cited above can give only the roughest of guides to what charges of several *solidi* meant in fourth-century North Africa. (They also underline the vertiginous disparities in wealth in the western half of the empire, where a middle-ranking senator might reckon on an annual income of at least 72,000 *solidi*.)[17] But they do again suggest that the decision to afford the fees for legal and administrative services as set out in the *ordo salutationis* would have been a serious matter for many peasant farming families. Only in some circumstances, when something as valuable or as necessary to their livelihood as their farmland, a slave, or a stock animal was at stake, might the expense of litigation be worth bearing. Even then, raising the necessary sums could involve the added risk of borrowing, perhaps (to compound these difficulties) against the often-unpredictable chance of a successful result, both in court and in executing any judgment. Only those smallholders fortunate enough to live near the provincial capital, and saved the punishing additional costs of litigating at a distance, might be able to consider taking some legal action. For the overwhelming majority of the population, judicial proceedings were in all likelihood possible only if a group decided to pursue some collective grievance. Individual losses had to be recovered by some means other than through the courts, or simply suffered in silence.

Unsurprisingly, litigation (usually on appeal) in the courts of the imperial capital was even more expensive. The *ordo salutationis* stipulated a surcharge of 100 *modii* for the conduct of a case overseas. According to John Lydus, in the early sixth century a plaintiff litigating in the praetorian prefect's court might expect to pay 37 *solidi* for a *postulatio simplex* alone. Only the wealthy could afford such high prices. Discounts were stipulated for some privileged groups (bureaucrats, guards, servants) attached to the imperial court. Before the *magister officiorum*, members of the household guard (*scholae palatinae*), their families, and slaves paid 6 *solidi* in administrative fees to defend a case (one *solidus* for the *executores*, 3 for the court officials at the trial itself, and 2 for the various bureaucrats involved in drawing up the court records and drafting the necessary legal documentation). Clergy in Constantinople, litigating as defendants before the praetorian prefect, paid no more than 2 *solidi* to the *executores*.[18] The advantages enjoyed

by these privileged groups were extended (on a less generous scale) to
the provincial courts. Members of both the *scholae palatinae* and the
sacra scrinia could be charged up to half the amount they might pay in
the capital. Clerics, according to a law issued by the emperor Leo in
472, were to pay no more than half a *solidus* to the *executores*.[19] Soldiers
(Anastasius decreed twenty years later), involved in a case before a military commander in one of the eastern provinces where they were
stationed, were to pay one *solidus* to the official responsible for the execution of writs and judgments, and no more than one *solidus* for all
court fees.[20]

Even at these reduced rates, the very levying of a charge set a level
below which even those who could afford to go to court might not consider legal action worthwhile. On the basis of the Timgad charge-
sheet, the costs in court fees alone (81 *modii* for a plaintiff, 59 for a defendant) meant that, even given a successful outcome, litigation on
matters worth less than these amounts would be a waste of resources.
An acute awareness of such a threshold lay behind one of the bitter attacks made by the Antiochene rhetor Libanius in his *Oration against
Tisamenus,* governor of Syria in 386. As part of a series of accusations of
avarice and extortion, Libanius singled out the governor's insistence
on dragging into court "matters worth a *solidus,* or a half, or a third of
a *solidus,* disputes which had remained dormant beneath the passage
of the years."[21] Tisamenus' alleged motive in compelling litigation was
the acquisition of funds to support an extravagant public building program. The logic of Libanius' complaint is clear. While the governor's
close attention to his judicial duties (ironically) resulted in greater accessibility to the courts, from the point of view of those involved, as
long as the costs of legal proceedings exceeded the value of the case,
such increased activity was unwelcome. Disputants in Antioch were
forced to obtain official justice to settle their differences. They unwillingly joined a queue whose costs outweighed its potential benefits. Under normal conditions, litigation on such relatively unimportant matters was (like poorer litigants) literally priced out of court.

For bureaucrats, too, the threat of heavy fines for any breach of
imperially imposed restrictions on access to the empire's judicial system could make certain cases prohibitively unremunerative. In 395
Arcadius and Honorius issued a law banning an acting praetorian prefect from dealing with "petty and trifling" matters, "concerning a run-

away slave, a theft (clearly apprehended in the act or not), concerning an animal which has been stolen, a slave, or thing, movable or moving, or goods seized by force, or concerning the boundaries of small plots of land, or concerning small farms."[22] The fine imposed on the members of the praetorian prefect's staff, if they permitted such cases to go forward to court, was 5 pounds of gold or 360 *solidi,* a sum ten times the amount they might expect to receive for legitimately issuing a *postulatio simplex.* More severely, in the early 490s an imperial edict of Anastasius (displayed as an impressive inscription built into a series of forts in southern Syria and Jordan and best preserved at Qasr el-Hallabat) prescribed fines of 10 pounds of gold for governors and 20 for their staff if they failed to settle cases "according to the statutory prescription" or, where appropriate, to refer judicial matters to military commanders in their provinces.[23] In 545 Justinian ruled that those officials successfully accused by litigants of receiving fees beyond those prescribed for the conduct of civil cases should be fined three times that amount and removed from office.[24] An earlier law, issued by Theodosius II and Valentinian III in 439, imposed a similar penalty of a quadruple fine (in addition to threats of divine punishment) on both parties to the transaction.[25] No doubt such equations had an effect on the way bureaucrats assessed fee-paying litigants. They introduced a second set of thresholds. Potential users of government services were not the only group restricted by the imposition of a regulatory mechanism based on the ability to pay. The threat of heavy fines could also price litigation out of court. Even if litigants were prepared to pay substantially above the publicly advertised rate, officials might not be willing to take the risk.

For later Roman bureaucrats, forever faced with a queue of those needing services much longer than they could ever process, the detailed stipulation of prices for administrative services was an effective method of regulating demand. The payment of money established clear cutoff points, automatically disbarring those unable to afford the costs of access to administrative or judicial services, and openly advantaging groups already connected with government by offering them discounted rates. The charging of fees for litigation acted as a significant barrier, preventing many from going to law in an attempt to pursue or resolve their disputes. Officials, too, required some means of both selecting and ordering the transactions in which they were prepared to participate. Unlike modern Western industrial states, later Roman society lacked either the human or the economic resources to make possible easy or near-universal access to government services. In fourth-century North Africa, the praetorian prefect's deputy (the *uicarius*) had an established staff of only 300 officials to process the complaints and problems arising from the governors' courts of five provinces, as well as to deal with revenue collection and all the other business of government. A provincial governor (such as Ulpius Mariscianus in Numidia) probably had an established staff of around 100.[26] Some method of exclusion was necessary if government was to function efficiently. A selection had to be made. Under these conditions, it was easier for central government to pay officials less and allow them to supplement their income by charging fees. It would have been cumbersome and inefficient (a waste of both time and resources) to have paid officials more and required them to remit the charges they collected to a central exchequer for subsequent redistribution as salaries.[27] A system of fees transferred transaction costs directly to the consumers of bureaucratic services. In turn, their ability to pay helped to regulate access to government.

Small-Town Societies

The payment of fees for administrative or judicial services did not inevitably lead to widespread rapacity. Of course, in the later Roman Empire (as in most societies ancient and modern) there were rogue government officials who, by any standards, could fairly be described as greedy, avaricious, or corrupt. But by and large it was not in the long-term interests of the majority of provincial bureaucrats to charge extortionate prices. For the most part, these were local men with local concerns. Many belonged to families which for several generations had had an important and continuing investment in the prosperity of their locality and in the maintenance of a highly esteemed and long-cherished social position. They greatly prized their membership in the small and self-regarding elite which dominated the life of most provincial towns.[28]

Most probably in the first few months of 363, about the same time as the *ordo salutationis* was fixed to the north side of the *curia* in Timgad, a much larger inscription (covering more than 3 square meters of limestone) was erected in the imposing main hall of the same building. This inscription, the so-called *album municipal,* offers a snapshot of one small-town society in the mid-fourth century. In six long columns, it recorded 283 names of those in some way connected with the local government of the town, ranked according to their status and position in that year.[29] The *album* opened with a listing of Timgad's grandees: 12 men who held high imperial rank (as *clarissimi* or *perfectissimi*), 5 named as patrons of the city, followed by 2 (one also a patron) serving during the course of the year in the prestigious post of chief priest *(sacerdos)* for the province of Numidia. Next followed the 3 senior municipal magistrates currently in office; then 32 names of those who had served their year as *flamen perpetuus* responsible for the maintenance of the imperial cult. Taken together, these men might comfortably be regarded as constituting Timgad's local ruling elite.[30] Next followed 153 names (133 survive) of those who might fairly have seen themselves as belonging to the town's "quality," even if in many cases they were significantly less wealthy than their higher-ranking colleagues. The first 10 listed in this group were the annual holders of junior offices and priesthoods. The remainder, though not in office in that year, had previously held posts (real or honorary) or had various, mostly hereditary, administrative or financial responsibilities for the town's government to be discharged by officeholding in a future year. Some had been exempted from fulfilling their municipal obligations, in most cases probably on grounds of insufficient wealth.[31] The final two columns of the *album* listed 11 Christian priests and 70 bureaucrats. Of these officials, 28 were attached to departments based in Carthage, 5 to the *officium* of the *uicarius* of Africa and 23 to the *officium* of the *praefectus annonae* (responsible for the supply of grain to the city of Rome). The remaining 42 were allocated to the provincial capital, Cirta, 37 to the governor and 5 to the *rationalis,* the imperial treasury official assigned to Numidia.

Given the size of the governor's administrative staff, a good proportion of those categorized as *officiales* on the Timgad inscription cannot have been in active service.[32] The list must also have included a sizable number of men who claimed immunity from some of the financial and administrative obligations of local government by securing bureaucratic rank either through hereditary succession or through a sinecure (perhaps obtained through influence or purchase). Some of those listed may also have acquired immunity on retirement from their posts, having served for at least the minimum specified period.[33] Claims to immunity were at times contested. Some were upheld, others denied by imperial legislation.[34] In this context, the listing of those with administrative posts (active or fictive) on the *album municipal* may in itself represent an attempt to regularize—and make public—a register of those whom the *curia* in Timgad accepted as immune. But such disputes should not be allowed to obscure the dense network of personal relationships which always existed between bureaucrats and the powerful in the provinces in which they served. Both belonged to the thin layer of landowners which dominated local, small-town life throughout the empire. In Timgad, fewer than 300 men had the necessary minimum requirement of property worth 300 *solidi* to qualify as members of the municipal council.[35] Taken together, these individuals perhaps represent sixty or seventy family groups out of a population of around 10,000.[36] And as their inclusion in the *album* demonstrates, many established provincial bureaucrats can reasonably be thought of as belonging to this municipal "upper crust."

Indeed, even to the most cursory reader, the stark simplicity of the *album* clearly displayed the close links between those on the municipal council in Timgad and those who were associated with the imperial bureaucracy in Carthage and Cirta. Four Timgad clans were particularly prominent: the Sessii, the Pompei, the Iulii, and the Claudii. Ten members of the Sessii are listed on the *album;* two as officials, eight in municipal government, four at its highest ranks. Sessius Cresconius, an official attached to the *praefectus annonae,* was most likely the son of the former senior magistrate (also called Sessius Cresconius) and the father of one of the most junior members of the council (also called Sessius Cresconius). Similarly, some members of the Pompei, the Iulii, and the Claudii held respected positions among Timgad's elite; others are listed as imperial officials in Cirta or Carthage. And there is an impressive number of other individual connections. One official, Flavidius Sudianus, attached to the staff of the provincial governor, has the same name as a former senior magistrate in Timgad, perhaps his father. One of Sudianus' colleagues in Cirta cited in the *album* as "Donatus, the son of Innocentius Abassi" is most likely the son of the Innocentius Abassi listed among the most junior members of the council. And so on across thirty-one identifiable family groups.[37]

These intimate connections are striking. Regrettably, it is impossible to distinguish which of those listed as *officiales* were in active service when the text of the inscription was drafted. Even so, the overwhelming impression given by the *album municipal* and its columns of names is that of a close association between those serving in the imperial bureaucracy and "the quality" in Timgad. Indeed, for many outside that exclusive small-town society, the categorization as *officiales* of those holding a sinecure or possessing hereditary immunity must have further strengthened the impression of a cosy relationship between those in post in Cirta and Carthage (or retired from active service) and those advertising on the *album* their superior social position in Timgad. Importantly, too, the connections between the municipal council and the governor's *officium,* as prominently displayed in the main hall of the *curia,* dulls any too sharply antagonistic view of the *album*'s relationship with the charge-sheet posted outside. After all, any local standing in the cool of the colonnade shading the north wall of the *curia* and attempting to calculate the risks and costs of litigation in the provincial capital might also reflect that he had a good chance of dealing with an official who—whatever his loyalties to his colleagues or his attempts to avoid the financial responsibilities of local government in his hometown—also retained close ties with Timgad and its ruling elite.

In addition to their social or familial connections, many local bureaucrats might be expected to have had an economic stake in the area where they lived and worked. Substantial fragments of two surviving registers from mid-fourth-century Egypt record landholders in the Hermopolite nome (a local administrative district centered on the town of Hermopolis, about 300 kilometers south of the delta). Two broad categories of owners are distinguished: those living in the West Citadel quarter of Hermopolis and those resident on the opposite bank of the Nile in the town of Antinoopolis. In these registers, various officials—some active, some no doubt retired—are listed as holding property alongside bishops, current and former municipal magistrates, those with military rank, professionals (doctors, lawyers, teachers of rhetoric, astrologers), artisans, and tradesmen (silversmiths, builders, potters, fullers, dyers, donkey drivers).[38] Among the 203 landowners recorded in the later and better-preserved register as resident in Antinoopolis, there are probably somewhere around 30 provincial officials (including some subclerical staff and some established grades familiar, like those cited on the *ordo salutationis,* from the great departments in Constantinople: *princeps, commentariensis, ab actis*).[39] Of these officials, about a fifth own properties larger than 100 *arouras* (one *aroura* = 2,756 square meters), which places them in the top 10 percent of landholders listed in this section of the register. The substantial majority have properties between 11 and 100 *arouras,* estates large enough to yield a rental income sufficient to support a family. These holdings place their owners in the top half of all landowners recorded as resident in Antinoopolis.[40]

Some officials were probably also involved in the sale and acquisition of land. The overall differences in holdings between the two registers, compiled perhaps five to ten years apart, indicate a greater change in ownership than might be expected as a result of inheritance or transfer within families, as gifts or dowries, or through confiscation by central government in default of taxes or other obligations. This would seem to suggest an active property market, at least among the town-dwelling landholders listed in these registers (although, of course, in any specific case the reason for the change in ownership is not known). Again officials are part of this general pattern: two of the *beneficiarii* (financial officials) resident in Antinoopolis reduced their holdings; one from 150 to 58.5 *arouras,* another from 80 to 75; a third added 4.5 *arouras* to his existing holding of 12. In the same period Gerontius, a *primipilaris* (probably a senior-ranking provincial official), and, among those listed as resident in Antinoopolis, one of the largest recorded holders of land in the Hermopolite nome, reduced his holding from 466 *arouras* to 8.[41]

With a few exceptions such as Gerontius, provincial bureaucrats, though comfortably in the top half of landowners listed on these registers, were far from having the most extensive holdings in their communities. On the later register, the largest recorded property in the Hermopolite nome belonging to an official resident in Antinoopolis is 292 *arouras;* the largest belonging to an official living in the West Citadel quarter of Hermopolis is 210 *arouras.* In this same area of the city, of the 238 individuals with full entries in the later register, 14 owned 200 *arouras* or more and 8 more than 500.[42] Clearly, here, too, the surviving evidence needs to be treated with some circumspection: the proportion of any one town-dweller's wealth invested in land is unknown; similarly (as Alan Bowman rightly points out), there are no data on "the quality of land and the quantity of yield and possible differences in modes of exploitation, levels of rental, and overhead costs." Moreover, many town-dwellers are unlikely to have relied on landholding as their sole source of income.[43] Even so, the general impression given by these registers is unlikely to be seriously misleading. They show that provincial bureaucrats were economically fully part of the community in which they lived. Moreover, as a group, officials (both retired and in post) were, by and large, among the better off in Hermopolis and Antinoopolis. Only a small minority might be able to compete with the wealthiest in their towns.[44]

The surviving personal documents once carefully filed away by the fourth-century Egyptian official Flavius Isidore (and detailing various of his business dealings and legal disputes) give a similar impression of one provincial bureaucrat's position in his local community. In 373, while serving on the staff of the governor of the Thebaid, Isidore had been instructed to deliver 238 *solidi* in taxes levied on the town of Hermopolis in lieu of army recruits to one Ammonas, an imperial treasury official attached to the court of the emperor Valens, at that time probably in Syria. In the event, as a result of a reduction in the tax, Isidore was instructed to return three-quarters of the sum (177 *solidi*). On the homeward journey (or, at least, so Isidore alleged) the money was stolen. The town council of Hermopolis, perhaps suspecting embezzlement, held Isidore responsible for the loss and petitioned the governor, demanding reparation. Isidore was ordered to pay compensation, even though he complained bitterly that any such sudden drain on his resources would bankrupt him. Nevertheless, he refunded 72 *solidi* and carefully kept the official receipt recording his payment.

That a provincial bureaucrat (guilty of financial irregularity or not) could manage to pay such a sum is itself worth noting, although there is no reason to doubt that it might have been difficult to raise without selling off land or other assets. Even setting aside any of Isidore's understandable exaggeration, 72 *solidi* was still a sizable amount. After all, in many towns it represented just under a quarter of the minimum property qualification for membership of the municipal council. Given the sums involved, this was the kind of case on which litigation might be considered worthwhile. Nor is it surprising that the town council of Hermopolis (still seeking the balance of 105 *solidi*) might have wished to appeal the governor's decision. In response, Isidore petitioned the emperors Valens, Gratian, and Valentinian II, seeking confirmation that his liability would be limited to the 72 *solidi* he had already paid. But it seems that his petition got no further than an official in the *sacra scrinia* (in this case, most likely the *scrinium libellorum et sacrarum cognitionum,* responsible for investigating cases submitted to the emperor). The petition was returned with a summary request for further information. Isidore drafted a second document in which he set out a more elaborate, but still rather vague, account of events. The outcome of the dispute is unknown. It may be that Isidore's petition was part of some wider strategy—possibly in collusion with the governor—to face down the town council, or perhaps he eventually capitulated and paid off the whole sum. At all events (whatever the truth of his fears of financial ruin), Isidore remained in business. A number of later documents in his dossier show him involved in leasing plots of land and entangled in a long dispute over an inheritance.[45]

For the most part, like Flavius Isidore or those recorded on the land registers from mid-fourth-century Hermopolis, the majority of established provincial bureaucrats were comfortably well off. Indeed, as the *album municipal* from Timgad shows, a good number serving on the staff of a provincial governor could be expected to own land worth more than 300 *solidi.* But there is little sign either of excessive wealth or of vast ill-gotten gains. Overall, it seems that provincial bureaucrats might fairly be thought of as being somewhat (but not too far) superior to local grammarians, described by Robert Kaster as "a group of men who might differ considerably in their individual situations but who would on the whole belong to the quality of their towns, respectable if unprepossessing members of the local elite."[46] And like grammarians, too, many officials (as the *album municipal* and the Hermopolite land registers clearly illustrate) were local men who had a stake in the area where they had lived and worked for most of their lives. They had no wish to wreck the economy on which they relied for fees (and in which they had invested, perhaps through buying and selling land) or to disrupt the traditional municipal society of which they were a recognized part. Their interests—even if they amounted only to a few acres of land or a few relatives in a nearby hometown—acted as a brake on the charges they were prepared to levy. Provincial bureaucrats were not outsiders looking for any opportunity to squeeze the locals dry. For the most part, it seems reasonable to suppose that the great majority were careful to charge their fellow provincials only what they judged the traffic would bear.

Pay and Display

Alongside the restraints imposed by the communities of which they were superior members, the public advertisement of centrally determined administrative and judicial fees further curbed the freedom of bureaucrats to set the terms on which they were willing to offer their services. Importantly, too, it also limited the ability of would-be litigants and others seeking access to government (or to avoid its demands) to negotiate their own independent arrangements. A sixth-century inscription from Beersheva, in southern Israel, laid down the sums due to officials on the staff of the local governor from taxes levied on the civilian population of various towns in the province of Palaestina Tertia and (where relevant) from units of regular soldiers *(comitatenses)* and frontier troops *(limitanei)* quartered in those settlements.[47] In a part of the now-fragmentary preamble to the list of prescribed amounts, an emperor, perhaps Justinian, expressed his confidence that the new charging regime would reduce the variations in the more arbitrary open market which it sought to replace.

> The emperor expressly decreed that through its public posting the contents of this edict should become generally known, in order that from now on, those from whom it is attempted to demand more may be confident that they will pay the fees as specified in this sacred imperial edict. Furthermore, the governor shall see to it that these regulations, which we have determined and made known through this sacred imperial decree, are closely followed. The regular soldiers under the military commanders [*duces*] for the time being, as well as the most loyal frontier troops under their disposition and the other taxpayers, shall pay year by year as follows:

From Mampsis	60 *solidi* and for the governor's staff 4 *solidi*
?	60 *solidi* and for the governor's staff 4 *solidi*
For the *uicarius*	50 *solidi*
?	40 *solidi* and for the governor's staff 3 *solidi*
?	30 *solidi* and for the governor's staff 3 *solidi*
?	24 *solidi* and for the governor's staff 3 *solidi*

. . . From the regular soldiers stationed at Zoara 50 *solidi* and for the governor's staff 4 *solidi*.

And from the association of taxpayers of the community of Zoara 100 *solidi*.[48]

The same principle of restriction and regulation lay behind an edict promulgated by the emperor Anastasius at the beginning of the sixth century. This law sought to manage the affairs of officials on the staff of the *dux* in command of soldiers stationed in the Pentapolis (on the coast of modern Libya). Three copies survive. Several fragments inscribed on marble were found in Apollonia (known in the later Empire as Sozousa), the provincial capital of the Pentapolis probably from sometime in the late fifth century.[49] The majority of the fragments came from the fifth- and sixth-century structures built in part out of, and in part over, the public baths. The disused warm room *(tepidarium)* was converted into a large hall. Together with its spacious adjoining chambers, this complex perhaps served some public or official function. The inscription may have been displayed in such a location.[50] Other copies of the decree were found built into the sides of two forts in the Pentapolis: one at Taucheira (modern Tukrah), the second and the best-preserved of all at Ptolemais (modern Tulmaythah).[51] Both of these versions were cut on rough sandstone blocks; only the provincial capital merited marble.

Anastasius' decree dealt for the most part with military matters. Its particular concerns were the disposition of various troops, as well as the regulation of the order of seniority and promotions of the civilian staff of the *dux.* A schedule appended to the main provisions of the law listed general payments to individual bureaucrats as well as specific charges for a range of administrative services. A fee of one *solidus* was payable for issuing the necessary paperwork confirming an enlistment *(probatoria);* the same charge was levied for the documentation required for a promotion or for the authorization of an extra ration or fodder allowance. Four *solidi* were payable for the compilation of the four-monthly reports on rations issued to the troops *(quadrimenstrui breues)* and 161 *solidi* to the staff en bloc at the new year (καλανδικά). The edict assured its readers that, as a result of posting these tariffs, "no more than those amounts which are thought to be necessary and are listed below" would be levied.[52]

Similar lists of fees and explanations for their public posting were on display in a later edict of Anastasius (perhaps issued in the early 490s), which aimed to control the tariffs levied on ships transporting various products, including oil, wheat, and wine, for public distribution in Constantinople. The sums were directly payable to the patrol vessels in the Hellespont under the commander of the straits (κόμης τῶν στενῶν), responsible for policing shipping to and from the imperial capital. The surviving copy of the edict, cut on a fine white marble slab, was displayed in the port of Abydos, the commander's headquarters, on the Hellespont's eastern shore. A list of the various amounts charged ships' captains was prefaced by a clear statement on the purposes and advantages of publicly advertising such detailed schedules.

> If anyone should dare to violate these regulations, we decree that he should be deprived of the post which he has obtained and be made subject to the lawful penalty, and that he who has command of the straits shall pay a fine of 50 pounds of gold if the rules laid down by our piety are violated in any way whatsoever. For we desire him to be vigilant and to be concerned closely with each and every matter, so that no one doing wrong may pass unnoticed. We have also decreed that the regulations should be displayed in these particular locations, and inscribed on stone slabs, and fixed in a place facing the sea, so that both the tariff collectors and the tariff payers may read this law, and, as a result, that the first group through fear may curb its greed, and the second may be confident that it will suffer no harm, and that the illustrious commander of the straits, ever facing the threat of punishment in these matters, might in fact expect to experience the same, should he prove negligent.[53]

Publicly posted charge-sheets were in many cases a more demonstrable and uncompromising expression of imperial intent than the set of similar laws on display to the much smaller and more specialist audience which might consult the legislation collected in the *Theodosian* and *Justinianic Codes*. (Something of this difference was recognized in a law issued by Constantine in 321; the immunity of retired palatine officials from taxation and curial obligations was affirmed, and these regulations were ordered to be engraved on bronze, "so that if [the aforementioned *palatini*] should be subject to such a claim, they may instantly flee for refuge to these tablets as to an immediate remedy, and they shall be freed from the threatened burden.")[54] The laws in the *Codes* detailing specific fees for administrative services (or in some instances denying officials the right to charge for particular tasks) dealt mainly with the amounts to be paid for the collection of revenue or on its receipt. A smaller number of surviving imperial laws covered particular administrative circumstances, some (discussed in Chapter 2) regulating the fees to be paid by officials on appointment or promotion, others by certain privileged groups involved in litigation.[55] As noted before (in Chapter 1), the editorial excisions of the *Codes*' compilers, who as a matter of course removed most of the prefaces to the laws they selected for inclusion, in most cases make the circumstances surrounding the drafting of any particular regulation impossible to reconstruct. These cuts also often mean that the applicability of any one law remains difficult to determine. But it seems safe to say that, in great part, the laws concerned with prescribing or preventing the payment for administrative or judicial transactions repeated the insistent concerns so clearly evident in the publicly inscribed edicts cited above. Local transactions were to be seen as unavoidably subject to the possibility of imperial interference. The ever-present threat of central government intervention was to play an inescapable part in regulating dealings between officials and taxpayers or litigants.

In 545 legislation issued by Justinian forcefully restated these imperial priorities. Litigants were required to swear on the Gospels "that they had neither given nor pledged anything at all to the judges in return for their support, nor to any other person to advance their case in anyway whatsoever, and that thereafter they would not give anything either themselves or through some other intermediary, with the exception of those sums which are to be given to their own attorneys for their support and those which our laws specify are to be given to other persons."[56]

A similar emphasis on the central importance of the imperial regulation of administrative charges was also well made in a law of Valentinian I, Valens, and Gratian issued to the praetorian prefect of Italy and Illyricum in 365. Fees for litigation were not to be charged on those happy days when "the delights of our auspicious proclamations are made known to provincials and whenever any announcement is disseminated throughout the world, whether the famous victories of our soldiers and the slaughter of our enemies or our triumphs are reported, or those consulships which we hold ourselves or confer on others."[57]

Provincial courts were to keep to imperial time. Moreover, this manifest concern to regulate administrative arrangements was to be seen to include both parties in any transaction. In 458 the emperor Majorian legislated to regularize the amounts paid by landholders in the Praetorian Prefecture of Italy to officials responsible for the collection of taxes. In fixing the sums, the emperor claimed to be taking account both of "the benefits enjoyed by officials as a proper reward for their labors," and of landholders, who, despite an increase in the amounts to be paid, would (it was alleged) be freed from "the many annoyances caused by the payment of fees." For each taxable unit of land a fee of 2 $\frac{1}{2}$ *solidi* was levied. The law set out in detail how the half *solidus* was to be distributed to the various municipal, provincial, prefectural, and imperial officials involved (perhaps in the same proportions as the other 2 *solidi*). The imperial financial officer was to receive half a *siliqua* (24 *siliquae* = one *solidus*), the tax collector one, the municipal and provincial officials 4, and the staff of the Prefecture $6\frac{1}{2}$ *siliquae*.[58]

Throughout the empire, these imperial laws (some with their often long and detailed schedules of fees) permitting or prohibiting the payment of money, or threatening officials who exacted more than the specified sums, were an important regulatory device. They were not an index of increasing official rapacity, or of a loss of central government control in the provinces, or of a once-covert sin now overtly legitimized and shamelessly on view, or of "old vices on a new scale."[59] They should not be assumed to be part of a long and unhappy imperial struggle against an inexorable tide of venality. Rather, like the charge-sheets inscribed and publicly posted at Timgad, Apollonia, Ptolemais, Beersheva, and the quayside at Abydos, the laws collected and put on more restricted display in the *Theodosian* and *Justinianic Codes* can also be read as a sophisticated—and deliberately admonitory—means of afforcing imperial power by limiting local variability. Through the manipulation of money payments, as the preface to the edict displayed in Abydos made uncompromisingly clear, central government intruded a system which enabled it to increase its chances of influencing the transactions of both officials in the provinces and those who sought access to the judicial or administrative services they could provide.

Imperially sanctioned charge-sheets offered a means of restricting the ability of bureaucrats to conclude their own independently negotiated agreements. The disruptive effect of money payments could be exploited as part of a wider strategy of countering the often strong links between local officials and those whom they governed. As had long been recognized by many in the Roman Empire, the payment of money could be seen as a single, impersonal transaction. It established no lasting relationship, no emotional ties, no need (for either party involved) for any further reciprocal obligation. Money could act as an emollient, softening conflict and reducing friction between bureaucrats and those who required (or wished to avoid) their services. As suggested in Chapter 3, it held out the opportunity of an immediate payoff without the necessity of becoming enmeshed in a complex and emphatically personal network of contacts. Against the undoubted and well-advertised advantages of clout and connections (so evidently on display in the long lists of names on the *album municipal* in Timgad), central government both actively promoted and widely advertised an alternative and sometimes competing means of ordering the queue of those seeking to attract its attention. For those standing in line, the payment of money opened the possibility of a different way of coming to terms with imperial government and its insistent demands.

From this point of view, inscriptions detailing various fees and charges can also profitably be read alongside a set of imperial legislation which moved to limit the contact between governors and "the quality" in the provinces. Governors, ruled Valentinian I, Valens, and Gratian in 369, were not to be taken by local grandees on pleasure trips to *deuerticula deliciosa*—"delightful retreats." Other legislation instructed them not to interview litigants in private or to receive afternoon courtesy calls at their official residences.[60] Governors were not to be posted to their home provinces or to purchase property in the province in which they served. Any marriage which they or a member of their family contracted was to be scrutinized for evidence of improper influence.[61] Of course, it would be naïve to think that these regulations were always closely followed, just as it would be simplistic to assume that litigants or taxpayers always paid officials the amounts laid down in imperial edicts, even when displayed in the *Codes* or, more publicly, in the forums of provincial towns. Indeed, a number of surviving imperial laws were specifically aimed at forcefully reiterating the amounts sanctioned by custom or imperial approval. (Similarly, the presence in the provinces of a centrally regulated officialdom with its own particular practices, routines, regulations, and esprit de corps helped to counter, rather than to replace or eliminate, the still powerfully binding personal and familial ties linking bureaucrats and those they governed.) Charge-sheets helped to hold in check the ability of officials and the locally powerful to make their own arrangements or to dictate their own conditions. Neither officials nor those demanding their services could ever count on setting their own terms freely.

Above all, publicly posted schedules of fixed fees and fines were a significant means of influencing the way in which official business was conducted. Indeed, the unstinting use of technical terms and the deliberately opaque legal language—which sometimes seems to have been beyond the competence of the mason responsible for cutting the text[62]—are further stark reminders that these inscriptions were not intended to make government either more easily intelligible or more broadly accessible. Rather, these proclamations (preserved on stone and in the *Codes*) offered central government another way of staking out its own position in the day-to-day running of the Empire. Carefully regulated schedules of fees and fines forcibly established fixed points in an open market. They emphasized that local transactions were always at risk of being cross-cut by central prescription. In provincial towns throughout the Mediterranean, publicly posted charge-sheets were indelible and intrusive reminders of the pressing presence of a distant imperial power. For all involved, they were yet another obstacle to be negotiated.

The Sale of Offices

For those in the later Roman Empire seeking office or preferment, success in many cases significantly depended, as it had always done, on clout and connections. *Suffragium*—influence, however obtained, exercised by family, friends, middlemen, and their well-placed contacts—was frequently a key factor in ensuring a successful career.[63] The orator Libanius set out clearly the basic rules and expectations governing the trading of such favors among those who valued and paraded their ability to persuade the powerful. Writing in 360 to secure the support of the *comes Orientis* Domitius Modestus in a municipal dispute involving the family of Zenobius (Libanius' former teacher), he opened with a series of pointed generalizations.

Those making an initial request for a favor expect to obtain it simply because it is their first request, and they cite in their support that maxim about the first good turn [demanding another]. I, however, have obtained many favors in the past; hence, I think, my confidence in obtaining one now. For if you do not accede to the request of someone on whom you have not previously conferred a favor, it might be said that he is not worthy of obtaining it. On the other hand, if you have often advantaged someone, you cannot henceforth debar him, or else you must be critical of your previous actions, concluding that they were spent to no worthwhile end.[64]

Libanius' surviving correspondence (more than 1,500 letters) reveals something of the time and effort invested by one grandee in the expansion, revision, and continual maintenance of a complex network of contacts. Correctly addressed in the uncontroversial banalities in which these often long-distance relationships were conventionally conducted, powerful men might be persuaded to advance the careers and causes of friends, relatives, old classmates, former pupils, other litterateurs, and fellow citizens.[65] For Libanius, the extent of his correspondence was itself an impressive indication of the range of his influence. To exchange letters with men of high rank was to have his own position affirmed. These were greatly anticipated and much-prized tokens of his own importance. The failure of a correspondent to write might make Libanius feel nervous or depressed. By contrast, the receipt of letters from a praetorian prefect or some other senior official was something publicly to be celebrated. When in 390 a letter arrived from Quintus Aurelius Symmachus (a leading senator in Rome and urban prefect in 384), Libanius, at least according to his reply, hurriedly had the text translated into Greek and sent three friends with copies into the streets of Antioch so that they might "fill the city to the brim with this gift of Fortune" to the applause of his admiring supporters and the annoyance of his detractors.[66] A copy of the reply was carefully filed. Later it was included in the selection of letters published posthumously as a permanent and well-edited memorial to Libanius' superior social standing and his success as an influential patron and middleman.

High-ranking officeholders could find themselves involved in a similarly vast correspondence. Like Libanius, they were continually responding to (selecting from or choosing to ignore) the endless stream of letters received from those who hoped to influence them. And, in turn, they sought their own favors. Over a quarter of the 900 surviving letters of Libanius' distinguished correspondent Symmachus were directed to well-placed acquaintances who might be of help in finding posts for his protégés. Writing to Virius Nicomachus Flavianus (in turn *quaestor sacri palatii,* twice praetorian prefect, and consul), Symmachus, with accustomed well-turned elegance, put his request:

> Many people speak well of the merits of Sexio, who formerly governed Calabria. As a result of these, they have requested that I should recommend him to your patronage [*suffragium*]. It is part of your customary good nature to regard as worthy of your affection those whom others have found agreeable. I ask you then, that if nothing stands in the way of satisfying the wishes of those who make this request, you allow Sexio to profit from my words and the hopes of many.[67]

This pattern is repeated again and again. The openly partial exercise of personal preference in the allocation of posts remained a recognized and well-tried method of establishing and strengthening ties between the powerful and their supporters. As John Matthews has observed, it would not have occurred to these men "to deny the propriety of influence—*suffragium*—in the promotion of perceived and reliable virtue."[68] Those (like Symmachus and Libanius) who portrayed themselves as influential in secular affairs, or those well-educated bishops (like Augustine, Basil of Caesarea, Synesius of Cyrene, and Theodoret of Cyrrhus) equally eager to advantage themselves by advancing the causes of their dependants, subordinates, family, and friends, offered in their published and highly polished collections of letters example after example of the skillful deployment of the long-hallowed language of friendship and the carefully regulated exchange of favors.[69]

But in the later Empire (as explored in Chapter 1), the smooth and successful operation of a system of securing advancement through the influence of the powerful and their trading of favors could be cross-cut by a set of imperial legislation which gave explicit priority in appointment or promotion to those with claims of seniority or merit. It could also be disrupted by the sale of offices.[70] Retiring officials in a number of palatine departments continued the practice (well established among *apparitores* in the first two centuries A.D.) of selling their positions to their subordinates. John Lydus is also clear that officials on the staff of the eastern Praetorian Prefecture expected as a matter of course to pay fees for a formal certificate of appointment *(probatoria)* and to the official responsible for the maintenance of the department's personnel registers. In some circumstances, other offices, including provincial governorships, might also be purchased through middlemen who sold their influence *(suffragium)* to the highest bidder. These brokers either paid a cut from their fee into the imperial treasury or had themselves purchased the right to appoint *(beneficium)* from the emperor. In the late fifth century, Zeno and his eastern praetorian prefect Sebastianus (in office from 476 to 480, and again in 484) were alleged to have had the system well worked out. The contemporary historian Malchus, who later comprehensively condemned Zeno's reign and regarded the emperor himself as "a hostelry for all vices,"[71] offered one disapproving version of this arrangement. "There was nothing in the palace which he did not buy and sell. If Zeno conferred a position upon one of his courtiers, like a dealer in public offices, he [Sebastianus] bought it from him for a small sum and sold it on to others for more, giving the proceeds of his theft to Zeno."[72]

The sale of offices (like the payment of money for access to judicial or administrative services) was also subject to often-complex imperial regulation. In 362 the emperor Julian legislated to prevent litigation for the recovery of monies paid out in exchange for recommendations (whether or not they had led to an appointment): "If any person should attempt to recover, or should be convicted of having recovered, such a sum, whatever he paid shall remain the possession of his broker [*suffragator*]."[73] It may be this law which is referred to by the fourth-century historian Ammianus Marcellinus. In late 361 some Egyptians arrived in Constantinople to petition the emperor and the praetorian prefects, "demanding after almost seventy years the exaction of sums which they alleged they had given, justly or otherwise, to many people." Julian refused to see them. Instead he ruled that "no broker [*suffragator*] should be subject to claims about payments which it was recognized he had properly received."[74] In 394 Theodosius I again affirmed the legal validity of such agreements, ruling that contracts to exchange gold, silver, movables, and urban or rural property in return for a recommendation were enforceable in the courts.[75]

The legality of agreements involving the direct purchase of an office was clearly set out by Justinian in a law issued in 528 which dealt with a creditor's rights to reclaim a loan spent by his debtor on purchasing a post. (Again, a loan for such a purpose was to be legally recognized, and the creditor's rights upheld.) If the office had been purchased for a child or a relative, the creditor could demand from the current incumbent either the amount of the loan or an amount equal to the current market price of the office. If the post had been purchased for someone outside the debtor's family, the creditor still had a valid claim. After the debtor's death (if the loan was still outstanding), a creditor was entitled to receive from the officeholder either the sum "generally acceptable to those currently in post" or the amount payable to purchase the *beneficium* (the right to appoint) from the emperor.[76]

Like publicly posted charge-sheets, a sophisticated legal and financial framework (most clearly on view in the laws collected in the *Codes*) circumscribed the ability of candidates and their brokers to bargain freely. Imperial legislation acted to limit the play of other factors (such as the superior social standing of one of the parties) involved in any transaction, emphasizing the validity and enforceability of agreements based on the payment of money. Further restrictions on the ability of buyers and sellers of offices to negotiate independently were imposed by more direct imperial involvement. Emperors could act as their own brokers or, like Zeno, sell the option to appoint, demanding a share of the profits. Less subtly in 372, Valentinian I ordered the decapitation of a governor who had dared lobby for another province. The broker (the general Flavius Theodosius) was dismissed with a punning imperial witticism: *Abi, comes, et muta ei caput, qui sibi mutari prouinciam cupit*—"Go, commander, and change his head, since he wished to change his province."[77]

Alongside such dramatic interventions, a series of imperial rulings also restricted the ability of those involved to make their own arrangements by specifying the tariffs to be paid for specific posts. Zeno directed that those granted the honorary title of consul should pay the huge sum of 100 pounds of gold (7,200 *solidi*) toward the construction and maintenance of aqueducts in Constantinople.[78] An earlier fifth-century law aimed to regulate appointment and promotion practices in the *sacra scrinia* under the administrative control of the *magister officiorum*. A new entrant was required to pay the head of the *scrinium* (or his heirs, assignees, or creditors) 250 *solidi*, and the deputy head 15 or 20 *solidi*, depending on the custom of the different *scrinia*. In 535 Justinian ordered that any member of the *sacra scrinia* wishing to join the *adiutores* (principal assistants) serving under the *quaestor sacri palatii* was to pay 100 *solidi* to the retiring *adiutor*.[79]

The most comprehensive surviving schedule of charges was issued earlier the same year. It set out the amounts payable to various officials in the palace and the eastern Praetorian Prefecture responsible for securing an appointment (perhaps by presenting the candidate's name to the emperor) and for issuing the necessary documentation. The sums payable for forty-eight governorships were carefully and separately listed. Governors of provinces with the rank of *spectabilis* were to pay 76 *solidi* in all: 9 *solidi* to officials from the imperial household; 24 to the *primicerius notariorum* (the head of the palace secretariat, in charge of compiling the *notitia dignitatum*, the official register of all senior appointments); 3 to his principal assistant *(adiutor); and 40 to the staff of the Prefecture.[80] On the face of it, this represented a substantial reduction in fees for which, in some cases, Justinian also offered compensation. One example is preserved in an edict issued in 536 upgrading the governorship of Phoenice Libanensis to *spectabilis* rank and detailing the post's responsibilities. The edict also provided for 10 pounds of gold (720 *solidi*) drawn from the revenues of the province to be paid annually to the *primicerius notariorum* to cover (as the law explicitly noted) that official's previously purchased *beneficium*, the right to appoint to the governorship.[81]

Justinian's reforms were not aimed at the complete elimination of the sale of offices. Rather, they sought to enforce imperial control over these transactions by cutting out or buying off the middlemen and by directly regulating the fees paid by incoming officeholders. As a result, at least according to the justification offered in the preamble to the legislation of 535, the amounts paid by officials for their posts would also be substantially reduced. Ten years later, in 546, a parallel scheme was promulgated to regulate the cost of episcopal appointments by directly linking the fees payable to the expected annual revenue of the see. On their consecration, the five most senior bishops in the Empire (the patriarchs of Rome, Constantinople, Alexandria, Antioch, and Jerusalem) were to pay no more than twenty pounds of gold to the Church. The cost of ordination to other bishoprics was expressed as a sliding scale. When the annual revenues of the see were more than 30 pounds of gold, the successful candidate was to pay 400 *solidi;* between 10 and 30 pounds, 300 *solidi;* between 5 and 10 pounds, 250 *solidi;* between 3 and 5 pounds, 42 *solidi;* between 2 and 3 pounds, 18 *solidi;* below 2 pounds of gold, no charges were to be levied. Again middlemen were cut out. These sums paid by a newly appointed bishop went directly to colleagues involved in his consecration and to other specified church officials.[82]

The sale of offices had several practical advantages for imperial government. It was a simple way of raising revenue. It was also another means of financing the administration by supplementing official salaries. Allowing retiring bureaucrats to sell their own offices yielded a lump sum which, along with significant taxation immunities, helped to compensate for the lack of superannuation or state pension. (Any attempt to alter the balance of these arrangements, as Justinian's legislation admitted, was a costly charge on imperial revenues.)[83] More broadly, the disruptive effect of monetary payments on local or individual arrangements was, as far as possible, to be exploited and controlled. Importantly, too, like the public display of detailed charge-sheets, the greater government regulation of the sale of offices in late antiquity marks out a significant elaboration of a practice well established in the Principate.[84] Again, it would be overhasty to assume that imperial interference in these arrangements always constricted bureaucrats' or emperors' (or brokers' or bishops') ability to bargain. That would be to exaggerate the levels of systematic central control possible even in the later Empire, and to expect too much from laws which in their operation and effect are better read as tactical rather than prescriptive. From that point of view, it is perhaps unsurprising that the contemporary polemicist Procopius (as always, in his *Secret History,* unremittingly hostile to Justinian's policies) was able to claim that, within a year of the promulgation of the schedule of set fees in 535, the emperor "proceeded more shamelessly than before to negotiate the prices of offices, not in some obscure spot, but publicly in the forum."[85]

Given the inescapable limitations on the range and extent of its power, central government's involvement in the sale of offices, as with the public posting of schedules of fines and fees, is again perhaps best understood as an attempt to limit unregulated negotiations by pegging a series of fixed points in an open market. A regulatory mechanism based on a candidate's ability to pay helped to counterbalance conventional methods of establishing priority in the queue of those lobbying to join the imperial bureaucracy. The creation of alternative avenues for appointment or promotion also widened the options available to emperors and central government in the selection of staff. Above all, the sale of offices ensured that the influence of the great, exercised through friendship and favors, was no longer always the surest means of obtaining office or preferment. Confronted by an imperial government attempting to force the displacement of traditional methods of organizing power, many opted to take advantage of alternative ways of coming to terms with its demands. Something of that shift in expectations, by all concerned, was nicely reflected in a gradual blurring in the meaning of *suffragium*. As it had done in the early Empire, *suffragium* continued to mean the influence exercised by the powerful; but by the end of the fourth century it had also come to mean (and often indistinguishably) the money paid by a candidate to secure a post.[86]

Cautionary Tales

For many of those fearing displacement, the imposition of a new and potentially disruptive means of regulating access to government could be seen as an unwanted intrusion into traditionally justified ways of organizing power. Hostile reactions were inevitable. In the late fourth century the orator Libanius bitterly disapproved of the way in which purchased influence upset long-standing relationships in the city of Antioch and its surrounding territory. In his oration *On Patronage* (most probably composed around 390), Libanius complained that his role as patron to tenants on his estates had been usurped by the local military commander, who had been presented with "barley, corn, ducks, and fodder" in return for his support in a court case.[87] Libanius contrasted the halcyon days of the early Empire (and its networks of obligation based on honor) with his own times, when offices were hawked by street traders and when rank and proper order were destroyed.[88] Moreover, in Libanius' view, this new method of forming a relationship, trading influence for payment like "meat and vegetables,"[89] was typical of the questionable behavior of imperial bureaucrats. In his opinion, such cavalier disregard for long-established arrangements was only to be expected from officials whose fathers had been (at best) fullers, bath attendants, and sausagemakers.[90]

These sentiments were echoed by other commentators. In the late 390s the military magnate Stilicho (who, after the death of Theodosius I in 395, had consolidated his influence over the young emperor Honorius in Milan) commissioned the poet Claudian to write a set of invectives exposing the faults of those highly placed officials in Constantinople who had strongly resisted Stilicho's attempts to extend his "protection" to include the new eastern emperor Arcadius and his court. In his piece attacking Eutropius, Arcadius' *praepositus sacri cubiculi* (head of the imperial household) and consul in 399, Claudian included, as part of a long catalogue of shameless abuses, the sale of offices. In a neatly turned exaggeration of some imperial legislation, Claudian imagined that Eutropius had drawn up and publicly displayed his very own charge-sheet: "A schedule fixed above the open doorway to his house lists provinces with their prices; so much for Galatia, Pontus goes for so much, such an amount buys Lydia. Should you wish to govern Lycia, then put down thousands; if Phrygia, add a little more."[91] Similarly, in his poem attacking Rufinus, eastern praetorian prefect in the mid-390s, Claudian claimed that he, too, had been unrestrained in his indiscriminate peddling of favors:

> Everything was put up for sale. He revealed secrets, deceived those who depended on him, and sold high-ranking posts which had been solicited from the emperor . . . And yet as Nereus [the Ocean] knows no increase from the innumerable rivers which flow into him, and though here he drains the Danube's surge, here in summer engulfs the waters of the Nile with its seven mouths, yet he always remains exactly the same, so Rufinus' desires could not be sated by floods of gold.[92]

Such trenchant moralizing must, as always, be put firmly in context. It is dangerous to assume that these carefully contrived condemnations convey a clear or uncomplicated impression of either the ordinary experience or the general attitude of contemporaries. Claudian's accusations of Eutropius' administrative corruption were part of a highly rhetorical picture of depravity and iniquity. Eutropius was glutton, ingrate, perjurer, pander, pervert and, above all, a eunuch.[93] In what Alan Cameron has characterized as "the cruellest invective in all ancient literature," Claudian mercilessly exploited age-old prejudices against a group widely regarded as personifying every vice.[94] The opportunity to combine political satire with (not particularly subtle) sexual innuendo was too good to ignore.

> Always new things, always grand things does he love, and taste individually with a swift sense. He fears nothing from the rear; to cares standing watch on all sides he is open, night and day. He is smooth and easy for suppliants to move, and in the middle of passion he is nonetheless very soft. He denies nothing and offers himself even to those who don't ask. Whatever the spirit desires he cultivates and hands over to be enjoyed; whatever you love, that hand will give. In common to everyone he performs his service, and his might delights to be bent. This too he has brought to birth by his plans and the desert of his labors, he accepts the consular robes too as rewards of his clever right hand.[95]

So, too, in Claudian's *Against Rufinus,* which (as Harry Levy has observed) fell squarely within "a well-established rhetorical tradition concerning the stereotype of a tyrant."[96] Rufinus was a foster child of the Furies, released on the world by hell's "numberless monsters" to extinguish a Golden Age.[97] He was coward, barbarian, destroyer, madman, murderer, and miser. Even Hades was defiled by his presence. Cerberus barked in vain to prevent him entering. The judge of the dead was at a loss.

> What punishment is sufficient to match such crimes? Indeed, what shall I find that is suitable for them all when each by itself outstrips any penalty? . . . To look on him is enough. Have pity now on our eyes and cleanse the realms of Dis. Drive him with whips beyond the Styx, beyond Erebus, consign him to the empty abyss beneath the infernal prison of the Titans, beneath the farthest reaches of Tartarus and the depths of Chaos where lie the foundations of blackest night.[98]

Given Claudian's aims and methods, one should be wary of singling out for approval his remarks on Eutropius' and Rufinus' venality simply because they seem more closely to reflect modern Western attitudes to public morality. That would be to privilege in isolation one particular element in a wide-ranging and self-consciously artificial critique. Accusations of corruption (like those of deformity, degeneracy, extravagance, excess, and perversion) were part of a complex and highly charged rhetoric of execration. Indeed, Claudian's abusive versions of Eutropius and Rufinus were no more credible than his portrayal of Stilicho as the longed-for savior of Rome, a general whose military prowess and popularity put him on par with the gods and the great men of old.[99] In his conquests and disposition, Claudian's Stilicho was a second Scipio, an indomitable hero whose triumphal entry into Rome in 400 was the return of a victorious Mars from war.[100]

These neatly contrasting caricatures of Stilicho's virtues and Eutropius' and Rufinus' vices were skillfully and explicitly rhetorical. They were pieces produced to order to please a powerful patron, penned in partisan response to Stilicho's signal failure successfully to advance his cause in the eastern empire. Moreover, in its turn, Claudian's well-phrased abuse should be set against the admiration for Rufinus' foresight, rhetorical skill, bravery, and humanity expressed by both Symmachus and Libanius (no less). The latter even planned to write a panegyric in Rufinus' honor.[101] And again, in turn, Claudian's polished praises of Stilicho should be set against a sharply contrasting version in the *New History* of the sixth-century historian Zosimus. In his moralizing exposé of the workings of two rival Christian regimes, this pagan sympathizer refused to allow any significant difference between the court of Arcadius in Constantinople and the court of Honorius in Milan.

> From now on, the whole empire devolved on Arcadius and Honorius, who, although they seemed to exercise power, they did so in name only. Complete control over the empire was vested in Rufinus in the east and depended on the advice of Stilicho in the west. All cases were decided by them as they pleased, and the victorious party was he who paid money for the judgment, or through some other personal connection gained the judge's favor . . . Some offered them gifts as a way of escaping false accusations; others gave away their property in order to gain office or to purchase some other means of ruining the cities. With every sort of vice current in the cities, wealth flowed in from every direction to the households of Rufinus and Stilicho.[102]

These stereotypes were also deployed and elaborated by bishops and ecclesiastical historians. For Philostorgius, most probably writing in the 440s, the rise and fall of the hated Rufinus offered a worthy moral lesson. After a career notable only for its venality, he was justly assassinated by soldiers acting in the interests of good government. In

Philostorgius' memorable tale, the prefect's corpse was mutilated and his severed right hand carried through the streets of Constantinople. Stopping anyone they met, his murderers demanded "something for the Insatiable One."[103] Similar accusations of bribery and corruption were leveled by Palladius, the biographer of John Chrysostom (bishop of Constantinople at the turn of the fourth century), against John's many critics, and especially against Theophilus of Alexandria, his most vocal and effective ecclesiastical rival.[104] For Chrysostom, the sale of offices and influence was part of a contrasting picture of the imperfections of this sinful life and the glories of the next.[105] Joined to a well-worn litany of the evils of worldly government, it was yet another demonstration of the purity of the true Church and its servants against the many snares set by their ungodly opponents. In this context, it is not at all surprising that such groups as Priscillianists, Donatists, and Arians were regularly accused by the orthodox of venality, bribery, or simony.[106] It was only to be expected. They were, after all, heretics.

The vigorous defense of a strongly held position was also key to Libanius' oration *On Patronage*. His reaction to being taken to court and losing in public, in front of the governor, was predictably trenchant. He blamed his humiliation on his tenants' newfound supporter (the local military commander) and the immorality of his methods, trading influence for payment like "meat and vegetables." There was a proper and time-honored way of going about such things. Libanius presented a moralizing *"tableau émouvant"* (to quote Jean-Michel Carrié) in the finest classical tradition.[107]

> For it is not proper for a slave who demands justice for wrongs he has suffered to look to one person and then to another, and to present himself before someone who is not his owner and ask his help, while ignoring his master . . . But suppose that those to whom they actually belong, by the will of God cease to be powerful. Then it is better that they should live their lives in their masters' weakness and put up with their fate rather than purchase such a power as this and show up their landlords. Take the example of a woman: if she belonged to two men, she would be more powerful, but you would not be pleased at her having the one in marriage and the other in adultery.[108]

Others (not surprisingly) assessed the situation differently. Indeed, for those men like the military commander, not themselves part of the local Antiochene elite, the establishment and strengthening of rival networks of influence based on the payment of goods and services allowed them quickly to profit from their powerful and prestigious positions. It provided them with an effective means of buying into the human and economic resources which had traditionally been the well-guarded preserve of municipal grandees. As Peter Brown has noted, the acquisition of support in the countryside "was the only way in which men whose careers lay on the fringe of the traditional landed aristocracy could gain access to the one permanent source of wealth and prestige in the ancient world, to the land."[109] Hence the commander's willingness (in return for suitable remuneration) to represent Libanius' tenants in the governor's court, or more generally to use his clout in the resolution of the monotonous round of rural disputes over field boundaries, water courses, and irrigation channels.

For Libanius, some of whose estates had been in the family for four generations, the disruption caused by the availability of alternatives to his preferred version of landlord-tenant relations deserved only caustic recrimination.[110] From his perspective, an unchallenged, exclusive relationship with his tenants was self-evidently attractive and morally defensible. Libanius dreamed of a cosy, comfortable world free of trouble and complaint; a world in which the landlord was firmly in control and alternatives could not be bought. Like Claudian's invectives against Eutropius or Rufinus, Libanius' stress on the ethical superiority of conventional methods of initiating and maintaining a relationship aptly suited his own position. It was intended to defend a particular view of Antiochene society. It both furthered and justified his own interests.[111]

But one should hesitate before taking sides in this dispute: before condemning the tenants and their supporters as corrupt, or before endorsing Libanius' complaints, accepting his social critique, and applauding his crusading stance against the purchase of influence. For Libanius' tenants, the possibility of securing the backing of the local military commander was clearly preferable to a selfless loyalty which recommended that they "should live their lives in their masters' weakness and put up with their fate." Against the unceasing reciprocal obligations of traditional personal networks the payment of money offered them a less open-ended and more impersonal alternative. It allowed a relatively rapid realignment of social ties and obligations. It held out the possibility of a more flexible and less oppressive arrangement. Such a relationship with a powerful man must have seemed an attractive antidote to the long-term, suffocating exclusivity so self-righteously propounded by landowners like Libanius. At any rate, for those tenants seeking some means of improving their existing position, the possibility of buying access to alternative and perhaps more effective sources of influence was worth (at least in the first instance) a speculative down payment of barley, corn, ducks, and fodder.

Of course, some of those seeking to force access to government or further their causes could on occasion resort to more expensive measures. In June 431 at the Council of Ephesus, Cyril, bishop of Alexandria, took advantage of the late arrival of his opponents to badger his assembled colleagues into denouncing Nestorius, bishop of Constantinople, and rejecting his theological views. The council affirmed Cyril's contention that at the moment of conception in Mary's womb the human and divine natures of Christ had been inseparably linked; and that Mary could therefore rightly be called *Theotokos,* "she who gave birth to God." But Cyril also relied on Theodosius II (who had previously proved intransigent) to back these decisions. In the immediate aftermath of the council, it was important that the emperor not waver from his initial inclination to condemn Nestorius and to remove his supporters from their sees. Only then could a compromise between the two factions be worked out.

At court in Constantinople, Cyril continued to rely on the influence of the empress Pulcheria and the holy man Dalmatius. But to make doubly sure that the emperor would move toward unity on terms acceptable to the anti-Nestorian party, Cyril through his agents also rained down persuasive *benedictiones*—"blessings"—(in his phrase) on powerful officials and their families, on the eunuchs in charge of the imperial household *(praepositi sacri cubiculi),* and on those of their subordinates *(cubicularii)* rumored to be closest to the emperor. In all, 1,080 pounds of gold (77,760 *solidi*) were dispensed: among the recipients, 100 pounds of gold was paid out to Heleniana, the wife of the eastern praetorian prefect; 100 each to the *magister officiorum* and the *quaestor sacri palatii;* 50 pounds to the *praepositus* Paul; 200 to the *praepositus* Chryseros; to the *cubicularii* Scholasticius, Domninus, and Romanus, 100, 50, and 30 pounds of gold respectively; to Marcella and Droseria, *cubiculariae* in the empress Pulcheria's household, 50 pounds each. And along with the cash came an impressive array of presents. The *cubicularius* Romanus received "four large rugs, four sofa covers, four tapestries, six covers for stools, two for thrones, six curtains, and two thrones of ivory." The *praepositus* Chryseros was also greatly blessed: "six large carpets, four medium-sized ones, four large rugs, eight sofa covers, six table cloths, six large woven hangings, six small hangings, six covers for stools, twelve for thrones, four large curtains, four thrones of ivory, four stools of ivory, six benches, six large plaques, and six ostrich eggs."[112]

In reviewing these lists of exotic gifts, no doubt selected with the varied tastes, ranks, and influence of the recipients in mind, it is important to remember that Cyril was immovably convinced of the rightness of his cause. For him and his supporters, depleting the church treasury at Alexandria to provide presents for influential courtiers ensured a just conclusion to a long and bitter doctrinal dispute. It was (as Peter Brown has observed) "a small price to pay for the peace of the church." As Lionel Wickham, the most recent modern editor of Cyril's correspondence on the Nestorian controversy, has remarked: "The bankrupting size [of these gifts] is the sincerest testimony to Cyril's wish for a united Church and should, in fairness, bring him credit."[113]

Eschewing such costly ways of pressing their claims, others sought instead to influence the powerful by repeated volleys of letters. These still had currency. Their glittering rhetoric reiterated the enticing and supposedly more lasting advantages of long-standing, traditional relationships founded on clout, connections, and a shared self-interest. As J. H. W. G. Liebeschuetz has noted, "Clearly, neither Libanius nor the officials he addressed saw a sharp division between their obligations as friends and their duties as administrators or judges."[114] In the summer of 358 Libanius wrote again to one of his closest friends, Aristaenetus, whom the emperor had recently appointed as *uicarius Pietatis* (deputy for the eastern praetorian prefect in the diocese of Pontica in northern Turkey). Libanius wrote on behalf of Nicentius, the outgoing governor of Syria, who had been fined by the prefect Hermogenes for his failure to deliver supplies to the fort at Callinicum on the Euphrates (Raqqa in modern Syria). The facts of the matter are unclear, and Libanius offered only a brief summary before blaming the whole affair on the lies and deceptions of others. His real point was to persuade Aristaenetus to convince the prefect to reverse his decision, both because of their mutual friendships and on the grounds of justice. (Libanius, like Cyril of Alexandria, had no doubts about the rightness of his cause.) Earlier in the year, when Nicentius had arrived in Antioch to take up his post, he had shown himself a strong supporter of Libanius, who, in turn, was pleased to pass on the good news to Aristaenetus: "He has certainly delighted our city with his attentions to me, and me with his recollections of you, for he too repeated the praises of those who know you well: 'that they have not yet seen anyone like you.' He recounted many things about you, adding that he could not tell the whole of it." The prefect Hermogenes was also to be praised for his philosophy, his learning, and, above all, his choice of Aristaenetus: "I congratulate both of you: you because you have such authority willing to support you, and him because, in choosing the friend he should, he gains credit for his judgment." On such reasoning, the solution to Nicentius' difficulty was inescapably self-evident. As Libanius, here getting to the nub of the matter, pointedly observed to Aristaenetus: "You then, having been so befriended, as far as you are able must not hesitate to assist him [the prefect] by your advice; and you may do so now, for by furthering the cause of one friend who has been wronged, you may prevent another friend from making a mistake."[115]

Advantageous networks of influence and favor might be further strengthened by a common provincial origin. On joining the eastern Praetorian Prefecture in the early sixth century, John Lydus greatly benefited from membership in a group of successful fellow Lydians headed by the prefect Zoticus. Thirty years later, a clique of Cappadocians dominated the financial side of the Prefecture and were strongly favored by the then prefect John the Cappadocian. Similarly, in the fourth century it is possible to trace the rise of Pannonians under their countryman the emperor Valentinian I, and of Spaniards under Theodosius I.[116] Family ties mattered, too. The Gallic rhetorician Ausonius, tutor to the emperor Gratian, and elevated to the consulship by his former pupil in 379, obtained positions in the imperial administration for a number of his relatives from his native Bordeaux. His immediate family enjoyed even greater success. Ausonius secured a Praetorian Prefecture for himself, one for his son, Hesperius, and one for his octogenarian father, Julius.[117]

In such cases, it is all too tempting to take sides. But wherever our modern sympathies might lie (with either the winners or the losers), it is important to remember that for many contemporaries both the probity and appropriateness of these means of gaining preferential access to government were often uncertain and frequently disputed. It is possible, for example, to imagine that not all of those garrisoning the frontier fort at Callinicum would have appreciated the influential intervention of a famous (and decidedly unmilitary) orator supporting his friend the governor from the distant safety of Antioch. Equally, the success of men like Ausonius' aged father cannot always have been welcomed by those whose careers had been stymied or stalled by the rapid advancement of particular families or provincial coteries. The deep resentment of John Lydus at the inexorable rise (as he saw it) of Cappadocians on the financial side of the Prefecture ran as a constant and bitter thread through his autobiography. For John—here crudely recycling some of the stereotypical abuse so brilliantly deployed by serious literary figures like Claudian—these men were violent, ignorant, unspeakable perverts. John Maxilloplumacius, the Cappadocian sent out to John Lydus' hometown of Philadelphia, deserved only the most overdrawn of insults:

> This shark-toothed Cerberus, though he brought ruin to all alike, chewed up my Philadelphia so finely that after him, because it had been stripped not only of money but also of its people, henceforth it could take no advantage of any opportunity for a change for the better . . . And would that by himself he had devoured just that one province alone, and that others such as himself, and even worse than him, had not passed through each city and its territory, sucking up money no matter where it might have been buried, and dragging behind them an army of accursed wretches and a horde of Cappadocians.[118]

Opinion was also divided on the use of money to purchase advantage. Nestorius himself had no doubt that Cyril of Alexandria had bribed his way to victory both at the Council of Ephesus and later at the imperial court.[119] These accusations were frequently repeated in the doctrinal disputes of the next 100 years. The document listing the gifts distributed by Cyril's agents in Constantinople formed part of a sixth-century dossier which aimed both to discredit Cyril and to lampoon the tactics he had used to establish the orthodoxy of his own Christological claims.[120] Such dislikes ran deep. A forged letter, probably faked around the same time the dossier was compiled (and falsely attributed to Theodoret, bishop of Cyrrhus, northeast of Antioch), attempted imaginatively to recapture how one contemporary Nestorian sympathizer might have reacted to the welcome news of Cyril's death in 444.

> This man's demise brings joy to those still living, but perhaps it also brings sadness to the dead, and there is a fear that, oppressed by his company, they might send him back to us again . . . This must, therefore, be averted, and your Holiness [John, bishop of Antioch] must undertake to do this with the greatest possible speed and order those responsible for the care of the dead to bring a huge and very heavy stone and place it on his grave, so that he may not return to this world a second time.[121]

For others (some perhaps disbelieving the Nestorians' allegations, some disregarding them, some, like recent scholarly apologists, choosing to view his gift giving as justifiable) Cyril remained, in the words of one admiring late-antique biographer, a man whose "conduct was excellent, and humility great. And he never ceased to study theology, nor to meditate upon the words of the doctors of the orthodox Church . . . For he was like a bee which goes forth to feed upon every plant and tree, and collects what is profitable for itself, until it has filled its bag with pure untainted honey."[122]

For some, Cyril's "sweeteners"—his "blessings"—so liberally bestowed on the court at Constantinople, were problematic chiefly because of their sheer scale, rather than because he had attempted to exploit the possibilities money afforded for advancing the Church's cause. In the early fifth century, Augustine (who would no doubt have disapproved of Cyril's excesses, and, given his strictures on the often-oppressive behavior of large local landholders, perhaps of some of Libanius' opinions as well), defended the common practice of paying officials for access to the courts.[123] Writing in 414 to the high-ranking official Macedonius (in post as *uicarius Africae*), Augustine contrasted the unjust gains of lawyers who were paid to argue dishonestly and to deceive judges, with the fees paid court officials "according to the accepted custom." He doubted the probity of the former but supported the latter, even when people complained about having to pay. Augustine commented knowingly: "Most people do not want to give due credit to their doctor or to pay a workman his wages, yet when these people receive what they are properly owed from the unwilling, they do not acquire anything as the result of any wrongdoing; rather, it would be wrong not to give it to them."[124]

A similar argument in support of the charging of fees by bureaucrats was advanced by the historian Priscus of Panium. While on a diplomatic mission to the court of Attila the Hun in 449, Priscus related how he had fallen into conversation with a Greek merchant who had been captured eight years before at the sack of Viminacium (on the Danube east of modern Belgrade), but who now lived freely among the Huns and rejected his previous life within the Roman Empire. One of the points debated in this rather contrived exchange of views (which its author was always going to win) was the former merchant's objection to paying for justice: "no one will grant a hearing to someone who has been wronged unless he makes a down payment to the judge and to his court officials." Priscus' reply was straightforward: the payment of money to court officials was a simple regulatory device; it should be viewed as no more complicated or threatening than any other advantageous market transaction.

> There is also a prescribed sum of money which these men should receive from those contesting a case in court . . . Is it not proper to support someone who comes to your aid and to repay his goodwill, just as the feeding of a horse benefits the horseman, and the care of cattle benefits the herdsman, and dogs the hunter, and other animals those who keep them for their own protection and profit; and is it not proper whenever court fees have to be paid, even though the case has been lost, to blame that cost on one's own wrongdoing rather than on someone else?[125]

The lack of embarrassment surrounding many transactions involving the payment of money for access to government is both striking and important. As A. H. M. Jones wryly remarked of the sums (carefully calculated in *modii* of wheat) listed on the charge-sheet posted in the forum at Timgad, "even two bushels of wheat could hardly be unobtrusively slipped into the palm of an expectant-looking official."[126] A similar transparency can also be seen in transactions aimed at securing influence or advancement. In a written contract dated February 2, 345, Aurelius Plas, an army veteran and resident of Dionysias, a small garrison town in Middle Egypt, undertook to reimburse the former camp commandant Flavius Abinnaeus for any expenses incurred by him in securing the promotion of Aurelius' son to a junior command. The matter was a simple one; the agreement was concluded and signed openly. Aurelius Plas demonstrated his good faith by swearing "before God."[127]

Certainly these attitudes seem closer to those paraded by John Lydus, who, like most of his fellow bureaucrats in the eastern Praetorian Prefecture, clearly expected, as a matter of course, to be paid by those demanding his services, and expected to pay his senior colleagues on appointment and promotion. For John, the fee-income a bureaucrat earned from his official activities could be regarded as "both reasonable and acceptable to the law"; a flourishing administrative department was easily recognizable by "the limitless influx of earnings coming from the documents which were being processed."[128] An unabashed openness is again simply assumed in a wide range of imperial legislation, which treats the payment for money as another means, among many others, of regulating access to government services and of promoting a competitive advantage against more-traditional means of organizing power and influence. And it is a frankness indisputably on display in the detailed schedules of fees posted in the centers of provincial towns. Indeed, the very public presence of these inscriptions again emphasizes that in the later Roman Empire the payment of money was not always or inevitably regarded as a half-concealed, grubby, under-the-counter deal, shameful for all involved.

Importantly, too, the use of clout, connections, money, or their various combinations was part of a much wider set of overlapping possibilities. In late antiquity, those seeking to influence government officials to gain advantage might also think it prudent to present their cases to otherworldly authorities in the hope that they, too, might be able to offer some assistance. In mid-fourth-century Arabia a man called Proclus litigated before the local military commander *(dux Arabiae)* in the provincial capital Bostra (now Busra in southern Syria). The circumstances surrounding this suit are unknown, as are any other strategies Proclus may have used to advance his cause. What remains is a long text, some forty-five lines, inscribed in tiny Greek letters interspersed with magic signs on a thin sheet of gold the size of a modern credit card. Proclus appealed to a deity, mysteriously called "the

Name," to ensure his victory over the *dux,* his principal legal adviser *(assessor)*, and the opposing parties in the dispute. Aside from, or in addition to, any advantages this world might offer, there was still the chance that those more powerful in the next might come to a petitioner's aid, whatever the merits of his case.

> Holy and strong, mighty and great-powerful Name, give favor, glory, victory to Proclus whom Salvina bore, before Diogenianus, *dux Arabiae* at Bostra, before Pelagius the *assessor,* and before all men small and great; before gods, before spirits, in order that he might be justifiably or unjustifiably victorious in any judgment . . . And may no one act against, or speak against, or deliberate against him, in anything at all. But give him victory, favor, glory, power to the one bearing your glory; now, now; quickly, quickly. Amen.[129]

Like magic, belief in the power of Christianity (and the ability of God to intervene favorably in the affairs of this world) might at least for its holiest and most-committed adherents prove a superior means of dealing with government and its demands. In the early fifth century, Melania the Younger had been one of the wealthiest women in the Western empire. She had persuaded her husband to join her in a life of chastity and sold off many of her estates and freed her slaves. She had stayed for seven years in North Africa, establishing a friendship with Augustine, founding monasteries, and (seemingly without any sense of moral paradox) offering money to young people if they agreed to follow a life of continence and to heretics if they agreed to embrace orthodoxy.[130] In 417 Melania moved to Jerusalem, and in 436 she was persuaded to travel to Constantinople by her distinguished uncle Rufius Volusianus, a former urban prefect of Rome and praetorian prefect of Italy and Africa. No doubt thanks to her powerful connections, Melania was able to obtain a warrant which entitled her to use the public post *(cursus publicus)* for her journey. In Tripolis (modern Tripoli in Lebanon) Messala, a *curiosus* in charge of the post, was reluctant to release animals for the large entourage which accompanied the holy woman and which was clearly not traveling on official business. Confronted by this bureaucratic difficulty, Melania retired to a *martyrium* sacred to Leontius and kept vigil by the saint's relics. Meanwhile, as she prayed, her trusted friend and hagiographer the priest Gerontius sought to help matters along by paying the official 3 *solidi.*

We left that place and had traveled just under 7 miles when the afore-mentioned *curiosus* came after us in complete confusion and, question-ing us, asked, "Where is the priest?" Since I was unaccustomed to travel-ing, I was afraid that he had again come to retrieve the animals, and, dismounting, I asked him why he was so troubled. He replied, "I am ea-ger to have the honor of meeting the great woman." Then, when he saw her, he fell to the ground and seized her feet amidst many tears and began to speak: "Forgive me, O servant of Christ, that I, ignorant of your great holiness, put off the release of the animals" . . . He at once took out the 3 *solidi* which I had handed over to him as a fee and begged me to take them back from him.

Messala went on to explain that all night both he and his wife had had terrifying visions of Leontius. They had run to the *martyrium* and found it empty and had then set off along the road to find Melania and return the money. "And when we all entreated her to tell us plainly the reason, the saint answered, 'All night I prayed to the holy martyr Leontius that he might show us a favorable sign for this jour-ney. And behold, although I am unworthy, my request has been granted.'"[131]

For most people attempting to advance themselves or their causes, the choices between competing tactics were rarely so clear-cut. Many preferred to add an appeal to divine aid to a series of other, more mundane strategies for success. Equally, it was wise, even for the holi-est, to be prepared to adopt a range of tactics. At the beginning of her saintly career in late 407 or early 408, Melania had sought an audience in Rome of Serena, the wife of Stilicho, as a means of securing her in-fluence in obtaining from her son-in-law the emperor Honorius an edict instructing imperial officials in the provinces to act as agents in the disposal of Melania's vast estates. (Melania and her husband, Pinian, legally both still minors, feared that without such imperial sup-port their possessions would be divided up among their acquisitive rel-atives and not, as they wished, sold to benefit the poor.) On receiving Serena's assurances that she would intercede before Honorius, the holy couple responded by showering both her and her court officials with a series of εὐλογίαι—"blessings": crystal vases, precious orna-ments, rings, silver, and silks. Serena, recognizing Melania and Pinian's holiness, refused to accept them. "The empress then ordered the *praepositus* and two other high-ranking eunuchs to accompany them on their return with every honor, having made the former swear by the well-being of her most blessed brother [the emperor Honorius] that neither they nor anyone else from the palace would agree to take even one *solidus* from them."[132]

Such actions were exceptional: that is, after all, the point of the story. As Cyril of Alexandria appreciated, not everyone always recognized that holiness was more persuasive than money. Promises of rewards in the world to come often needed to be buttressed by immediate and more-tangible blessings. Moreover, as Cyril was also acutely aware, clout, contacts, and favors remained potent and effective means of securing appointment, advancement, and access to government. No doubt, too, Melania and Pinian's wealth and high social status had also been crucial factors in their being granted an audience with the mother-in-law of an emperor. Few, no matter how holy, enjoyed such an easy entrée to the imperial court.

Indeed, what marked out the later Roman Empire was not by any means the absence of traditional channels of influence, or of those prepared to argue their ethical superiority. It was, rather, the active and successful promotion of alternative routes to power. That was a process which involved both clashes and conflicts; but it also involved both accommodation and compromise. In attempting to understand everyday experience in the later Empire, that middle ground, where different currencies of power jostled and overlapped, is perhaps more revelatory than the deceptive clarities of the accomplished moralist or the ecstatic experiences of the divinely favored. For Mark the Deacon, the biographer of Porphyry, bishop of Gaza in Palestine, that holy man's ability to work carefully through the intricacies of court politics (using and combining various tactics as he progressed) was itself worthy of admiration. At the turn of the fourth century, Porphyry secured the help of the empress Eudoxia in persuading her husband, Arcadius, to order the closure of pagan temples in Porphyry's see. Initial approaches were unsuccessful. The emperor professed himself reluctant to disrupt an otherwise peaceful community which paid its taxes regularly. Only after Eudoxia had given birth to a son did a suitable opportunity for cornering the emperor arise. On the day of the baptism, Porphyry was to be outside the church at the front of the crowd. As the imperial procession emerged, Porphyry rushed forward and presented a petition, listing his demands, to the courtier carrying the baby boy. That man (well briefed beforehand) put the petition into the child's hands and declared that it had been approved. Arcadius had little option but to issue an edict for the closure of the temples in Gaza in both his own and his infant son's names.

But such dramatic incidents require careful staging and considerable planning. Porphyry's success was the result of long negotiation and continual pressure. Arriving in Constantinople in late 400, he had relied on the good offices of John Chrysostom, himself friendly with Amantius, a high-ranking eunuch in Eudoxia's entourage. (Amantius was apparently prepared either to overlook or to risk circumventing the recent sharp antagonism between empress and bishop.) Having used his powerful contacts and their connections to gain admission to Eudoxia's presence, Porphyry persuaded her of the rightness of his cause and, as a demonstration of his own high standing with a heavenly king, declared that the child she was carrying would be born alive and healthy. Eudoxia agreed to lend her support. She also gave Porphyry money to defray the costs he had incurred in securing access to her presence. Suitably grateful (and to the evident admiration of his biographer), the saintly Porphyry, in a shrewd combination of available tactics, left the imperial audience chamber blessing Eudoxia and scattering gold coins at the feet of her *decani*—the empress' doorkeepers.[133]

Power Plays

The variety of ways of forcing access to power in late antiquity should come as no surprise. Nor should the range of conflicting views of contemporaries on the use of money or of influence in pursuit of that end. The latter is a neat and not-unexpected corollary to the growth of a system in which success frequently demanded the skillful selection or combination of various, often seemingly contradictory, tactics. Set in this wider frame, what some might call "corruption" or "venality" or "nepotism" does not so unquestionably appear as a practice whose very persistence stands as certain evidence of a deeply flawed administration on the brink of decline. For those whose principal advantage lay with their family, their friends, and their connections, any other means of advancement constituted an unwelcome intrusion into a world tightly bound by the civilities of recommendation and the promotion of protégés and their causes. On this view, those who remained unmoved by such long-hallowed ties were incontestably immoral. But for those without such advantages (or for those wishing to improve their position or to reduce the influence of any rival) the payment of money offered an effective alternative or supplementary method for securing a post or getting their grievances heard. It is important to remember that, whatever the colorfully entertaining accusations leveled by their opponents, not all who sold recommendations for office or purchased preferment for themselves or their causes were immoral, undeserving, or utterly self-seeking. Nor is there any justification for the claim that officials who had bought their positions were, on the whole, any less competent than those who had risen through the ranks or had been advanced by the *suffragium* of powerful friends. Some individuals were well deserving; some causes worthwhile; others not. The same might be said of those who exploited their contacts and family connections to help them get on in the world.

Moralizing aside, the payment of money to officials in the later Roman Empire was, first and foremost, a clear-cut, practical, and efficient method of ordering the queue of those seeking administrative or judicial action. In a system designed only to process a tiny proportion of the demands which could potentially have been made on the empire's government, the requirement that officials be paid was a simple method of determining the allocation of scarce resources. In the majority of cases, litigation, as in most societies ancient and modern, remained something which only the well-off were able to contemplate seriously. Moreover, given the understandable difficulties in achieving access to government in the first two centuries A.D., there is no particular reason to think that the active promotion of money payments in the later Empire further restricted the ability of those in the provinces to get their concerns heard by central government.

The regulation of the payment of money for office or administrative services also offered central government the opportunity to underwrite an alternative method of establishing priority among those pressing for access. (Indeed, the effectiveness of this tactic in part rested on the twin assumptions that the payment of money could be an important element in administrative transactions and that officials expected to derive a substantial part of their annual income from such charges.)

Schedules of fees and fines were publicly posted in the center of provincial towns and on government buildings. This openness neatly marks out a shift between the early and later Empires in both the operation and the expectations of government. The payment of money was undeniably a factor in ensuring the advancement of some (often spectacularly visible figures) in the Principate. Yet there is no indication that imperial government in the first two centuries A.D. was ever involved to the same degree in the systematic legislative legitimation or regulation of either the sale of offices or the charging of administrative fees. But there were limits to central government's intrusive impact in late antiquity. These were, in part, an inevitable consequence of a set of inescapable physical and technological constraints on the most basic machinery of government. In part, they were imposed by those throughout the Roman Empire who understandably clung tenaciously to their deeply ingrained traditions of organizing power and preference around clout and connections. The result was a system of rule—and of response to rule—whose range of tactics and moral judgments seems closely to reflect an unresolved tension between sometimes conflicting, sometimes complementary, ways of dealing with government and its demands.

Nor were these irresolutions without their advantages. They widened the available alternatives for action or avoidance on all sides. The payment of money, like the use of influential connections and the various other means of securing advancement, was integral to the workings of later Roman government. For some, such as Libanius' tenants, the possibility of establishing links with a local military commander through gift giving offered a welcome chance of circumventing the exclusive relationship advocated by their landlord. By contrast, for others, the local and family ties between provincial bureaucrats and those of "quality" in the towns acted as a welcome curb on the activities of central government. In turn, for central government and its agents, the payment of fees or the sale of offices offered a means of limiting the influence of local networks and their particularities. But this, too, was a process to be carefully regulated. After all, the continued importance of networks of personal favor as a means of controlling preferential access to government and its resources also helped make it possible for a small number of officials to run a large empire.

In a similar manner (as John Lydus' autobiography nicely exemplifies), those well-educated young men from a prosperous municipal background who joined the imperial administration also became part of a particular organization with its own specific work practices, complex hierarchies, and internal ethics. These distinctive features (among others) helped to underline the sharp and advantageous differences between officialdom and the world outside. Membership in the imperial bureaucracy brought with it a new set of personal connections, moral obligations, and self-interests which might displace more-traditional priorities and allegiances. This, too, was a matter of continual counterbalance and countermove. As John's own fond memories of Philadelphia reminded his readers, he still maintained strong ties with his hometown. Alongside undoubted loyalties to his department and his colleagues, he expected to establish close and mutually beneficial links with others in Constantinople who had also come from good families in the same region.

There was no quick, clean break between early and later Empires. Traditional sites of influence and prestige unashamedly based on clout and connections proved tight knit and remarkably tenacious. Customary rights and privileges continued to be recognized and upheld. Some of the empire's educated elites, men like John Lydus or those listed on the *album municipal* in Timgad, preserved or bettered their positions, their local standing, their prospects, and their incomes by joining the imperial bureaucracy. Others loudly resisted and bitterly resented the displacement of time-honored channels of control. This sometimes uncomfortable mix of priorities, tactics, and moralities is in itself an important register of change. Like the hectoring, cartoon rhetoric of Claudian or Libanius (firmly convinced of the rightness of their cause, but not always entirely confident in their own positions), it represents a significant shift in the ways in which power was both organized and regulated in the Roman Empire.

To be sure, on some occasions, central government's attempts to exploit the resources of the Mediterranean world continued to be checked, canalized, shaped, and distorted by the well-tried methods of mobilizing support and influence so amply illustrated in the letters of Symmachus, Augustine, Libanius, and their colleagues. But in the later Empire, traditionally organized networks of clout and connections—for all their continued strength and importance—could no longer so comfortably be relied upon to bring success for those who wished to advance or to protect their position. As Libanius' rebarbative complaints sharply indicate, their unchallenged supremacy was sometimes less well assured. The promotion and detailed regulation of money as a means of acquiring office or influence cut across the ability of those dealing with officials to negotiate freely on their own terms. It rendered less certain customary ways of getting things done. It challenged the easy expectations of those who had always assumed that they would benefit from their well-placed contacts.

In the more unsettled world of late antiquity, to direct or to deflect central government power demanded the deployment of a complex set of tactics. For all involved, the promotion of different, more impersonal criteria for the allocation of government resources offered new alternatives. It created and supported new possibilities for regulating access to administrative services, for determining appointment to office, and for the effective exercise of influence. In turn, these new possibilities threatened both the security and the reliability of strategies which relied principally on longer-term and emphatically personal ties. In some circumstances, the payment of money might be used in coalition with, or as a supplement to, other methods of securing position or advantage. In 374 Basil of Caesarea wrote to his fellow bishop Amphilochius of Iconium (also in the southern hinterland of Asia Minor) offering to help seek an exemption from civic duties for an important member of his congregation. They, with the assistance of the Almighty, had to decide tactics, "so that we may set about asking this favor from each of our friends in power, either as a gift or for some moderate price, however the Lord may help us forward."[134] Money, of course, as Basil and Amphilochius well knew, could not purchase everything. It had both its uses and its limits. The successful in the later Roman Empire—themselves neatly mirroring the tactics of central government—combined or shifted between different currencies of power. This demanded skill, experience, and good luck (or divine favor). Above all, as far as circumstances dictated or permitted, it was a matter of finding the right currency at the right time. Of central importance, for all concerned, was the ability to use, to combine, or to block the various different options which it was hoped might work to their best advantage—as well as to praise by admiring supporters, or to vilification by disappointed rivals.

CHAPTER 5

Autocracy and Bureaucracy

Allowing someone to live or killing him, enriching or impoverishing him, honoring or debasing him, these six handles are what the ruler grasps.

— *The Book of the Lord Shang* (Chinese—probably third century B.C.)

If one day all my ministers resigned, I would say to my chauffeur—be minister.

—King Hassan II of Morocco

The Six Handles of the Lord Shang

The transformation from the Principate to late antiquity was marked by a change in the way the Mediterranean world was ruled. For central government, the formation and promotion of an enlarged and sophisticated bureaucracy held out the attractive possibility of a more detailed and penetrating level of control. More formal structures permitted the development of an elaborate hierarchy of command, the more reliable allocation of tasks, and a greater degree of specialization. A more permanent organizational framework (as John Lydus' autobiography so clearly reveals) helped to focus loyalties, reinforce internal solidarities, and encourage a binding esprit de corps. In turn, the carefully regulated payment of money for administrative services, the officially sanctioned sale of offices, and the establishment of standardized, military-style grades, ranks, and privileges helped both in strengthening the bureaucracy and in the imposition of this new pattern of power and its forcible intrusion into the provincial towns of empire.

That later Roman emperors in many ways supported the growth of this "elaborate centralised machine" (to quote A. H. M. Jones), and were acutely aware of its advantages, there should be no doubt.[1] As previous chapters have suggested, this was a concern repeatedly evidenced in court ceremonies and their magnificent representations, in John Lydus' account of the eastern Praetorian Prefecture, in publicly displayed edicts and inscriptions, and in the legislation collected in the *Justinianic* and *Theodosian Codes*. It was a powerful imperial preoccupation reflected in the surviving political histories of late antiquity, with their seemingly inexhaustible fascination with courtly intrigue and the rise and fall of influential officials. More than anywhere else, the close relationship between emperors and bureaucrats was clearly on show in Constantine's purpose-built "New Rome." Constantinople represented a physical and emotional break with (old) Rome and the long tradition of imperial rule it represented. Within a recognizable framework—imposing forums, palaces, libraries, baths, aqueducts, an imperial mausoleum, a Hippodrome modeled on the Circus Maximus, a Senate House, a Golden Milestone—the new capital enshrined in its architecture a new system of government and a new religion. The possession of the *palladium* (the ancient talisman of Athena brought by Aeneas from Troy and taken by Constantine from Rome), the presence of the relics of Christ (said to have been unearthed in Jerusalem by Constantine's mother, Helena), and the public display of classical statuary and art plundered from other cities together triumphantly proclaimed Constantinople the epitome of the Mediterranean world.[2]

Importantly, too, this New Rome on the Bosphorus was designed and built to function as the administrative hub of empire. The concentration in the Great Palace of a byzantine complex of audience halls, council chambers, judicial tribunals, imperial secretariats, and state archives expressed in concrete form the intimate reliance of emperors on their officials. This vast imperial citadel was to be distanced from the houses of private citizens. In 409 Honorius and Theodosius II instructed the urban prefect of Constantinople that buildings which had encroached on land surrounding the palace were to be demolished: "for the imperial residence requires extensive grounds hidden from all the world, so that within its precincts there shall be a place to dwell only for those who have been selected for the due requirements of our majesty and for the government of the state."[3] Marveling at this Forbidden City, John Chrysostom encouraged his congregation to imagine heaven with its angelic inhabitants as a place with its own similarly strict moral code. Violators could expect severe penalties, "just as in imperial palaces . . . if one brought in a prostitute and enjoyed her, or was overcome by too much wine, or committed any similar indecent act, one would suffer extreme punishment."[4]

Officials associated with the imperial household and the great departments of state (such as the Praetorian Prefecture, the *sacra scrinia*, and the *quaestor sacri palatii*) shared something of that aura of sanctity which surrounded an emperor. Their authority and position were made clear to all (as John Lydus was ever eager to emphasize) by their numerous retinue, fine uniforms, and their impressive insignia of office. They were expected to set themselves apart from ordinary men. "The dignity of the palace" (to quote a law issued in 357 by Constantius II) demanded that they not hire themselves out as gladiators.[5] Nor were freedmen, Jews, or the heterodox to be permitted in their ranks. In two laws issued at Constantinople in 395 (one to the eastern praetorian prefect, the other to the *magister officiorum*) Arcadius and Honorius ruled that heretics and any who shared their "religious madness" should be deprived of their posts, "and you shall order that they, along with those with whom they have connived at the subversion of our laws and of our religion, shall not only be removed from the imperial administration, but also kept outside the walls of this city."[6]

Bureaucrats who reached retirement could expect (in the pleasing phrase of a law of the emperor Constantine) to be "deluged with privileges." They were granted important legal rights and wide-ranging immunity from taxation.[7] Such advantages were regarded as just and fitting rewards for faithful *palatini* (who staffed the most important administrative departments located in and around the Great Palace): "for after proofs of loyal service undertaken in our sight they shall obtain complete repose."[8] In the striking terminology of a law issued in 425, those "entitled to be admitted to the secret chamber of our imperial council [*consistorium*], to be involved in official business, and to approach our oracle" were to enjoy (both in office and thereafter) a superior rank in their own communities.[9] Imperial legislation ensured that bureaucrats remained a privileged group. The lengthy inscription erected outside the town hall in Timgad in Numidia, which listed the various fees payable by litigants in cases brought before the court of the provincial governor in Cirta, also detailed the strict order of precedence to be observed by those attending the governor's morning levees *(salutationes)*. The first to be presented were high-ranking officials, retired or in service, as well as those with equivalent honorary status such as the civic grandees listed at the head of Timgad's *album municipal*. In second place followed the *princeps, cornicularius,* and any *palatini* sent out on missions from Constantinople. Third were the *coronati,* those who had served in the prestigious annual post of *sacerdos*, chief priest of Numidia (two are listed in the *album*). Next, led by its senior members, came the administrative staff both of the governor and of the *rationalis* (the imperial treasury official assigned to the province) along with civic magistrates and the local council, presumably of Cirta, where this decree was originally displayed. Fifth, and the last to be admitted, were the *supernumerarii*, unsalaried juniors not yet formally registered on the staff of either the governor or the *rationalis*.[10]

The *ordo salutationis* (as this inscription is known) clearly advertised the importance of officials as well as their close links with "the quality" both in the capital Cirta and in the province's other main towns like Timgad. For bureaucrats—given the difficulties which confronted those in the Roman Empire seeking access to government—the guarantee of comparatively easy contact with the local governor, even if in such a strictly ceremonial form, was a much-prized privilege. The most senior officials in a province (the majority retired from active service) could also expect much more than the studied courtesy of a formal greeting at a morning *salutatio*. As Arcadius and Honorius, confirming earlier imperial rulings, reminded the eastern praetorian prefect Flavius Caesarius in 396, those who had served in the *sacra scrinia* were permitted to exercise "at will and without notice the right to enter a governor's secretariat and to sit in court with any governor."[11]

On some occasions, in addition to the award of immunities and privileges, emperors might lavish exaggerated public praises on high-ranking officials. (And, in turn, as the citation read out by the prefect Hephaestus on John Lydus' retirement demonstrates, such extravagant imperial pronouncements could provide models for those senior officials' laudatory addresses to members of their own staff.)[12] In prolix terms, Constantius II eulogized the achievements and capabilities of the eastern praetorian prefect Flavius Philippus, who in 351 had been stripped (perhaps mistakenly) of his office after confusion over his relations with the usurper Magnentius. Philippus had died soon afterward, in exile and disgrace. An official letter from the emperor to the proconsul of Asia, inscribed and displayed in the monumental center of Ephesus, grandly proclaimed what amounted to an imperial apology:

Innate virtue has this excellent consequence for men of proven loyalty, that when such a man is always alert in furthering the interests of his emperor and of the state, the glory of that endeavor compensates for the troubles of his life, and besides, as regards fame, he may be considered to have sought to obtain for himself this recognition: that by merit in the service of his emperor he has succeeded as a result of hard work and diligence . . . Therefore, we who strive to match such great and distinguished merits as his, since we are resolved and it is fitting, we decree that monuments dedicated to this great man [Flavius Philippus] are to be erected in wealthy cities . . . and gilded statues be set up for the same . . . and in our state let the memory of that man be everlasting, he who by his own labors ever advanced the glory of our state.[13]

Effective governance in late antiquity inevitably involved a close dependence on officials. This inescapable necessity was neatly summed up in the late fourth century by Synesius of Cyrene, bishop of Ptolemais (modern Tulmaythah on the coast of Libya), in his tract *On Kingship:* "Now to seek to know each place, each man, and each dispute would require a very thorough survey, and not even Dionysius [of Syracuse], who established his rule over a single island—and not even the whole of that—would have been capable of performing this task. But through a few officials it is possible to pay attention to many concerns."[14] Yet for all its undoubted advantages in broadening the scope of imperial authority, the continued advancement of bureaucrats and bureaucracy (even in terms less rhetorically enthusiastic than Constantius II's) also confronted emperors with a range of difficulties. At its simplest, as Synesius recognized, the problem was one of delegation and independence. The successful functioning of any administration requires officials sufficiently empowered to make decisions in their own right. Moreover, a balance must be struck between the fulfillment of external goals (such as the collection of taxes, the allocation of resources, and the administration of justice) and the expenditure of time and effort on the comparatively much less productive tasks of internal surveillance, cross-checking, and supervision. No organization can possibly manage a complex range of operations—which no single person could ever hope to accomplish alone—while remaining under the direct control of one man. In the later Roman Empire, the success of bureaucracy as an effective system of government demanded the delegation of power to independent officials. Emperors had no option but to depend on secondhand advice or information; no choice but to count on often far-distant subordinates to carry out their commands. Delegation was an inescapable corollary of imperial rule.

But delegation might also be seen as a dangerous and frequently unpalatable necessity. Power emancipated was power lost. Authority relinquished to a particular department or to a high-ranking official might encourage or strengthen rivals. Indeed, it might so far remove emperors from the actual business of government that they could become, in Louis XIV's memorable phrase, mere "rois fainéants," prisoners of an administrative system which monopolized and controlled important policymaking information.[15] Max Weber wryly noted Bismarck's annoyance upon finding that the Prussian state bureaucracy (which he had been instrumental in creating) carried on, seemingly unconcerned, without him: "Upon his resignation, he saw to his surprise that they continued to manage their offices unperturbed and unaffected, as if he had not been the mastermind and creator of these creatures, but rather as if one person in the bureaucratic machine had been replaced by another."[16]

In the later Roman Empire, the conflict between the competing demands of bureaucracy and autocracy exerted a double pressure. On the one hand, for emperors to subordinate themselves to regulation, to delegate power, or to conform to the demands of order was to strengthen the bureaucracy at the cost of their own independence and authority. On the other hand, for emperors to resist the constraints imposed by a more institutional pattern of rule was to assert their own personal preferences at the cost of that certainty and reliability necessary for administrative efficiency. Undoubtedly a well-regulated bureaucracy allowed emperors to rule more effectively, but its claims to autonomy, its drive for orderliness and systematization, and its emphasis on convention and regulation also threatened to limit their authority. The art of successful rule was, in part, the art of incomplete and uncertain delegation. The exercise of imperial power sometimes entailed the ability to destroy established patterns or to prevent their formation, to create chaos, and to confound expectation. Intermittent terror and instability allowed emperors both to manage and to undermine their administration. It added force to their insistent claim that the continued importance of officialdom in the government of empire was dependent upon them personally and upon the vicissitudes of imperial will.

This closely interlocking relationship between emperor and officials was delicate and easily broken. Both sides sought to exploit their own advantages, each playing on the weaknesses of the other. Both sides, too, were forced to accept trade-offs, compromises, and failures. Faced with these pressing and inevitable difficulties, various emperors achieved varying degrees of success. They were as often victims of this situation as they were its masters. Their power of intervention was in continual danger of being hijacked by those whom it sought to dominate. Weak emperors became the isolated servants of officials whom they could no longer control. More subtly, too, throughout the later Empire emperors struggled to prevent their own gradual entrapment in a highly structured and convention-bound court society. Autocratic independence was much more difficult to maintain in a world dominated by formal institutions. Bureaucracy, with its predictable rules and established norms, had little room for the caprice of autocracy. Emperors risked being pavilioned in splendor within an inaccessible court; trapped unwillingly in a shimmering web of ritual, their capacity, their inclination, and simply their time for intervention subordinated to an endless round of pomp and circumstance.

Centralization

The majestic courtly ceremonies described by John Lydus or by the sixth-century poet Corippus, or so opulently depicted on the Missorium of Theodosius I, on the frescoed walls of the temple of Ammon in Luxor, or on the mosaics depicting Justinian in Ravenna were all unquestionably focused on the brilliant image of the emperor himself. The poet Ausonius, consul in 379, compared an imperial audience to standing before God; both inspired "a quiet dread and a reverent awe."[17] The imperial countenance itself illuminated the world. In the words of one orator celebrating the appearance of Constantine before a cheering crowd in Trier: "Immortal gods! What a day then shone forth upon us . . . when you passed through the gates of this city."[18] To meet the imperial gaze was to risk blindness, like those who dared to look directly at the sun. Scarcely less dazzling was the sight of the "shining throng of courtiers" who accompanied an emperor, flanking the painted tetrarchs in Luxor or crowding round the imperial presence in the apse of San Vitale.[19] For John Chrysostom, closeness to an emperor, like nearness to God, was always greatly to be desired: "for we regard those as blessed who are near him and have a share in his speech and mind, and partake of the rest of his glory."[20]

These memorable images of imperial magnificence etched in purple and gold reflect something of the "fantastic degree" of centralization (again to quote A. H. M. Jones) which characterized later Roman government.[21] The careful disposition of monarch and court emphasized both the centrality of the emperor and, for those who desired power, wealth, and position, the overwhelming importance of proximity to that center. In the fourth century, high-ranking officeholders, military commanders, and influential members of the imperial household were known collectively as *proximi*—"those who are nearest."[22] To be sure, this concentration of power was to a great extent an inevitable result of the establishment of an institutionalized bureaucracy whose senior officials were resident in the imperial capital. But centralization also protected an emperor's position. The glittering attractions of the court and the location of key bureaucratic departments in or near the Great Palace helped emperors to maintain an explicitly personal stake in an expanding administration. It increased the likelihood that they might successfully assert their will, sometimes violently, against the wishes of their advisers. It kept open the possibility of an idiosyncratic, or even whimsical, response to embassies or petitions. Above all, centralization enforced the attendance of high-ranking officials at court. Their presence not only openly emphasized their dependence upon imperial favor for appointment and promotion; it also offered an emperor, aided by palace intrigue or personal rivalries, a better chance of policing or punishing the powerful who claimed to rule the empire in his name.

An emperor's influence was most keenly felt in the world of the *potestates excelsae,* the "lofty powers" who surrounded the throne and took part in the debates and discussions of the *consistorium* (the imperial high council).[23] In formal terms, emperors emphasized their role in the selection of these senior officials through the requirement that documents authorizing their appointment bear the imperial signature.[24] If possible, as commemorated on the Missorium of Theodosius, *codicilli* were to be presented by the emperor himself. In practice, emperors maintained the attraction of their persons and their court by ensuring that proximity brought success. This is an insistent theme of both ancient and modern writing on late Roman politics and its shifting patterns of influence, support, and opposition. Among contemporaries, ever jockeying for position, it was widely assumed that close association with an emperor, for all its self-evident risks, also held out the chance of the greatest rewards.

In the mid-fourth century, the high-flying bureaucrat Anatolius owed a series of posts to his well-timed appearances. Having been proconsul of Constantinople in 354, he journeyed to the court at Milan and continued to press for preferment. He seems to have been offered the Urban Prefecture of Rome and to have turned it down. In 355 he returned eastward on a brief visit to Seleucia, on the southeastern coast of Asia Minor (where he may have had estates), but by the beginning of winter he was back in Italy lobbying for office and was, in 357, appointed to the Praetorian Prefecture of Illyricum.[25] In similar vein, in 369 the decidedly unmilitary senator and orator Quintus Aurelius Symmachus (later urban prefect of Rome) was granted the honorary rank of *comes tertii ordinis* as a result of touring the empire's northern defenses with Valentinian I.[26] More generally, emperors might favor their compatriots (in the fourth century, a group of Pannonians was particularly prominent under Valentinian, Spaniards under Theodosius) or grant promotion to the provincial associates or family of an already established official.[27]

Meteoric rises were matched by sudden falls. For those too closely connected to a previous regime the consequences could be severe. The emperor Julian, on taking the throne in 361, purged the leading advisers of his predecessor. According to the fourth-century historian Ammianus Marcellinus, a show trial, which condemned both innocent and guilty alike, was followed by a general expulsion from the Great Palace of all Constantius II's attendants and household staff. Several who had hitherto enjoyed successful careers were burned alive.[28] Yet even without incurring imperial displeasure, high-ranking officials could not have expected to remain in office for long. In practice, senior posts were held only briefly and irregularly. On average, praetorian prefects in the fifth century were replaced after eighteen months, urban prefects after little more than a year. Longer stints or further terms were exceptional.[29] From an emperor's point of view, despite obvious costs in efficiency and the accumulation of experience, a highly centralized system with a rapid turnover of personnel both prevented the powerful becoming entrenched in their positions and underlined the importance of imperial goodwill in securing and holding office.

For Christian writers, the perilous position of those who served the emperor understandably inspired instructive homilies on the fragility of temporal power and its rewards. In 399 the eunuch Eutropius fell unexpectedly from favor. As *praepositus sacri cubiculi*, Eutropius ran the imperial household and, after 395, had become the dominant influence at the court of Arcadius in Constantinople. In 398 he commanded, as a civilian and without any prior military experience, a successful expedition against the Huns in Asia Minor and was rewarded the following year with a consulship. In that same year, no doubt nervous at the coalition of civil and military authority in a eunuch who had privileged access to the emperor, a rival court faction succeeded in deposing him and demanded his execution. Terrified, Eutropius fled the imperial palace and took refuge in the adjoining church of Hagia Sophia. The next day John Chrysostom preached one of his finest sermons. This was a morality tale too good to pass over in silence. John took as his text Ecclesiastes 1.2.

> *Vanity of vanities, all is vanity* . . . Where now are the resplendent trappings of your consulship? . . . Where are the cheers which greeted you in the city, where the acclamations in the Hippodrome and the flatteries of the spectators? . . . Where now your feigned friends, where your parties and your dinners, and those who courted your power, doing and saying everything to win your favor? . . . These were all nighttime dreams, dispelled at daybreak; they were spring flowers, all withered with the end of spring; they were a shadow which has passed, smoke which has dispersed, bubbles which have burst, cobwebs which have been swept away.[30]

The sermon was a brilliant tour de force. With Eutropius in full view, trembling and holding tightly to the altar pillars—"more frightened than a hare or a frog, fixed firmly to that column there, without bonds, held fast by his fear rather than by a chain"—the congregation, proclaimed John, had come to witness "human nature convicted and the hazard of worldly affairs exposed."[31] The penitent Eutropius was not executed but exiled to Cyprus. The edict instructing the eastern praetorian prefect Aurelianus to organize his deportation was another memorable piece of late-antique legislation. It made its point force-

fully. Nor did it shy from exploiting the same stock rhetorical caricatures of eunuchs and their pernicious influence which had been so
artfully deployed by the poet Claudian (from the distant safety of Milan) in his pungent attacks against Eutropius' corruption and abuse of
power.

> His splendor has been stripped away and the consulate delivered from
> foul muck and from the need to remember his name and its filthy squa-
> lor. This has been done so that, once every item of business he trans-
> acted has been revoked, silence may fall for all time and the stain on
> our age may not be made visible by his name being listed among the
> consuls . . . We direct that all statues, all likenesses, whether they be of
> bronze, or of marble, or painted (or of whatever material these images
> may be made), should be obliterated from all cities, towns, and from
> public and private places, so that this blot on our age may not defile the
> gaze of those who look upon it.[32]

Precipitous falls demand high-flown rhetoric. The reality was scarcely
less dramatic. A few months after his exile, Eutropius was recalled
from Cyprus, tried before Aurelianus, condemned, and beheaded.

For that shrewdly perceptive historian Ammianus Marcellinus, the
sometimes dangerous shifts in imperial policy were reminiscent of the
bloody staged fights between gladiators and wild animals in the am-
phitheater. Within Ammianus' courtly world, itself bounded by the
precise, formal rigidities of imperial ceremonial, emperors—like "untrained beasts" in the arena[33]—could swing without warning from acting on the (sometimes incorrect) advice of their officials to violently
rejecting their recommendations in favor of independent action. Constantius II, Valens, and Valentinian I were each capable of moderation
and self-control as well as of excessive cruelty. "While in the conduct of
affairs he [Constantius] was comparable to other moderate emperors,
yet if he got hold of any inkling, no matter how trivial or groundless, of
an aspiration to imperial power, in his endless investigations (in which
he gave equal weight to right and wrong) he easily surpassed the savagery of Caligula, Domitian, and Commodus."[34] At their extremes, attempts to reconcile these conflicting aspects of imperial rule resulted
in paradox and further uncertainty. Valentinian having referred a case
to the Roman Senate, which, "weighing the matter in the scales of justice, found out the truth," was incensed when the death sentence he

had imposed was commuted to exile. Constantius followed his own personal preferences "as if they were the most impartial laws." When he doubted the strength of imperial power, it was his closest advisers (*proximi*) who assured him that "there was nothing so troublesome that his overwhelming ability and good fortune bordering on the heavenly could not triumph as usual." Nor was the seemingly milder approach to justice by Constantius' successor any less uncertain or haphazard. When in a rape case the victim's parents objected to his showing any leniency, Julian was said to have remarked: "Justice might impugn my clemency, but it is proper for an emperor of the most forgiving disposition to be above all other laws."[35]

The exercise of imperial power as illustrated by Ammianus takes his readers into a Looking Glass world where nothing is quite what it seems. This is a place where false information was sometimes treated as fact, where right and wrong could be indistinguishable or inverted, where clemency could disguise or promote cruelty, where sorrow or violence might bring rejoicing, and where men were afraid to offer good counsel because of uncertain (and often perverse) consequences.[36] In such an isolating, terrifying atmosphere, even the walls of an empty room were feared in case they might overhear a secret.[37] Under such circumstances, who could predict with certainty the resolution of any issue or rely with confidence on what appeared to be the truth? In a striking literary mirror image of a world turned upside down, Ammianus left his own summary assessments of emperors open. His obituary notices, in their formal juxtaposition of long-recognized categories of virtue and vice, held out the promise of a systematic and orderly method of evaluating imperial policies and achievements. That promise remained unfulfilled. In their careful construction, Ammianus' obituaries artfully reflected something of the ambiguities of imperial power. Any resolution is the readers'. And that judgment must inevitably remain provisional.

Then died Valens . . . of his merits, known to many, we shall now speak, and of his defects. He was a loyal and constant friend . . . a most impartial guardian of the provinces, protecting each of them from harm as he would his own household . . . He combined generosity with moderation . . . He distinguished sharply between justice and injustice . . . He had an uncontrollable desire for great wealth and being unwilling to undertake any hard work his great austerity was more of a pretense. He was inclined to cruelty . . . There was one thing also which could not be endured: though he wished to appear to conduct all legal disputes and judicial investigations in accordance with the laws and referred the examination of these matters to judges (either to those normally assigned to such cases or to those specially selected), nevertheless he allowed nothing to be done contrary to his own caprice. He was in other ways unjust, hot-tempered . . . idle and sluggish.[38]

In Ammianus' view, it was those in the palace nearest the emperor who stood the greatest chance of experiencing firsthand the often destructive unpredictability of their actions. In his portrayal of Valentinian, Ammianus concentrated in particular on his rages and vile temper. Here was an emperor who had condemned officials guilty of only minor infractions to be burned alive, who had ordered the death of an attendant who had accidentally let slip a hunting dog, and who commanded that a groom who had failed properly to control a horse which he wished to mount should have his right hand cut off. Here, too, was an emperor whose ferocious outburst of abusive anger when confronted by barbarian ambassadors at court in 375 led to a seizure and his untimely death.[39] Most notoriously of all, Valentinian was rumored to have kept two man-eating bears in cages outside his bedroom in the imperial palace. He assigned servants to look after them, particularly to ensure that their savagery was not dulled through overfeeding. The emperor even gave these bloodthirsty beasts affectionate names: Mica Aurea and Innocentia, "Goldflake" and "Innocence." It is attractive to read this grim story of Valentinian's pets as a black parody of the emperor's intimate relationship with his closest advisers and high officials (often compared by Ammianus in their own capricious cruelty to wild animals). It is a sharp parallel which cuts both ways. Even the influence of these murderous bears was short-lived. After they had performed excellent service as executioners at court, Valentinian instructed that they should be released. "Finally, after he had seen many burials of the corpses which Innocence had dismembered, as she was good and well-deserving, he discharged her and let her return to the forest unharmed, hoping that she would have cubs like herself."[40]

Despite such dark uncertainties (which contemporaries such as

Ammianus Marcellinus warned could suddenly eclipse the dazzling magnificence of the court), those skillful or lucky enough to secure imperial favor might also enjoy—if only for a short while—substantial rewards. In late 340 or early 341 an Egyptian soldier, Flavius Abinnaeus, petitioned the emperor Constantius II. The issue was a simple one. Four years earlier, Abinnaeus had been selected to escort an embassy of Blemmyes (a Nubian tribe) to the imperial court at Constantinople. The mission was successful. He saw the emperor on at least one ceremonial occasion, when, kissing the hem of the imperial robe, he had adored the purple. After accompanying the ambassadors on their return journey, Abinnaeus was ordered to conduct a detachment of new recruits from Egypt to Hierapolis in northern Syria. In 339 or 340 he again visited the court, probably in residence at Antioch. On this occasion Constantius granted Abinnaeus a promotion and conferred on him the command of the garrison at Dionysias, in the Upper Thebaid in Middle Egypt. But, when, on his return to Alexandria, Abinnaeus presented himself for service, he was told that for the same post there were other nominees, supported by the commander of military forces in Egypt, the *dux et comes* Valacius. Abinnaeus had only one claim to priority over these local rivals. He played it to the full. Petitioning the emperor, he explained the situation, as he saw it: "But when your sacred letter was produced before the *comes* Valacius his office replied that other men had presented letters of this sort. Since it is clear they have been advanced by influence [*ex suffragio*], but I by your sacred decision . . . may your clemency deign to order that I be appointed to . . . Dionysias, and remove those who through influence have obtained promotion to that camp."[41]

Valacius capitulated, but only in the face of a direct imperial instruction. By the end of March 342 Abinnaeus was in post at Dionysias. Two years later Valacius seized an opportunity to discharge him on the grounds that he had finished his tour of duty. A brusque letter of dismissal made Valacius' position clear. Abinnaeus again prepared an appeal to the emperor. But this time he may not have had to travel all the way to court. Sometime in 345, Valacius was killed. (He suffered a severe fall in a riding accident and was badly bitten by his companion's horse.) Abinnaeus may have been able to take immediate advantage of his untimely death. After all, he still had (to quote T. D. Barnes) "an imperial letter of appointment which stated no fixed term for his command, while his supplanter may have had nothing more efficacious than a letter from the *dux et comes* Valacius." However it was managed, Abinnaeus was successful in asserting his claim. He was back in post by May 346 and was still in charge at Dionysias five years later.[42]

With whom should one sympathize in this Egyptian soap opera? Some have sided with the harassed Flavius Abinnaeus, applauding the success of this "deserving candidate of humble status" who had served long and hard, and finally obtained a post which he merited.[43] But what of Valacius? For him, Abinnaeus was an unwanted interloper, someone who had been mostly absent from Egypt for four years only to reappear with a special grant of imperial favor which he claimed gave him the right to be preferred above those who were, no doubt, Valacius' loyal supporters. It is unlikely that those men, unexpectedly elbowed out of the queue for promotion, welcomed Abinnaeus' return or were attentive listeners to his stories of court and Constantinople.

The petition of an insignificant figure like Flavius Abinnaeus was an important token of the possible extent and range of imperial power and of the perceived ability of emperors, should they so choose, to affect even minor matters in a small provincial garrison town. It reinforced the impression that contact with the court was what really counted. It provided opportunities for emperors to demonstrate their claim to universal authority and beneficence by cutting through obstacles imposed by those with more limited influence. Above all, the high level of centralization in later Roman government might act to weaken local sites of authority whose rulings could be canceled or overturned without warning to the substantial benefit of those few who—despite the many difficulties—managed to gain access to an emperor.

In late April 348, Ammon, an educated lawyer from the Egyptian town of Panopolis (about 200 kilometers downstream from modern Luxor), said farewell at the quayside in Alexandria to his brother. Aurelius Harpocration, trained in rhetoric, intended to visit the imperial court, probably in Antioch. (He planned to be away for about four months, and left three female slaves in Ammon's safekeeping.) Harpocration was confident that proximity to court and emperor would help him conclude favorably a dispute with the *archiereus*, the high priest of Alexandria and all Egypt, the Roman official responsible for the regulation and administration of the (non-Christian) priesthood in the province. At issue was the succession of Ammon and

Harpocration's nephew, Horion, to the hereditary priesthood *(prophe-teia)* of the Panopolite nome, a position which had been held by Horion's father, also called Horion. In making its case, the family relied on an imperial ruling from Diocletian (perhaps issued during his time in Egypt in the late 290s) in favor of such hereditary rights. The customary "investiture fee" for the confirmation of such an appointment had also been paid to the office of the *archiereus*. Some pressure had been put on the high priest to accept Diocletian's decision (at least as represented by Ammon's family). He had, it seems, been offered more money and also sent a copy of the emperor's judgment. But the *archiereus* still refused to allow Horion to take up his father's post. Confident of success at court, Harpocration told Ammon to pass on his advice and assurances to their mother in Panopolis. It is Ammon's letter home which survives.

> And as he [Harpocration] was about to depart he gave me many instructions, to go up now to Panopolis, saying "Why are you spending still more money with the high-priest in order to get the office for the boy, why in short . . . do you continue to approach the high-priest's office about this? For I ought to get it abroad from the emperor for him," and at the sea when he was about to embark on the boat he swore, "Whether you receive it from the high-priest or not, I will get the office for the boy from the emperor; and after Horion's death no other person will be appointed *prophetes* in Panopolis except the son of Horion. Let those hostile to the gods therefore learn their own fate."[44]

Despite his brother's confidence, Ammon—perhaps at his mother's request—continued to press his nephew's claim in Alexandria. On behalf of Horion, he drafted a petition (perhaps never submitted) to the prefect of Egypt which again set out the main arguments on which the family relied: the payment of the required fee and the ruling of Diocletian. Ammon carefully emphasized the unimpeachable authority of such a decision. "It was the emperor who decided long ago, and we offered to him [the *archiereus*] the imperial rescript, which decides all things for all men."[45] The result of Ammon's efforts on behalf of Horion is unknown. So, too, is the outcome of Harpocration's attempts at court. They may not have lived up to his expectations. (Ammon perhaps allowed himself a knowing smile in quoting verbatim his elder brother's bombastic claims. They may not have come as any surprise to his mother back in Panopolis.)

As things turned out, Aurelius Harpocration died abroad within a few months of leaving Egypt. It was not at first certain that he had left a will. As a result, Ammon found himself involved in a legal dispute over the ownership of Harpocration's slaves. An imperial official, Eugeneios, had arrived in Alexandria and claimed the slaves on the grounds that Harpocration had died intestate (and that therefore his property fell to the *res priuata,* the imperial treasury). Eugeneios had a warrant signed by the emperor allowing him to take the slaves for himself unless it could be established that Harpocration had a legally valid heir. (Eugeneios also pressed the nice legal point that since the slaves were technically without a master, he had in effect gained ownership by taking them into his possession.) A compromise was struck: Eugeneios and Ammon agreed to divide the inheritance. But when it became clear that Harpocration had in fact left a will, Ammon, now legally his heir, sought to repudiate the agreement. His surviving archive contains nine successive drafts of a petition to the *rationalis* (the chief financial official in Egypt in charge of administering all property belonging to the state) in which he presented his case for the ownership of the slaves. Ammon also emphasized his brother's close relations with the court, noting his many panegyrics delivered in the emperors' praise, neatly glossing over whether or not Harpocration had ever actually spoken in the imperial presence: "From Greece to Rome and from Rome to Constantinople, and from one country to another, traversing virtually most parts of the earth he [Harpocration] did not cease proclaiming the victories of our gloriously triumphant emperors and delivering royal orations everywhere."[46]

For Ammon these were important points. In a dispute with an imperial official some counterclaim of a connection with court and capital was no doubt well worth making. Again, the outcome of this case is not known; but it is striking that in both matters in which Ammon (himself an educated lawyer) was closely involved, he chose, as a significant part of the presentation of his brief, to emphasize the links—however tenuous—between his family and emperors, both past and present. Of course, in practice, few provincials, especially those not already part of the municipal elite or without friends in the right places, ever adored the purple or were ever able to air their grievances outside their own small communities. Perhaps Aurelius Harpocration, like his contemporary Flavius Abinnaeus, might have succeeded in bringing his case to the attention of Constantius II. (His hopes may after all have been more than mere idle boasting to a younger brother.) Certainly, such possibilities could never have been entirely excluded. And possibilities—however tenuous—mattered. Buttressed by the occasional well-advertised success or by the advancement of those known to enjoy an emperor's favor, they helped to ensure both the irresistible pull of the court, and its insistent presence in the minds of provincials seeking to present their claims to local authorities in the most favorable light.

It is something of that strong sense of an imperial center which also dominates Ammianus Marcellinus' version of fourth-century emperors: their distinct personalities, their often-unpredictable actions, and the continual tension between them and their high officials. Whatever the accuracy of any of the particular incidents he chose to relate, Ammianus offered his readers a complex and lasting impression of imperial power, its operation, risks, and limitations. Away from court and capital, no doubt many in the empire were unable to name the current emperor, or to distinguish one emperor from another, or even to conceive of the magnificence of the Great Palace at Constantinople; but that does not mean that they were insensible to a model of society which placed at the center of its imperial gaze an emperor and the *potestates excelsae* who surrounded him. This was a world (to quote J. H. W. G. Liebeschuetz) in which "the idea of emperor loomed powerfully and fearfully."[47] Memorable anecdotes of emperors' cruelty or clemency, or the stories of provincials who had approached the "divine imperial oracle," these tales continually retold—like brilliant ceremonies, repeatedly reenacted—helped both to construct and to reinforce a model of society focused on emperors and the imperial court. Above all, the centralization of power held out an open-ended promise of success for anyone fortunate enough to make contact. In the imagination of contemporaries, an emperor might intervene in any situation—if only he were told.

The Emperor in the Later Roman World

Roman emperors, despite their own grandiloquent claims and the hopes of those seeking advancement or redress, were not omnipotent.

The extent of their power was tightly circumscribed by a range of physical and technological limitations, and compounded by the difficulties arising from the painful slowness of communication and the absence of any sophisticated methods of data storage or retrieval. The free flow of information to central government was further restricted by those who feared that their advice might be interpreted as hostile criticism of the emperor or his policies. In John Lydus' partisan account of the administrative reforms of John the Cappadocian, it was only the empress Theodora who dared speak out. Others were not prepared to risk criticism of a praetorian prefect.[48] Similarly, Ammianus Marcellinus regarded it as worthy of note that the *quaestor sacri palatii* Flavius Eupraxius was able to quell Valentinian I's rages and persuade him to act with greater clemency.[49]

Others were not always so successful in their attempts to counsel emperors. Responding, in 384, to a report from Quintus Aurelius Symmachus, which questioned the selection of officials in the Urban Prefecture of Rome and recommended revised criteria for future appointments, Valentinian II witheringly observed: "There must be no questioning of an imperial judgment: it is a kind of sacrilege to doubt whether the person whom the emperor has selected is worthy."[50] In the light of such a reaction, it comes as no surprise that, in the late 360s, the anonymous author of *de rebus bellicis* (a pamphlet offering ingenious advice on a wide range of civil, fiscal, and military affairs) advanced his case tentatively, observing the excellence of the emperors and their government while nervously suggesting improvements. "Most sacred emperors, the good of your state, ever fortunate under the inspiration of heaven, demands that on suitable occasions suggestions should be made to ensure that your divine plans may be brought to divine conclusions . . . Therefore, most merciful emperors . . . consider it proper for you to take notice of the useful projects with which the foresight of the divinity has inspired my mind."[51]

By contrast, on some occasions the very risks involved in criticizing imperial policy, combined with unreliable records and inefficient communications, could allow those sufficiently daring, or sufficiently far distant, to ignore imperial directives or knowingly supply an emperor with false or misleading information. In the 360s Romanus, military commander in Africa, evaded any proper inquiry into his refusal to defend the city of Lepcis Magna (on the Libyan coast) against raids from desert tribes unless the townsmen equipped his troops with provisions and four thousand camels. He forestalled an embassy sent by the provincials to Valentinian I by dispatching a swift messenger to the *magister officiorum* Remigius (also a relative of Romanus by marriage). Although the deputation was successful in presenting its grievances to the emperor, Remigius was able to obfuscate the issue and to delay any investigation. Meanwhile the attacks continued. The emperor, learning of this, reopened the case, sending a court official, the *notarius* Palladius, to interview prominent local spokesmen. They showed him the devastation the raids had caused and complained of the lack of proper military intervention. But Palladius, too, was suborned by Romanus. The evidence from Lepcis Magna was deliberately distorted and suppressed. Palladius (in Ammianus' words) "through the wicked art of lying" convinced Valentinian that the complaints were groundless. The emperor, misinformed and misguided by his own (supposedly loyal) officials, in the belief that there was no irregularity, left Romanus, Remigius, and Palladius unpunished. Instead, for giving false information to an imperial official and thereby attempting to deceive the emperor, he ordered the provincial spokesmen's tongues to be torn out.[52]

In principle, the solution to such imperial difficulties was simple. The orator Themistius, speaking before Constantius II in March 347, advised the cultivation of friendships.

> For the emperor, who must hear many things, see many things, and at the same time pay attention to many things, his two ears and his two eyes and his body (which contains one soul) are very little indeed. But if he is rich in friends, he will see into the distance and will hear things which are not close to him, and he will know what is far off—like the seers—and he will be present at the same time in many places—like a god.[53]

In practice, things were more difficult. Permanent links between central government and other departments were enforced through the requirement that established officials receive their certificates of appointment (*probatoriae*) from the palace secretariats (*sacra scrinia*) and through the regular submission by governors of reports summarizing their financial and judicial activities.[54] This close relationship between center and periphery was further strengthened through the dispatch from Constantinople of palatine bureaucrats to oversee the collection of various taxes and to supervise the operation of the public post.[55] Ideally, *palatini* on tours of duty in the provinces were to conduct their business without the threat of interference from either praetorian prefects or governors.[56] Outside this more regulated system of reporting and inquiry, direct contact could also be established with a variety of other official sources. The laws collected in the *Theodosian Code* preserve some direct interchanges between emperors and provincial governors. These queries or requests seem to have been submitted without prior vetting by the relevant *uicarius* or praetorian prefect (although presumably they still had to pass through the *sacra scrinia*).[57]

Normal channels of communication and command might also be circumvented by entrusting special missions to two groups within the palatine bureaucracy: the *notarii* (principally clerks and shorthand writers serving as an imperial secretariat) and the *agentes in rebus* (principally messengers and supervisors of the public post under the control of the *magister officiorum*).[58] In 359 Constantius II instructed the two *agentes* sent out to each province not to conceal "anything which you see being done in the state."[59] Similarly, *notarii* like Palladius in the "Romanus affair" acted as imperial representatives in a wide range of diplomatic, military, ecclesiastical, and administrative matters. The creation of separate corps whose members could be employed as reporters, ambassadors, or negotiators offered the possibility—not always realized—of securing a systematic flow of reliable and independent information. At the same time, *notarii* and *agentes* were encouraged to inform on the activities of other officials. The establishment of potentially conflicting lines of control (paradoxically) increased the chances that emperors' wills would be enforced. Expanding the number of bureaucrats involved in cross-checking the conduct of their colleagues helped to reduce the likelihood that any one department or individual would be able to plan or conceal actions contrary to the imperial interest.

This broad remit, combining the conduct of confidential missions with the surveillance of other departments' activities, made both *agentes* and *notarii*, like modern tax inspectors or auditors, easy targets for those already highly critical of the growth of centralized bureaucracy. For the distinguished Antiochene orator Libanius, avowedly old-fashioned in his attitudes, *agentes* were the ubiquitous "eyes of the emperor,"[60] interminable "snoopers" who, instead of seeking out genuine misconduct, terrorized provincials. These were "sheep-dogs who had joined the wolf pack," men who like shopkeepers at the start of a day knew how to drum up business: "they would lead on respectable citizens with handsome youths and then cause them to fear disgrace, or would plant evidence of magical practices on those who were completely innocent." *Notarii*—"these Cerberuses, these many-headed monsters"—were vilified in similar textbook displays of traditional rhetorical terms of abuse: "It was impossible for anyone to live near them; no one who met them could speak to them without being robbed or plundered . . . they went about the common enemies of anyone who possessed anything worth having, whether horse, slave, fruit tree, field, or garden."[61]

For the most part, the reality was more prosaic. There were perhaps (on the crudest of estimates) somewhere around 1,200 *agentes in rebus* in the imperial administration, the great majority operating openly.[62] Even if the number was substantially greater, given the size of the empire, the difficulties of communication, and the volume of information involved, it is unlikely that these officials could ever have functioned effectively as a "secret service or internal security police force."[63] Even so, as Libanius' lurid criticisms suggest, the very independence of such officials raised continual doubts about their trustworthiness. Julian, on coming to power in 361, was alleged (at least by Libanius) to have reduced drastically the numbers of serving *agentes* and *notarii*.[64] Other emperors, acutely aware of the problem, tried to guard their guards by carefully restricting the movements and activities of officials sent out into the provinces. In 416 Honorius and Theodosius II instructed Flavius Palladius, the praetorian prefect of Italy and Illyricum, that

> any person selected [to be sent on business into the provinces] . . . to further the collection of any tax whatsoever shall know that within the limit of a year he must finalize his accounts, return to his designated superior, and demonstrate to him his effectiveness . . . But if, after the period of a year has elapsed, he should delay and be found to be a plunderer preying on the vitals of that region, then he shall be stripped of his belt of office [*cingulum*] and expelled from the imperial administration . . . If he should fail to return [after completing his tour of duty],

he shall be bound with iron fetters and put in the charge of the provincial office staff, and with a report of the case he shall be turned over to the appropriate investigating authority.[65]

The responsibility for important tasks might also be shuffled, sometimes unpredictably, between departments and officials. In 395 the emperor Arcadius stripped the eastern Praetorian Prefecture of some of its jurisdiction over the *cursus publicus* (the public post), the *scholae palatinae* (the palace guard), and the *fabricae* (the imperial arms factories), which it had acquired under the influential prefect Rufinus. These duties were transferred to the *magister officiorum*. As John Lydus' account of the Prefecture under Justinian clearly shows, the possibility of shifts in administrative competence was naturally attractive to aggrandizing officials and, if carried too far, was potentially dangerous for emperors. John's view of the loss of his own department's control in these three key areas was curt and uncompromising: Rufinus had overreached himself and "wrecked the Prefecture by his despotic rule."[66] The assignment of variable, indistinct, or overlapping responsibilities also helped to ensure that no one group of officials could become too independently powerful. Strategically sensitive areas were arbitrarily split. The importance (and danger) of *fabricae* was reflected in the fragmentation of their administration. Oversight of the collection of raw materials was entrusted to the Praetorian Prefecture; the day-to-day running of the factories fell within the jurisdiction of the *magister officiorum*, except that the Prefecture cross-checked the suitability of new staff, exercised some control over workers' wives and families, and was involved in the transportation of finished products. The prime responsibility for *fabricae* seems to have seesawed between these two departments. The factories' administration was further complicated by the involvement of one of the empire's two chief financial officers, the *comes sacrarum largitionum,* and by the presence of supervisors sent out directly from the palatine departments.[67]

These organizing principles of irregularity and disruption were widely applied. Divisions cut across functions as diverse as, for example, the issuing of warrants *(euectiones)* for the public post and the maintenance of its infrastructure (split between the praetorian and urban prefects, and the *magister officiorum*); the compilation of reports on frontier troops (split between their commanders and the *magister officiorum*); and the drafting of imperial legislation (split between the *quaestor sacri palatii* and the *magister memoriae,* the head of one of the *sacra scrinia* from which the *quaestor* seconded his staff).[68] In 365, in a dispute over the management of the supply and distribution of corn (the *annona*) in Rome, Valentinian I and Valens ruled on the respective duties of the urban prefect and the *praefectus annonae.* Their response, in A. H. M. Jones's delightful phrase, was a "masterpiece of ambiguity."[69]

> We charge the aforementioned Prefecture with a duty of oversight and care; but not in such a way that the office of the *praefectus annonae* shall be obscured, but that both authorities, as far as their respective remits allow, shall supervise the *annona.* Their partnership in this task shall be such that the lower-ranking shall recognize the merits of his superior [the urban prefect]; and the superior authority shall show that he knows, from the very title of that official, what is properly due to the *praefectus annonae.*[70]

Within the imperial administration, many comparatively minor tasks were also frequently distributed in a miscellaneous or patchwork fashion. The issuing of *probatoriae* to lower-ranking officials was divided, again to quote A. H. M. Jones, in "a quite arbitrary way" among the *sacra scrinia.* Alongside other varied duties, the *scrinium memoriae* dealt with the appointment of *agentes in rebus,* palatine officials in the financial departments, and junior military commands; the *scrinium epistularum* with the staff of praetorian and urban prefects, proconsuls, and *uicarii;* and the *scrinium libellorum* with officials attached to senior military commanders.[71] To some extent, this confusion of often-conflicting competences was a product of the administration's rapid growth (and subsequent reorganizations), but it was also the result of a deliberate imperial reluctance to demarcate clearly areas of responsibility. The history of individual offices and departments in the later Roman Empire is rarely one of the slow accretion or systematization of particular jurisdictions. More often, it is one of continual shifts and changes.

The overlapping of responsibility for various functions also increased the likelihood that departments (perhaps in the hope of enlarging their own sphere of operation) might monitor more effectively the work of rivals and superiors. A system of penalties for unauthorized administrative acts imposed fines both on a provincial governor (or *uicarius* or praetorian prefect) and on his staff. Given this double sanction, it was no doubt hoped that it would be in the interests of officials to scrutinize the decisions of their superiors, and vice versa. But the advantages of mutual surveillance might also on some occasions shade into collusion.[72] Some of that risk could be reduced—but not always, and never entirely—by the regular deployment of well-tested officials in checking the actions of others. The general principle of using *agentes in rebus* or *notarii* for a range of sensitive missions, cutting across all other departments, was given particular force with the regular transfer of senior *agentes* to the post of *princeps officii* in the Praetorian Prefectures, the two Urban Prefectures (Rome and Constantinople), all vicarates, and a small number of high-ranking provinces. Their position was an ambiguous one. On the one hand, along with the other internally promoted senior officials, such as the *cornicularius* or *primiscrinius,* the *princeps,* as head of department, worked closely with the prefect (or *uicarius* or governor). On the other hand, the *princeps* was also well placed to keep watch on these men and their affairs and to report back to the *magister officiorum,* to whom as an *agens in rebus* he remained ultimately responsible.[73] A similar pattern of the secondment of the *princeps officii* from another department was common practice across a wide range of *officia,* both civil and military.[74] Reflecting on the history of the eastern Praetorian Prefecture, John Lydus (himself a former *cornicularius*) had no doubt of the reason for this system of appointment: it was a deliberate restriction on the activities of the Prefecture by an emperor who feared the autonomy of a powerful department.[75]

Similar tensions were also played out in the selection, appointment, and promotion of officials. In 315, in a law issued to the *consularis aquarum* in Rome, Constantine confirmed that "the order of promotion is to be so observed that the senior-ranking official in a department is he who was first in obtaining his appointment from the emperor."[76] Likewise staking out a claim for a well-ordered administration, some imperial legislation was concerned (to quote the emperor Leo in a law issued to his *magister officiorum* in the early 470s) that appointments should be made *non passim nec licenter*—"neither indiscriminately nor arbitrarily."[77] In 534, in establishing a Praetorian Prefecture in Africa, Justinian's legislation set out the grades, ranks, and salaries of 396 personnel:

In the *scrinium* of the *commentariensis,* twelve men allocated 17 *annonae* and 14½ *capita,* which is equivalent to 143 *solidi,* to be distributed thus: one *commentariensis* to receive 3 *annonae* each worth 5 *solidi* and 2 *capita* each worth 4 *solidi,* which is equivalent to 23 *solidi.* Beneath him there are to be three men, each to receive 2 *annonae* each worth 5 *solidi* and 1 ½ *capita* each worth 4 *solidi,* which is equivalent to 48 *solidi.* The remaining eight men are each to receive one *annona* worth 5 *solidi* and one *capitum* worth 4 *solidi,* which is equivalent to 72 *solidi.*[78]

Even if in most cases the circumstances which caused a specific law to be issued are irrecoverable, more generally it is possible to locate in both the *Justinianic* and *Theodosian Codes* legislation which, like Justinian's law of 534, both actively promoted and openly displayed a commitment to a well-organized and tightly regimented officialdom. (Here again, as suggested in Chapter 1, these laws should be seen as preserving individual moments in a more complex series of trade-offs. For the most part, they tend to isolate and authorize one particular tactic or the actions of one particular group.) Importantly, too, these regulations, with their clear stress on order and rationality, were part of a wider, more complicated, and less consistent set of imperial rulings. As illustrated in Chapter 1, the *Codes* also preserve a number of laws which entitle certain higher-ranking officials in the central administration on retirement to have some say in the selection of their successor or to appoint a son or brother to a junior post in the same department. Alongside seniority and inheritance, merit and competence might be represented as relevant criteria for securing advancement; although it is not clear that any easy distinction could always be made between competence and length of service, both in many cases covered by the single term *meritum.* In some instances, those claiming seniority were recognized over those advanced by imperial favor or on the recommendation *(suffragium)* of their influential supporters. In others, emperors upheld the priority of those who had come to their notice or had been promoted over those who had served for longer in the same department. In some cases, imperial legislation might both permit and regulate the payment of money as a means of securing preferment—a practice also known as *suffragium.* In other circumstances, such payments were prohibited. But even here, as in the uncertain determination of merit or long service, these rulings frequently exploited a well-known ambiguity. In restricting the operation of *suf-*

fragium, a number of laws could equally well (and perhaps knowingly by all concerned) have been understood to refer to the operation of influence, to the payment of money, or to both.[79]

Sometimes compromises were struck. In 380 Gratian, Valentinian II, and Theodosius I, in a law issued to the *magister officiorum,* laid down a system of promotion for *agentes in rebus* founded on strict seniority: "no greater number shall advance to any rank of honor than the number of *agentes in rebus* which each year retires from the department, their exertions having come to a final end." Despite this ruling, the emperors also reserved to themselves the right to promote two *agentes* annually on any basis. The edict recognized (with what degree of irony it is impossible to tell) that in promulgating two clearly inconsistent schemes for promotion, the emperors had in their own legislation arrogated to themselves the seemingly paradoxical right to "exceed the force of their own law."[80]

This blurred spectrum of possibilities significantly reduced the autonomy and security of officials. Neither ability, nor seniority, nor inherited right, nor influence, nor the payment of money (the last two often confusingly covered by the single term *suffragium*), nor some combination of these was ever a sure guarantee of advancement. A potentially threatening department might be weakened by the insistence on promotion by seniority or merit (not themselves always easily distinguished), rather than by the recommendation of senior officers or other influential persons. Candidates not in existing networks of influence might be brought into a department through the purchase of office. Conversely, a favored individual might be allowed to reinforce his position by recommending the appointment of friends, family, or associates. Taken together, imperial laws present a bewildering variety of tactics reflecting continual shifts and lasting uncertainties in the reasons for appointment and promotion. On some occasions there was no attempt to set out unambiguous provisions or to indicate a clear-cut preference for any specific criteria. Inheritance, the payment of money, merit, and seniority all competed, jostled, and overlapped. In a decree of February 26, 445, issued to the *magister officiorum* Nomus, the emperors Theodosius II and Valentinian III ordered

that any person who performs administrative duties in the *sacra scrinia* shall obtain his position on the basis of his service [*meritum*]. And we decree that all those over and above the number of established officials who work in the same *scrinia* [that is, *supernumerarii*] are to be promoted so that, as far as their ranking is concerned, the order in which they are to be allotted an established position which has fallen vacant is such that it is to be assigned to the longest serving. It is evident that it is utterly forbidden for anyone, when he is later in the time of his appointment, to seek to gain the position of one ahead of him, unless perhaps, it might be the case that there is a person who, held back by the time of his appointment, is superior in terms of his work and, supported by the testimony of the fifteen senior members of the *scrinium* and confirmed by their solemn oath, is judged more worthy of being given precedence. We also decree that this rule be observed, except by the sons of the heads of departments. And indeed we determine that it is possible for each head to give priority to one of his sons, who, as regards length of service, shall have preference [*suffragium*], so that even if he is known to have paid little attention to the imperial administration, he shall be protected from those appointed subsequently with the advantages of experience [*laborum merita*]. Notwithstanding this, we order a person who has been granted an established position also to pay 250 *solidi* to the head of department . . . But if any of the *supernumerarii* who has been due to succeed to an established position, in order not to pay the money, wishes to decline that established post, freedom is granted to substitute the next candidate in order of appointment upon payment of the aforementioned sum of money.[81]

Similarly interconnected patterns of permission and prohibition can be traced in the surviving laws dealing with the payment of money as a means of forcing access to government. A number of edicts, some surviving in the *Codes,* others inscribed and publicly displayed (like those at Apollonia, Ptolemais, Beersheva, in the forum at Timgad, and by the harbor at Abydos), set out in careful detail the amounts to be paid to various officials involved in a wide variety of tasks such as revenue collection and receipt, the conduct of court cases, and the drawing up and issuing of various documents. At the same time, the extent and effectiveness of this particular method of regulating access was undercut by its often seemingly contradictory relationship with other tactics endorsed and promoted by imperial legislation. In 331 the emperor Constantine issued an edict "to the provincials":

The grasping hands of officials shall immediately be stopped, they shall stop I say; for if after due warning they have not stopped, they are to be cut off by the sword. Access to the governor's court should not be for sale; entrance should not be purchased; the secretariat should not be brought into disrepute by bidding; the appearance of the governor should not be at a price. The ears of the governor shall be open equally to the poorest and to the wealthiest. There shall be no plundering when matters are brought before the court by the official known as the *princeps officii*. The assistants of the aforementioned *princeps officii* shall not be implicated in the shakedown of litigants . . . and the unsated greed of those who deliver court records to the parties involved in a case shall be curbed.[82]

Other laws inveighed against those "enriched by despoiling the provincials," against the "extremely perverse and venal treachery" of some officials, or, with threats of flogging and dismissal, against the avarice and extortion of those who exceeded the imperially prescribed fees for their services.[83] "We extinguish . . . the brands of this pernicious fire, and we do not permit it to rage further to the destruction of those whom it has exhausted."[84]

This colorful and highly charged language, especially when compared with the terse clarity praised in many modern legal systems, underlined one of the aims of this legislation. This was neither the clinical exactitude of a law expecting undisputed conformity, nor the hysterical blustering of an impotent government. (No doubt those who drafted and supported Constantine's edict were fully aware that the charging of fees for services formed the substantial bulk of an official's annual income.) Rather, like glittering imperial ceremonies, the grand parades of regimented bureaucrats, and the impressive schedules of officials in detailed rank order, the sweeping moral condemnation of the payment of money for access to government was another example of that "dramatic exaggeration" (to borrow a phrase applied by Ramsay MacMullen to late-antique art) which helped powerfully to mark out one idealized version of later Roman government.[85] Imperial laws such as Constantine's edict, with its combination of rhetorical grandeur and graphically described brutality, were intended to leave an immediate and indelible impression on the minds of those who read or heard them. In a world of hazardous and difficult communication, the shocking, the forceful, and the magnificent helped to drive the point home.

Such laws—not all phrased in the memorably grandiloquent terms of Constantine's edict of 331—were also aimed at regulating the actions of officials and of those trying to gain access to government or to avoid its demands. Like carefully calibrated charge-sheets prescribing particular tariffs for specified services, or legislation laying down the criteria for appointment or promotion, they can usefully be seen as another form of harassment, another potentially unwelcome intervention in the affairs of both bureaucrats and litigants, another block on their ability independently to reach their own agreements or to dictate their own conditions. Importantly, too, the ability to pay as a means of determining the allocation of government resources remained one option among a number of alternatives—some conflicting, others complementary. The use of money payments and the undoubted advantages it offered had always to be set against other available possibilities, against the pressures exerted by those who continued successfully to rely on more-traditional methods of advancing themselves and their causes, and against the pressing need to establish and maintain order in a centralized and increasingly bureaucratic empire.

Such kaleidoscopic patterns of support and subversion were neatly captured by the commissioners charged with the compilation and editing of the *Justinianic* and *Theodosian Codes*. In both cases, in the extensive sections dealing with the imperial administration, they included a range of legislation which would allow any reader to see at once something of the variety and variability of responses to the concerns raised by the establishment of a centralized bureaucracy, to the continued importance of traditional ways of exercising influence, and to emperors' insistence on their own autocratic power to intervene in any matter without pretext or warning.[86] In that sense, the *Codes* captured in miniature something of the continual pressures and the constant play of various tactics which surrounded both the workings and the failings of government in the later Roman Empire. Something of those same pressures, at least from an emperor's point of view, was also recognized by the historian John of Antioch, who in the seventh century wrote a chronicle of world events from Adam and Eve to the deposition of the emperor Phocas in 610. In his account of Anastasius (later excerpted in the great tenth-century Byzantine encyclopedia, the *Suda*), John pointed out that this emperor, "in his unbridled desire to raise money," had created difficulties for himself by overenthusiastically promoting the sale of offices. Anastasius almost went too far, relentlessly and all too predictably pursuing one particular tactic. Instead of protecting his autocratic position against those whose principal advantage lay in their clout and connections, or against a well-organized bureaucracy with too settled and certain criteria of appointment and promotion, the emperor, in single-mindedly selling so many offices, risked routinizing one particular way of securing preferment. As a result, Anastasius came dangerously close to limiting his own capacity for independent action. By standardizing one method of gaining access to office, as John shrewdly noted, the emperor permitted the establishment of what, in effect, amounted to another "aristocracy."[87]

The Balance of Disadvantage

Many of the complexities and confusions which characterize later Roman bureaucracy reflect a careful and often uncomfortable relationship between the maintenance of an administration which enabled a greater degree of control to be exercised over empire, and the preservation of some measure of imperial autonomy. In the face of competing and sometimes irreconcilable interests, emperors' strength ultimately lay in ensuring that the chances of their succeeding in enforcing their will (though never entirely guaranteed) could equally never entirely be discounted. Possibilities—however tenuous—mattered. In an uncertain world only emperors, as they repeatedly insisted, stood a chance of resolving what for the majority of those caught up in later Roman government remained a shifting set of tactical possibilities to be played, as far as they were able, to best advantage.

In 384 Quintus Aurelius Symmachus, then urban prefect of Rome, was required to adjudicate in a dispute over the appointment of one of the *archiatri* (state-funded physicians) in the city. In 370, elaborating a law issued two years earlier, Valentinian I had ruled that a new appointee should be selected by a vote of existing officeholders and be counted the most junior in order of precedence.[88] But in 384, when a vacancy arose, one John, claiming to have once been a doctor at court, petitioned for the post and the second-most-senior rank. In support of his application he presented a special imperial grant of title. The doctors appealed to Symmachus. Some were prepared to compromise, suggesting that John might be accorded a seniority which took into account his years of service to the emperor. Others argued that his grant clearly contravened previous legislation. In the background was the suspicion that John's *curriculum vitae* might itself be a forgery. Asked to provide proof of his time in the palace, he claimed that his documents of appointment *(codicilli)* had been stolen when his house was burgled. In such a situation, faced with apparently contradictory imperial pronouncements and the possibility that John's grant of title might not be genuine, Symmachus refused to adjudicate. He referred the whole matter to Valentinian II. He closed his covering letter by deferentially explaining his failure to decide the issue: "Therefore, disturbed by these uncertainties and venturing neither to quash the decree of your divine father nor to counter a particular imperial grant, I have left the final decision in this case to the divine judgment of your godhead; I have appended the depositions of the parties involved and I await what your royal counsels may determine."[89]

A similar problem arose in the case of a disputed appointment to the position of *tribunus suarii fori* (the official in charge of the pig market in Rome). A candidate, again with a special grant of imperial title, demanded that he be confirmed in office without delay. The incumbent, who according to Symmachus was now an old man, "relying on a law which has prescribed specific times for these posts," refused to resign. In this case Symmachus upheld the force of the special imperial grant. But he was also careful to refer the general issue to the emperor: "I decided to consult the sacred oracle of your godhead: Is it right to uphold the law and to allow new appointments as tribunes to be delayed, or rather, putting my loyalty to you first, should the old appointees be removed from office?"[90]

The unwillingness or inability of high officials independently to resolve inconsistencies by the application of a standard set of recognized rules was key to the maintenance of imperial influence within later Roman bureaucracy. It drew attention to the central importance of emperors' decisions in establishing rights or conferring legitimacy. Even powerful aristocrats like Symmachus were not prepared to risk wrongly second-guessing imperial intentions or incorrectly dismissing as a forgery an authentic document. As the emperors Leo and Anthemius noted in 468 at the opening of a long and detailed ruling on property law, it was "in the nature of imperial majesty" that it should "by unlocking ambiguity issue decrees which are to be followed."[91] The superiority of imperial pronouncements was not to be doubted. They proclaimed their own sanctity: "sacred" documents issued from the "imperial oracle."[92] In 470 Leo emphasized to his *magister officiorum* that the imperial signature was always to be written in a specially manufactured purple ink.[93] Edicts sent to the empire's cities were read out publicly, often in the theater. They had a dramatic effect. According to John Chrysostom, a normally rowdy audience stood in silence, straining to hear the sacred commands, fearing what they might contain. In furthering his family's claim to a hereditary priesthood in Panopolis, Ammon, more confident than his brother of being able to secure success locally, reported to his mother that he expected the high priest in Alexandria to give way once he had received a copy of Diocletian's ruling. "Nothing prevails against the letter of Diocletian . . . now also [the high priest himself] in fear awaits the imperial document." Basil, bishop of Caesarea, writing to a friend in the early 360s, joked that he treated the latter's previous letter as an imperial missive: "I paid it due reverence as if it were some proclamation from the emperor, and when I broke the seal, I stood in awe at the sight of it."[94]

As urban prefect in Rome, Symmachus, awestruck or not, was even wary of contradicting special imperial grants which he strongly suspected had been illegally obtained. In dealing with a request from the *mancipes salinarum* for some relief from their public obligations, Symmachus found that a number of *mancipes* (who for an annual fee contracted for the working of the salt pans at Ostia) had already obtained exemptions from the emperor. The validity of these concessions was open to question. They had allegedly been issued as a result of the influence *(suffragium)* of Macedonius, *comes sacrarum largitionum* in 380 and *magister officiorum* in 383. But whatever his own views on the merits of the case, as in the matter of John's claim to be appointed as one of the *archiatri*, Symmachus was not prepared to deal with the matter definitively. Before summarizing the issues for Valentinian II, he carefully remarked, no doubt by way of surety, that "it is open only to your clemency to revoke rescripts unfairly issued."[95]

Symmachus' refusal to decide finally on the force of apparently illegally obtained imperial rulings deserves some sympathy. After all, the emperor might have known, and even approved, of Macedonius' actions. In response to queries from even their highest-ranking subordinates, emperors themselves did not always offer a clear-cut resolution. In an edict issued in 428 to Proculus, urban prefect of Constantinople, perhaps replying to a similar query to that posed by Symmachus a generation before in Rome, Theodosius II and Valentinian III ruled:

> If, contrary to the scope of this decree, any general grant of imperial favor or any specific decision concerning an immunity should have been procured by any department, person, association, or profession, it shall have no force. But if such grants have been presented and if it should be the case that they have also been accepted by the most honorable [senatorial] order, they may again be considered, whenever appropriate.[96]

In such circumstances, the risks for any officeholder of making the wrong decision were great. Even suspicion that an official was acting contrary to imperial interest, as the eastern praetorian prefect Flavius Philippus found to his fatal cost, was enough to ensure disgrace, tempered in this particular case only by the extravagant praises of a contrite emperor, loudly repentant once Philippus was safely dead. But not even the permanence of an imperial apology could be guaranteed. Despite Constantius II's insistence that the prefect's virtues should be remembered forever, within fifty years of its public display in Ephesus the grand inscription in his honor had been turned upside down and reused as a paving slab.[97]

These difficulties and doubts (on all sides) were exaggerated in the pressurized atmosphere of a highly centralized court. Imperial inaction, ignorance, or incompetence were frequently portrayed in Ammianus Marcellinus' penetrating account of fourth-century emperors as the result of faulty sources, deliberate misinformation, or the lack of reliable reports. As the Romanus affair in North Africa neatly illustrated, imperial power could sometimes be thwarted by officials who flagrantly disobeyed clear instructions or who deliberately blocked reports on their activities. At court, informers were always ready to play on fears that even seemingly dependable officials could not always be trusted. Yet the reliability of informers and their information was also ever open to doubt. It was always possible that they had been motivated by the hope of reward or advancement.[98]

The truth of some matters was always difficult to determine. In the aftermath of the fall to the Persians in 359 of the fortress town of Amida (on the Tigris River in far western Turkey), the general Ursicinus was rumored to be responsible for the loss. A commission was set up to investigate the allegation, but was (at least according to Ammianus, a strong supporter of the general) so influenced by the *praepositus sacri cubiculi* Eusebius that it "veered away from the truth, and closely scrutinized some minor matters far removed from its proper business." Ursicinus' reaction was uncompromising. He let it be known that, as far as he was concerned, the emperor, "so long as he bemoans what he has learned from fraudulent reports to have happened in Amida, and so long as he is influenced by the opinion of eunuchs, not even he in person with all the finest troops in his army will be able next spring to prevent the break up of Mesopotamia." These words were duly reported to Constantius II. The emperor, "without investigating the issues or allowing any opportunity for the matters which had been kept from him to be brought into the open," immediately ordered Ursicinus to resign his commission.[99]

For Ammianus Marcellinus, such dangerous uncertainties powerfully dominated the relationship between an emperor and his officials. Some courtiers like Flavius Eupraxius might deserve praise for their frankness in the face of imperial anger; but equally emperors could sometimes be misled by a too-easy willingness to follow the advice of those who surrounded them. Constantius II was said by Ammianus to have relied on two officials in particular to keep him informed: Paul, a *notarius,* known as "the chain"; and Mercurius, a *rationalis,* dubbed the "Count of Dreams."

> Paul was surnamed *catena* because he was unbreakable in linking together series of false accusations, deploying himself in an amazing variety of schemes, just as some expert wrestlers in their bouts are accustomed to display excessive skill. Mercurius was called *comes somniorum* because, like a slinking, snarling dog, vicious within but submissively wagging its tail, he would frequently join the company at banquets and meetings. If anyone had mentioned to a friend something which he had seen in his sleep (when nature wanders more freely), Mercurius would give it a more sinister gloss with his poisonous skills and pour it into the wide-open ears of the emperor.[100]

Paul's influence did not last. To Ammianus' approval he was burned alive as part of the purge of palace officials which followed Julian's entry into Constantinople in 361.[101] But for all his deep-seated dislike of men like Paul and Mercurius, Ammianus was also acutely aware of the paradox that emperors who acted successfully to prevent too great a degree of independence in their subordinates might also, as a result, ignore, distrust, or simply discourage accurate and honest advice. Concluding a catalogue of some of Valentinian I's more savage and arbitrary behavior, Ammianus wryly commented: "Some emperors therefore commit these and similarly unrestrained acts with a lofty disdain because they do not permit their friends any opportunity of correcting their ill-conceived thoughts and deeds."[102]

In 355 Silvanus, the infantry commander at Cologne, became the center of a complex plot. As in the Romanus affair, its intricacies are important in Ammianus' portrayal of imperial power. Dynamius, a minor official at court, had sometime previously requested from Silvanus letters of recommendation (*commendationes*). He then expunged the writing, leaving only Silvanus' signature. Above it Dynamius wrote a new text indicating that Silvanus was relying on officials at Milan to support his leadership of a revolt. The praetorian prefect of Gaul (later alleged to have been aware of the deception), presenting himself to Constantius II "as a most vigilant guardian of his safety," showed him this letter in private. The emperor immediately ordered Silvanus' arrest and recall. Several further forgeries eventually led to a closer scrutiny of the documents. Ammianus continues: "On examining the writing more carefully and discovering a sort of shadow of the previous markings, what had happened was understood: that the earlier text had been altered and, in accordance with the aim of this patched-together forgery, other material had been added, quite different from that which Silvanus had dictated." But by then, Silvanus, learning that he had been disgraced, had decided (although it had never been his intention) that he had no option but to revolt. In Ammianus' neatly constructed version of this usurpation, Constantius II was committed to a series of actions by forged documents on which he had mistakenly relied; Silvanus was committed to rebellion by documents he had never seen. Only Silvanus' death finally expunged both their mistakes.[103]

The delight of Ammianus' tale lies in the duping of an emperor by his officials. In Constantinople, more sinister tales of illicit influence by the powerful were part of the currency of a court society. At the beginning of the fifth century, Eudoxia's influence with her husband

Arcadius was alleged to have played a key role in securing the exile of John Chrysostom.[104] Similarly, in the theological disputes of the late 350s, Constantius II, apparently "won over most of all by the women" in the imperial household, supported Basil, bishop of Ancyra, and ordered the removal of a number of high-ranking churchmen (including Eudoxius of Antioch) from their sees. Basil, it was also claimed, prevented Eudoxius' appeal from reaching the emperor by seizing the bishop's envoy on his journey from Antioch. The emperor, eventually learning of Basil's illegal furthering of his cause, was said by the ecclesiastical historian Philostorgius to be "amazed and struck with grief."[105] There were also stories of the improper influence exercised by eunuchs who waited on the emperor in private. It was widely rumored that Constantius II's decision to execute his cousin and heir-apparent Gallus was the result of a whispering campaign by those who "while performing duties of an intimate nature" knew how to play upon the emperor's fears.[106]

Not all these dark tales were told by those aiming to blacken the reputation of an emperor by portraying him as too easily susceptible to the often ill-intentioned advice of those who surrounded him. Supporters (or at least those claiming to be so) also gave such stories credence as a means of explaining away imperial policies with which they disagreed. The emperor, it might be argued, had simply been wrongly advised. John Lydus was thus able simultaneously to praise Justinian and to vilify his close associate John the Cappadocian, by claiming that the emperor was unaware of his praetorian prefect's actions and behavior.[107] The early fifth-century ecclesiastical historians Socrates, Sozomen, and Theodoret attributed some imperial lapses in orthodoxy (as they saw it) to poor advice. In defense of some of Constantine's less praiseworthy actions (chiefly the exile of the anti-Arian polemicist Athanasius, bishop of Alexandria), Theodoret, in a learned aside, observed that even the prophet David had once been deceived by Ziba, formally a trusted servant in Saul's household.[108] Sozomen, Socrates, and Theodoret all suggested that Constantius II's support for the Arian cause was the result of the skillful wiles of deceitful heterodox bishops. In Sozomen's view, they had successfully turned an emperor whose natural disposition was to favor orthodox Christianity.[109]

Such stories, too, on some occasions must have been attractive to emperors. In the midst of the Nika riots in early 532 (in which some of the major public buildings in Constantinople were burned to the ground) the emperor Justinian sought to calm the crowd by acceding to demands that he sack his chief advisers. The dismissal of John the Cappadocian, the urban prefect Eudaemon, and the *quaestor sacri palatii* Tribonian offered all involved an opportunity to dissociate the emperor—unsuccessfully as it turned out—from the unpopular policies which some claimed had caused the unrest.[110] A similar attempt to detach himself from responsibility for another unfortunate incident was made in the late fourth century by Theodosius I. In mid-390 the emperor was widely criticized following the deaths of 7,000 people in the hippodrome in Thessalonica, modern Thessaloniki in northern Greece. The killings were said to have been ordered in retribution for the murder of the commander of the Gothic garrison in the city. The details of the summary slaughter, its causes, and chronology are confused. It seems likely that whatever imperial instruction was issued in Italy it was (perhaps deliberately) misinterpreted, most probably by troops on the ground determined to avenge their commander. For church historians like Sozomen, this bloody narrative formed the dramatic backdrop for the famous public penance of Theodosius before Ambrose of Milan. In this version of events, a sorrowful emperor bent the knee to a powerful bishop, seeking forgiveness for his anger, which had been the true cause of the massacre.[111] Others—equally determined to absolve Theodosius—claimed that he had been inclined to clemency but at a secret meeting had been persuaded by his advisers to authorize the retributive killings.[112] Even Ambrose hesitated to blame an emperor unequivocally. He was (by his own admission) ready to accept the "official version" of events: that Theodosius had countermanded his original instruction, but that the order had arrived too late.[113] The excuse was an old one. Constantius II was said to have sent a letter authorizing Gallus' release, but it, too, had been delayed (this time by eunuchs at the imperial court), regrettably arriving only after his cousin had been executed.[114]

Blaming others for imperial policies helped both to distance and to exonerate emperors from the consequences of their actions. Responsibility could be shifted on to those more easily expendable. But for all its attractions, such a tactic remained two-edged. While it might successfully deflect criticism from an emperor, it did so at the inescapable cost of promoting the impression of an isolated and gullible ruler overly reliant on the advice and opinions of others. Certainly—whether told to damn or to exculpate—these colorful stories of emperors seemingly at the mercy of their wives, eunuchs, heretical churchmen, or courtiers stand in sharply dissonant counterpoint to the splendid impression of unruffled majesty so harmoniously conveyed by imperial laws, images, or ceremonial. But one should beware too strong a contrast. The growth of a highly centralized system of rule (continually emphasized by solemn rituals and the frequent appointment and dismissal of officials) ensured that the court remained the glittering focal point of the late Roman political system. Above all, the concentration of the powerful around the throne underscored emperors' determination to retain a personal stake in the government of empire. It kept them in close contact with those whose own position remained largely dependent on imperial favor. Yet, against these clear advantages, a high degree of centralization also inevitably restricted emperors' ability to gather a wide range of information. It exacerbated the problems of long distances and slow communication. At court, it unavoidably gave considerable authority to family, friends, and officials.

Some emperors countered. They relied on highly privileged officers to perform special missions and to report directly on events outside the palace. But in so doing, as the Romanus affair starkly revealed, they risked being misled even more seriously by those purporting to give "accurate" accounts. In response, emperors moved, as far as they were able, to define and regulate the operation of their "trusted" agents and to threaten transgressors with harsh penalties. Of course, there were limits. Too many safeguards or double-checks could paralyze imperial rule. By turns, those who acted contrary to emperors' interests always chanced detection, and usually death. In an acutely imagined scene, Ammianus Marcellinus neatly summed up the difficulties which faced emperors attempting to police the activities of their officials. Valens, having declared his intention to act as a judge in private lawsuits, was dissuaded by the eastern praetorian prefect Domitius Modestus, himself acting to prevent any imperial scrutiny of a lucrative market in the sale of verdicts. "Modestus, with a forced and deceptive demeanor, declared that the minutiae of private suits were far beneath the heights of imperial concern. Valens, thinking that the examination of myriads of cases was devised to degrade the loftiness of his power (as advised), completely gave up hearing such matters. By so doing, he opened the doors to robbery."[115]

This emperor was fooled. Modestus was a shrewd judge of risks, or perhaps just lucky. The *notarius* Palladius (the powerfully backed, barefaced liar in the Romanus affair) did not enjoy such sound judgment or such good fortune. Following Romanus' fall from favor, among his papers was found a letter in which Palladius admitted that, in reporting to the emperor the situation in Africa and the grievances of the townspeople of Lepcis Magna, he had "spoken to the sacred ears that which was not true." He was immediately arrested. At one of the halting stations on the way to Constantinople, while his guards were at prayer, Palladius—grimly recognizing the inevitable—hanged himself from a beam.[116]

Holding a Wolf by the Ears

The later Roman Empire was before all things a monarchical state. The position of the emperor, so brilliantly emphasized by courtly ceremony and its surrounding litany of praise, was central both to its system of rule and to contemporary political thought. Imperial intervention (real or imaginary) at any time, at any place, or on any pretext could never be entirely excluded. Indeed, given the restrictions imposed by the vastness of empire, the slowness of communication, and the technological limitations of a preindustrial state, it might convincingly be argued that later Roman emperors were remarkably successful in imposing their will on the Mediterranean world. But such assertions should not be too crudely phrased. The exercise of imperial power in the later Empire involved the continual and often difficult negotiation of sometimes conflicting sets of interest and advantage. Emperors moved to strengthen and justify their own position by (for example) arrogating to themselves certain ceremonies, symbols, and language, and insisting on their exclusivity, and by ensuring that those close to the imperial person or loyal to imperial policy were well rewarded. Those who benefited (and those who sought or hoped to benefit) were keen to collude in the promotion of an image of imperial power whose continued efficacy guaranteed them further advancement. By contrast, those excluded or disadvantaged tended to portray emperors as misinformed fools or murderous despots.

Paradoxically, the same tactics which might help to secure an emperor's position could also weaken it. The concentration of imperial power at the center exacerbated its tendency to drain away at the edges of empire. Strong men in provinces far distant from Constantinople frequently could do as they pleased. Those who enjoyed influential connections were often able to deflect unwelcome inquiries into their activities. In the imperial capital, the confinement of emperors within a court society difficult of access increased their dependence on family, followers, and officials for information and advice. Emperors risked being trapped by the very advantages of centralization which had made both their court and the imperial bureaucracy attractive. Nor were these risks lightly to be dismissed. A brief cautionary tale contained in the Syriac *Chronicle of Pseudo-Joshua the Stylite,* written at the very beginning of the sixth century, succinctly illustrated some of the difficulties any ruler, in this case a provincial governor, might face in attempting to enforce his will against deeply entrenched bureaucratic interests. (Another story could no doubt be told by emperors of the fate of intractable bureaucrats.) Outside his headquarters in Edessa, in northern Syria, Alexander, governor of Osrhoene, placed a box with "a hole in its lid" for the deposition of written complaints. He hoped that the townspeople would communicate their concerns and grievances to him directly, without having to go through his staff. "And he wrote above it that anyone wishing to make something known, which he could not do easily in public, should put it in writing and drop it inside the box without fear. On this account he learned many things, for many people wrote notes and put them in it."[117] In addition, on Fridays Alexander dispensed justice, ignoring his officials and their fees, discarding procedural niceties, and disposing of any complex legal documentation. But in the face of what must have been strong opposition from his staff, Alexander's radical experiment was short-lived. On his departure, administrative normality was quickly restored. Local bureaucrats reasserted their control over the flow of information and the allocation of government services. In short, having seen off Alexander, they got rid of his box.

Emperors as far as they were able (and sometimes with greater success than their governors) also moved to counter the twin threats of ignorance and isolation. The continual rise and fall of favorites, the reliance on certain groups of well-tested officials who could be sent into the provinces on confidential missions, the brief tenure of most senior administrative posts, and the unpredictable shifts in imperial policy ensured that the advantages of loyalty could be broadly (if unevenly) distributed. New men might always hope for advancement, often by exposing the faults of those already in office. Importantly, too, emperors ensured that the penalties for flouting or misdirecting imperial power were severe and memorable. Just as the attractions of loyalty were both displayed and enhanced by the splendor of the emperor and his retinue, and by the ranks, titles, and praise lavished (at least temporarily) on trusted officials, the consequences of disfavor were also loudly proclaimed. By widely advertising the beneficial or punitive consequences of imperial intervention, emperors sought to maintain the belief that similar actions could be repeated without warning anywhere in the empire. Threats and inducements, and the hopes or fears they inspired, were vital to the maintenance of imperial authority. They helped to bridge that perilous gap between the concentration of power around an emperor and his court, and the equally pressing need for some effective degree of control over the empire as a whole.

The development of an elaborate and hierarchically structured administration was also an important factor in the establishment and maintenance of imperial power. It improved the collection and collation of information from all parts of the empire. It permitted the more effective enforcement of imperial regulations and the more efficient assessment and allocation of revenue. That emperors, of necessity, relied on bureaucrats to manage the day-to-day operations of government was also recognized in the tale of the governor of Osrhoene. However laudable Alexander's tactic of circumventing his officials by permitting the posting of petitions in a box, he soon found that he had to cope with a sudden surge in his workload. Without a staff to organize, control, and prioritize the flow of official business, Alexander was pressed by those in the city, and those who came into Edessa from the surrounding countryside, demanding that he give judgment "on uninvestigated cases going back more than fifty years."[118]

Alexander's extreme actions and their consequences neatly illustrate some of the central structural tensions which shaped later Roman government. For emperors, as for provincial governors, the clear advantages of government by bureaucracy continually had to be set against the threat that, in the face of such an impressive administrative machine, the range and extent of imperial power might be significantly limited. It might (as in Alexander's story) be channeled in directions determined by the information or advice provided by officials, or simply dissipated in an endless, labyrinthine round of obscurantist regulation. Both emperors and bureaucrats responded to these pressures by shuffling, often unpredictably, between competing concerns. Departmental rivalries were exploited by arbitrary shifts in jurisdiction and personnel, and by carefully ill-defined administrative duties. Officials' fee-income was restricted by the promulgation of minutely detailed schedules of charges. Personal networks within departments were weakened by the more powerful attractions of imperial influence or by the outright sale of offices. Appointment and promotion were based on a set of often conflicting and ambiguous criteria: seniority, merit, money, inheritance, imperial favor. Complexity and inaccessibility were countered by moralizing edicts decrying "the miasma of detailed computations confused with inexplicable obscurity."[119] Importantly, too, officials' dependence on fees as the main element in their annual income ensured that they remained highly and personally vulnerable to sudden turns in imperial policy. And in the face of such deliberate uncertainties, emperors made it clear that in matters of doubt only they could rule definitively.

By comparison with a modern state, the system which emerged was hardly "efficient." Faced with the confusing and often-contradictory imperial pronouncements on the diverse and changing responsibilities of officials and their departments, or on the various requirements for appointment and promotion, or on the different means of gaining access to the courts, it is often tempting to recommend ways in which the operation of later Roman government might have been reformed. It is easy, for example, to agree with A. H. M. Jones that the appointment of officials might have been better managed if the significant role played by personal connections and influence had been properly formalized. "If the system of *suffragium* had been rationally organised, so that the great officers of state regularly recommended candidates for the lower posts 'under their disposition,' it might have been a reasonable method of selection."[120] Certainly, any such scheme would have greatly enhanced administrative efficiency. But in so doing it would also have risked restricting the ability of all those involved to advance, undercut, and play off one tactic against another.

But efficiency is only one way of judging success. For emperors, the inevitable waste of time and resources caused by duplication, cross-checking, the transfer of personnel, the short tenure of posts, the uncertainties of appointment and advancement, and the arbitrary division of tasks had to be weighed against an ever-present threat of isolation in the face of a more compact and streamlined administration. For bureaucrats, whatever the costs in time, manpower, and clarity, it was also undoubtedly in their interests to ensure the maintenance of a highly complex set of protocols whose arcane workings were opaque and impenetrable for any but an expert long trained in their peculiarities. Similarly, there were clear attractions in the continued operation of an administrative apparatus which, while it offered the protective benefits of collegiality, well-ordered departmental structures, and predictable career paths, also allowed ambitious officials to advance their careers by a range of other, some markedly less formal, tactics. As John Lydus' autobiography makes amply clear, bureaucrats were not themselves always interested in upholding formal rules or routinized procedures. In an often hostile and highly competitive environment they depended for success on a much broader, and at times conflicting, set of strategies. In some circumstances, officials might recognize the superior merits of regularity or seniority in determining promotion; in others, they might give priority to those with connections, talent, or the ability to pay. Endless maneuvering between tactics and their varied combinations was fundamental to the institutional shape of later Roman bureaucracy. These possibilities and their combinations—inevitably seesawing between different sets of priorities—were of central importance to emperors and bureaucrats. There were limits to the level of order which both sought to impose and to the degree of certainty both found desirable. Predictablity is, after all, only one way of managing or exercising power.

Indeed, for all involved, loyalty or subversion, promotion or disgrace was often a matter of risk. The wide distribution of rewards (some undoubtedly illegally or immorally acquired) was important both in maintaining a broad level of support for the system as a whole and in ensuring a continued willingness among participants to play for the advantages to be won. Most expected that government would "give" if pressure was properly applied.[121] Even emperors expected to be able to cut through their own administration and make contact directly with individuals in the provinces. In that sense, centralization, the growth of bureaucracy, and the set of tactical combinations deployed to limit some of their consequences together offered benefits to emperors as well as to those who sought to channel imperial power for their own ends. Such uncertainties also helped to resolve some of the contradictions between the rhetoric of ideal government (with its emphasis on an open accessibility to all) and the less accommodating reality of everyday practice. It promoted the possibility that access to emperors or their officials was always available in some new way as yet untried. Where there are no fixed rules, no option can be definitely excluded; no hope can be definitively dashed.

Of course, there were both successes and failures. Imperial power could be unfocused, misdirected, or simply ignored. Emperors were sometimes deceived, just causes were sometimes stymied, dishonest officials were sometimes caught and killed. In the face of competing and irreconcilable claims, emperors' strength ultimately lay in ensuring that the chances of their succeeding in enforcing their will, though not always certain, could never entirely be discounted. Looked at from that point of view, inconsistencies and unpredictable changes in imperial policy should not always be understood as undisputed indications of emperors' weakness, a growing loss of control, or the result of irresistible pressures from powerful provincials, courtiers, or officials. Sometimes these shifts were striking illustrations of imperial power. For emperors, an ability to exploit uncertainty, contradiction, and ambiguity could be the very stuff of autocracy.

Above all, in the later Roman Empire the centralization of government and the expansion of bureaucracy entailed the negotiation of the threats and advantages which both posed to imperial power. Emperors and bureaucrats (with varying degrees of success) were continually involved in a complex series of compromises, concessions, and trade-offs. For both, if taken too far, subversion, division, and disorganization were potentially self-defeating tactics. For emperors, to weaken the bureaucracy was to risk undercutting an important institution through which they ruled. To strengthen the bureaucracy was to risk the erosion of autocracy. Emperors were further hampered by the knowledge that if the bureaucracy ceased to function or was too greatly impaired in its workings, administrative chaos (and their own downfall) would result. These conflicts and options were rarely clear-cut. The political history of the later Roman Empire was in great part a product of the disputes and frictions which followed the establishment and growth of a bureaucracy with its own particular self-interests and institutional pathologies, and its problematic relationship with the exercise of imperial power. This was a knife-edge game whose results were frequently uncertain and sometimes unpredictable. In an unstable environment, the survival of individual emperors as significant players chiefly depended upon their success in preserving their own position in the face of these competing concerns. For them, as the early first-century emperor Tiberius once remarked—perhaps ruefully reflecting on the story of Romulus and Remus—ruling the Roman Empire remained "like holding a wolf by the ears."[122]

Epilogue
Last Judgments

Parce que c'est une erreur de croire que le pouvoir consiste exclusivement à faire faire des choses, à contraindre, à exercer de la puissance: le pouvoir est souvent une gesticulation, un autoritarisme à vide, une tragi-comédie destinée à donner une haute opinion du comédien.

—Paul Veyne

In the mid-fourth century the holy Egyptian monk Theodore had a vision.

> While he was praying an ecstasy came over him, and this is what he saw . . . All the brothers were lying down like resting sheep, and an angel was in their midst watching over them . . . in his hand he held a very bright and fiery sword; he was dressed in a tunic . . . large medallions adorned this very shiny and very fine tunic; and his belt was a palm's breadth in width, it was bright crimson and sent out innumerable rays.[1]

Whether this is an accurate description of an angel it is impossible to say. (Regrettably, there are always limits to any historical inquiry.) But it is a remarkably good description of a high-ranking bureaucrat in the later Roman Empire. In the fourth century, even a relatively junior official was easily recognizable by his white, long sleeved tunic, his heavy, military-style cloak *(chlamys)*, often decorated with brightly colored appliquéed or embroidered patches *(segmenta)*, and by his belt of office *(cingulum)*. As John Lydus would have been quick to point out, high officials were even more impressively uniformed. On grand ceremonial occasions, the eastern praetorian prefect wore a cloak striped with gold, a deep-purple tunic, an elaborately embellished crimson *cingulum,* and was girt with a sword.[2]

Such splendor was an important part of the imperial court. Through elaborate rites, the "permanent quasi-liturgical drama" (to quote Sabine MacCormack) which dominated so much of late Roman public life imposed a magnificent order on the world.[3] Pomp and power were inextricably linked. Like the tetrarchs in the temple of Ammon at Luxor or Justinian in the church of San Vitale at Ravenna, these exemplary images of emperors were often surrounded by high-ranking officials. Here were men (in Corippus' memorable phrase) whose countenances gleamed like the "golden shining stars in the curving sky." In a similar image, for Mark the Deacon (the biographer of Porphyry, bishop of Gaza, whose skill at court had secured an edict ordering the closure of pagan temples in his see), the dignitaries who escorted the imperial couple Eudoxia and Arcadius at the baptism of their son glittered in their finery "like stars which have come down to earth." In the sheer brilliance of their appearance, these courtiers could easily be confused with the angel of Theodore's nighttime vision.[4]

Nor should Theodore's dream be considered an eccentric or isolated experience. For holy men, visions of the divine which combined the outward and visible forms of both sacred and secular power were an accepted part of their religious experience. The holiest might even appear to their followers, or their enemies, clothed like Roman emperors in royal purple.[5] Caesarius, bishop of Arles in the early sixth century, compared the gospels with letters issued by a distant heavenly king.[6] For John Chrysostom, the city of God was like an imperial palace, adorned with innumerable courts and buildings. Here the righteous would stand, "not in the presence of a mortal king, but of him who is immortal, the king of kings and lord of lords. They do not have a leather belt around their waists, but that glory which is inexpressible."[7] Christ in the awesome splendor of the Second Coming could be compared to an emperor surrounded by his retinue processing in full ceremonial dress:

> The men in golden apparel, and the pairs of white mules caparisoned with gold, and the chariots inlaid with precious stones, and the snow-white cushions . . . and dragon-shaped standards fashioned from silken cloth, and the shields with their golden bosses . . . and the horses with their golden trappings and gold bits. But when we see the emperor, we lose sight of these. For he alone draws our gaze: the purple robe, and the diadem, and the throne, and the clasp, and the shoes—all the brilliance of his appearance.[8]

Heaven remained a very Roman place. It had been foreshadowed in this world. The visions of saints and holy men held out to those who believed in their powers faint images of the splendors which were to come.[9] In the second half of the fourth century, a long poem written in hexameter verse narrated the vision of the Egyptian monk Dorotheus, a Christian mystic who, "sitting alone in the palace in the middle of the day," dreamed that he was transported to a heavenly palace, which in architecture and personnel was closely modeled on its earthly, imperial counterpart. In the audience hall he saw God surrounded by his courtiers. The archangel Gabriel stood next to a figure described in strict bureaucratic terminology as the "Lord's *primicerius*" (πριμικῆρος ἄνακτος)—head of the corps of *notarii* who staffed one of the imperial secretariats. As a result of this audience, Dorotheus was enrolled as a new recruit in heaven's palace guard. But his subsequent failure to keep to his post and his attempts to deny (even before Christ) his dereliction of duty resulted in imprisonment and a severe beating: "my skin was covered in blood, my flesh was lacerated, and my bones showed through." As a result of Dorotheus' disobedience, God ordered his dismissal but was persuaded to reverse his decision by the intercessions of both Christ and Gabriel. After further trials of his courage, Dorotheus' vision ended with the final confirmation of his commission; his uniform was strikingly similar to that worn by members of the *scholae palatinae* who protected the emperor in the Great Palace at Constantinople. "I did not have simple clothing . . . but I was wearing a cloak made for me from two different sorts of linen. I stood with a kerchief around my neck and round my legs I wore long breeches and a multicolored belt."[10]

A similar concern with courtly forms and protocol was central to a sermon in praise of the archangel Michael delivered in 535 or 536 by Theodosius, briefly bishop of Alexandria in Egypt. In attempting to describe something of the hierarchy of heaven and Michael's place at its head, Theodosius was drawn continually to images of an emperor and his court officials. Michael was God's "Commander-in-Chief" and "the governor of the denizens of heaven, and also the beings of the earth."[11] As a mark of his rank he wore a belt "set with precious stone of great price" and "a glorious mantle, of the measure of the majesty of which no man can describe." In a splendid ceremony, God crowned Michael, marking him out as an archangel. "And he set upon the crown three seals in the form of the Holy Trinity, and the similitude of His image was upon the seals, so that the Archangel Michael might continue to invoke God at all times on behalf of His image."[12]

Such symbolism was significant. The courtly scene on the Missorium of Theodosius captured for one official the memorable moment when, standing before the imperial majesty, he received his *codicilli* in carefully veiled hands, like a sacred object. These ivory document cases handed in person to senior administrative officials on their appointment were carved on their outer face with a bust of the emperor. On formal occasions they were exhibited between burning tapers on a blue-cloth-covered table. Together with the grand ceremonial pen case and inkwell *(theca)*, also decorated with imperial portraits, *codicilli* proclaimed both the legitimacy of an official's acts and his close dependence on the emperor for his position.

Importantly, too, at least in Theodosius' version of Michael, those seeking the archangel's help could be certain that his position on the right hand of God was permanently assured. Unlike the imperial court, heaven was politically stable, at least after the expulsion of Satan and the rebel angels. The new order was fixed and unchanging.[13] There was no risk that Michael might suddenly be replaced by another more favored courtier. "He is not an earthly Commander-in-Chief who will come to an end, and whom the king can dismiss whensoever he pleaseth, but he is the Commander-in-Chief of the hosts of heaven, and he shall endure, with the King thereof, for ever."[14] On this basis, Theodosius encouraged his congregation to pray to Michael and to celebrate his festival day. Here was a heavenly official who could be trusted to intercede with his superior. In a neatly constructed passage, Theodosius imagined an objector to his sermon who might argue that neither praise nor prayers should be offered to Michael, but to God alone.

And I on my part will make answer unto thee, saying, Thou speakest well; a faithful man indeed is he whose faith is right towards his Lord. But hearken and I will tell thee. Let us take the case of a king who has taken possession of a certain country, and who hath a vast number of soldiers with him; wilt thou not find among all these hosts one man who is superior to all the rest, even though the king is over them all? And if it happen that the king hath an affection for some individual

among these royal troops he will bestow upon him honours and possessions. . . . And he hath power to approach the king at all times, and he
is able to deliver him from every evil thing, and from every danger, and
he is such a valuable member of his body-guard that other folk find favour through him. And thus it is with every man who giveth alms and
oblations unto God on the day of Michael; for the archangel taketh the
sacrifices and gifts from his hands, and presenteth them unto God as a
sweet-smelling savour, and he receiveth commands from God concerning these men.[15]

Michael's superior position was confirmed by eyewitness reports. A
late fifth-century Coptic text known as *The Book of the Investiture of the
Archangel Michael* claimed to preserve the record of a vision of heaven
as experienced by John the Evangelist. In this version, Michael had
gained his exalted position only after the expulsion of Satan. At dawn
on the following day, God had conferred on Michael all the honors
and offices once held by his now-disgraced predecessor.[16] Another vision of John, quoted in a homily attributed to Timothy II Aelurus, the
mid-fifth-century bishop of Alexandria, offered a detailed account of
Michael's role in the administration of this world:

Michael goeth inside the veil . . . and casteth himself down at the feet of
the Father, and worshippeth Him, and doth not rise up [again] until
the Father hath accepted his supplications and until He provideth the
means of subsistence for men and beasts, and water in the river [Nile].
For all the angels who are over the Powers of the earth are gathered together . . . outside the veil of the Father [and wait there] until the Archangel Michael cometh forth from inside the veil . . . and straightway the
angels who are over the operations of the earth know what [manner of
crops] shall be upon the earth.[17]

It was Michael, like some high-ranking official in the imperial court,
who received instructions from God, transmitting them to his angelic
subordinates. On Michael's administration the annual flooding of the
Nile depended. Such important business demanded the closest con-
sultation at the highest levels. For Egyptian readers of these texts no
responsibility could conceivably be greater than ensuring the fertility
of the land.

Such striking parallels between this world and the next were not always easily accepted, especially by some Christians. In the early sixth century, Severus, bishop of Antioch, objected to the portrayal of the archangels Michael and Gabriel "as princes or kings, with a royal robe in purple." In Severus' view, close comparisons between earthly and heavenly hierarchies could only devalue the mystery and true splendor of the latter. Such representations, he warned, were dangerously reminiscent of pagan descriptions of their gods.[18] Emphasizing similar concerns at the very end of the fifth century, John, bishop of Parallos in Lower Egypt, wrote a sharp refutation of *The Book of the Investiture of the Archangel Michael.* John recoiled from its vision of heaven, finding it suitable only for heretics who sought to mislead "uneducated people." The Archangel Michael had, John argued, existed since the beginning of time. It was a mistake to think that, like some earthly courtier, he had come to sudden prominence only with the fall of Satan. Such misconceptions were the direct result of a dangerous foisting of worldly affairs onto the mystery of the divine. For John, it was important to emphasize the great divide which lay between this world and the next.[19]

Yet for many concerned with gently coaxing the great mass of the faithful across that chasm, such strong claims of incomprehensible difference (however theologically attractive) needed to be tempered. Indeed for many Christians, encouragement and strength were derived from a more accessible image of heaven as this fallen world reached perfection. From that point of view, it is perhaps unsurprising that visions of divine omnipotence should be shaped by dominant images of imperial power. In the fourth century, the poet and biblical exegete Ephrem the Syrian elegantly captured the problem faced by those who wished to talk of such things:

> For him who would tell of it
>   there is no other means
> but to use the names
>   of things that are visible,
> thus depicting for his hearers
>   a likeness of things that are hidden.[20]

The didactic use of metaphors was widely advocated. John Chrysostom argued that "human illustrations . . . while insufficient to describe the things spoken of, and unable to reveal even half of their true proportions, nevertheless suffice, given the weakness of the hearers."[21] In the third of his surviving homilies *On the Incomprehensibility of God,* John went on patiently to explain archangels, and to deal with the difficult business of their wings: "Their wings reveal, as it were, the loftiness of their nature. Gabriel, for example, is shown flying, not because angels have wings, but so that you may know that he approaches human nature descending from the loftiest of places and from a way of life above."[22]

The mundane was no more than an imperfect analogue of the heavenly. The brightest imperial splendors of this world were no more substantial than "stage scenery and child's play."[23] God's accommodation to the weakness of his creatures allowed them, for a moment, to glimpse something of heaven.[24] In his description of the Second Coming of Christ, Chrysostom was careful to distinguish his powerful and comprehensible imagery from the inexpressible and unimaginable reality of that mystery itself. "For then you will not see any pairs of mules, nor golden chariots, nor dragon-shaped standards, nor shields, but those things which are full of great wonder, and create such amazement that the incorporeal powers themselves are astonished . . . What language can capture that blessedness, that brightness, that glory?"[25]

But no matter how careful the caveats, views of perfection in the next world inevitably depended on the visionary and his views of this world. The shining New Jerusalem of the apocalyptic revelation looked, in many ways, like the earthly city it was designed to replace. Perhaps in response to their own experiences of dealing with government (and with those who sought their aid in preference to an official tribunal), later Roman divines were captivated by visions of an afterlife characterized by its ceremonial order, its careful regimentation, and its bureaucratic exactitude. In another fourth-century dream, Pachomius, the founder of communal monasticism in Egypt, saw something of that perfection.

> At the death of a pious man, three angels whose rank corresponds to the measure of the dying man's conduct come to fetch him . . . The three angels are in ascending rank, and the one of lower rank always obeys the one whose rank is higher . . . God acts thus so that those angels who come to visit the man may lift him out of his body with proper patience, and lest some high-ranking angels, being sent to take someone who is of low rank by his practices, should treat him according to

the custom of earthly authorities. These authorities act with partiality, impressed by riches and empty glory . . . but the divine powers act in all things in accordance with right judgment, in conformity with the Lord's command and with the merit of the works that have been accomplished.

Similar administrative care was taken with the wicked. Pachomius' vision of hell included pitiless "torturing angels" with whips who rejoiced at the torments of the wicked and received each new batch of damned souls, who, in their turn, were "classified for punishments according to their deserts."[26] It was something of this bureaucratic order and punctiliousness (even in the punishment of transgressors) which Pachomius' successors attempted to mirror in his monasteries. In their structured communities, the monks were like angels, "drawn up in perfect order, robed in white."[27] New recruits were regimented in prayer groups and work gangs. Their day was timetabled and centrally controlled.[28] This discipline was extended to the natural world, chaotic and disorderly after the expulsion of Adam and Eve from Paradise. In the monastery gardens of fourth-century Egypt, even the windfalls were to be arranged in neat, straight rows under the fruit trees.[29] It was Pachomius, too, who appeared to his successor Theodore dressed in imperial purple.[30] Such symbolism was evidently powerful, even for a monk who had rejected the world. Indeed it was that same Theodore (a man who appears to have been peculiarly susceptible to visions) who witnessed the memorable sight of a Roman official posing as an angel; or at least an angel dressed as a Roman official; or perhaps both at once.

A grim concern with the judicial violence of the Last Judgment, again combined with a fascination for its bureaucratic exactitude, was also central to an apocalyptic work known as the *Vision of St. Paul*. Its composition is difficult to date. The core may have been written in the late second century; but the final, revised form (or at least so the preface claims) dates to 420.[31] Certainly, the circumstances of the text's discovery—again in its own version—were remarkable.

In the consulship of Theodosius II and Flavius Constantius, a certain high-ranking man was living at that time in Tarsus, in the house which had been that of St. Paul; an angel, appearing in the night, revealed it to him, saying that he should dig up the foundations of the house and should make known what he found. But he thought that these things were dreams. But the angel coming for the third time beat him and forced him to dig up the foundations. And digging he found a marble box, inscribed on the sides. There was the revelation of St. Paul, and his shoes in which he walked teaching the word of God. But he feared to open the box and brought it to the governor. When he had received it, the governor . . . sent it to the emperor Theodosius . . . When the emperor had received it he opened it and found the revelation of St. Paul. He sent a copy to Jerusalem, and retained the original himself.[32]

This was an appropriate foundation myth for such a text. St. Paul's visions were greatly enriched in meaning, and made more immediately terrifying, by their explicit imperial associations. It mattered to the author (and to its intended readership) that an emperor could be imagined to be concerned with this account of the world to come and might himself keep the autograph manuscript—perhaps along with St. Paul's shoes—in the imperial library in Constantinople.

In his vision, Paul had been greatly impressed by the detailed organization of the apocalypse. Sinners were carefully filed according to their misdeeds. In a text which in many ways prefigures Dante's *Inferno,* Paul was taken on a guided tour of hell by a guardian angel who (like any expert) explained at some considerable length the principles of classification involved:

And I saw there a river boiling with fire, and in it a multitude of men and women immersed up to the knees, and other men up to the navel, others even up to the lips, and others right up to their hair . . . And I asked the angel and said, "Who are these, sir, immersed up to their knees in fire?" He answered me and said, "These are they who, when they have gone out of church, busy themselves with talk of issues which should not concern them. Those who are immersed up to the navel are those who, when they have taken the body and blood of Christ, go and fornicate and do not cease from their sins until the day they die. Those who are immersed up to the lips are those who slander each other when they assemble in the church of God. Those immersed up to the eyebrows are those who nod to each other in their malice and plot against their neighbor.[33]

Nor were these meticulously graded punishments meted out lightly. The heavenly tribunal adopted a well-regulated procedure. Each soul appeared before the Lord God, who commanded a recording angel to present in evidence to the court the (no doubt often bulky) files containing the detailed records of that soul's unrepented wrongdoings. Against a soul who stubbornly refused to admit of its sins, Paul witnessed a particularly thorough angel in full administrative action: "And the angel of the sinful soul came, having in his hands a document, and said, 'These, Lord, in my hands, are all the sins of this soul from its youth right up until today, from the tenth year of its birth. And if you so command, Lord, I will relate its acts from the beginning of its fifteenth year.'" But even eternity is too short for some bureaucratic minutiae. The Lord God, speaking from the bench—like any perceptive and slightly sarcastic judge unwilling to slow down the judicial process just for sake of administrative detail—ordered the angel to get to the point: "And the Lord God, the just judge, said, 'I say to you angel, I do not expect of you an account of this soul since it was fifteen years old, but set forth its sins for the five years before it died and before it came hither.'"[34]

The emperor Theodosius—if he ever did read this text—would perhaps have greatly enjoyed God's reply to this overzealous heavenly court official. Like any wary emperor, the Lord God was unwilling to have the exercise of his power limited by tedious and painstaking protocols. He was not prepared (as Satan and his supporters found to their eternal cost) to permit divine omnipotence to be threatened by the establishment of an independent celestial hierarchy. Angels, like bureaucrats, had always to be watched. Even in heaven, as Paul observed, God had to remain ever vigilant in order to ensure that the Last Judgment did not become caught up in unnecessary red tape.

For ordinary people in the later Roman world, caught between these dissonant visions of this world and the next, the exercise of power (imperial or divine) must have seemed even more coercive, threatening, and uncontrollable. In a series of sermons preached in the late 380s, John Chrysostom offered his congregation a truly frightening vision of the Last Judgment. In February 387 the citizens of Antioch rioted, pulling down the statues of the emperor Theodosius I and his family. Some were smashed and mired with filth, some dragged through the streets in a crude parody of a grand ceremonial procession. This was a defiant act of rebellion.[35] The countless thousands of imperial images which adorned the shops, temples, courtrooms, and public places of the Roman world demanded respect and veneration.

Those approaching the emperor's portrait were expected to adopt the same awestruck attitude as if they stood before the emperor himself. Fifty years earlier, Athanasius, bishop of Alexandria, had once imagined what an imperial statue (albeit one versed in the theological subtleties of Christology) might say if it could speak: "The emperor and I are one. For I am in him, and he is in me. What you see in me, this you look at in him. And what you have seen in him, this you look at in me."[36]

Theodosius' reaction in the face of such sedition was predictably severe. He ordered the closure of the city's public baths, theaters, and hippodrome. An imperial commission was dispatched from Constantinople to investigate the causes of the rebellion and to punish its instigators. In the days following the "Riot of the Statues," John Chrysostom delivered a (perhaps not altogether welcome) series of homilies which combined striking rhetorical images of a panic-stricken populace with a strong apocalyptic theme. John reminded his congregation that he, too, had been an eyewitness of these terrible events. He had stood in the silent crowd outside the tribunal waiting for news of the commissioners' deliberations; he had seen Antioch's leading citizens shackled and imprisoned; he had pitied their once-pampered wives and daughters who now groveled on the pavement in front of the court house begging for mercy. For John, the fear which ran through the city was a forewarning of the Last Judgment. The terror inspired by the imperial commission was a mere shadow of things to come.

> For I saw . . . fulfilled through these works that saying: "All the glory of man is as the flower of the field. The grass withereth and fadeth away" [Isaiah 40: 6–7]. For then indeed wealth, and high birth, and distinction, and the patronage of friends, and family, and all in this life were found worthless, the sin and the breach of the law which had been committed having dispelled all this help . . . Then, looking at these things, I cast in my mind that fearsome tribunal; and I said to myself: If now, when men are judges, neither mother, nor sister, nor father, nor anyone else (even though innocent of the acts committed) has the power to deliver the accused, who will stand by us when we are brought to trial at the dread tribunal of Christ? Who will dare speak out? Who will deliver them when they are led away to those unbearable punishments?[37]

In these sermons in Antioch, and in later series on the books of the New Testament, John presented a detailed vision of the universal judicial proceedings and penalties which would follow the Second Coming of Christ.

> There is a judgment, there is a punishment, there is a resurrection, there is an investigation into what we have done. The Lord comes on the clouds . . . a river of fire flows before him, the undying worm, the unquenchable fire, the outer darkness, the gnashing of teeth . . . we must be dragged to the mouths of the furnaces, to the river of fire, to the darkness, to eternal punishments, lacking anyone to deliver us. For it is not, it is not possible, he [Christ] says, to cross over from this side to that: "between us and you there is a great gulf fixed" [Luke 16: 26]; and even for those who desire it, it is not possible to go across and stretch out a helping hand; but we must burn forever, no one aiding us, not even if it were father or mother.[38]

These punishments (which make some of the more violent passages in the *Theodosian Code* or Ammianus Marcellinus seem tame) were to be carried out to the letter. Divine threats of horrific tortures were always to be taken literally:

> Do you not see in this world soldiers who serve those in authority, how they drag men about; how they chain, how they whip them, how they pierce their sides, how they apply burning brands to torture them, how they dismember them? All these things are but playacting and jokes compared to the retribution which is to come. For these punishments are temporal; but there neither the worm dies, nor is the fire quenched.[39]

The final tribunal was presided over by the risen Christ. The accused were called to give a full account of themselves. Charges were read out, evidence presented, and a full judgment with reasons delivered. The staff of angels was untiring; all in that "array full of trembling" would be processed; all evidence—"thoughts and actions and everything"— would be revealed. Time was unlimited; one day equaled a thousand years.[40]

In the terrifying visions of John Chrysostom, Pachomius, and Paul, this world would end in a chilling administrative apocalypse. In their finely observed detail, these Last Judgments presented their readers and listeners with a transcendent version of later Roman bureaucracy perfected. For many, the similarities between the ultimate tribunal and even a provincial governor's court (not to mention the awesome majesty of an imperial audience hall) must have been both immediate and unmistakable. Doubly so. These parallels lent a present and comprehensible reality to a divine mystery. They also lent heavenly sanction to standard administrative procedures. Angels might believably appear as bureaucrats. But at the same time (while recognizing the impossibility of solving some of life's iniquities and inequalities) the tension in these apocalyptic visions between these closely congruent versions of this world and the next also exposed the inadequacies and the limitations of the mundane. No doubt some saw in such images the heavenly validation of earthly splendor and the magnificence of the imperial court. Others, some perhaps with a finer sense of irony, might see in that comparison only an acknowledgment of the antithesis between the two. It is, after all, the differences which ultimately give both these images their power. Comparisons—as always—cut both ways.[41]

But however striking the parallels between this world and the next, lasting perfection in the delivery of justice and administrative services, which later Roman bureaucracy could never hope to match, remained the exclusive province of the divine. Heaven on earth was a dream sometimes fleetingly to be glimpsed in the visions of holy men or in the glittering brilliance of the imperial court. Only Christ presiding over a tribunal at the end of this world could offer justice to all comers. Only then could the possibility of access—however tenuous—be definitely realized. For many in the later Empire, the administrative and judicial perfection of the apocalypse must have been a startling and alien vision, inspiring hope and diverting attention from present disabilities. Perhaps, too, as John Chrysostom suggested, such representations of the world to come, albeit "crass and human," achieved something of their purpose to "lead those who are earthbound to an understanding of the glory of the Only Begotten."[42]

But for others, the contrast with widely accepted, everyday practice must have been starkly and disturbingly clear. At the Last Judgment, there was to be no means of mollifying, tempering, or avoiding bureaucracy. Christ's court would hand down a decision untroubled by clout, connections, or money. (Not until the Middle Ages were the faithful offered indulgences as a means of purchasing advantage in advance of the next world.) Faced with an arresting vision of a heavenly administration, unresponsive to the various pressures which might in this world hold out the possibility of influencing an official decision, John Chrysostom's simple question—"Who will stand by us when we are brought to trial at the dread tribunal of Christ?"—became a potent and menacing threat. This was an apocalypse coldly terrifying in its isolation. It severed the often fragile ties which held late-antique society together. It rendered worthless its currencies of power and influence. It nullified the means by which emperors, officials, and those seeking to gain access to government (or to avoid its demands) expected to get things done. In this heaven there was no place for the endless jockeying for power, influence, or preferment—sometimes uncertain, sometimes unsuccessful—which dominated courtly politics and the exercise of imperial power; no room for the bitter rivalries and protective solidarities which shaped John Lydus' disappointed account of his time in the eastern Praetorian Prefecture. No doubt for some in the later Roman Empire, imagining a world to come with an inexorable and inescapable angelic administration and a truly omnipotent ruler had its attractions. But from the point of view of those skilled in the complexities of this world, such dazzling visions of heavenly perfection must also have presented a sobering and, at times, a most unwelcome prospect.

Notes

Citations of ancient texts follow the scheme in Jones, *LRE* III 394–406. Abbreviations for modern journals follow *Année philologique.*

Abbreviations

Jones, *LRE* = A. H. M. Jones, *The Later Roman Empire 284–602: A Social, Economic, and Administrative Survey,* 3 vols. (Oxford: Basil Blackwell, 1964)

Stein, *Officium* = E. Stein, *Untersuchungen über das Officium der Prätorianerpräfektur seit Diokletian* (Vienna, 1922; reprint, ed. J. R. Palanque, Amsterdam, 1967)

PLRE I = A. H. M. Jones, J. R. Martindale, and J. Morris, eds., *The Prosopography of the Later Roman Empire I: A.D. 260–395* (Cambridge, 1971)

PLRE II = J. R. Martindale, ed., *The Prosopography of the Later Roman Empire II: A.D. 395–527* (Cambridge, 1980)

PLRE III = J. R. Martindale, ed., *The Prosopography of the Later Roman Empire III: A.D. 527–641,* 2 vols. (Cambridge, 1992)

Prologue

Epigraph: Jones, *LRE* II 563.

1. Brown (1978) 48.
2. Matthews (1989) 253; see too (for example) Demandt (1989) 60–61; Jones, *LRE* I v; MacMullen (1964a) 311–312, (1976) 206–213; Brown (1978) 47–49, (1992) 7; Callu (1969) 1–2; Palme (1999) 117; and the positive evaluation of the late Roman legal system in Harries (1999) 96–98. The perception is an old one; see Edward Gibbon, *The History*

of the Decline and Fall of the Roman Empire, 3d ed., vol. I (London, 1777), 424–425, 464–465 = Womersley (1994) I 359, 390–391.

3. MacMullen (1986a) 512.

4. On this point, see in particular the valuable discussion in Schuller (1977) 387–392 and the brief remarks in Ausbüttel (1988) 202–203. For a contrasting approach to the one offered here, see importantly MacMullen (1988).

Part I. Introduction

Epigraph: Hopkins (1978) x.

1. Περὶ ἀρχῶν τῆς ʿΡωμαίων πολιτείας; the one surviving manuscript also offers the alternative title of Περὶ ἐξουσιῶν *(On Powers)*. The Latin title by which the work is usually known, *de magistratibus populi Romani,* is an early nineteenth-century coinage; Dubuisson (1991) 55.

2. The biographical sketch which follows draws in particular on Bandy (1983) ix–xxvi; Stein (1949) 729–734, 838–840; *PLRE* II 612–615; and Kaster (1988) 306–309, no. 92, who provides the best bibliography on John's career, to which should be added Caimi (1984), esp. 7–16, 46–83, 111–124; Evans (1996) 44–45; Jones (1949) 51–53; Maas (1992) 9–10, 28–37; Barnish, Lee, and Whitby (2000) 190. *De magistratibus* is edited with an English translation by Bandy (1983), who summarizes the manuscript tradition and previous editions of all three of John's surviving works at xxxix–lxxiv; see too Caimi (1984) 85–111. References in the text are to *de magistratibus;* translations are my own adapted from Bandy.

3. For more-detailed accounts, see usefully Jones, *LRE* I 370–372, 448–462; Ensslin (1954), esp. cols. 2453–77.

4. *PLRE* II 70, 1206–07.

5. Kaster (1988) 307; Maas (1992) 33–34; Caimi (1984) 57–59.

6. Stein (1949) 287–296; Evans (1996) 114–119.

7. Av. Cameron (1985) 242.

8. *PLRE* II 614; Maas (1992) 35; Caimi (1984) 80.

9. Photius, *Bibl.* 80 125a (ed. R. Henry, Paris, 1960), with Caimi (1984) 46–49; Bandy (1983) xiv.

10. Bandy (1983) xxviii–xxx; Caimi (1984) 66–79; Maas (1992) 10, 34.

11. Despite no explicit mention, on the basis of John's remarks in 3.25 (as well as the tone of his whole treatment of the office), I assume that his final post was as *cornicularius;* so Bandy (1983) xxii–xxiii; Stein, *Officium* 28–29, (1949) 838–839; Jones (1949) 53; Kaster (1988) 308; Caimi (1984) 82; Morosi (1977) 106; for doubts, Maas (1992) 36; *PLRE* II 614.

12. John's often-complex attitude to the past is explored in Carney (1971) II 35–45; Dubuisson (1991); and particularly in the elegant study by Maas (1992), esp. 38–52.

13. 1.10, 3.32, 3.63–64, 1.42. John's learned digressions are appreciated by Bandy (1983) xxxii–xxxiii; Caimi (1984) 141–147.

14. Photius, *Bibl.* 80 125a.

15. A connection dismissed by modern philologists as clearly false; see Caimi (1984) 203–204; Carney (1971) II 37–39; Jones, *LRE* I 601; Maas (1992) 89–92.

16. Caimi (1984) 111–124. I assume that John's remark that Justinian "prevailed over both the Persians and [their king] the lawless Khusro with gold at first, and then when he started warring again, with steel" (3.55) refers, first, to the "Endless Peace" negotiated in 532 and broken by the Persians in 540, and, second, to the treaty concluded in 545 after five more years of war. Both treaties, as John notes, involved the payment of considerable reparations to the Persians. This reading brings John's reference to Justinian's Persian campaigns into line with the other events summarized in 3.54–56, all of which can be dated well before 350; see Caimi (1984) 306–308. For indications of the lack of revision, see Bandy (1983) xxxiii–xxxv.

17. Carney (1971) II 81–82, 166–169. John deals in passing with the main events of Justinian's reign when they concern his career or affect the Prefecture: 3.1 (legal reform); 3.28, 3.47 (perhaps reusing some of the material from his history of the Persian campaign of 527–532); 2.2, 3.1, 3.54–56 (a rapid review of various wars, including a summary encomium of the emperor, perhaps reflecting something of his earlier panegyric); 3.69 (brief praise of Theodora); 3.70 (Nika riots). The surviving text breaks off at 3.76; but the list of contents (*pr.* 2.15–16) indicates that the sections immediately following would again have referred to the piety of Theodora and described the plague of 542.

1. All the Prefect's Men

Epigraph: The Cabinet Office Staff Handbook, Part I: *On Becoming a Civil Servant* (London: HMSO Cabinet Office, May 1987) at 1.

1. This chapter and the next owe a substantial debt to Jones, *LRE* I 321–606; Chastagnol (1960) 187–388; and Stein, *Officium.* Their work remains fundamental to any understanding of later Roman bureaucracy. In thinking about *On the Magistracies,* I have learned much from Carney (1971), esp. II 77–153; Maas (1992) 28–52, 83–96; and particularly from the elegant explication of many of John Lydus' obscurities in Caimi (1984). Useful formal accounts of later Roman bureaucracy are

offered by Demandt (1989) 231–255; Piganiol (1972) 343–359; Noethlichs (1981) 37–48. Both Noethlichs (1991) and Delmaire (1995) provide first-rate surveys of the structure and responsibilities of the palatine offices, Palme (1999) of the *officia* of provincial governors.

2. John retired during the prefecture of Hephaestus, in office from the
autumn of 551 until late 552 (Stein [1949] 786; *PLRE* IIIA 582–583).
The precise day on which he retired and on which those next in line
were promoted *(promotiones officii praetoriani)* is taken to be either December 25 (the date given by Cassiodorus for the Praetorian Prefecture of Italy) or April 1, the anniversary of Justinian's accession and
the date on which the *aduocatus fisci* (the senior crown counsel) in the
court of the urban prefect of Constantinople retired; see Cass. *Var.*
11.17; Just. *Nov.* 47.1.1 of 537; *CJ* 2.7.26.4 of 524 as subsequently
amended by the compilers of *CJ*; Stein, *Officium* 33 n. 1, (1949) 838–
839; Bandy (1983) xxiii; Morosi (1977) 135–136. On the basis of *CJ*
2.7.26.4, I have preferred the latter date.

3. Jones, *LRE* III 174 n. 67; Morosi (1977) 144–147; Caimi (1984) 82;
Stein, *Officium* 25–29, (1949) 731–732 n. 6; *PLRE* II 614; and see *CJ*
12.49.12 of 491–518. For the raising of an official's rank on retirement, see *C.Th.* 6.22.7.2 of 383 and Delmaire (1984) 145–149. For the
range of privileges enjoyed by officials, see Ensslin (1942) cols. 2540–
44; Delmaire (1989) 138–146, (1995) 24–27; Vogler (1979) 154–159;
Chastagnol (1960) 120–130; Jones, *LRE* I 488–490.

4. *Adoratio purpurae: C.Th.* 8.7.8 = *CJ* 12.52.1 of 365; *C.Th.* 8.7.9 of 366;
C.Th. 8.7.16 = *CJ* 12.53.1 of 385; Sinnigen (1957) 38; Vogler (1979)
152–153; Avery (1940), esp. 67–69. *Codicilli:* Delbrueck (1929) 3–8;
Berger (1981) 25–31, 175–183; O. Seeck *P-W* 4.1 (1900) cols. 179–80,
s.v. *"Codicilli,"* with Grigg (1979) 112–118.

5. Delbrueck (1929) 235–242, no. 62; Toynbee and Painter (1986) 27–
28, no. 16; Kiilerich (1993) 19–26, 68–70; MacCormack (1981) 214–
221; Berger (1981) 177–178; and the detailed discussions in Almagro-
Gorbea et al. (2000). For different interpretations of the images and
date, see Meischner (1996) and Canto (2000). I thank Professor Jaime
Alvar and the Patrimonio Nacional, Madrid, who allowed me in April
1997 to inspect the Missorium in the course of restoration. In thinking about images of later Roman ceremonial, I have learned much
from Elsner (1995), esp. 157–245; MacCormack (1981), esp. 267–275;
McCormick (1985); MacMullen (1964b).

6. Kelly (1998a) 168–169; Jones, *LRE* I 566; Noethlichs (1981) 20–34;
Palme (1999) 101–102. *Agentes in rebus: CJ* 12.20.3 of 465–466; Jones,
LRE I 578; Clauss (1980) 24; Hirschfeld (1893) 423–433. Cavalry

ranks: 1.48, 3.2, 3.7. Fictive enrollment as soldiers: *C.Th.* 8.4.12 = *CJ* 12.57.4 of 372; *C.Th.* 6.36.1 = *CJ* 12.30.1 of 326; Stein, *Officium* 15–16.

7. Dimitrov (1960), esp. 353–354, (1962), esp. 35–40, 48–52; more generally on uniforms, see Delbrueck (1929) 36–40; Chastagnol (1960) 221–222; MacMullen (1964b) 445–451. At 1.17, John gives a detailed description of *campagi*.

8. Elsner (1995) 173–176; Kalavrezou-Maxeiner (1975), esp. 230–238, 244–246; Monneret de Villard (1953), esp. 85–95; M. Reddé in El-Saghir et al. (1986) 27–31; Deckers (1973), esp. 8–17, 25–28, (1979), esp. 621–47, whose suggestion that the procession converged on the niche I follow here. Some of the frescos were sketched by the Egyptologist J. G. Wilkinson, who visited the site in the late 1850s. Wilkinson's sketches are now in the Griffith Institute, Oxford. The existence of the canopy, suggested by Monneret de Villard (1953) 89 and Kalavrezou-Maxeiner (1975) 230–231, was challenged by Deckers (1979) 614–617, but has now been persuasively established; see M. Reddé in El-Saghir et al. (1986) 29, figs. 30–32. I follow Reddé's suggestion (at 30) that the canopy covered an altar or—more likely—an empty throne.

9. Barnes (1982) 62, (1996) 543–544.

10. Elsner (1995) 177–188; MacCormack (1981) 259–266; Barber (1990), esp. 33–35. Deichmann (1976) 180–187 offers the best description.

11. Av. Cameron (1976) 1–2, (1980) 536–539; *PLRE* IIIA 354–355; Kaster (1988) 261–263, no. 37. On the scenes from Corippus, see Av. Cameron (1975), esp. 137–140. Translations of Corippus follow Av. Cameron (1976).

12. Corippus, *Laud. Just.* 3.191–199.

13. Chalke: Mango (1959), esp. 30–34, 97–98. The mosaics are known only from the description given in Proc. *Aed.* 1.10.12–20. Augusteion and Justinian's Column: Proc. *Aed.* 1.2.1–12; Mango (1959) 42–47, 174–179; Janin (1964) 59–62, 74–76; Müller-Wiener (1977) 248–249. *Consistorium:* Guilland (1955) 107–108; Ebersolt (1910) 39–43; Vogt (1935) 45. The precise location of the principal buildings in the palace complex, including the *consistorium*, is unknown. For a reconstruction based on descriptions in the tenth-century *Book of Ceremonies*, see the plans at the back of Vogt (1935); but see too Mango (1959) 23, fig. 1; Janin (1964) 110–112; Müller-Wiener (1977) 229–237; and especially the discussion in Bardill (1999).

John does not indicate in which of the many splendid spaces in the Great Palace he had his audience with the emperor and received his *codicilli*. I have imagined this ceremony taking place in the *consistorium*. But, as in many palaces, there are a number of grand locations which may be used on different occasions for receiving dignitaries, ambassadors, and high-ranking officials. John's retirement ceremony might have taken place in the open air on the large terrace known as the Tribunal or Delphax, adjacent to the *consistorium,* or perhaps in the Augusteus, a large, impressive hall in the southeast corner of the palace complex; on these, see most conveniently Bardill (1999) 219–221, 227; Guilland (1950), (1948) 167–169; and more generally Hunger (1986), esp. 3–5.

14. Corippus, *Laud. Just.* 3.204–213.

15. Ibid. 3.245–253.

16. Ibid. 3.257–263.

17. Ibid. 3.164, 3.182–183, 3.244.

18. *C. Th.* 6.22.6.

19. Corippus, *Laud. Just.* 3.179–187.

20. Scott (1972) 441–445. For other illustrations of this "ample style" in official documents, see MacMullen (1962). For more general discussions of John's fascination with the details of administrative procedure, see Jones, *LRE* I 601–602, (1949) 52; Scott (1972) 445–446.

21. For attempts to decipher John's list, see Bandy (1983) 340–341; Caimi (1981) 322–349. See too Caimi (1984) 386–418 on the cluster of technical terms in 3.66.

22. Boak (1937) col. 2048.

23. John's κομποφακελορρημοσύνη is a stylishly self-conscious imitation of Aristophanes, *Frogs* 839 (ed. K. Dover, Oxford, 1993) κομποφακελορρήμων, one of Euripides' insults to Aeschylus.

24. Stein, *Officium* 20; Jones (1949) 47–48 rightly challenging John's chronology. In 3.35 (as in 3.2–4) John uses *adiutores* in its old-fashioned sense to refer generally to established members of staff; see Stein, *Officium* 15.

25. For the marching order on such occasions, see Aug. *Sermo* 66.1 (*PL* 38: 431) for a (much smaller-scale) provincial procession.

26. *C. Th.* 9.19.3 with Marichal (1952).

27. On the rank and responsibilities of the *secretarius,* see Stein, *Officium* 35–37; Morosi (1978) 137–138.

28. *CJ* 7.45.12; Th. II, *Nov.* 16.8.

29. On the displacement of Latin, see Barnish, Lee, and Whitby (2000) 202–203; Dagron (1969), esp. 36–46; Jones, *LRE* II 988–991; Liebeschuetz (1972) 246–255; Mihăescu (1973), esp. 144–147; Hahn (1907) 696–703, 712–714. Cyrus: *PLRE* II 336–339; Dagron (1974) 268–272. On the language of Justinian's legislation, see Honoré (1978) 134–137.

30. Just. *Nov.* 7.1.
31. On this passage, see Rochette (1997).
32. Jones, *LRE* I 601, II 989, (1949) 52, suggests that in the eastern Praetorian Prefecture, save for the Thracian diocese, Cyrus' reforms replaced Latin altogether, and that John's references to its use were to be understood as referring to a time before Cyrus' tenure. Given John's own account of the early part of his career, such a sweeping reform under Cyrus seems unlikely. At 3.27, John explicitly states that he wrote *suggestiones* in Latin; for the *personalia* he refers the reader to his previous explanation at 3.20. I assume that the two formulae quoted by John (3.3, 3.12) also continued in use. At 2.12 = 3.42, John states that Cyrus' decision affected only τὰς ψήφους—the edicts issued by the prefect and the judgments handed down in his court.
33. Dubuisson (1991) 56–57, (1992) 130–131; Jones, *LRE* II 991; Stein (1949) 732; Carney (1971) II 48 all offer unflattering assessments of John's linguistic ability. Bandy (1983) xxxiii; Maas (1992) 32 are more complimentary. For John's sometimes faulty philological discussions, see Dubuisson (1992) 125–130. For his literary sources and habitual citation of learned works, see Bandy (1983) 445–446; Caimi (1984) 147–199; Carney (1971) II 47–76; Klotz (1927) cols. 2212–16; Maas (1992) 119–137; Tsirpanlis (1974) 487–489.
34. *CJ* 12.49.10 of 490; for the date, see *PLRE* II 131.
35. Jones, *LRE* III 178–179 n. 94; Pedersen (1970), esp. 177–190; Noethlichs (1981) 88–94. In those laws in which such terms as *labor, industria, meritum, fides, probitas,* and *sudor* are explicitly linked with seniority, long service, or status it may be that some separate test of ability or competence was required. The clearest examples are *C.Th.* 1.5.8 of 378; *C.Th.* 1.9.1 = *CJ* 1.31.1 of 359; *C.Th.* 1.9.2 = *CJ* 1.31.2 of 386; *C.Th.* 1.9.3 of 405; 7.3.1 of 393; *CJ* 12.19.7 of 445. In other instances, the force of the contrast is much less certain; see *C.Th.* 6.14.1 = *CJ* 12.12.1 of 372; *C.Th.* 6.24.10 of 427; 6.27.23 of 430; 6.29.4 of 359; *C.Th.* 6.32.1 = *CJ* 12.25.1 of 416; *C.Th.* 8.1.2 of 331. In most cases, the distinction seems to be principally between those actively serving in their departments, as opposed to longtime absentees, those holding honorary positions, or those who through status or profession were not permitted to become imperial officials; see *C.Th.* 6.10.4 of 425; 6.14.2 of 397; 6.18.1 of 412; 6.22.6 of 381; 6.22.8 of 425; 6.24.6 of 395; 6.26.11 of 397; 6.27.19 of 417; 7.3.2 of 409; 8.7.10 of 369; Val. III, *Nov.* 30.2 of 450. In some cases, no more than service in a department seems to be meant; see *C.Th.* 6.10.1 = *CJ* 12.7.1 of 380; *C.Th.* 6.25.1 = *CJ* 12.18.1 of 416; *C.Th.* 6.26.1 of 362; *C.Th.* 6.26.14 = *CJ* 12.19.4 of 412; *C.Th.* 6.27.3

of 380; 6.27.7 of 395; 6.27.13 of 403; 6.27.16 of 413; 6.27.20 and 21 both of 426; *C.Th.* 6.28.3 = *CJ* 12.21.1 of 386; *C.Th.* 6.35.5 of 328; 6.35.7 of 367; 6.35.8 of 369; 6.35.10 of 371 or 374; 6.35.11 of 381; 7.1.7 of 365; 12.1.5 of 317; Val. III, *Nov.* 28.1 of 449; 30.1 of 450; *CJ* 12.19.8 of 445.

36. *C.Th.* 8.7.1 of 315; some further examples: *C.Th.* 6.7.1 = *CJ* 12.4.1 of 372; *C.Th.* 6.7.2 = *CJ* 12.4.2 of 380; *C.Th.* 6.8.1 = *CJ* 12.5.1 of 422; *C.Th.* 6.10.2 of 381; 6.24.7 of 414; 6.24.8 of 416; *C.Th.* 6.24.9 = *CJ* 12.17.2 of 416; *C.Th.* 6.24.10 of 427; 6.24.11 of 432; *C.Th.* 6.26.4 = *CJ* 12.19.1 of 386; *C.Th.* 6.32.1 = *CJ* 12.25.1 of 416; *C.Th.* 6.33.1 = *CJ* 12.26.1 of 416; *C.Th.* 6.35.13 = *CJ* 12.28.4 of 386; *CJ* 12.19.13.2 of 522–526.

37. *C.Th.* 6.27.14 = *CJ* 12.20.1 of 404.

38. *C.Th.* 1.6.12 = *CJ* 1.28.5 of 424; some further examples: *C.Th.* 1.9.1 = *CJ* 1.31.1 of 359; *C.Th.* 6.18.1 of 412; 6.22.1 of 326; 6.22.2 of 338; 6.24.3 of 365; 6.24.7 of 414; 6.26.11 of 397; 6.27.3 of 380; 6.27.19 of 417; 6.29.4 of 359; 6.30.3 of 379; *C.Th.* 6.33.1 = *CJ* 12.26.1 of 416; *C.Th.* 7.20.13 of 407; *CJ* 12.7.2.4 of 474.

39. *C.Th.* 6.26.17 = *CJ* 12.19.6 of 416; *C.Th.* 6.26.7 of 396; *C.Th.* 6.26.8 = *CJ* 12.19.3 of 396. Some further examples of limited tenure of posts: *C.Th.* 6.26.6 of 396; 6.26.11 of 397; 6.30.3 of 379; 6.30.14 of 396; *C.Th.* 6.30.21 = *CJ* 12.23.11 of 416; *C.Th.* 6.30.22 of 419; *C.Th.* 6.32.1 = *CJ* 12.25.1 of 416; *C.Th.* 6.33.1 = *CJ* 12.26.1 of 416; *C.Th.* 6.34.1 = *CJ* 12.27.1 of 405; Val. III, *Nov.* 30.1 of 450; *CJ* 12.7.2.1 of 474. On length of service, see *C.Th.* 6.27.19 of 417; *C.Th.* 6.28.8.1 = *CJ* 12.21.4.1 of 435. These laws are sometimes cited as evidence of career length, but they only establish the right to retirement with certain honors after a designated period. They neither enforce compulsory retirement nor indicate how long officials could, or were expected to, serve.

40. *CJ* 12.19.10.

41. *CJ* 12.20.3 of 465–466; some further examples of the regulation of department size: *C.Th.* 1.12.6 = *CJ* 12.55.2 of 398; *C.Th.* 1.13.1 = *CJ* 12.56.1 of 394; *C.Th.* 1.15.12 of 386; 6.27.23 of 430; 6.30.15, 16, and 17, all of 399; Th. II, *Nov.* 7.4.1–3 of 441; *CJ* 12.20.5 of 465–466; 12.57.9 of 402–407; Just. *Nov.* 10, 24.1, 25.1, 26.2.1, 29.2, all of 535; Just. *Ed.* 8.3.2 of 548; 13.2 of 539; and see too Pedersen (1970) 177 n. 52; Noethlichs (1981) 66. Number of annual promotions: *C.Th.* 6.27.3 of 380; *C.Th.* 6.30.8 = *CJ* 12.23.8 of 385; *C.Th.* 6.30.9 of 385.

42. For returnees, see *C.Th.* 6.27.3.1 of 380. For joint positions, see Stein, *Officium* 17; *C.Th.* 8.1.15 of 415; 8.1.17 of 433; *CJ* 12.19.10 of 470; for some exceptions: *CJ* 12.20.5.1 of 465–466; 12.33.5.4 of 524. For re-

peated tenure, see *C.Th.* 6.32.1 = *CJ* 12.25.1 of 416; *C.Th.* 8.1.16 = *CJ* 1.51.6 of 417; *C.Th.* 8.4.10 of 365; *C.Th.* 8.7.18 = *CJ* 12.59.2 of 386; for some exceptions, *C.Th.* 6.28.8 = *CJ* 12.21.4 of 435; and see Pedersen (1970) 184 n. 79; Noethlichs (1981) 100–102. For the prohibition on moving departments, see *C.Th.* 6.30.5 = *CJ* 12.23.5 of 383; *C.Th.* 8.4.8 of 364; 8.4.18 of 394; 8.4.23 and 24 both of 412; 8.4.25 of 409; *C.Th.* 8.4.30 = *CJ* 12.57.12 of 436; *C.Th.* 8.7.16.1 of 385; 8.7.19 of 397; Val. III, *Nov.* 7.3 of 447; for some exceptions, Val. III, *Nov.* 22.1–2 of 446; Noethlichs (1981) 97–100. For prohibited groups, see *C.Th.* 8.2.1 = *CJ* 10.71.1 of 341; *C.Th.* 8.4.21 of 410; 8.4.29 of 428; Noethlichs (1981) 59–63.

43. On the duties, rank, and privileges of the *primicerius notariorum*, see the laws collected at *C.Th.* 6.10; Jones, *LRE* I 574–575; Vogler (1979) 195–197. The full title of the *notitia* is given at *Not. Dig. Occ.* XVI.5, *Or.* XVIII.4.

44. The *notitia* is discussed in more detail in Kelly (1998a) 163–166. Both Jones, *LRE* III 347–380, and articles in Goodburn and Bartholomew (1976) provide helpful introductions to the complexities of the text. Brennan (1996) offers an important and perceptive understanding of the document as a whole. For recent contributions to the debate on the dating of the *notitia*, see Mann (1991); Zuckerman (1998a); and especially Kulikowski (2000), stressing at 360–361 that the original text of the surviving version of the *notitia* covered the whole empire.

45. The dioceses and provinces as catalogued in the *notitia* are conveniently tabulated in Jones, *LRE* III 382–390 and Map II; for the grouping into prefectures and dioceses, see I 371–374. The *notitia* does not include a separate entry for each governor, but offers examples for the various ranks; *Not. Dig. Or.* XLIII–XLIV, *Occ.* XLIII–XLV.

46. Only the illustrations for the praetorian prefects of Illyricum and Italy are preserved; *Not. Dig. Or.* III, *Occ.* II. The urban prefect of Rome shared the same *insignia; Not. Dig. Occ.* IV. The entry for the urban prefect of Constantinople is missing from the surviving manuscripts. For the formal trappings of the prefect's office, see Berger (1981) 25–37, 175–197; Chastagnol (1960) 201–203; John mentions the state carriage at 2.3, 2.14; see too Symm. *Rel.* 4 and 20 with Vera (1981) 152.

47. *Not. Dig. Or.* XII, XVIII, XIII, *Occ.* X, XVI, XI.

48. For the *officium* of the eastern praetorian prefect, see *Not. Dig. Or.* II.59–71 with Stein, *Officium* 57, 62; Chastagnol (1960) 233–240; Morosi (1977) 106–113. The *adiutor* is most simply understood as an alternative designation for the *primiscrinius;* see Stein, *Officium* 57–58; Jones, *LRE* III 172 n. 58. Examples of provincial *officia* are given at *Not.*

Dig. Or. XLIII–XLIV, *Occ.* XLIII–XLV (with some variations in the seniority of the *adiutor*). The eastern *officia* also include an *a libellis*, probably responsible for receiving petitions and perhaps for correspondence with other officials. On these *officia*, see Jones (1949) 48–49, *LRE* I 565–566, 592–594; Ausbüttel (1988) 186–192; Barrau (1987) 85–89; and especially Palme (1999). The civilian *officia* listed in the *notitia* are usefully tabulated by Seeck (1876) 335.

49. The schedule in *CJ* 12.23.7 (quotation from §2) modifies that of 384, which survives in part as *C.Th.* 6.30.7. The two texts should not be conflated; see the important discussion in Delmaire (1989) 146–158. The functions of the various groups of officials listed are discussed in detail in Delmaire (1989); for a brief summary, see King (1980) 142–146.

50. Littmann, Magie, and Stuart (1910) 29, frags. 1–7, quotation from lines 7–9; the schedule of positions at line 11 and following; limits on tenure at line 21 and following. For recent additions to the text, see Kennedy (1982) 41–48, no. 10; Marcillet-Jaubert (1980); and D. Feissel, *BSAF* (1992) 213–216, with discussion of the edict's date at 215. Matching fragments suggest that apparently identical edicts were inscribed in nearby Bostra (Sartre [1982] 107–119, nos. 9045–46), the surviving text covering the same parts of the edict cited above; at Imtan (Waddington [1870] 480, no. 2033); and at Salkhad (Dussaud and Macler [1903] 655, no. 35).

51. For the *notitia dignitatum*, see especially Brennan (1996) 154–158; for the *Codes*, Barnish, Lee, and Whitby (2000) 166.

52. 3.58–61; Joh. Lydus, *Ost.* 53; *Mens.* 3.20–21, 4.2, 4.58; Maas (1992) 30–31.

53. *PLRE* II 613; Stein (1949) 838. Sergius: Caimi (1984) 56, 224–225; Stein (1949) 838. John's reference at 3.30 is to the first-century B.C. Sicilian historian Diodorus Siculus 1.13.3.

54. *CJ* 12.19.13.2 of 522–526; Just. *Nov.* 35.7–10 of 535.

55. *CJ* 12.20.5.2 of 465–466; see too Noethlichs (1981) 64.

56. *C.Th.* 6.27.8 of 396.

57. *C.Th.* 6.27.4 of 382; *C.Th.* 1.9.1 = *CJ* 1.31.1 of 359; see too *C.Th.* 6.27.19 of 417; *CJ* 12.19.7 of 445.

58. *C.Th.* 6.27.9; see too *C.Th.* 1.9.2 = *CJ* 1.31.2 of 386; *C.Th.* 6.24.5 of 392.

59. *C.Th.* 6.32.2 = *CJ* 12.25.2. In this law I understand the reference to unestablished staff *(supernumerarii)* to refer to those appointed by imperial favor beyond the established numbers laid down for each grade, rather than (as in the Praetorian Prefecture or the *agentes in rebus*) to a separate corps of those waiting for vacancies to arise. This seems to be the view of Jones, *LRE* I 571; but see Dunlap (1924) 213–214.

60. *C.Th.* 6.27.3. For some other examples of careful compromises between influence and seniority, see *C.Th.* 6.24.3.1 of 365; 6.24.5 of 392; 6.27.8 of 396; 7.20.13 of 407; 7.21.1 of 320.

61. *C.Th.* 6.27.8.2; see too *CJ* 2.7.23.2 of 506; *C.Th.* 7.22.3 = *CJ* 12.47.1 of 331, with Stein, *Officium* 13; Pedersen (1970) 179–180 nn. 67–68.

62. *CJ* 12.19.7.1; for the date, see Honoré (1998) 173.

63. *C.Th.* 7.2.1 of 383 with Stein, *Officium* 7–8; see too *C.Th.* 6.27.4 of 382.

64. Zos. 4.52; Eunap. 57 (ed. Blockley [1983] 82); *Chron. Pasch. a.* 393 (*PG* 92: 776A); *PLRE* I 171, 746–747, 876–878. For the immediate background, see Cameron (1970) 81–82, 490; Cameron and Long (1993) 180; Dagron (1974) 255–257; Liebeschuetz (1990) 89–90; *PLRE* I 778–781.

65. Hedrick (2000) 128–129; Grégoire (1923) 151–154; Roueché (1989) 47–52, nos. 25–27, and 63–67, no. 63 (Aphrodisias); L. Robert, *Hellenica* 4 (1948) 51–52 (Side); *IGC* 290 (Myra); *IGC* 293*bis* = *ILS* 8844 (Sidyma); *CIG* 4816 = *IGR* I 1225 = *ILS* 8809 (Antinoopolis); *ILS* 821, Bruns (1935) 30–32, Abb. 33–34 (Constantinople). Tatianus was governor of the Thebaid in the 360s and prefect of Egypt, 367–370; see Lallemand (1964) 247–248, 251–252.

66. *C.Th.* 9.38.9.

67. Oliverio (1936) 141, §III line 13; Waddington (1868) 426; see too *C.Th.* 6.8.1 of 422; 6.26.17.1 of 416.

68. *PLRE* IIIA 404–406. Dioscorus' career and world are splendidly evoked in MacCoull (1988); see esp. 9–15 for a brief biography (quotation from 15) and 58–63, 150–159 for a kindly assessment of Dioscorus' abilities as a poet. The quotation comes from an hexameter *encomium* on Romanos, H12 in MacCoull's catalogue; the translation is MacCoull's at 69–70.

69. *PLRE* II 881–882; Maas (1992) 78–82; Caimi (1984) 257–273; Stein (1949) 371, 456. This Phocas is, it seems, to be distinguished from his homonym, *magister militum* in 528–529 and one of the commissioners charged with the compilation of the *Justinianic Code;* see *PLRE* IIIB 1029 and the discussions in Caimi (1984) 263–266; Guilland (1958) 276; Honoré (1978) 47 n. 66.

70. For the Nika riots, see Jones, *LRE* I 271–272; Evans (1996) 119–125; Stein (1949) 449–456; and the reconstruction of events in Greatrex (1997), esp. 71–72. For the rebuilding of Hagia Sophia, see Evans (1996) 216–217; Stein (1949) 456–460.

71. Bandy (1983) xliv; Caimi (1984) 90–91.

72. References conveniently collected in *PLRE* II 882. On these trials, see Maas (1992) 70–72; Chuvin (1990) 132–135; Stein (1949) 369–373.

73. Caimi (1984) 260; Maas (1992) 81.

74. Caimi (1984) 257–262; Lamma (1947) 86; Carney (1971) II 88 n. 16, 133 n. 16.
75. Maas (1992) 92.
76. Caimi (1984) 252–257; Maas (1992) 86, 92–96; and especially Av. Cameron (1985) 242–248.
77. References conveniently collected in *PLRE* IIIA 633–634; Stein (1949) 480–483.
78. John's criticism of Rufinus has been questioned on the grounds that all these reforms can be shown to predate his prefecture (*cursus publicus:* Clauss [1980] 45–46; Stein, *Officium* 63–64; *scholae palatinae:* Boak [1924] 60–63; Frank [1969] 49–50). Much ingenuity has been devoted to suggesting that John misunderstood the imperial legislation on which he based his claim, legislation which John indicates was originally included in the *Theodosian Code,* but omitted in a later edition (2.10 = 3.40). Stein (1920) 222–223, *Officium* 44 (and others listed in Sinnigen [1962] 369 n. 1) proposed that John had misread the consular dates in the legislation he consulted and was in fact citing laws dating from 341 or 346 (which he incorrectly assigned to 395 or 396 and associated with the fall of Rufinus). Vogler (1979) 134–135, 201 n. 192, 207–209 suggested that John may have confused Rufinus (praetorian prefect, 392–395) with Vulcacius Rufinus, who held a series of prefectures under Constantius II in the 340s and 350s (*PLRE* I 782–783). Delmaire (1989) 32–38 has argued strongly for a praetorian prefect Rufinus in office in 326. He further suggests, (1995) 76–77, that it was legislation addressed to this prefect which John mistakenly transferred to the Rufinus in office 392–395. But the quest for a single set of reforms may be misplaced. Given both the shifts in administrative duties and the pressure of interdepartmental rivalries, it would be unwise to insist on the permanence of any attested changes in jurisdiction, or indeed to presume that their first attestation in the surviving sources necessarily fixes the date of their introduction. In the case of Rufinus, it may be that, having served as *magister officiorum* immediately before being appointed eastern praetorian prefect, he retained some of the responsibilities of his former post. On his assassination in 395, these divisions were restored, perhaps in a law which set out the two departments' administrative structures and responsibilities more explicitly (or in a more consolidated form) than before. It may be this law which John read; for discussion, see Boak (1924) 36–37, 78–79; Clauss (1980) 50–51, 120–122; James (1988) 290–294; Sinnigen (1962) 373–375; Giardina (1977a) 16–17.

These are possibilities only. John himself is perhaps too eager to blame Rufinus for a series of disadvantageous changes to the Prefecture's responsibilities. Certainly, John's unambiguous assertion (at 3.32) that before the emperor Arcadius the *princeps officii* (the head of all the administrative staff in the Praetorian Prefecture) had not at any time been seconded from the *agentes in rebus* is (either by negligence or design) demonstrably incorrect. The practice was in place at least by 355 (Amm. 15.3.7–9 with Giardina [1977a] 40–42) and possibly earlier, perhaps in some *officia* dating back to Constantine; see Sinnigen (1962) 375–376; Giardina (1977a) 13–18; Chastagnol (1960) 219; Delmaire (1995) 110–111; Jones, *LRE* I 579.

79. Demosthenes: *PLRE* II 353–354; Stein (1949) 245. Marinus: *PLRE* II 726–728; Caimi (1984) 214–218, 223–227.

80. John the Cappadocian: *PLRE* IIIA 627–635; Caimi (1984) 243–257; Guilland (1958) 282; Lamma (1947); Stein (1949) 435–449, 463–483; Maas (1992) 87–88; Barnish, Lee, and Whitby (2000) 196.

81. For the problematic text of this passage, see Bandy (1983) 116, 297. For an excellent introduction to late-antique invective, see Long (1996) 78–105.

82. *Pomp.* 40.4. Plutarch's account of Pompey's male companion Demetrius is much less forthright than John's comparison might suggest.

83. The quotation is from Euripides, *Hecuba* 570 (ed. J. Diggle, Oxford, 1984), and nicely ironic for those aware of the context (Talthybius' account of the sacrifice of Iphigenia).

84. Briareus was one of the primeval giants, the son of Gaia and Uranus; see Homer, *Iliad* 1.401–404; Hesiod, *Theog.* 147–149; Joh. Lydus, *Mens.* 4.3.

85. *PLRE* IIIA 626; Stein (1949) 448.

86. Καππαδόκαι φαῦλοι μὲν ἀεί, ζώνης δὲ τυχόντες | φαυλότεροι · κέρδους δ᾽ εἵνεκα φαυλότατοι · | ἢν δ᾽ ἄρα δὶς καὶ τρὶς μεγάλης δράξωνται ἀπήνης, | δή ῥα τοτ᾽ εἰς ὥρας φαυλεπιφαυλότεροι. Also quoted with some minor variants in *Anth. Gr.* 11 no. 238 lines 1–4 (ed. R. Aubreton, Paris, 1972). In *Anth. Gr.* this poem is attributed to Demodocus of Leros (a fifth- or fourth-century B.C. author of a number of witty verses on national characteristics); but the pointed references to later Roman officeholding seem here to indicate a more contemporary (perhaps sixth-century A.D.) authorship; see Cameron (1993) 295, 331.

2. The Competition for Spoils

Epigraph: Handbook for the New Civil Servant (London: HMSO Civil Service Department, 1980) at 6.

1. The *solidus* (first struck under the emperor Constantine at the begin-

ning of the fourth century) was the standard gold coin of the later Empire; 72 *solidi* equaled one Roman pound (about 327 grams) of gold.

2. At some point in his first year, John was also selected to serve as a chief administrative officer *(chartularius)* to the *adiutores* of the *ab actis* (3.26). Depending on the precise timing of his appointment, John's tenure may have extended some months beyond the end of Zoticus' term in office and his own first year on the judicial side; see *PLRE* II 612–613; Kaster (1988) 306–307; Maas (1992) 31–32.

3. *CJ* 1.27.1.24–28; see generally Jones, *LRE* I 590–591; Morosi (1977) 138–141; Stein, *Officium* 19, 74–75; and especially Puliatti (1980) 59–82 (on the background to the reforms), 82–90 (on the administrative structure of the new Prefecture), 90–97 (on salary scales).

4. Jones, *LRE* III 89–90 n. 65; Stein (1949) 466–467 n. 4; Hendy (1985) 178–181; Puliatti (1980) 95–96, tav. 5 list the salaries cited in the Justinianic legislation.

5. Just. *Nov.* 102.*pr.* and 3; 103.*pr.* both of 536; *Nov.* 8.*pr.* of 535.

6. *CJ* 1.27.1.24; the senior officer on the judicial side of the African Prefecture was the *primiscrinius*.

7. The purchasing power of the *solidus* is difficult to gauge, and it fluctuated across time. The sixth-century figures quoted here (from Jones, *LRE* I 447–448, II 858; Patlagean [1977] 377–409, esp. 380–396) have no pretensions to accuracy. They are crude indicators of scale, nothing more.

8. *CJ* 12.19.7.2 of 445; 12.19.11 of 492–497.

9. There is some evidence that senior retiring officials might be paid a bonus, perhaps roughly equivalent to their salary, in their final year in post; see Stein, *Officium* 19; Jones, *LRE* I 591; Morosi (1977) 142–143.

10. Jones, *LRE* I 605.

11. Boak (1924) 38–41; Clauss (1980) 78–80.

12. See Chapter 4, note 20.

13. *CJ* 1.3.25.2–3.

14. Jones, *LRE* I 498–499.

15. Just. *Nov.* 23.3 of 536.

16. John's figure refers to the number of *exceptores* in the department at any one time (so Stein, *Officium* 18), not to the number of annual recruits. Following Stein, I assume that John's figure includes *supernumerarii*. Their number is difficult to determine. A law issued in 399 (*C.Th.* 6.30.15), prescribing the number of personnel permitted to serve in the *officium* of the *comes sacrarum largitionum* in the eastern half of the empire allowed for 224 on the established staff and 610 *supernumerarii*. By the sixth century, the number of established staff

had risen to 443; see *CJ* 12.23.7 with Delmaire (1989) 146–158. Regrettably, the number of *supernumerarii* is mentioned only in the first law of 399. If the total number of officials in this department remained roughly steady (at just over 800), then by the sixth century half of the staff was established. If the same proportions held for the judicial side of the Praetorian Prefecture, then—at least on John's figures—there would at any one time have been around 500 established officials and a roughly equal number of *supernumerarii*.

17. *CJ* 1.27.22–38; Stein, *Officium* 18; Morosi (1977) 138.

18. Jones, *LRE* III 173 n. 60; Caimi (1984) 45.

19. What follows is no more than a thumbnail sketch of the principal features of Justinian's administrative and legal reforms of the 530s; a number of areas (especially Armenia, Cappadocia, and Egypt) had their own particular variations on these basic themes. Useful overviews of Justinian's reorganization and its aims are offered by Jones, *LRE* I 280–283, 482–484, 494–495; Bonini (1989) 35–39; Hendy (1985) 178–181; Puliatti (1980) 30–34; Stein (1949) 463–480; and by various contributors to *Cambridge Ancient History*, vol. XIV, ed. Av. Cameron, B. Ward-Perkins, and Michael Whitby (Cambridge, 2000) at 574, 590–592, 613–615, 672. The administrative changes are discussed in more detail in Gitti (1932) 59–79; Haase (1994) 75–105; Justinian's legal reforms (as treated by John) in Caimi (1984) 292–366, whose understanding of John's references to *causae sacrae*, esp. 292–313, 351–359, I have followed in preference to Turpin (1982) 201–224. Bonini (1989) 17–18, 122–123 provides an ample bibliography.

20. On these ranks and their privileges, see Koch (1903) 10–33; Guilland (1967) 27–36.

21. In practice, since there was also a right of appeal from *uicarii*, litigants normally preferred to appeal directly to the superior prefectural court; see Jones, *LRE* I 281.

22. *CJ* 7.62.32.1 with Caimi (1984) 292–302, 344–359, esp. 354–357.

23. Just. *Nov.* 126.

24. Caimi (1984) 313–320; Legohérel (1965) 99–101.

25. Just. *Nov.* 8.2–3 and 5; Haase (1994) 27–31.

26. The basic scheme is outlined in Just. *Nov.* 23.3 of 535 (on the text and date, see Caimi [1984] 322–324; Stein [1949] 805–810; Jones, *LRE* III 136 n. 28). For the details, see Just *Nov.* 24.5 (Pisidia); 25.6 (Lycaonia); 26.5 (Thrace); 27.2 (Isauria); 28.8 (Helenopontus); 29.5 (Paphlagonia) all of 535; 30.10 (Cappadocia Prima); 31.1.3 (reorganization of Armenia with the upgrading of two of the four governors); 103.1 (Palaestina Prima) all of 536; see too *Nov.* 102.2 (Arabia); *Ed.* 4

(Phoenice Libanensis) both of 536, which promote the existing provincial governors to *spectabilis* rank but do not mention specific amounts for determining jurisdiction on appeal (for the date of *Ed.* 4, see Stein [1949] 466 n. 3). Four of these newly upgraded governors also had the right to hear appeals from neighboring provinces whose governors were of lower rank: *Nov.* 30.10 (Cappadocia Prima); 31.1.3 (the two governors of *spectabilis* rank in Armenia); 103.1 (Palaestina Prima). From these decisions, there was no further right of appeal. For the raising of the threshold for appeals, see Just. *Nov.* 103.1 with Jones, *LRE* I 483; Stein (1949) 469. One exception to this scheme is worth noting: if the magistrate at first instance was of equal rank to the governor (that is, also a *spectabilis*) or superior, any appeal—no matter what the value of the matter—was to be heard by the joint tribunal of praetorian prefect and *quaestor sacri palatii* in Constantinople (*Nov.* 23.4; see too 24.5, 25.6, 26.5, 28.8, 29.5, 30.10).

27. Just. *Nov.* 26 (Thrace); *Ed.* 13.1 (Egypt), see Stein (1949) 476–480; Jones, *LRE* I 281; Keenan (1977), (2000) 613–615. The *quaestor exercitus* controlled five provinces: Moesia Secunda and Scythia on the Danube (both detached from the diocese of Thrace), Caria in Asia Minor, the Aegean Islands, and Cyprus (*Nov.* 41). When he was based on the Danube frontier, appeals from Moesia and Scythia were heard by the *quaestor* sitting alone. Appeals from the other provinces were heard in Constantinople by the *quaestor* (if he was resident in the city) or his representative. On the model of the praetorian prefect, the *quaestor exercitus* or his representative sat jointly with the *quaestor sacri palatii* (Just. *Nov.* 50 of 537); see Stein (1949) 474–475; Barnish, Lee, and Whitby (2000) 183–184.

28. Some of the original competence of the *comes Orientis* seems to have been restored by 542 (Just. *Nov.* 157); the *uicarius* of Pontica was reinstated in 548 (*Ed.* 8); and a *uicarius* for Thrace was in post by 576; see Jones, *LRE* I 294, 374; Stein (1949) 747–756.

29. Just. *Nov.* 8 *Notitia* 1–48; Bonini (1989) 72–75; Jones, *LRE* III 116 n. 94; Kolias (1939) 54–64 with a useful tabulation of the various offices and charges at 56–57. As the list of governors indicates (and particularly the presence of the *uicarius longi muri* at §5), this schedule was issued midway through the series of reforms detailed above.

30. *CJ* 1.27.1.19 of 534.

31. Malalas 18.67 (ed. J. Thurn, *CFHB* 35, Berlin, 2000).

32. Jones, *LRE* III 142 n. 64; Stein (1949) 438. A fragment is perhaps preserved in a brief quotation of a law addressed to the eastern praetorian prefect Julianus (*PLRE* IIIA 729–730). One amount is recorded.

The fee payable to *executores* for delivering a summons was prescribed: "Thanks to an imperial decision, for cases up to the value of 100 *solidi*, it is decreed that half a *solidus* is to be given; if the value of the case is greater, then the fees are to be higher" (*CJ* 3.2.5 of 530). But, regrettably, this directive lacks any context; neither the court nor the class of litigants is mentioned.

33. *CJ* 1.27.1.20; Just. *Nov.* 8.7.

34. Just. *Nov.* 17.3 and 5.2 of 535; 80.6, 82.7, 86.9 all of 539; 124.1 and 3 of 544; *Inst.* 4.6.25.

35. *CJ* 7.62.32.2 (for *epistulares*); see too Just. *Nov.* 23.4 of 535. That the Prefecture provided at least some of the staff at court hearings is also strongly suggested by John's description of some of the joint tribunal's forms and procedure, particularly his account of the methods of time-keeping, which were the responsibility of the *primiscrinius* (2.16).

36. Just. *Nov.* 20.*pr.* with Caimi (1984) 337–340; Turpin (1982) 218–219.

37. Just. *Nov.* 20.1–4 and 6. With one exception (at §5): on the grounds that the governorship of Syria Prima had been raised to *spectabilis* grade because of its amalgamation with the *comes Orientis,* the provisions of the 440 law were agreed to apply. In the conduct of these appeals, the *epistulares* were permitted to share the administration of the joint tribunal's business with the *exceptores.* But it may indicate something of the tough negotiations between these two departments that this principle was not applied either to Phrygia Pacatiana or to Galatia Prima (at §6), although these governorships were also raised to *spectabilis* grade as a result of their amalgamation with the vicarates of Asiana and Pontica respectively (now redundant posts, which, like the *comes Orientis,* had previously ranked in their own right as *spectabilis*).

38. Caimi (1984) 364–365; Turpin (1982) 220.

39. Caimi (1984) 256–257, 359–366; *PLRE* IIIA 631.

40. John's weak pun is worth recording: καὶ χόρτον ἀντὶ χάρτου γράμμασι φαύλοις.

41. *C.Th.* 7.12.2 = *CJ* 12.42.2; see too *C.Th.* 1.9.3 of 405; 6.24.5 of 392; 6.27.15 of 412; 6.27.23.1 of 430; 8.1.2 of 331; Val. III, *Nov.* 30.2 of 450; *CJ* 12.7.2.2–3 of 474; 12.17.3 of 450. Jones, *LRE* I 604, (1949) 50 suggests that "absenteeism was rife."

42. *CJ* 12.34.1.

43. For this reading of 3.27, and particularly John's use of the term βουλή to refer to the *consistorium,* see Caimi (1984) 51–55. Caimi's reading of John is convincing; but imperial laws may themselves be more precise in their terminology; see Caimi (1984) 52 with Vincenti (1986) 63–66. The "temple of justice which is called the *secretum*" to which John also

refers at 3.27 is the prefectural court (as at 3.11, 3.65, 3.66), not the *consistorium;* see Chastagnol (1960) 381–382; Caimi (1984) 369 n. 166.

44. Caimi (1984) 56; Delmaire (1995) 44–45, 55–56, in part revising Stein, *Officium* 46–51, (1949) 737–739.

45. *CJ* 12.33.5 of 524 (quotation from §1 with exceptions listed at §4); 12.33.8 of 531–534; see too 12.20.5.1 of 465–466. On the *memoriales,* see Stein, *Officium* 8 n. 1; Caimi (1984) 430–432.

46. Jones, *LRE* I 605, (1949) 50 suggests that "pluralism was common"; see too Stein, *Officium* 17; Chastagnol (1960) 223–224.

47. *C.Th.* 14.9.3 = *CJ* 11.19.1 of 425; see Lemerle (1971) 63–64; Jones, *LRE* I 707–708; Fuchs (1926) 1–8; Chastagnol (1960) 284; Evans (1996) 27. On the Auditorium, see Janin (1964) 174–176.

48. Stein, *Officium* 18. Following his appointment to a chair, John is sometimes described as "an absentee"; so Kaster (1988) 308; Maas (1992) 35–36. But absentees were not entitled to receive fee-income, and John's complaints clearly indicate that he expected so to benefit (3.25, 3.30, 3.66–67).

49. *CJ* 1.27.1.42 of 534; see Kaster (1988) 116–123; Puliatti (1980) 86.

50. *C.Th.* 6.21.1 = *CJ* 12.15.1 of 425.

51. There is a possibility that John's enjoyment of the dowry resulting from his marriage may not have lasted as long as this. Married in 511 or 512, at the start of his career, John reveals at *Mens.* 4.89 that his wife married young and sadly died young. No children are ever mentioned. Unless the marriage contract stipulated otherwise, the legal assumption seems to have been (at least in some cases) that on a wife's death in a childless union half the dowry would be returned to her father or his testamentary heirs; see Kaser (1975) 189; Arjava (1996) 59. John is silent on this subject as well as on any subsequent remarriage.

52. *C.Th.* 8.7.7 = *CJ* 12.57.2 of 356; see too *C.Th.* 8.7.21 = *CJ* 12.59.6 and 12.49.7 of 426; *C.Th.* 8.7.22, 8.7.23 both of 426; *CJ* 12.59.9 of 470–474; 12.59.10 of 471–472; with further examples in Noethlichs (1981) 67. Stein, *Officium* 8–9; Caimi (1984) 19 suggest that here John deliberately misrepresented the legal position. Even so, imperial laws such as *C.Th.* 8.7.22, which granted amnesty to those in post who had gained their position without the necessary imperial approval, at least indicate that the argument of the judicial side was worth making, if only for the advantage of those who had already been appointed without *probatoriae.* Vogler's suggestion, (1979) 174–175, that 3.67 refers to *C.Th.* 8.7.7 stretches John's text, and its obviously contemporary references, too far.

53. The post of *matricularius* was not a separate official position, but was a

responsibility undertaken by one of the department's senior retiring officers *(princeps officii, cornicularius, primiscrinius)* within the context of their joint oversight of the department's personnel registers; see Stein, *Officium* 56.

54. The most important discussions of the internal structure of the eastern Praetorian Prefecture are Caimi (1984) 16–46; Ensslin (1954) cols. 2478–95, esp. 2488–94; Morosi (1977); Palme (1999) 105–111. Jones, *LRE* I 586–592; and Stein, *Officium,* remain fundamental. For a more detailed treatment of the arguments canvassed here, see Kelly (forthcoming b).

55. This understanding of the *Augustales* was first proposed by Jones, *LRE* III 172–173 n. 60, with minimal discussion. John's dating of these reforms may be faulty. Stein, *Officium* 43–44, noted that a law issued under Valentinian I (*C.Th.* 8.7.8 of 365) referred to *deputati,* the term John says was used to describe the fifteen most senior *Augustales* (3.10); but in John's defense, see Sinnigen (1962) 379–381.

56. Stein, *Officium* 34–36; Ensslin (1954) cols. 2489–90; Jones, *LRE* I 602–603; Morosi (1978) 129–138.

57. For similar sentiments in imperial laws, see *C.Th.* 6.10.1 = *CJ* 12.7.1 of 380; *C.Th.* 6.22.8.1 of 425; 6.27.16.1 of 413; 6.27.19 of 417; 6.28.6 of 399; 8.1.1 of 343; Val. III, *Nov.* 28.1 of 449; *CJ* 12.19.15.2 of 527.

58. These figures are impressionistic only, to give a crude and highly schematic sense of scale. I base these rough estimates on the model life tables argued by Saller (1994) 12–42, esp. 22–25; Frier (2000) 788–791 as most appropriate for the Roman world. For a perceptive critique of the limitations of model life tables as guides to Roman demography, see Scheidel (2001), esp. 3–11.

59. This passage is difficult to understand. The reading adopted (οὐδὲ γὰρ εὐχερὲς ἦν τὸ τηνικαῦτα, τῶν βασιλέων ἅμα τῇ βουλῇ δίκας ἀκροωμένων, τοὺς πάντα ἀρίστους ὑπηρετεῖν) follows an emendation suggested by Stein, *Officium* 43 n. 1; Caimi (1984) 420 n. 107, but here understood to refer to the *Augustales* rather than, following Stein, to officials already serving the imperial court. Bandy's reading (τοὺς πάντας ἄριστα ὑπηρετεῖν) essentially yields the same meaning, but without the euphemism.

60. *CJ* 12.19.10 of 470–474.

61. *CJ* 12.19.13 of 522–526; 12.19.15 of 527; Just. *Nov.* 35.1–3 of 535.

62. For traces of these disputes in imperial legislation, see the laws collected at *C.Th.* 6.28.

63. Stein, *Officium* 46; Teitler (1985) 270–271 n. 3; Kraus (1960) 45–47; Sinnigen (1957) 66.

64. Boak (1924) 78–79.

65. Stein, *Officium* 66–70; Ensslin (1954) cols. 2494–95; Caimi (1984) 23–24.

66. Jones (1940) 152–153, *LRE* I 236, 457; Stein (1949) 210–215; Caimi (1984) 216–218; Liebeschuetz (2001) 108–109; and especially Chauvot (1987), stressing that in practice the precise role and responsibilities of *uindices* varied from city to city.

67. John does not explain the link between *uindices'* activities and the loss of judicial work. Caimi (1984) 414–415 suggests that John's complaint should be broadly interpreted. It may be that in some cases *uindices* were able to resolve disputes before the parties resorted to litigation in the prefect's court. It may be too that the conversion of the bulk of land taxes into gold and the imposition of strict restrictions on compulsory purchase, both policies pursued under Anastasius, helped more clearly to establish some fiscal liabilities; see Jones, *LRE* I 235, 460. A similar vague connection with a decline in cases heard on appeal is made with the refusal by the praetorian prefect Demosthenes (in office 521–522 and again in 529) to remit taxes (3.42). If, as Chauvot (1987) 275 suggests, *uindices* were organized into a corps of officials attached to, or even drawn from, the staff of the Prefecture, John may also have viewed Marinus' reforms as a harbinger of the unwelcome prominence which the financial side and its officials (the *scriniarii*) would assume under John the Cappadocian.

68. *CJ* 1.27.1.24–27 with Stein, *Officium* 61–62; Morosi (1977) 112–113; Puliatti (1980) 89–90. On the elimination of the *princeps officii* and *cornicularius*, see Delmaire (1995) 115–116; Caimi (1984) 374–380; Kelly (forthcoming b), revising Stein, *Officium* 4–6.

69. *C.Th.* 8.9.2.

70. The payment of salaries en bloc to a department seems to be assumed by Justinian's legislation, which in some cases went on to prescribe the way in which the sum was to be divided up; see *CJ* 1.27.1.22–40, 1.27.2.19–34 both of 534; Just. *Nov.* 24.6.1, 25.6.*ep.*, 26.5.1, 27.2.*ep.* all of 535; 80.8 of 539; 102.2, 103.1 both of 536; Just. *Ed.* 13.3–4 and 18 of 539. Some degree of redistribution seems also to be implied in Procopius' polemical and highly generalized account of Justinian's moves to reduce bureaucrats' incomes (*HA* 24.31–33). For fees en bloc, see Maj. *Nov.* 7.1.16 of 458. For fines, see *C.Th.* 6.10.1 = *CJ* 12.7.1.1 of 380; *C.Th.* 6.18.1 of 412; 6.26.16 of 410; *C.Th.* 6.28.4 = *CJ* 12.21.1.2 of 387 with further examples collected in Noethlichs (1981) 222–228; Jones, *LRE* III 181 n. 105. For income to heirs, see *CJ* 12.19.11 of 492–497 (concerning *proximi*, the heads of the *sacra scrinia*); *CJ* 12.20.3.1 of

465–466 (concerning *ducenarii,* the highest service grade for *agentes in rebus*); *C.Th.* 6.24.11 of 432 (concerning *protectores domestici,* the palace guard). These were unlikely to have been long-lasting charges on the corporate fund: in 416 Theodosius II and Honorius ruled that *proximi* should serve for only one year; *C.Th.* 6.26.17 = *CJ* 12.19.6. The law of 432 concerning *protectores* specifically prescribed that only the income for the balance of the year in which the officer died was payable to his children or close relatives.

71. Stein, *Officium* 36 n. 2; Chastagnol (1960) 252–253; Kelly (1994) 161–163.

Part II. Introduction

Epigraph: Finley (1983) 84.

1. Chastagnol (1978) 75–76, quoting lines 12–22. The listing of dignitaries and their order of admission to the governor's presence (lines 4–12) gives this inscription its conventional modern title, *ordo salutationis.* For find-spot, description, and date, see Chastagnol (1978) 75–78; Boeswillwald, Cagnat, and Ballu (1891–1905) 47, and generally on the forum, 1–92 with an excellent plan at plate VI; for a detailed description of the *curia,* 32–45 and plate VII. Also on Timgad, see usefully Lepelley (1979–81) II 444–476; Fentress (1979) 126–132.

   Ulpius Mariscianus celebrated his appointment as governor of Numidia A DOMINO NOSTRO | INVICTO PRINCIPE IVLIANO (lines 3–4), phrasing which nicely echoes the inscription on the hexagonal base of the statue of Julian in front of the *curia:* DOMITORI HOSTI | VM INVICTO | IMP[ERATORI] (*CIL* VIII 2387, lines 1–3; with Boeswillwald, Cagnat, and Ballu [1891–1905] 65–66; Lepelley [1979–81] II 450, no. 13).

2. For some thoughtful and interesting characterizations of provincial government on which this thumbnail sketch is based, see (very selectively) from a now-substantial literature Nörr (1966), esp. 76–114; Garnsey and Saller (1987) 20–40; C. P. Jones (1978) 95–103; Millar (1983), esp. 79–84; Ando (2000), esp. 49–70. The "essential passivity" of emperor and central government is the insistent theme of Millar (1992), esp. 6, 10, 266–267, 270–272, 617. The importance of patronage to the maintenance of the system of rule is well brought out in MacMullen (1988), esp. 96–121; Millar (1992), esp. 275–276, 470–477; Wallace-Hadrill (1996) 296–306; and particularly in Saller (1982) and the essays collected in Wallace-Hadrill (1989).

3. Lendon (1997) 1–27; on the importance of fear to the success of Ro-

man rule, see MacMullen (1986b), (1988) 84–96; on the imperial cult, see especially Price (1984) and more generally on the political resonances of civic religion, Gordon (1990); Beard, North, and Price (1998) I 206–210, 348–363.

4. Pflaum (1950) 67; Brown (1978) 48.

5. Lendon (1997) 6–7.

6. Brown (1992) 12.

7. Lendon (1997) 7.

8. In thinking about the third century, I have found—again very selectively from a substantial literature—the following particularly helpful, Callu (1969), esp. 314–343, 475–483; Christol (1986), esp. 35–54; MacMullen (1976), esp. 195–213; Malcus (1969) 233–237; Drinkwater (1987) 239–256; Potter (1990), esp. 3–18; Hopkins (1980), esp. 116–124. On the imperial budget, see usefully Duncan-Jones (1994) 33–46.

9. For estimates of the numbers of the different kinds of personnel involved, see for example MacMullen (1988) 144; Garnsey and Saller (1987) 26; Pflaum (1950) 102; Duncan-Jones (1994) 37; Eck (1980) 16; Austin and Rankov (1995) 151–152; Palme (1999) 100–101.

10. Jones, *LRE* III 341–342 n. 44 with revisions proposed by Heather (1994) 18–20, (1998) 189; see too MacMullen (1988) 144; Bagnall (1993) 66. These figures might be further increased if older, much higher estimates for the staff of the Praetorian and Urban Prefectures were included; see Stein, *Officium* 18; Chastagnol (1960) 228; Morosi (1977) 138. Jones's estimate of 1,000 officials staffing each of these departments seems too low, especially if John Lydus' remark (at 3.66) that there were 1,000 *exceptores* on the judicial side of the eastern Praetorian Prefecture can be taken as reliable.

11. MacMullen (1976) 100–101.

12. Jones, *LRE* I 406.

13. Noethlichs (1981) 3–18, 34–37 offers an instructive comparison between later Roman and modern Western bureaucracies.

14. Heather (1994) 11–25, quotation on 20, (1998) 195–197; see too Teitler (1985) 64–68; Vogler (1979) 197; Jones, *LRE* I, 547–552; and the important discussions in Dagron (1974) 147–190, esp. 154–163; Chastagnol (1992) 233–291.

15. Matthews (1975) 101–107, quotation on 102.

16. Brown (1992) 9–34, quotation on 33, perceptively recognizes this resilience to change and its importance; see too the useful discussion of the impact of these changes on local elites in Heather (1994) 25–33, to be read alongside Whittow (1990) and Liebeschuetz (2001) 104–202.

3. Standing in Line

Epigraph: Hansard (Commons), vol. 144 at col. 990.

1. Cassius Dio 69.6.3; see Millar (1992) 3–4, 546. The story is a common one; see Plu. *Demetr.* 42.3–4, *Mor.* 179C–D = *Regnum et imperatorum apophthegmata* Philip §31; Stobaeus, *Anth.* 3.13.48 (ed. O. Hense, Berlin, 1894). It also has a long afterlife; see especially Lightfoot (1889) I 3–6.

2. Jos. *AJ* 18.170–171; Plu. *Demetr.* 42.2. Some imperial refusals to receive petitions and embassies were part of a carefully calculated strategy of silence. In 325 at the Council of Nicaea (the first ecumenical council convoked by the Christian convert Constantine to debate the alleged heresy of Arius), the emperor, in order to emphasize the need for unity in the Church, ordered the incineration of the petitions which had been presented to him by various rival bishops and their supporters on the day before the council was to begin its deliberations; see Soc. 1.8.18–19 (*GCS* n.f. 1: 20).

3. Eck (1980) 6–7; Ausbüttel (1998) 159–161. Modern British government requires around half a million bureaucrats to service a roughly comparable population. On October 1, 2002, the Home Office had a fulltime staff of 19,860, the Lord Chancellor's Department (responsible for the administration of justice) 11,390, and the Department of Work and Pensions 125,510; see *The Civil Service Year Book*, 39th ed. (London: TSO, 2003) 585–593. The federal government of the United States employs more than three million civilians, the fifty state governments 4.5 million more (Lendon [1997] 2–3).

4. Barnish, Lee, and Whitby (2000) 170.

5. Rome to Ravenna, *Coll. Avell.* 14–16, 33 (*CSEL* 35: 59–63, 79–80), an exchange of correspondence between the urban prefect of Rome and the emperor Honorius in late 418 and 419 seeking to resolve a disputed papal election, Jones, *LRE* I, 402–403; Antioch to Constantinople, Lib. *Or.* 21.12, 15–19, the transmission in March 387 by the *magister officiorum* Caesarius of his report on the "Riot of the Statues"; Ulm to Sirmium, Zos. 3.10.2–3, the vanguard of Julian's eastern advance in summer 361, Paschoud (1979) 92–93. The surviving literary evidence for communication times by land and sea is conveniently collected in Friedländer (1921–23) I 333–342; Casson (1995) 281–296; Riepl (1913) 157–235. For a survey of the early medieval period, see McCormick (2001) 64–119 and Part IV.

6. For the known transmission times of imperial edicts in the later Empire, see Jones, *LRE* I 402–403, III 91–93 n. 76, with those dispatched

from Milan to Rome listed at 91; see too Duncan-Jones (1990) 17–23; Ando (2000) 121–122; Matthews (2000) 183–185; Ausbüttel (1998) 163–166; Stoffel (1994) 161–165.

7. Val. III, *Nov.* 27.
8. Plin. *NH* 15.75 and 19.3.
9. Symm. *Rel.* 11; see too Riepl (1913) 235–240.
10. Duncan-Jones (1990) 26.
11. Ibid. 7–17, 25–29, esp. table 10; Jones, *LRE* I 403.
12. Jos. *BJ* 2.203; *AJ* 18.303–309.
13. Skeat (1964) xxiv; *P.Panop.Beatty* 2, lines 109, 116, 126, 134. On the face of it, there is nothing in the content of these letters (compared with others in the archive with much slower transit times) which might indicate the need for particular urgency in dispatch or reply.
14. Skeat (1964) xx, xxiii–xxv; the slowest are *P.Panop.Beatty* 2, lines 176, 179, 245, 249.
15. Duncan-Jones (1990) 28.
16. See usefully (with much material from outside Egypt) Ando (2000) 80–96, 351–362; Burton (1975) 103–104; Austin and Rankov (1995) 155–161; Barnish, Lee, and Whitby (2000) 180–181; for Egypt, see particularly Cockle (1984); Burkhalter (1990); Haensch (1994). The surviving evidence is meticulously surveyed in Haensch (1992), esp. 245–254 for "letter books" similar in format to *P.Panop.Beatty*, and 254–263 for the archiving of written replies to petitions.
17. *P.Herm.Landl.* G and F = Sijpesteijn and Worp (1978); for general description and date, see Bowman (1985) 139–144; Bagnall (1993) 72; Sijpesteijn and Worp (1978) 5–7, 21–23.
18. The check marks are best visible in Sijpesteijn and Worp (1978) Tafelheft II, plates XIII, XV, XXI, and XXXII–XXXIV; the *marginalia* on plate XXVII. The editors take Z as an abbreviation of ζ(ήτει). For the use of check marks in first- and second-century Egyptian tax registers, see *P.Mich.* IV.1 and the editorial introductions to *P.Cair.Mich.* 359; *P.Princ.* I 9; *BGU* IX 1891; *P.Col.* II 1 recto 2. *P.Ryl.* II 185 is a good example of a more comprehensive ledger compiled from a number of specialized registers. Further examples of labeling and cross-referencing are conveniently collected in Austin and Rankov (1995) 158–160.
19. *P.Panop.Beatty* 2, lines 128–134 (trans. following T. C. Skeat).
20. Ibid., lines 145–152.
21. Ibid., lines 211–214.
22. Ibid., lines 62–63; see too 11–15. Immediacy is an insistent demand; for example, lines 13, 21, 33, 53–54, 66–67, 73–74, 78–79, 88, 90, 114, 197–198, 216–218, 251, 255, 271; see Lewis (1991) 170–173.

23. Joh. Lydus, *Mag.* 3.20. John's point is, of course, that the carefully compiled summaries of each case prevented the complete loss of the court records of any proceeding.

24. Th. II, *Nov.* 1.1 of 438; see Harries (1999) 8–10.

25. Matthews (1993), esp. 31–44, refined and elaborated in his magisterial analysis of the *Theodosian Code,* (2000), esp. 280–293, with the attractive suggestion (at 288–289) that imperial archives may have supplied a greater proportion of the more recent material collected by the editors of the *Code.* For a contrasting view, arguing that the *Code* was compiled chiefly from copybooks (which recorded outgoing legislation) in the imperial archives in Constantinople and Rome or Ravenna, see Sirks (1993), esp. 49–56. For the mainly archival sources of the much more limited law codes complied in the 290s, see Corcoran (2000) 29–31.

26. Nor should cases of detailed administration be thought of as confined to Egypt, see Haensch (1992) 260–263 and the useful survey of some recent discoveries of papyrus documents in the Roman Near East in Cotton, Cockle, and Millar (1995).

27. Jones, *LRE* I 602.

28. Ibid. 406. Of course, there are exceptions to each of these generalizations (some of them discussed by Jones at 407–410). But, as Jones emphasized, these failures in government ought to be seen against the background of considerable and consistent achievement. See too the assessment of the effectiveness of imperial government in the eastern Empire in the fifth and sixth centuries in Barnish, Lee, and Whitby (2000) 184–186.

29. Cic. *Planc.* 63.

30. *C.Th.* 12.12.9.1 of 382; see too *C.Th.* 1.16.2 of 330; *C.Th.* 12.1.9 = *CJ* 10.32.16 of 324; *C.Th.* 12.12.3 of 364; *Dig.* 50.7.5.6; for the Principate, see conveniently Millar (1992) 380–382; Williams (1967).

31. Williams (1974) 93–98; Millar (1992) 241–242, 475–477; more generally on petitions, see usefully Millar (1992) 240–252, 507–549; Garnsey (1970) 65–85; Ando (2000) 375–385.

32. *P.Lond.* inv. 1589 (G. A. Souris, *Hellenika* 40 [1989] 155, quotation from line 4); Millar (1992) 636.

33. Just. *Nov.* 49.*pr.*2 of 537; in this case, Justinian's response was to permit a longer time for appeals; see too *Nov.* 50 of 537 with Barnish, Lee, and Whitby (2000) 183–184.

34. Suet. *Tib.* 52.2.

35. Philo, *Leg.* 364–365; for the background see Sly (1996) 167–177.

36. Cassius Dio 71.6.1; see too Millar (1992) 4–12.

37. Bagnall (1993) 161–172; Hobson (1993); and especially Harries (1999) 172–190.
38. Versnel (1991) 80–81.
39. Mitford (1971) 253–255, no. 130 = Gager (1992) 136–137, no. 46 (trans. following J. G. Gager); for further examples and discussion, see conveniently Gager (1992) 116–150, 175–199; Versnel (1991) 81–90; for some Christian examples, see Meyer and Smith (1994) 183–225.
40. Burton (1975) 106.
41. *P.Ryl.* II 74 (edict of M. Petronius Mamertinus, prefect of Egypt, 133–135) giving notice that the assizes south of Coptos in Upper Egypt were canceled (interestingly) through "insufficient time" (line 5).
42. *P.Oxy.* XXXVI 2754, lines 5–7 (edict of Sulpicius Similis, prefect of Egypt, 111); see too *P.Oxy.* XLII 3017 (edict of Ti. Pactumeius Magnus, prefect of Egypt, 176–177) ordering litigants instructed to present their cases before his tribunal to do so within ten days or forfeit their right to a hearing; see Foti Talamanca (1979) 232–239, 279–283.
43. Burton (1975) 101–102; more generally on the assize system in Egypt, from an extensive and detailed literature, see Lewis (1981), (1983) 189–195; Foti Talamanca (1974), esp. conclusions at 160–164, 198–201; Haensch (1997).
44. *P.Oxy.* XXII 2343 with Lewis (1976) 8–9, (1983) 189. The surviving text is a copy of Nemesianus' second petition.
45. *P.Oxy.* XXXI 2597, quotation from lines 3–10, third or fourth century (trans. following J. W. B. Barns); see too the sixth-century case (*PSI* I 76) discussed in Keenan (1975) 244–246.
46. Williams (1974) 96–97; Garnsey (1970) 67–68; Lewis (1981) 125–126; Foti Talamanca (1979) 178–196, 249–258; Millar (1992) 514–515.
47. Bagnall (1993) 170–171; for a discussion of those petitions to the prefect of Egypt which specifically request the delegation of a case to another official, see Foti Talamanca (1979) 131–144.
48. For delays in litigation see most conveniently J. M. Kelly (1966) 118–125 for the early Empire, and Jones, *LRE* I 494–496 (adding Symm. *Rel.* 41.2) for the later.
49. *In Flacc.* 97–101.
50. Thompson (1952) 6; on date and addressees, see Cameron (1979); Giardina (1989) XXXVII–LII.
51. Roueché (1989) 87–89, no. 53, quotation from lines 1–7 (trans. C. Roueché); see too L. Robert, *Hellenica* 4 (1948) 116; *PLRE* II 160–161.
52. *IRT* 588 (from Lepcis Magna, statue base in the Forum Severianum), quotation from lines 2–4; *IRT* 111 (from Sabratha, statue base in the forum in front of the *curia*), quoting lines 5–8; *CIL* VIII 27 = 11025 =

ILS 787 (from Gigthis); see too Lepelley (1979–81) II 352, 369–370, 377, discussing the likely purpose of the mission. For the Principate, see the useful survey of evidence in Millar (1992) 375–463.

53. The exception is the rare case in which an unfavorable official reply to one city was inscribed by one of its rivals as a public testimonial to the latter's advantage, see Reynolds (1978) and (1982) 104–106, no. 13, and 113–115, no. 14; Ando (2000) 94–95; Eck (2000) 269–270.

54. Val. III, *Nov.* 1.3.2.

55. *C.Th.* 11.29.1.

56. *C.Th.* 1.5.3; see too *C.Th.* 2.26.2 = *CJ* 8.4.5 of 330; *C.Th.* 9.1.14 = *CJ* 9.2.13 of 383; *C.Th.* 9.10.3 = *CJ* 9.12.7 of 319; *C.Th.* 11.30.6 = *CJ* 1.21.2 of 316; *C.Th.* 11.30.17 = *CJ* 1.21.3 of 331; *Sirm.* 15 of 411; Marc. *Nov.* 1.8 of 450.

57. Jones, *LRE* I 483–484; J. M. Kelly (1966) 118; Monks (1957) 759–760.

58. *P.Yale* I 61, lines 6–7, with Foti Talamanca (1974) 179–184; Lewis (1981) 121.

59. Joh. Lydus, *Mag.* 3.13; see too Anon. *de rebus bell. pr.*15–16 (ed. A. Giardina, Milan, 1989); compare (for the first century) Suet. *Vesp.* 10; Sen. *Cons. Polyb.* 6.5.

60. Marc. *Nov.* 1 of 450.

61. Millar (1967) 18.

62. Fro. *Aur.* 4.7.1.

63. *C.Th.* 1.16.7 of 331; see too *C.Th.* 9.1.4 of 325; *Pan. Lat.* 4.34.4, 7.5.1 (ed. R. A. B. Mynors, Oxford, 1964); and the valuable comments in Eck (2000) 271–277.

64. MacMullen (1988) 99.

65. *Dig.* 1.16.9.4.

66. In addition to the works on patronage cited above, Part II Introduction, note 2, see Garnsey (1970), esp. 65–90, 221–233; de Ste. Croix (1954) 38–44; J. M. Kelly (1966) 42–68; Lendon (1997) 36–73; Corcoran (2000) 241–244.

67. For discussion, see Eck (1982), esp. 149–151; Schuller (1982b) 202–203; Brunt (1975) 127–142; Saller (1980), esp. 55–57, (1982), esp. 79–117; Pflaum (1950) 195–209; Rouland (1979) 514–532; Lendon (1997) 185–191.

68. Plin. *Ep.* 2.13.4–8 and 10; and see Cotton (1981) 237–238.

69. Cic. *Quinct.* 72.

70. Pflaum (1948), esp. 12–28, quotation from col. 2, lines 12–13; the presents are listed at col. 3, lines 9–13.

71. MacMullen (1988) 126.

72. Plin. *Ep.* 4.9.6; Brunt (1961) 227, no. 39.

73. Plin. *Ep.* 2.11.23; Brunt (1961) 227, no. 37.
74. Plin. *Ep.* 4.9.17–18.
75. *Dig.* 1.16.6.3.
76. See most conveniently on *apparitores,* Purcell (1983); Cohen (1984); Jones (1949) 38–42; MacMullen (1988) 124–126; Millar (1992) 66–69. On *frumentarii,* Clauss (1973) 82–117; Austin and Rankov (1995) 136–137. On imperial freedmen, Treggiari (1969) 153–159; Jones (1949) 43–44; Weaver (1972) 224–296; Millar (1992) 69–83; Boulvert (1970) 374–437, (1974) 113–180 with the important remarks by G. P. Burton, *JRS* 67 (1977) 162–166. Imperial freedmen are best understood as forming part of the imperial household, rather than as constituting a separate, embryonic civil service; see Wallace-Hadrill (1996) 297–299; Lendon (1997) 19–20.
77. Purcell (1983) 128–138; Cohen (1984) 39–48. For the suggestion that *apparitores* may also have worn some kind of uniform, see P. Habel, *P-W* 2.1 (1895) col. 194, s.v. *"Apparitores."*
78. Purcell (1983) 139; Jones (1949) 41; for Horace, see Suet. *Poet.* 24(c) (ed. A. Rostagni, Turin, 1956); Taylor (1925) 165–167; Armstrong (1986).
79. *Dig.* 31.1.22 (quoting Celsus); see too 4.4.3.7, 32.1.11.16 (quoting Ulpian), 19.1.52.2 (quoting Scaevola), 31.1.49.1 (quoting Paul).
80. Cassius Dio 60.17.8.
81. Suet. *Vesp.* 23.2; further examples collected in Collot (1965) 188–190; Liebs (1978) 168–169; Schuller (1980) 62–64.
82. Cic. *Verr.* 3.184.
83. Plin. *Ep.* 9.5.3.
84. *SHA AS* 36.2; see too 23.8, *AP* 11.1, *Elag.* 10.3. Admittedly, a story from a late fourth-century text; although the phrase *fumum uendere* goes back at least to the first century A.D.; see Mart. 4.5.7 with the comments of Goffart (1970) 149–150.
85. Tac. *Hist.* 1.2.3.
86. References conveniently collected in Purcell (1983) 132–133, 136, 140–141; Jones (1949) 41 (on *apparitores*); Clauss (1973) 104–109 (on *frumentarii*); Boulvert (1970) 438–442; Friedländer (1921–23) I 40–52 (on freedmen).
87. Cassius Dio 64.3.4(1).
88. *SHA Gord.* 13.7.
89. Plin. *Ep.* 7.29.3 and 8.6.17.
90. Millar (1992) 69.
91. Ibid. 70; see too Weaver (1972) 263–264, 282–284.
92. Purcell (1983) 138–142, 152.

93. Aur. Victor, *Caes.* 39.44 (ed. F. Pichlmayr, Leipzig, 1970). See the protests of Clauss (1973) 103–105; unheeded, for example, in Austin and Rankov (1995) 136–137.

94. For a range of estimates, see Clauss (1973) 83; Austin and Rankov (1995) 152.

95. *Tab.Vindol.* II 225, quotation from lines 18–24.

4. Purchasing Power

Epigraphs: Ghanaian proverb quoted in Le Vine (1975) 43; Duke of Wellington quoted in *Report from the Select Committee on Army and Navy Appointments,* in *The House of Commons: Reports from Select Committees* (1833), VII no. 650 at 274.

1. This chapter elaborates ideas briefly sketched in Kelly (1998a) 175–180. In thinking about some of the issues involved I have learned much, and profited greatly, from some recent work on "corruption" in the later Roman Empire. For the most part, these approaches have stressed that any understanding which seeks to do more than simply moralize should be closely tied to a categorization of late-antique bureaucracy, in both its operation and organization, as falling (in Weberian terms) between a fully rational administration and a patrimonial system. See Noethlichs (1981), esp. 214–222; Schuller (1982b); Boulvert and Bruschi (1982), esp. 426–429; and in particular the excellent discussions in Migl (1994) 192–193, 208–237; and Schuller (1989). Similar views of Roman bureaucracy (though not in such overtly formalist terms) have also been suggested in important articles by Veyne (1981) and Demougeot (1986). More generally see the useful discussion in Barnish, Lee, and Whitby (2000) 186–193. For a strikingly different approach from that elaborated in this chapter, see MacMullen (1988), esp. 148–197.

2. *C.Th.* 7.11.2 of 417; 8.5.21 of 364; see MacMullen (1962) 366–367.

3. Le Vine (1975) 56; *P.Flor.* III 297, line 290; following a suggested reading in Johnson and West (1949) 297.

4. Mommsen (1884) 632–633. An as-yet-unpublished sixth-century inscription from Caesarea Maritima in Palestine which listed "the fees permitted for specific procedures" was found in 1993 in the vicinity of the imperial revenue office, itself probably part of an administrative and judicial complex adjacent to the governor's official residence; see Holum (1995) 344 n. 40; Patrich (1999) 93–94, fig. 28.

5. In the *officia* of provincial governors, the titles of officials, their rank-

order, and their duties mirrored with only minor variations those of the eastern Praetorian Prefecture; Jones, *LRE* I 593–594; and the detailed study in Palme (1999) 103–111.

6. The technical language of this part of the *ordo salutationis* is not always easy to understand (and may not have been much easier for many contemporary readers without specialist legal training). The version offered here owes much to the excellent study by Chastagnol (1978), esp. 81–83. In particular I follow Chastagnol (at 83) in understanding the *contradictio* (at line 29) to refer to the presentation of opposing cases in court, rather than as Jones, *LRE* I 497, to the rebuttal issued by the defendant. The interpretation is difficult, but unless both parties paid at this stage, the unlikely result (especially in a legal system seeking to limit litigation) would be that the cost in fees to a defendant would be greater than to a plaintiff.

Payment by a defendant seems to be taken for granted in the laws in *Justinian's Code* dealing with privileged classes of bureaucrats and others associated with the palace. The most detailed sets out the administrative fees to be paid by a *castrensis* (a member of the domestic staff of the imperial household) to defend a case before the *magister officiorum.* A single payment of one *solidus* is to be made to the *executores, ultra conuentionis . . . ad usque ad finem litis*—"from the *conuentio* (the summons) right through to the conclusion of the case" (*CJ* 12.25.4.2 of 474). Jones, *LRE* I 497–498, assumed that a defendant who wished to contest an action paid the *executor* a fee on receipt of the summons issued by the plaintiff.

Further sums (as with the other officials involved) were probably levied by the *executor* for the service of a summons outside the provincial capital, with higher rates for longer journeys. Regrettably, the surviving text breaks off at the point where any such charges may have been specified. For the attractive suggestion that some part of the fee-income due senior officials was redistributed, see Mommsen (1884) 640.

For other variations in the understanding of the *ordo salutationis,* see Jones (1949) 51, *LRE* I 497; Harries (1999) 100; Mommsen (1884) 640–642. These deal with matters of procedural and legal detail, and although, as a consequence, they affect the precise calculations for the charges levied on plaintiffs and defendants, they do not greatly alter the broad picture presented here of the overall cost in fees for litigation. Chastagnol (1960) 375–378; Kaser and Hackl (1996) 566–570 offer a helpful, brief account of the complex procedural stages in a civil case.

A fragment of a second, and much less well-preserved, slab (found in the same area as the *ordo salutationis*) appears to belong to the same decree. It lays down regulations for criminal actions and the maintenance of prisoners; see Lepelley (1979–81) II 458–459 and Chastagnol (1978) 87–88, who suggests that it went on to stipulate fees to be paid bureaucrats and lawyers involved in the administration of criminal cases.

7. Chastagnol (1978) 83–86.

8. The costs in *modii* for a successful plaintiff are composed as follows: 10 for the *postulatio simplex;* 10 for the costs associated with issuing the summons; 22 for the *contradictio;* 35 for final judgment; 2 for the *libellensis;* and 2 for the *executor.* These figures are deliberately conservative. For the whole process of litigation, they include only one charge of 2 *modii* each for the *libellensis* and the *executor;* and they exclude any payment for the papyrus used in drawing up the necessary documentation. The higher fee paid by a plaintiff in Timgad litigating in the provincial governor's court in Cirta also excludes any surcharge which may have been levied by the *executor* for service outside the provincial capital; see Chastagnol (1978) 82, 86; Mommsen (1884) 640. The costs for defending a case are similarly conservative; I have not included any charge which might have been payable by the defendant to the *executor.*

9. The distance (confirmed by modern maps) is calculated from the *Antonine Itinerary,* a second-century list of distances by road between major towns in the Roman Empire; *Ant. Int.* 40.7–41.2 (ed. O. Cuntz, Leipzig, 1929); see Miller (1916) cols. 936–937. One Roman mile = 1,478 meters.

10. For the estimate, see most conveniently Hopkins (1980) 118. One *modius Italicus* in North Africa = 7.03kg of wheat; see Duncan-Jones (1982) 370, table 18.

11. In Carthage in 367–368, following a serious famine, the proconsul of Africa purchased wheat on the open market at a rate of 30 *modii* to the *solidus* (Amm. 28.1.17–18). In 445 the emperor Valentinian III fixed 40 *modii* to the *solidus* as the official rate for the purchase of military supplies in Numidia and Mauretania (Val. III, *Nov.* 13.4); see Chastagnol (1978) 82 n. 18; Jones, *LRE* I 445–446; de Jonge (1948).

12. *C.Th.* 7.13.7.2 of 375.

13. *P.Ness.* III 89 with Patlagean (1977) 393–395; Mayerson (1986) 142.

14. *Dig.* 48.2.10.

15. *P.Ness.* III 18, 20, and 33; see Patlagean (1977) 381; *P.Lond.* V 1711, lines 72–74 (of 566–573); further examples in Montevecchi (1936) 39–54, esp. those discussed at 43, 47, and 54.

16. Joh. Lydus, *Mag.* 3.60.

17. Jones *LRE*, I 554–557; Hendy (1985) 201–204.
18. Joh. Lydus, *Mag.* 3.25. Discounts for *scholae palatinae*, *CJ* 12.29.3.1–2 of 484–491; for clergy, *CJ* 1.3.25.2–3 of 456, further reduced in *Nov.* 123.28 of 546. *Castrenses* (*CJ* 12.25.4.2–3 of 474), *agentes in rebus* (*CJ* 12.21.8.3 and 8 of 484), and members of the *sacra scrinia* (*CJ* 12.19.12.1 of 503–518) were also charged similarly discounted rates for litigation before the *magister officiorum;* for the details, see Jones, *LRE* I 497–499; Karayannopulos (1958) 172.
19. *CJ* 12.29.3.3 of 484–491; 12.19.12.1 of 503–518; 1.3.32.5 of 472.
20. *CJ* 12.35.18.2–2*a* of 492 with Jones, *LRE* I 488. A later edict of Anastasius, also concerned with regulating the payments to the civilian staff of a *dux* (in this case of Libya), laid down that soldiers appearing as defendants should, in cases worth up to 100 *solidi,* have to pay no more than half a *solidus* in court fees; see Oliverio (1936) 142, §IX lines 37–38, with editor's commentary at 158–159.
21. Lib. *Or.* 33.14. For the background to this oration, see Long (1996) 86–88; Petit (1956) 504–505.
22. *C.Th.* 2.1.8.
23. Littmann, Magie, and Stuart (1910) 33–34, frags. 15–19, quotation from line 4; a higher rate of 20 pounds was prescribed for governors in provinces along the eastern frontier from Euphratensis to Palaestina, and 30 for their staff (lines 5–7).
24. Just. *Nov.* 124.2; see too *Nov.* 8.7 of 535.
25. *CJ* 9.27.6.1.
26. *C.Th.* 1.15.12 of 386; *CJ* 12.57.9 of 407; for the date, see Honoré (1998) 95; Jones, *LRE* I 594.
27. This basic principle was recognized (at least in part) by the early third-century jurist Ulpian, who remarked that the action of some governors in sending the proceeds derived from the sale of the personal effects of executed prisoners to the imperial treasury was "somewhat overzealous." It was much better, he advised, to retain such monies in a fund for the use of the staff *(ad utilitatem officii)* than to remit them centrally *(Dig.* 48.20.6; see too Jones [1949] 45).
28. Jones, *LRE* I 595; Palme (1999) 117–120.
29. For text and discussion see above all Chastagnol (1978), esp. 13–14, 22–39; Lepelley (1979–81) II 459–470. In dating the *album* to 363, I have followed Chastagnol (1978) 35–37, 40–48; Lepelley (1979–81) II 467–468; but see H. Horstkotte, *BJ* 182 (1982) 661–662, proposing a later date of 365 or 366.
30. Chastagnol (1978) 22–31; and the important observations of Lepelley (1979–81) I 202, 318–325, II 462–463.
31. Lepelley (1979–81) I 212–213, II 465; Chastagnol (1978) 31–33. The

last set of names (some now missing) in the fourth column may have included some of the sons of members of the municipal council listed above. These *praetextati* may have been permitted to attend certain meetings and formal occasions; see Chastagnol (1978) 33; Lepelley (1979–81) I 197–198, II 465, 467. For a first-rate discussion of the municipal magistracies and the role of the *curia,* particularly the financial obligations and judicial, fiscal, and administrative duties of its members, see Lepelley (1979–81) I 149–235; see too Jones, *LRE* I 724–737; Schubert (1969), esp. 299–308.

32. Veyne (1981) 339–340; the point still holds good even assuming a sizable number of *supernumerarii* in the governor's *officium.*

33. Veyne (1981) 340, 344–349; Chastagnol (1978) 37–38.

34. Jones, *LRE* I 743–744; Millar (1983) 93–95.

35. Again this figure gives only a crude sense of scale. The minimum property qualification varied from town to town, and there is no surviving evidence from fourth-century Africa. I use the figure cited in a law of Valentinian III (*Nov.* 3.4 of 439), which is conventionally assumed to be of "general application"; see Jones, *LRE* I 738–739, quotation from 738; Lepelley (1979–81) I 198–199.

36. Chastagnol (1978) 50–57, 89.

37. Sessii: col. 1, lines 9, 21, 30; col. 2, line 15; col. 3, lines 46, 47; col. 4, line 36; col. 5, lines 6, 39; col. 6, line 28; the three Sessii Cresconii are at col. 1, line 21; col. 5, line 6; col. 6, line 28. Flavidius Sudianus and father at col. 2, line 31; col. 5, line 41; Donatus and father at col. 4, line 24; col. 5, line 35. For further examples, details, and discussion, see Chastagnol (1978) 38–39, 70–74; Lepelley (1979–81) II 468–470; Leschi (1948) 83–86. These data yield only a rough picture. Close family groups can be identified in only a minority of cases.

38. Sijpesteijn and Worp (1978) Index IV, 161–164.

39. Only an estimate: the result of some unclarity in the register's terminology and the use of the same ranks and grades in both the army and the bureaucracy; see Bagnall (1992a) 52–53. Again, the broad impression of the registers offered here is unlikely to be affected seriously by the "softness" of these numbers.

40. The figures for the overall pattern of landholding in the Antinoopolite section of *P.Herm.Landl.* F, using only complete entries, are taken from Bowman (1985) 159, table IVB.

41. Landholdings in *P.Herm.Landl.* G at lines 333–334, 383, 322, and 339–342 respectively with Bowman (1985) 162–163, table VIIIB. More generally on the changes in land ownership between the two registers, see Bowman (1985) 154–155; Bagnall (1993) 72–73.

42. *P.Herm.Landl.* F lines 60–61, 707–708 (both *primipilares*). Other fig-

ures for the Hermopolite section of this register again from Bowman (1985) 159, table IVB.

43. Bowman (1985) 149; Bagnall (1992b) 130.

44. See generally the elegant studies of the data on Egyptian landholding in Bagnall (1992a), esp. 52–54, (1992b), esp. 137–143, usefully summarized in (1993) 68–71.

45. Dispute over allegedly stolen money: *P.Lips.* 34, 35, and 61 (= *W.Chr.* 187) with U. Wilcken, *APF* 3 (1906) 563–564 and *APF* 4 (1907–08) 187–189. On this confused and complex case, see Zuckerman (1998b) 86–91, whose reading of the petitions in Isidore's dossier would strongly suggest a scam, also involving the local governor, to defraud the town council of Hermopolis of the 177 *solidi* in remitted tax; see too Jones, *LRE* I 596; Bagnall (1993) 65. Isidore's other business interests are known from *P.Lips.* 17, 20–23, 37; see Keenan (1994) 445–446. Further examples of the resources and economic interests of individual bureaucrats in late-antique Egypt are usefully discussed in Jones, *LRE* I 595–596, 599, II 895; Keenan (2000) 617–625; for a rare example from Asia Minor, see Roueché (1989) 73–75, no. 41.

46. Kaster (1988) 123; see too the useful discussions in Ausbüttel (1998) 177–179; Barrau (1987) 96–100.

47. Alt (1921) 4–8, no. A.1; see too Abel (1909) with photograph at 88, and the editor's introduction to *P.Ness.* III 38 (C. J. Kraemer). Other fragmentary inscriptions also from Beersheva appear to continue the list of taxation payments and fees in the same format; Alt (1921) 8–13, nos. A.2–4; F.-M. Abel, *RBi* n.s. 17 (1920) 260–265; with Mayerson (1986) 147–148. Unfortunately it is not known how any of these inscriptions (perhaps all part of the same edict) was originally displayed. The largest fragment—the result of clandestine digging—was purchased from a dealer in Jerusalem; others were seen during the construction of a new settlement near Beersheva, perhaps on the old town's Byzantine site.

My understanding of this inscription follows Mayerson (1986), who suggests that it records a supertax imposed on both the military and civil population in the three Palaestinian provinces. (The latter group was generally taxed through a κοινὸν τῶν συντελεστῶν, an association of local citizens responsible for seeing that quotas were met.) The extra revenue was perhaps levied to support a series of reforms in provincial administration promulgated by Justinian in 536 (*Nov.* 103) and collected by *uicarii* on behalf of the proconsul, the newly elevated governor of Palaestina Prima charged with general oversight of the three provinces.

48. Alt (1921) 4–8, no. A.1, lines 1–7; col. ii, lines 8–13; and col. iii, lines

2–3. The translation of the preface is tentative. It is based in part on the reconstructions and suggestions of Alt (1921) 5–6; Abel (1909) 90–95; Mayerson (1986) 143. Neither the name of the emperor issuing the decree nor the name of the official to whom it was addressed survives. Following Abel (1909) 97; Alt (1921) 7; Mayerson (1986) 148, I have assumed that δοῦλοι in these lists refers to officials on the staff of the provincial governor.

49. On the *dux* and the status of the city, see Goodchild (1976a) 253–255; Pedley (1976) 20–21; for the inscription, Reynolds (1976) 309–312, no. 37, with tav. LXVI.

50. Goodchild (1976b) 184–187 and fig. 2 at 178; F. Chamoux, *CRAI* (1955) 333–334.

51. Taucheira: Oliverio (1936) 135, no. 139, with tav. LII; Ptolemais: Oliverio (1936) 136–163, no. 140, with tav. LIII–LVI; for a revised text of §§I–X, see Reynolds (1976) 311–312; on the fort, see Goodchild (1953) 74 with plate VII, nos. 5 and 6.

52. Oliverio (1936) 143, §XIV, lines 70–83, quotation from lines 59–61; see Jones, *LRE* I 598; the fragment of this edict from Taucheira also preserves the schedule of fees. On καλανδικά, see Karayannopulos (1958) 174; on *quadrimenstrui breues*, see Jones, *LRE* III 94 n. 81.

53. Durliat and Guillou (1984) 583–584, quotation from lines 1–16, with photograph at 582; I follow their understanding of this inscription and suggestions for its dating (at 585–586); see too Dagron (1985) 451–455. On the post of the κόμης τῶν στενῶν, see Ahrweiler (1961) 239–243. A late fifth- or early sixth-century inscription from Seleucia Pieria, the port of Antioch in Syria (much more fragmentary than the regulations from Abydos, and seemingly lacking any extended explanatory preface), laid down the amounts due to the *curiosi litorum* (the inspectors of ports responsible to the *comes sacrarum largitionum*) for checking ships' cargoes. The different amounts (only two survive) seem to be related to tonnage and destination; see Dagron (1985) 435–451; Delmaire (1989) 289–290.

54. *C.Th.* 6.35.4; see too *C.Th.* 14.4.4.4 of 367 and generally, on the public display of laws, Corcoran (2000) 246–248; Matthews (2000) 195–199; Williamson (1987).

55. See *C.Th.* 1.31.2 of 370; 6.4.21.3 of 372; 6.24.3 of 365; 6.29.5 of 359; 6.30.11 of 386; *C.Th.* 6.31.1 = *CJ* 12.24.1 of 374; *C.Th.* 7.4.28 = *CJ* 12.37.12 of 406; *C.Th.* 8.4.6 of 358; 8.4.9 of 368; 8.4.27 of 422; 11.1.29 of 401; 11.17.3 of 399; *C.Th.* 12.1.192 = *CJ* 10.32.59 of 436; *CJ* 12.49.13 (undated); Just. *Nov.* 130.1 of 545; further examples in Noethlichs (1981) 195–198.

56. Just. *Nov.* 124.1; see too *CJ* 1.27.1.17, 1.27.2.12 and 17 all of 534;

9.27.6.1 of 439; Just. *Nov.* 8.7, 17.3, both of 535; 80.6, 82.7, both of 539; 161.1 of 574. For a detailed study of *Nov.* 8 and 17, see Haase (1994) 15–74.

57. *C.Th.* 8.11.3; see too the other laws collected at 8.11.

58. Maj. *Nov.* 7.16 of 458 with Jones, *LRE* I 468; see too *C.Th.* 6.4.27 of 395; 10.1.11 of 367; 12.6.3 of 349; Val. III, *Nov.* 7.1.1 of 440. On the regulation of the supply of meat to Rome, see the legislation collected at *C.Th.* 14.4 with Chastagnol (1960) 325–330. Further examples conveniently surveyed in Karayannopulos (1958) 172–175.

59. MacMullen (1988) 153; Schuller (1975) 14.

60. *C.Th.* 1.16.12; *C.Th.* 1.16.6 = *CJ* 1.40.3 of 331; *C.Th.* 1.16.9 of 364; 1.16.10 of 365; 1.16.13 of 377; *C.Th.* 1.20.1 = *CJ* 1.45.1 of 408.

61. Home province: *CJ* 1.41.1 (late fifth cent.); 9.29.3 of 385. Purchases: *C.Th.* 8.15.5 of 368; 8.15.6 of 380; with exceptions in Val. III, *Nov.* 32 of 451. Marriage: *C.Th.* 3.6.1 = *CJ* 5.2.1 of 380; *C.Th.* 3.11.1 = *CJ* 5.7.1 of 380; and see Jones, *LRE* I 399–400.

62. Oliverio (1936) 136–139; Littmann, Magie, and Stuart (1910) 34, 38; Waddington (1868) 424; Reynolds (1976) 309.

63. See for example the comments of de Ste. Croix (1954) 44–45; Frank (1967); Jones, *LRE* I 392–393; Matthews (1989) 270–271; Krause (1987) 50–58.

64. Lib. *Ep.* 101.1–2; the maxim quotes Sophocles, *Ajax* 522 (ed. H. Lloyd-Jones and N. G. Wilson, Oxford, 1990).

65. Liebeschuetz (1972) 192–198; Petit (1957) 158–188.

66. Lib. *Ep.* 1004.1–5, quotation from §4.

67. Symm. *Ep.* 2.43 (ed. J.-P. Callu, 4 vols., Paris, 1972–2002); for further examples, see Matthews (1974) 61–64; Roda (1986).

68. Matthews (1989) 270.

69. For a sympathetic evocation of this epistolary world, see Van Dam (2003) 131–138. For the letters of Augustine, see the discussion and full bibliography in J. Divjak, "*Epistulae,*" in *Augustinus-Lexikon*, ed. C. Meyer, vol. 2:5/6 (Basel, 2001) cols. 893–1057; for Basil, Patrucco (1982); Treucker (1981); Rousseau (1994) 158–169; for Theodoret, Wagner (1948), esp. 129–140; for Synesius of Cyrene, Roques (1989).

70. On the sale of offices in late antiquity, see in particular the useful discussions in Liebs (1978); Collot (1965); Kolias (1939); Krause (1987) 58–65; and the helpful, briefer treatments in Jones, *LRE* 391–396; Vogler (1979) 247–252; Migl (1994) 223–226.

71. Malchus 3 (ed. Blockley [1983] 408); and see usefully, on Malchus' version of Zeno, Blockley (1981) 79–82.

72. Malchus 16.2 (ed. Blockley [1983] 424); on Zeno see too Agath.

5.15.4–6 (ed. R. Keydell, Berlin, 1967). The openly pagan historian Zosimus accused Theodosius I of freely selling offices through middlemen; see Zos. 4.28.3–4; Eunapius 72.1 (ed. Blockley [1983] 116–118); Jones, *LRE* I 393–394; and generally Chauvot (1986) 144–147; Kolias (1939) 23–42; Liebs (1978) 170–173. For other polemical observations (some by panegyrists blackening a previous reign), see for example Zos. 2.38.3; Proc. Gaz. *Pan.* 11–12; Priscian, *Pan.* lines 204–205 (both ed. A. Chauvot, Bonn, 1986).

73. *C.Th.* 2.29.1 with Goffart (1970); Barnes (1974); Schuller (1994). For a reading of this law as an attempt to ban or, at the very least, to discourage the purchase of *suffragium,* see Andreotti (1975) 12–25; Collot (1965) 195–198; Liebs (1978) 174–182; Jones, *LRE* I 393.

74. Amm. 22.6, quotation from §§2 and 5.

75. *C.Th.* 2.29.2 = *CJ* 4.3.1; see Andreotti (1975) 4–11; Liebs (1978) 182–183.

76. *CJ* 8.13.27; see too Just. *Nov.* 53.5 of 537. The text of 8.13.27.1 is complicated; I understand the latter provision for setting the sum due the creditor (quod pro isdem militiis pro tenore communis militantium placiti uel diuinae sanctionis tale praestantis beneficium dari solet) as usefully distinguishing between the amount charged by an office-holder entitled to sell his post to his successor, and the amount charged by the emperor for the right to appoint to the equivalent post.

At least on some occasions, a judge seems to have been prepared to recognize the claims of an unsuccessful candidate for a post to recover at least some of the money paid over to a *suffragator.* A case tried in Rome by Pope Gelasius in the late fifth century was brought by one Eucharistus against Faustus, to whom he had paid 63 *solidi* to advance his candidature for the see of Volaterrae. Eucharistus had not in the end been successful in securing preferment, and sought to recover the money. Faustus counterclaimed for the expenses he had incurred in promoting Eucharistus' cause. In reaching a judgment, Gelasius recognised the validity of both claims and ordered Faustus to repay only the balance. *Epistolae Pontificum Romanorum Ineditae,* ed. S. Loewenfeld (Leipzig, 1885), no. 22, pp. 11–12; Jones, *LRE* II 910.

77. Amm. 29.3.6.

78. *CJ* 12.3.3.1 of 474–491; 12.3.4.1 of 476–480 or 484.

79. *CJ* 12.19.7.2 of 445; Just. *Nov.* 35.5–6.

80. Just. *Nov.* 8 *Notitia*; see too *Nov.* 24.6.1, 25.6.*ep.,* 26.5.1, 27.2.*ep.,* 28.7, 29.5 all of 535; 30.11.1 of 536. Justinian's legislation on the sale of offices is usefully discussed in Jones, *LRE* I 394–395; Kolias (1939) 43–67;

Liebs (1978) 161–167; Bonini (1989), esp. 22–34; Collot (1965) 216–220; Haase (1994) 16–19.

81. Just. *Ed.* 4.1.

82. Just. *Nov.* 123.3 and 16; see too *Nov.* 56 of 537; Kolias (1939) 71–75; Jones, *LRE* II 909–910.

83. Just. *Nov.* 8.*pr.*1 of 535; 161.2 of 574.

84. See generally the important discussion in Schuller (1980) 68–71.

85. Proc. *HA* 21.18; see Bonini (1989) 97–105.

86. de Ste. Croix (1954) 48.

87. Lib. *Or.* 47.13.

88. Ibid. 18.135 and 47.22.

89. Ibid. 1.109.

90. Ibid. 42.24–25. Unsurprisingly, the accuracy of Libanius' remarks has been doubted; see Pack (1935) 65–67; Teitler (1985) 64–68; Vogler (1979) 63–64.

91. Claudian, *in Eutrop.* I 201–205; see too I 167–170, II 585–590 (ed. J. B. Hall, Leipzig, 1985); for the background to this piece, see Cameron (1970) 124–155; Long (1996) 149–177, 221–262.

92. Claudian, *in Ruf.* I 179–180, 183–187; for the background, see Cameron (1970) 63–76.

93. Some choice passages: Claudian, *in Eutrop.* I 1–23, 110–137, 252–271, II *pr.* 21–32; for a discussion and taxonomy of Claudian's abuse, see Christiansen (1969) 92–101; Döpp (1980) 161–174; and especially Long (1996) 107–146. More generally the position of eunuchs and the invective they provoked are discussed in Guyot (1980) 157–176; Scholten (1995) 186–195; Hopkins (1963), esp. 64–69, 78–80; Liebs (1978) 183–186; Matthews (1989) 274–277.

94. Cameron (1970) 126.

95. Claudian, *in Eutrop.* I 358–370 (trans. Long [1996] 142); see too I 24–31, 287–307, 317–345, II 24–94.

96. Levy (1971) 54.

97. Claudian, *in Ruf.* I 25–175 (quotation from 29), 354–387.

98. Ibid. II 517–519 and 521–526, with Cerberus at 457; see too I 196–256, II 7–21, 130–136, 317–323, 410–439.

99. Some choice passages: Claudian, *in Eutrop* II 501–515; *in Ruf.* II 293–322; *de cos. Stil.* I 24–35, 138–147, 291–313, II 1–5, 100–172, III 51–71; see too Döpp (1980) 175–198; Levy (1958). For a catalogue of Claudian's categories of virtue, see usefully Christiansen (1969) 16–26, 117–120.

100. Claudian, *de. cos. Stil.* III *pr.* 21–24, II 367–370; *in Ruf.* II *pr.* 13–20; *de bello Getico* 138–144.

101. Lib. *Ep.* 1106.6–7, 1111; Symm. *Ep.* 3.81–91. Symmachus skillfully and quickly revised his views after Rufinus' fall; *Ep.* 6.14.1 (ed. J.-P. Callu, Paris, 1995).
102. Zos. 5.1.1–2.
103. Philostorgius 11.3 (ed. J. Bidez and F. Winkelmann, Berlin, 1981).
104. Pall. *Dial.* 8, 13–16 (*S.Chrét.* 341: esp. 158–162, 292–294, 304–306); see too Soc. 6.2.5–10 (*GCS* n.f. 1: 312–313). For the trading of similar accusations in the 360s by Ursinus and Damasus in their rival bids for the papacy, see *Coll. Avell.* 1.5–6 (*CSEL* 35: 2–3); and again at the turn of the fifth century between Laurentius and Symmachus, see Theophanes 143 (ed. C. de Boor, Leipzig, 1883); Stein (1949) 134–142. For a disputed episcopal appointment on a humbler, provincial scale, see Syn. *Ep.* 66 (ed. A. Garzya, Turin, 1989); other instances are usefully collected in MacMullen (1986c) 338–341.
105. Joh. Chrys. *Hom. ad pop. Ant.* 13.2 (*PG* 49: 138); *Hom. in Matth.* 56.4 (*PG* 58: 555); *Hom. in Ep. I ad Thess. c. IV* 6.4 (*PG* 62: 433–434); *Hom. in Ep. II ad Tim. c. II* 5.3 (*PG* 62: 628); *de Lazaro Conciones* 4.4 (*PG* 48: 1011–12).
106. Anti-Priscillian: Sulp. Sev. *Chron.* 2.48.5 (*CSEL:* 1: 101); anti-Donatist: Aug. *Ep.* 66.1 (*CSEL* 34.2: 235–236); anti-Arian: Greg. Naz. *Or.* 21.21 (*S.Chrét.* 270: 152–154); Soc. 1.27.7–10 (*GCS* n.f. 1: 76–77); Theod. *HE* 1.4.1–6, 4.22.9 (*GCS* 44: 8–10, 252).
107. Carrié (1976) 162; for the background to this oration, see Garnsey and Woolf (1989) 162–163; Liebeschuetz (1972) 201–208; Brown (1971) 85–86; Harmand (1955), esp. 173–183; Pack (1935) 45–52; and particularly Carrié (1976) 169–172, who stresses the importance of giving full weight to Libanius' rhetorical intentions, constructions, and reuse of both stock images and traditional topics. For Libanius' shame at losing the court case, see *Or.* 47.11–16.
108. Lib. *Or.* 47.21–24, quotations from §§21 and 24.
109. Brown (1971) 86.
110. Lib. *Or.* 47.13.
111. For further examples of such moralizing tactics, especially in legal texts, and a complementary approach to that adopted here toward accusations of corruption (through the payment of money or the exercise of influence) against provincial governors acting in their judicial capacity, see the important discussion in Harries (1999) 163–166.
112. *Collectio Casinensis* 293–294, quotation from §294, lines 15–18 (*ACOec.* 1.4: 222–225); for this incident, see Brown (1992) 15–17; Wickham (1983) xxi–xxvi, xxxi–xxxv; Jones, *LRE* I 346; on the gifts and their recipients, see Batiffol (1919) 159–173; Wickham (1983) 66–67; refer-

ences to "blessings" in *Collectio Casinensis* 293.4; see too *V. Mel.* 13 (*S.Chrét.* 90: 154, line 3).

113. Brown (1992) 17; Wickham (1983) xxv.

114. Liebeschuetz (1972) 195.

115. Lib. *Ep.* 364, quotation from §§2–3 with a nice tag from Homer, *Od.* 4.269; *Ep.* 21, quotation from §§2–3. On this incident and those involved, see most conveniently Seeck (1906) 85–87, 173–174, 220; *PLRE* I 104, 423, 628. Nicentius visited Libanius in Antioch in 360 and Libanius hoped that a friendship with the *comes Orientis* Domitius Modestus might lead to a new posting (*Ep.* 193). Aristaenetus was killed in an earthquake at Nicomedia in August 358. The limits of Libanius' influence in such cases are neatly exposed (despite his elegant excuses for failing to write) in *Ep.* 957.

116. Matthews (1975) 35–49, 107–115, (1989) 271–274; Lenski (2002) 56–67; Chastagnol (1965).

117. *PLRE* I 140–141 (Ausonius 7), 427–428 (Hesperius 2), 139 (Ausonius 5), 1134–35 (Stemma 8); Hopkins (1961); Matthews (1975) 69–76; Sivan (1993) 131–141.

118. Joh. Lydus, *Mag.* 3.58 and 61.

119. Nestorius, *The Bazaar of Heracleides* 384–389, 478–481 (trans. G. R. Driver and L. Hodgson, Oxford, 1925, pp. 279–282, 349–351).

120. Batiffol (1919) 154–159.

121. *PG* 83: 1489–92; *ACOec.* 4.1: 135–136, quotation from 135, lines 24–29. For a discussion of the letter's authorship, see Richard (1941–42), esp. 421. The letter's sentiments are as crude as its forgery; John of Antioch, its alleged addressee, died in 440, four years before Cyril.

122. *History of the Patriarchs of the Coptic Church of Alexandria, PO* 1: 429 (trans. B. T. A. Evetts). For a useful discussion of the complexities of this text and its authorship, see den Heijer (1989), esp. 3–7, 138–139 (on the biography of Cyril); Johnson (1977).

123. Aug. *Sermo* 107.8–9 (*PL* 38: 630–631), 85.6–7 (*PL* 38: 522–523), *Ep.* 22*.2–4 (*CSEL* 88: 113–315), *En. Ps.* 39.7 (*CCSL* 38: 430).

124. Aug. *Ep.* 153.23–24 (*CSEL* 44: 423–424).

125. Priscus 11.2, lines 407–510, quotations from 451–453 and 476–483 (ed. Blockley [1983] 266–272) with Blockley (1981) 55–59.

126. Jones (1949) 51.

127. *P.Abinn.* 59, quotation from line 14; see Bell et al. (1962) 121–122; Liebs (1978) 173; Rémondon (1965) 140–141.

128. Joh. Lydus, *Mag.* 3.76, 3.15.

129. Kotansky (1991) 42–43, quotations from lines 11–19, 41–45 (trans. following R. Kotansky).

130. *V. Mel.* 29 (*S.Chrét.* 90: 182–184). For the background to this text, see Clark (1984), esp. 92–115, 129–136. For a similar story, see *V. Theod. Scy.* 76 (ed. A.-J. Festugière, Brussels, 1970).

131. *V. Mel.* 52 (*S.Chrét.* 90: 226–228); Jones, *LRE* I 580.

132. *V. Mel.* 10–15, quotation from §13 (*S.Chrét.* 90: 144–158, quotation from 154); see Clark (1984) 100–102; Batiffol (1919) 175–176. *V. Mel.* at §§12 and 13 refers to Honorius as Serena's brother.

133. *V. Porph.* 36–49, *decani* at §40 (ed. H. Grégoire and M.-A. Kugener, Paris, 1930); see Holum (1982) 54–56; Jones, *LRE* I 344–346. The authenticity of this saint's life, often doubted, is vigorously defended in a full discussion by Trombley (2001) I 246–282.

134. Basil, *Ep.* 190.2 (ed. Y. Courtonne, 3 vols., Paris, 1957–66); MacMullen (1986c) 339.

5. Autocracy and Bureaucracy

Epigraphs: The Book of the Lord Shang quoted in Metzger (1973) 247; King Hassan II quoted in Waterbury (1973) 553.

1. Jones, *LRE* I 406. This chapter in part elaborates ideas first sketched out in Kelly (1994), (1998a) 157–175, and (1999) 172–181. In working through these issues, I have learned much from, and am particularly indebted to, the rich and thoughtful discussions in Ando (2000) 336–405; Brown (1992) 7–34; Barnish, Lee, and Whitby (2000) 200–202; Harries (1999) 77–98 on the conflict between rules and power in late antiquity; Heather (1994) 25–33 on the social and political role of *honorati;* and especially Migl (1994) 176–208 on the representation and operation of imperial power in the fourth century.

2. Dagron (1974), esp. 34–37, 86–92; Krautheimer (1983) 41–61; Mango (1985), esp. 23–50; Janin (1964) 21–26; Kelly (1999) 170–172, (forthcoming a). On the description of Constantinople as a "New Rome," see Dagron (1974) 43–47; and especially Calderone (1993) 733–744.

3. *C.Th.* 15.1.47 = *CJ* 8.11.17; see Dagron (1974) 92–97.

4. Joh. Chrys. *Hom. in Joh.* 5.4 (*PG* 59: 60).

5. *C.Th.* 15.12.2.

6. *C.Th.* 4.10.3 of 426 (freedmen); 16.8.16 of 404, 16.8.24 of 418 (Jews); 16.5.25 and 29 (heretics); see Delmaire (1989) 133–138; Stein, *Officium* 10–11.

7. *C.Th.* 6.36.1 of 326 = *CJ* 12.30.1.

8. *C.Th.* 6.35.8 of 369.

9. *C.Th.* 6.22.8.1.

10. Chastagnol (1978) 75–76, lines 6–12; for discussion, see 79–81;

Mommsen (1884) 634–638; Delmaire (1989) 161 n. 64; and generally Liebeschuetz (1972) 188–189. I understand the problematic description of the fifth group as officiales ex ordine (line 12) to refer to *supernumerarii* rather than, following Chastagnol (at 81), to those *officiales* also members of the municipal council *(ordo)* of Cirta, here designated as a separate group, perhaps because of their continued liability to fulfill their curial obligations in their hometown; see too H. Horstkott, *BJ* 182 (1982) 663.

11. *C.Th.* 6.26.7; see too *C.Th.* 6.26.5 = *CJ* 12.19.2 of 389; Liebeschuetz (1972) 189–191.

12. Joh. Lydus, *Mag.* 3.30.

13. Swift and Oliver (1962) 247–248, lines 2–6 and 30–37; for the background, *PLRE* I 560, 696–697.

14. Syn. *de Regno* 27 (ed. A. Garzya, Turin, 1989). Dionysius, ruler of Sicily in the fourth century B.C., was often portrayed by ancient writers as the epitome of the tyrant. He was particularly notorious for his inability to trust his friends and subordinates; see for example Plut. *Dion.* 9; Cic. *Tusc.* 5.58 repeated in Amm. 16.8.10; see too 14.11.30, 15.5.37, 29.2.4.

15. Louis XIV, *Mémoires pour l'instruction du Dauphin* (1661), ed. C. Dreyss, vol. 2 (Paris, 1860) 373.

16. Max Weber, *Wirtschaft und Gesellschaft: Grundriss der verstehenden Soziologie,* 5th rev. ed., ed. J. Winckelmann (Tübingen, 1985) at 570–571.

17. Auson. *Gratiarum Actio* 1.2 (ed. R. P. H. Green, Oxford, 1991).

18. *Pan. Lat.* 5.7.6; see too *Pan. Lat.* 6.7.5, 11.8.3–5, 11.10.4; Eus. *V. Const.* 1.43.3 (*GCS Eusebius Werke* 1.1: 38); MacCormack (1981) 17–39, 45–50. For similar imagery used of governors, see Men. Rh. 378, 381 (ed. D. A. Russell and N. G. Wilson, Oxford, 1981).

19. *Pan. Lat.* 6.17.1, 10.3.2.

20. Joh. Chrys. *ad Theodorum Lapsum* 1.12 (*S.Chrét.* 117: 144); see generally McCormick (1986) 252–258.

21. Jones, *LRE* I 403.

22. Amm. 14.11.1, 15.8.2, 30.4.1; Gutsfeld (1998) 88–89.

23. Amm. 28.6.9; Brown (1992) 10. On the *consistorium*, see usefully Jones, *LRE* I 333–341; Delmaire (1995) 29–39; de Bonfils (1981) 25–39; Kunkel (1968–69) 242–246; Weiss (1975) 6–38; Vogler (1979) 216–220; on praetorian prefects, see in particular Gutsfeld (1998) 85–98.

24. *C.Th.* 6.7.1 = *CJ* 12.4.1 of 372; *C.Th.* 9.27.1 = *CJ* 12.1.12 of 380; *C.Th.* 13.11.11 of 406; 15.14.8 of 389; see too Jones, *LRE* I 378, III 81 n. 28; Noethlichs (1981) 21 n. 104.

25. Lib. *Ep.* 311, 391.13–16, 423.3, 492; see *PLRE* I 59–60; Petit (1955)

385–386; Seeck (1906) 59–63. The proconsul of Constantinople had responsibility for the running of the city and presided over the Senate until 359, when the office was replaced by the more prestigious position of urban prefect; see Dagron (1974) 215–226.

26. Matthews (1975) 32; *PLRE* I 866.
27. See Chapter 4, note 116.
28. Amm. 22.3–4 with Matthews (1989) 92–93; Thompson (1947) 73–79; Vogler (1979) 147–148.
29. Jones, *LRE* I 380, 690; Chastagnol (1960) 187–188; Dagron (1974) 284. A similar impression of high variability in tenure, with some periods of rapid succession, is also given by the lists of known holders of other major palatine offices; see for example Delmaire (1989) 105–111; Clauss (1980) 139–143; Harries (1988) 171–172.
30. Joh. Chrys. *in Eutrop.* 1 (*PG* 52: 391). For the incident, see Soc. 6.5.4–7 (*GCS* n.f. 1: 317); Soz. 8.7.3–6 (*GCS* 50: 360); Zos. 5.18.1–3; and more generally on Eutropius' career, *PLRE* II 440–444; Liebeschuetz (1990) 96–110 with Cameron and Long (1993) 161–175.
31. Joh. Chrys. *in Eutrop.* 3 (*PG* 52: 393–394).
32. *C.Th.* 9.40.17; see Hedrick (2000) 98–101; on the authorship of the law, see Honoré (1998) 90–91.
33. Amm. 15.3.23, 14.9.9, 29.1.27. On this imagery, see Matthews (1989) 258–261; MacMullen (1964b) 441–445; Barnes (1998) 107–110; Blockley (1975) 183–184.
34. Amm. 21.16.8. An exhaustive catalogue of Ammianus' examples of imperial moderation and excess forms the substance of Seager (1986) 1–83; see too the discussions in Drexler (1974) 85–103; Sabbah (1978) 437–453. For Ammianus' presentation of imperial power, see the perceptive discussions in Valensi (1957), esp. 91–106; Tassi (1967); and in particular Matthews (1989) 231–278; Barnes (1998) 129–165.
35. Amm. 28.1.23, 16.10.12, 15.8.2, 16.5.12. Even Julian (the emperor in his virtues most closely compared by Ammianus to the "good emperors" of old) could also display signs of inconsistency, excess, immoderation, and injustice. Some examples: Amm. 21.12.25, 22.7.3–4, 22.9.1, 22.9.12, 22.10.6, 25.4.18–21; and see further on this theme Blockley (1975) 77–96; Drexler (1974) 101–103; Matthews (1989) 251–252; Thompson (1947) 79–86; and especially Fontaine (1978) 53–64.
36. Some examples: 14.1.5, 14.5, 14.7.21, 15.2.9, 15.3.2, 26.10.11–14, 27.7.9, 29.1.18–22, 29.2.12–20.
37. Amm. 14.1.7.
38. Amm. 31.14.1–7, quotation from §§1–2 and 5–6; see too 21.16.1–19 (Constantius II); 25.4 (Julian); 30.8–9 (Valentinian I). On the unre-

solved nature of these obituaries, see usefully Blockley (1975) 35–49; Matthews (1989) 112–114, 237–241, 468–470; Niccoli (1976).

39. Amm. 27.7.5, 29.3.3, 30.5.19, 30.6; further examples collected in Seager (1986) 24–29, 43–49.

40. Amm. 29.3.9. For a passionate account which vividly conveys the terror imperial power could inspire, see Alföldi (1952) 28–47.

41. *P.Abinn.* 1, quotation from lines 11–13.

42. On Abinnaeus' career, see Barnes (1985) 369–373, quotation from 373, (1993) 96. Valacius' death is reported in Ath. *V. Ant.* 86.4–7 (*S.Chrét.* 400: 356–358); *Hist. Ar.* 14.4 (ed. H.-G. Opitz, Berlin, 1940); see also *PLRE* I 929.

43. Jones, *LRE* I 392.

44. *P.Ammon* I 3, col. iv, lines 14–22 (trans. Willis and Maresch [1997] 33). For the background to this dispute, see the editors' introduction, esp. 20–22, 42, 47–48. On the functions and duties of the *archiereus,* see usefully Stead (1981) 412–416. Diocletian visited Panopolis in his progress up the Nile in late 298; see Skeat (1964) xii–xv; for the movements of the imperial court in 340s, see Barnes (1993) 219–220.

45. *P.Ammon* I 4, line 32 (trans. Willis and Maresch [1997] 53).

46. Willis and Maresch (1997) 138. The translation is the product of a hypothetical combination by the editors of the nine surviving drafts of the petition (*P.Ammon* 7–15). As the editors stress (at 82), this composite is illustrative only; a final draft of the petition may never have been written or delivered. For the details of the litigation and the legal issues involved (only a much-simplified sketch is offered here), see 59–67; for the role of the *res priuata* in such cases, see Delmaire (1989) 201. In *P.Ammon* 6, line 3, Eugeneios is described as a μεμ[ορ]άριος, strictly speaking, a member of the *scrinium memoriae,* one of the *sacra scrinia.* The editors (at 76) tentatively suggest that Eugeneios may also have been a *notarius.* This seems unlikely: it is not so far, as the editors note, an attested combination of posts, and would, at least in principle, seem to run counter to the administrative concerns which led to the creation and promotion of the *notarii.* For Harpocration's rhetorical career, see Browne (1977) 190–196. He also held posts as "*procurator* and *curator* in the notable cities of Greece" (*P.Ammon* 13, line 26); this may perhaps refer to a stint as an official of the *res priuata* (Delmaire [1988] 132–133, no. 63, and generally on the duties involved [1989] 212–215) and so add to Ammon's stress on Harpocration's courtly connections; but it is more likely to refer to some municipal office (see Delmaire [1989] 211 n. 8, revising his earlier view). For recent discussion of the *curator ciuitatis,* see usefully Liebeschuetz (2001) 110–111, 192–195.

47. Liebeschuetz (1972) 106.
48. Joh. Lydus, *Mag.* 3.69.
49. Amm. 27.7.6, 28.1.25; see too 14.1.10, 15.5.37–38, 16.7.4–8, 27.7.7; for another similarly outspoken *quaestor,* see Proc. *HA* 9.41.
50. *C.Th.* 1.6.9; Symm. *Rel.* 17; see Vera (1981) 131–133.
51. Anon. *de rebus bell. pr.,* quotation from §§1 and 8; see MacMullen (1962) 376.
52. Amm. 28.6.1–24, quotation from §20; see Matthews (1989) 383–387; Blockley (1969) 417–419; Warmington (1956). On the problematic chronology of Ammianus' account, see Demandt (1968).
53. Them. *Or.* 1.17c (ed. H. Schenkl and G. Downey, Leipzig, 1965); for the date, see Vanderspoel (1995) 71–77.
54. Reports: Jones, *LRE* I 403–405; Vogler (1979) 253–254. *C.Th.* 1.16.3 of 319 required provincial governors to submit semiannual reports of judicial proceedings to the praetorian prefects. *C.Th.* 1.10.7 = *CJ* 1.32.1.2 of 401 expected governors to file detailed four-monthly financial returns *(quadrimenstrui breues).* Reports on the proceedings of the Senate at Rome were dispatched to the imperial court every month; Symm. *Rel.* 24.1. An annual assessment was also required from the urban prefect on the progress and merits of university students studying in Rome; *C.Th.* 14.9.1 of 370 with Chastagnol (1960) 287–288.
55. Collection of tax: on the activities of those officials sent out from the Praetorian Prefecture, see Jones, *LRE* I 450–451, 456–458, 589, III 118 n. 98; Ensslin (1954) cols. 2468–69; on those sent out from the office of the *comes sacrarum largitionum* and the *comes rei priuatae,* see Delmaire (1995) 127–134, offering a summary of his magisterial survey in (1989) 239–418, 597–701.
56. *C.Th.* 6.30.1 of 379; *C.Th.* 6.30.4 = *CJ* 12.23.4 of 378; *C.Th.* 6.30.6 = *CJ* 12.23.6 of 383; *C.Th.* 6.30.10 of 385.
57. Jones, *LRE* I 374–375, listing laws with "local allusions" at III 80 n. 22.
58. *Notarii:* Teitler (1985) 21–26; Vogler (1979) 192–197; Jones, *LRE* I 572–575; Clauss (1980) 22–23; Delmaire (1995) 52–53. *Agentes in rebus:* Clauss (1980) 27–32, 45–51; Jones, *LRE* I 578–580; Vogler (1979) 197–210; Holmberg (1933) 104–130; Boak (1924) 68–80; Delmaire (1995) 97–109.
59. *C.Th.* 6.29.4.
60. Lib. *Or.* 18.140, taking rather too seriously a joke in Aristophanes, *Acharnians* 94 (ed. A. Sommerstein, Warminster, Wilts., rev. ed., 1984); see too Herodotus 1.114.2.
61. *Agentes in rebus:* Lib. *Or.* 18.135, 140, 136, 138; *notarii:* ibid. 134, 131.

62. This estimate is avowedly speculative. In 430 Theodosius II and Valentinian III reduced the number to 1,174 (*C.Th.* 6.27.23); the emperor Leo in the mid-460s to 1,248 (*CJ* 12.20.3). Neither law indicates how large the numbers were before these cutbacks; see Clauss (1980) 24–26.

63. Sinnigen (1959) 238. The point is well and convincingly made in Clauss (1980) 72–75; Drinkwater (1983) 360–367; Giardina (1977a) 64–72; Purpura (1973) 231–242; Schuller (1975) 3–8; Teitler (1985) 236–237 n. 32; Delmaire (1995) 116–118. The opposing case is put in Blum (1969), esp. 1–8; Vogler (1979) 184–192; Sinnigen (1959), revising more moderate views in (1957) 18, 112.

64. According to Libanius, Julian cut the number of *notarii* to four and the number of *agentes* to seventeen (*Or.* 2.58). Given Libanius' open partiality toward Julian and his exaggerated rhetorical style, it is difficult to know how far to trust these figures. For doubts and discussion, see Boak (1924) 69; Clauss (1980) 25; Jones, *LRE* I 129; Teitler (1985) 60; and especially the skepticism of Kolb (1998) 353–355. It may be that the reduction in the number of *agentes in rebus* should be linked to Julian's short-lived reforms of the *cursus publicus*. In 362, in a clear attempt to reduce the responsibilities of the *magister officiorum*, the emperor restricted the right to issue warrants for the use of the public post to the praetorian prefect (*C.Th.* 8.5.12); see Clauss (1980) 49; Stein, *Officium* 63. Even so, given the wide range of activities undertaken by *agentes*, any close connection between the reform of the *cursus publicus* and a significant reduction in their number seems on the face of it unlikely. Nor should the extent of Julian's changes be overestimated; see Kolb (1998) 354; to be preferred to Stein (1920) 211–214. Libanius' further claim in the same oration that by 381 there were 520 *notarii* and "a very large number" (μύριοι) of *agentes in rebus* does not inspire much confidence either. For what it is worth, as with many high-ranking officials at the beginning of his reign, it may be better to see Julian as aiming at the retrenchment and replacement of existing *notarii* and *agentes* (perhaps with some reduction in numbers), rather than—as Libanius would have it—their virtual elimination.

65. *C.Th.* 8.8.9 = *CJ* 12.60.3; see too *C.Th.* 1.10.7 = *CJ* 1.32.1 of 401; *C.Th.* 6.29.5 of 359, 6.29.6 of 381, 6.29.12 of 415; *C.Th.* 7.4.35 = *CJ* 12.37.15 of 423; *C.Th.* 7.12.2 = *CJ* 12.42.2 of 379; *C.Th.* 8.8.7 = *CJ* 12.60.2 of 395; *C.Th.* 10.4.1 = *CJ* 3.26.9 of 326; *C.Th.* 12.6.11 = *CJ* 10.72.4 of 366; *C.Th.* 12.6.32.2 = *CJ* 12.60.5 of 429; *C.Th.* 13.11.11 of 406; Val. III, *Nov.* 7.1 of 440; 7.2 of 442; Maj. *Nov.* 2.2 of 458; further examples in Delmaire (1989) 160–166; Monks (1957) 763–772; Noethlichs (1981)

113–116, 144–146; Ensslin (1954) col. 2464; Giardina and Grelle (1983) 267.

66. Joh. Lydus, *Mag.* 2.10 = 3.40. See Chapter 1, note 78.

67. For the details, see Foss (1979) 280–281. Boak (1924) 86–89; James (1988) 273–274, 291–294; and Delmaire (1995) 86–90 all agree that the divided responsibility in the management of the *fabricae* goes back to the inception of the *magister officiorum* under Constantine; but see the reservations in Giardina (1977a) 66–69. For the suggestion that this is a late fourth-century reform, see Jones, *LRE* I 369, III 75 n. 8; Clauss (1980) 52–53.

68. See generally Migl (1994) 227–234. *Cursus publicus:* Stein, *Officium* 61–67; Clauss (1980) 45–51; Boak (1924) 74–80; Holmberg (1933) 86–94; Vogler (1979) 176–177; Chastagnol (1960) 239–240; Stoffel (1994) 8–12; and especially Kolb (1998), emphasizing that Julian's legislation on the public post should be seen as part of a general pattern of imperial regulation rather than as a specially motivated "reform program." Frontier troops *(limitanei):* Boak (1924) 89–91; Clauss (1980) 54–55. Drafting of imperial legislation: Harries (1988) 159–164; Matthews (2000) 178–180.

69. Jones, *LRE* I 690.

70. *C.Th.* 1.6.5 = *CJ* 1.28.1; see Chastagnol (1960) 297–300; Giardina (1977b).

71. Clauss (1980) 18; Jones, *LRE* I 576.

72. Examples from the *Codes* of "double fines" are usefully catalogued in Noethlichs (1981) 223–225; see too *P.Panop.Beatty* 2, lines 11–15, 61–63. On the risks and advantages of such a system of penalties, see Vogler (1979) 254–257; Blockley (1969) 403–405, 414–416; and in particular Rosen (1990), esp. 288–292.

73. Both the role and status of these so-called *principes agentum in rebus* have been much discussed. Delmaire (1995) 111–112 offers a useful summary of the debate. The most important recent contribution is by Giardina (1977a) 13–72, esp. 21–55, with valuable refinements in Clauss (1980) 32–39; Delmaire (1995) 112–116.

74. Jones, *LRE* I 406, 593, 597; Clauss (1980) 39–40; Delmaire (1989) 222.

75. Joh. Lydus, *Mag.* 3.23.

76. *C.Th.* 8.7.1.

77. *CJ* 12.59.9 of 470–474.

78. *CJ* 1.27.1.22–38, quotation from §25.

79. I agree with MacMullen (1988) 265 n. 85, refining the observations of de Ste. Croix (1954) 39–40, that *suffragium* meaning "a purchased recommendation" cannot unambiguously be attested before 338 (*C.Th.*

12.1.25). Such a shift in meaning must have been gradual. *Suffragium* in *C.Th.* 1.32.1 = *CJ* 11.8.2 of 333; *C.Th.* 11.30.6 = *CJ* 1.21.2 of 316; *C.Th.* 12.1.20 of 331 could refer to purchase, influence, or both; but note also two laws in which *suffragium* meaning "a purchased recommendation" requires specific qualification: *suffragio comparato* in *C.Th.* 12.1.5 of 317; *honorem uenali suffragio* in *CJ* 12.32.1 = *C.Th.* 6.38.1 of 312–337. I am much less confident than Collot (1965), especially the laws cited at 192–194; and Liebs (1978) 171–172 that *suffragium* in imperial legislation after 338 always refers to purchased recommendation or advantage, rather than to the exercise of influence (however obtained), or—at least in some cases—to both. Some laws seem clearly ambiguous: *C.Th.* 1.9.1 = *CJ* 1.31.1 of 359; *C.Th.* 6.22.3 of 340; 6.22.6 of 381; 8.5.46 of 385; *C.Th.* 8.7.16 = *CJ* 12.53.1 of 385; *C.Th.* 11.12.3 = *CJ* 4.61.6 of 365; *C.Th.* 12.1.36 = *CJ* 10.65.4 of 343; *C.Th.* 12.1.42 of 354; 12.1.43 of 355; 12.1.44 of 358; 12.1.70 of 365; 12.6.7 of 365. *Suffragium* meaning "purchased recommendation" could be used in contexts in which its meaning was clear. For *suffragium* distinguished from *gratia*: *C.Th.* 6.24.3 of 364; 12.1.75 of 371; *suffragium* distinguished from *ambitio*: *C.Th.* 6.22.2 of 338; 6.24.5 of 392; 6.29.4 of 359; *C.Th.* 6.30.7 = *CJ* 12.23.7 of 384; *C.Th.* 7.20.13 of 407; *C.Th.* 12.1.118 = *CJ* 10.32.41 of 387. Such a meaning might still, at least in some circumstances, require specific qualification (*C.Th.* 7.1.7 of 365; 8.1.1 of 319); and in some cases, qualification does little to clarify any ambiguity; see the references to *suffragium emendicatum* in *C.Th.* 6.27.19 of 417; *C.Th.* 6.30.7 = *CJ* 12.23.7 of 384; *C.Th.* 9.1.15 = *CJ* 9.2.14 of 385; *C.Th.* 12.1.75 of 371.

80. *C.Th.* 6.27.3.
81. *CJ* 12.19.7; for the date, see Honoré (1998) 173.
82. *C.Th.* 1.16.7; see too *C.Th.* 1.5.1 of 325; *C.Th.* 1.5.9 = *CJ* 1.26.3 of 389; *C.Th.* 1.16.3 = *CJ* 7.49.2 of 319; *C.Th.* 1.16.6 = *CJ* 1.40.3 of 331; *C.Th.* 1.16.11 of 369; 1.31.2 of 370; 2.1.6 of 385; 9.1.4 of 325; *C.Th.* 9.27.1 = *CJ* 12.1.12 of 380; *C.Th.* 9.27.5 = *CJ* 9.27.3 of 383; *C.Th.* 9.27.6 = *CJ* 9.27.4 of 386; *C.Th.* 10.1.16 of 399; 11.7.11 of 365; 13.5.36 of 412; Val. III, *Nov.* 23.6 of 447; Maj. *Nov.* 2.2 of 458; further examples in Noethlichs (1981) 162–164, 182–188, 190–191; Corcoran (2000) 239–244.
83. *C.Th.* 8.4.22 of 412; *C.Th.* 9.40.14 = *CJ* 9.47.21 of 385; Maj. *Nov.* 7.16 of 458.
84. Val. III, *Nov.* 1.3.3 of 450; see too *C.Th.* 7.4.35 = *CJ* 12.37.15 of 423; *C.Th.* 8.1.4 = *CJ* 12.49.1 of 334; *C.Th.* 8.10.2 = *CJ* 12.61.2 of 344; *C.Th.* 9.27.3 = *CJ* 9.27.1 of 382; Maj. *Nov.* 2.1 of 458. Generally on the regu-

lation of tax collection, see the examples catalogued in Noethlichs (1981) 134–150.

85. MacMullen (1964b) 452.

86. See the valuable discussions in Honoré (1998) 142–149; Archi (1976) 45–54; Matthews (2000) 57–71 on the inclusion of conflicting and inconsistent laws in the *Theodosian Code.*

87. *FHG* IV fr. 215 (ed. C. Müller, Paris, 1885); *Suda* A no. 2077 (ed. A. Adler, Leipzig, 1928).

88. *C. Th.* 13.3.9 = *CJ* 10.53.10 refining 13.3.8; see Chastagnol (1960) 289–291.

89. Symm. *Rel.* 27 quotation from §4; see Nutton (1977) 208–210. *C.Th.* 13.3.13, issued three years later in 387 by Valentinian II, Theodosius I, and Arcadius to the urban prefect Pinianus, is conventionally taken to be the reply to Symmachus' query. But it is not clear that it answers the particularities of the case with any certainty. The method of selection for *archiatri* set out in the legislation of 368 and 370 was confirmed. Any appointments contrary to this scheme made as a result of imperial grants which had been falsely obtained (inpetratis subrepticiis) were to be rescinded. All well and good, but what of genuine imperial grants?

90. Symm. *Rel.* 22; see Chastagnol (1960) 193–194. Regrettably, the emperor's reply does not survive.

91. Anth. *Nov.* 3.1.

92. Some examples: *C.Th.* 2.1.9 of 397; 2.4.5 of 389; 11.12.4 of 407; 11.13.1 of 383; 11.16.16 of 385; 11.21.3 of 424; 13.11.12 of 409; 16.5.51 of 410; *C.Th.* 16.7.7.3 = *CJ* 1.7.4.3 of 426; *C.Th.* 16.10.8 of 382; Symm. *Rel.* 22, 27.2 (of the special imperial grant of title for the post of *archiatrus* originally presented by John).

93. *CJ* 1.23.6.

94. Joh. Chrys. *Hom. in Gen.* 14.2 (*PG* 53: 112), 44.1 (*PG* 54: 406); *Hom. in Matth.* 1.8 (*PG* 57: 24); *P.Ammon* I 3, col. iv, lines 24 and 26–27 (trans. Willis and Maresch [1977] 33); Basil, *Ep.* 3.1; see Matthews (2000) 187–190; Ando (2000) 106–108.

95. Symm. *Rel.* 44, quotation from §1; see Chastagnol (1960) 362.

96. *C.Th.* 6.2.26.

97. Swift and Oliver (1962) 248, lines 35–37; F. Miltner, *JÖAI* 44 (1959) 287.

98. Blockley (1969) 414–415.

99. Amm. 20.2, quotation from §4; see Matthews (1989) 46–47, 57–66; Blockley (1969) 405–407.

100. Amm. 15.3.4–5; see too 14.5.6–9, 19.12.1–7. For further examples in

Ammianus of courtiers attempting knowingly to mislead emperors, see 15.1.2–3, 15.3.7–11, 15.5.37, 16.7.1–3, 16.8.3–7 (both failures), 17.11.1–4, 29.1.10–11, and those instances collected in Blockley (1969) 406–410; Noethlichs (1981) 203–205.

101. Amm. 22.3.11.

102. Amm. 27.7.9.

103. Amm. 15.5, quotation from §§5 and 12; on this incident, see in particular Drinkwater (1994); Hunt (1999), esp. 52–55; Kelly (1994) 168–169; Matthews (1989) 37–38; Blockley (1969) 408.

104. Soc. 6.15, 18 (*GCS* n.f. 1: 336–338, 341–343); Soz. 8.16, 20 (*GCS* 50: 370–371, 376–377); see too Holum (1982) 69–78; Liebeschuetz (1990) 198–222, showing Eudoxia at the center of a complex coalition of interests.

105. Philostorgius 4.8, 10; more generally on the influence of Constantius II's wife, Eusebia, see Wieber-Scariot (1998), esp. 115–130.

106. Amm. 14.11.2–4, quotation from §3; see too Zos. 2.55.2; Julian, *Ep. ad Ath.* 272D; Philostorgius, 4.1. See too the plots against Constantius' successor Julian: Amm. 17.11.1–4; Julian, *Ep. ad Ath.* 274A–B, 282B–D; Dunlap (1924) 264–270; Vogler (1979) 211–216; see generally Guyot (1980) 145–157; Scholten (1995) 76–95, (1998) 53–63.

107. Joh. Lydus, *Mag.* 3.69.

108. Theod. *HE* 1.33 (*GCS* 44: 89); see too Soc. 1.35.3 (*GCS* n.f. 1: 85) The ambiguity of David's reaction on learning of Ziba's deceit perhaps makes this parallel less attractive than some readers of Theodoret might have expected; see 2 Sam. 16.1–4 and 19.24–30.

109. Soz. 3.18, 4.2.1 (*GCS* 50: 132, 140); Soc. 2.27.1 (*GCS* n.f. 1: 136); Theod. *HE* 2.3.6–8, 2.13.1–2, 2.27 (*GCS* 44: 96–97, 123, 158–162); on these passages, see Urbainczyk (1997) 159–167, esp. 160–161. Further examples in Hedrick (2000) 220–222; Long (1996) 97–105.

110. See especially Greatrex (1997) 71–72. The tactic was an old one; for some examples from the Principate, see Cameron (1976) 185–187; Nippel (1995) 88; Millar (1992) 374.

111. Soz. 7.25.1–7 (*GCS* 50: 338–340). There is a large literature on the many complexities of this incident; see in particular Matthews (1975) 234–236; McLynn (1994) 315–330; Brown (1992) 109–112.

112. Paul. *V. Amb.* 24 (ed. M. Pellegrino, Rome, 1961).

113. Amb. *Ep. extra coll.* 11(51).6 (*CSEL* 82.3: 213–214); see McLynn (1994) 318, 322.

114. Philostorgius 4.1; Zonaras 13.9 (ed. L. Dindorf, Leipzig, 1870).

115. Amm. 30.4.2.

116. Amm. 28.6.26–27.

117. *The Chronicle of Pseudo-Joshua the Stylite* §29; trans. Trombley and Watt (2000) 27.
118. Ibid.
119. Val. III, *Nov.* 1.3.2 of 450.
120. Jones, *LRE* I 391.
121. Brown (1992) 14.
122. Suet. *Tib.* 25.1.

Epilogue

Epigraph: Veyne (1981) 341.

1. *Bohairic Life of St. Pachomius* 84 (*CSCO* 89, *Scriptores Coptici* 7, Louvain, 1925) 84; trans. Veilleux (1980) 110–111.
2. Joh. Lydus, *Mag.* 2.13.
3. MacCormack (1981) 8.
4. Corippus, *Laud. Just.* 3.182–183; V. Porph. 47. See in particular Mango (1984) 40–45 on the iconography of St. Michael.
5. *Bohairic Life of St Pachomius* 144; Theod. *Hist. Rel.* 1.12 (James of Nisibis) (*S.Chrét.* 234: 188).
6. Caesarius, *Serm.* 7.2–3 (*CCSL* 103: 38–39).
7. Joh. Chrys. *Hom. in Ep. I ad Thess. IV* 6.4 (*PG* 62: 434); see too *Hom. in Matth.* 1.8 (*PG* 57: 23–24); *Catechesis* 1.1 (*PG* 49: 223); Cyr. Hiersol. *Procatech.* 1 (*PG* 33: 332A–333A).
8. Joh. Chrys. *Hom. in Rom.* 14.10 (*PG* 60: 537); see too *Hom. in Joh.* 12.1 (*PG* 59: 82); *de Incomp.* = *de Christi Div.* 12.4 (*PG* 48: 809); *Hom. in Gen.* 5.6 (*PG* 53: 54); further examples in Setton (1941) 187–195.
9. Amb. *Exc.* 2.109 (*CSEL* 73: 311–312); Joh. Chrys. *ad Theodorum Lapsum* 1.11 (*S.Chrét.* 117: 144).
10. *P. Bodm.* 29, quotations from lines 4, 49, 150–152, and 329–334 (ed. Kessels and van der Horst [1987] 320–344). For the date and discussion of the various military and bureaucratic ranks, offices, and uniforms, see Bremmer (1988), esp. 85–86, (2002) 128–133; see too W. Speyer, *RLAC* 12 (1983) cols. 1258–61, s.v. "Gürtel."
11. Theodosius, *On St. Michael the Archangel* 29 (ed. and trans. Wallis Budge [1915] 908); see Orlandi (1971), esp. 178–180, 182–183. More generally on the (arch)angelology in Coptic texts, see Müller (1959), esp. 8–35 and 161–218 on Michael.
12. Theodosius, *On St. Michael the Archangel* 9 and 30; trans. Wallis Budge (1915) 898 and 908.
13. Theodosius, *On St. Michael the Archangel* 20–30.

14. Ibid. 7; trans. Wallis Budge (1915) 897.

15. Theodosius, *On St. Michael the Archangel* 45–46; trans. Wallis Budge (1915) 918.

16. *The Book of the Investiture of the Archangel Michael* (*CSCO* 225, *Scriptores Coptici* 31, Louvain, 1962) §1 for the vision, §§6 and 12 for the investiture. For other, similar accounts, see Müller (1959) 174–175, 208–209; Crum (1903) 396–397; van Lantschoot (1947).

17. Timothy of Alexandria, *Discourse on St. Michael the Archangel* 144 (ed. Wallis Budge [1915] 512–525); trans. at 1027, including supplements; see too Müller (1959) 161–162.

18. Sev. Ant. *Hom.* 72.365 (*PO* 12: 83–84; trans. M. Brière). Severus' views were also cited at the Council of Nicaea II in 787; see J. D. Mansi, *Sacrorum Conciliorum nova et amplissima collectio,* vol. 13 (Florence, 1767) col. 184C.

19. van Lantschoot (1946) 320 and 325–326; see too Brown (1992) 145, (1995) 74.

20. Eph. Syr. *Hymni de paradiso* 11.5 (*CSCO* 174, *Scriptores Syri* 78, Louvain, 1957); trans. Brock (1990) 155.

21. Joh. Chrys. *Hom. de capto Eutrop.* 9 (*PG* 52: 404).

22. Joh. Chrys. *de Incomp.* 3.5 (*S.Chrét.* 28*bis:* 212); see Lim (1995) 171–177. For a discussion of John's theology and its antecedents, see usefully J. Daniélou's introduction to *S.Chrét.* 28*bis.*

23. Joh. Chrys. *Hom. in Ep. II ad Cor.* 26.5 (*PG* 61: 582).

24. Joh. Chrys. *de Incomp.* 2.3–4 (*S.Chrét.* 28*bis:* 154–166).

25. Joh. Chrys. *Hom. in Rom.* 14.10 (*PG* 60: 537–538); see too *Hom. in Ep. I ad Thess. IV* 6.4 (*PG* 62: 434); *ad Theodorum Lapsum* 1.11–12 (*S.Chrét.* 117: 140–146).

26. *Bohairic Life of St. Pachomius* 82 and 88; trans. Veilleux (1980) 105–106 and 115.

27. Ruf. *Hist. Mon. (G)* 8.19 (Apollo) (ed. A. J. Festugière, Brussels, 1971); Joh. Chrys. *Hom. ad pop. Ant.* 17.1 (*PG* 49: 173).

28. See usefully Chitty (1966) 22–27; Rousseau (1985) 77–104, emphasizing that the monastic rule attributed to Pachomius was largely devised by his successors. On the bureaucratic parallels, see Ruppert (1971) 233–337.

29. *Pachomii Praecepta* 77 (ed. A. Boon, Louvain, 1932); see Brown (1978) 96.

30. *Bohairic Life of St. Pachomius* 144.

31. On the dating and composition of the text, which survives in a wide variety of languages and versions, see the useful summaries in Himmel-

farb (1983) 16–19; Piovanelli (1993) 37–45. Arguments for a second-century date (with a later revision) are canvassed in Silverstein and Hilhorst (1997) 11–12; Rosenstiehl (1990), esp. 207–210; and, for a late fourth- or early fifth-century date, Piovanelli (1993) 45–54. In dating the revision of the text to 420, I have followed the emendation to the consular names in the text suggested in Silverstein (1962), esp. 337–345; and Silverstein and Hilhorst (1997) 18–19 n. 3.

32. *Visio Pauli* 1–2, in the "Long Latin" version of the text from a manuscript in Paris, ed. Silverstein and Hilhorst (1997) 66–68. The account of the finding of the text is placed at the end of the Syriac version (ed. G. Ricciotti, *Orientalia,* n.s. 2 [1933] 1–25, 120–149 at §52; trans. J. Perkins, *JAOS* 8 [1864] 183–212 at 209–210).

33. *Visio Pauli* 31 (Silverstein and Hilhorst [1997] 136–138).

34. Ibid. 17 (Silverstein and Hilhorst [1997] 106). See too the version of this passage in the Coptic text: "And at that moment the angel came into the midst, with a bill of indictment of its sins in his hand, and he said, 'My Lord, the sins which this soul hath committed since its youth are in my hand; dost Thou wish me, O my Lord, to recite its sins from the time when it was ten years old?' And the Judge said unto the angel of the soul, 'O angel, I do not seek to know what sins it hath committed since the time when it was ten years of age or fifteen; on the contrary, I only ask thee concerning the sins which it hath committed in this year, the year in which it died'" (ed. Wallis Budge [1915] 534–574); trans. at 1046–47.

35. For good accounts of the "Riot of the Statues," see Browning (1952); Downey (1961) 426–433; Petit (1955) 238–244; French (1998); and especially van de Paverd (1991) 15–159.

36. Ath. *Contra Arianos* 3.5 (*PG* 26: 332); see Ando (2000) 239. On imperial portraits, see generally Setton (1941) 196–211; Kruse (1934) 23–50; Hopkins (1978) 221–231; MacCormack (1981) 67–73; Ando (2000) 232–253. On their destruction, see especially the perceptive remarks in Stewart (2003) 267–298.

37. Joh. Chrys. *Hom. ad pop. Ant.* 13.1–2 (*PG* 49: 136–139), quotation from 13.2.

38. Joh. Chrys. *Hom. in Ep. I ad Thess.* IV 9.5 (*PG* 62: 454) and *Hom. in Hebr.* 31.4 (*PG* 63: 218).

39. Joh. Chrys. *Hom. in Ep. II ad Cor.* 9.4 (*PG* 61: 466).

40. For these visions of the Last Judgment, see Joh. Chrys. *Hom. in Ep. II ad Cor.* 10.3–4 (*PG* 61: 471–472); *Hom. in Ep. ad Rom.* 3.1, 5.6, 25.6 (*PG* 60: 411, 430, 635–638); *Hom. in Matth.* 79.1–2 (*PG* 58: 717–720); *Hom. in*

Joh. 34.3 (*PG* 59: 196–197); *ad Theodorum Lapsum* 1.12 (*S.Chrét.* 117: 146–152), quotations from *Hom. in Ep. II ad Cor.* 10.3 (*PG* 61: 471); *Hom. in Joh.* 42.4 (*PG* 59: 244). See too Caesarius, *Serm.* 82.3 (*CCSL* 103: 338–339), 222.3 (*CCSL* 104.1: 141); Aug. *Civ. Dei* 20, esp. 21 and 24 (*CCSL* 48: 736–740, 744–747).

41. Brown (1981) 62–63.
42. Joh. Chrys. *de Incomp.* 4.4 (*S.Chrét.* 28*bis:* 250).

Bibliography

Abel, F.-M. 1909. "Épigraphie grecque palestinienne." *RBi* n.s. 6: 89–106.

Ahrweiler, H. 1961. "Fonctionnaires et bureaux maritimes à Byzance." *REByz* 19: 239–252.

Alföldi, A. 1952. *A Conflict of Ideas in the Late Roman Empire: The Clash between the Senate and Valentinian I.* Trans. H. Mattingly. Oxford.

Almagro-Gorbea, M., J. Álvarez Martínez, J. Blázquez Martínez, and S. Rovira. 2000. *El disco de Teodosio.* Estudios del Gabinete de Antigüedades 5. Madrid: Real Academia de la Historia.

Alt, A. 1921. *Die griechischen Inschriften der Palaestina Tertia westlich der ʿAraba.* Wissenschaftliche Veröffentlichungen des deutsch-türkischen Denkmal-schutz-Kommandos 2. Ed. T. Wiegand. Berlin.

Ando, C. 2000. *Imperial Ideology and Provincial Loyalty in the Roman Empire.* Berkeley: University of California Press.

Andreotti, R. 1975. "Problemi del "suffragium" nell'imperatore Giuliano." In *Atti dell'Accademia romanistica Costantiniana: I convegno internazionale (Spello, Foligno, Perugia) 18–20 settembre 1973.* Università degli studi di Perugia. 3–26.

Archi, G. G. 1976. *Teodosio II e la sua codificazione.* Storia del pensiero giuridico 4. Naples.

Arjava, A. 1996. *Women and Law in Late Antiquity.* Oxford.

Armstrong, D. 1986. "*Horatius Eques et Scriba: Satires* 1.6 and 2.7." *TAPhA* 116: 255–288.

Ausbüttel, F. M. 1988. *Die Verwaltung der Städte und Provinzen im spätantiken Italien.* Europäische Hochschulschriften 343. Frankfurt am Main.

———— 1998. *Die Verwaltung des römischen Kaiserreiches: von der Herrschaft des Augustus bis zum Niedergang des Weströmischen Reiches.* Darmstadt.

Austin, N. J. E., and N. B. Rankov. 1995. *Exploratio: Military and Political Intelligence in the Roman World from the Second Punic War to the Battle of Adrianople.* London: Routledge.

Avery, W. T. 1940. "The *Adoratio Purpurae* and the Importance of the Imperial Purple in the Fourth Century of the Christian Era." *MAAR* 17: 66–80.

Bagnall, R. S. 1992a. "Military Officers as Landowners in Fourth Century Egypt." *Chiron* 22: 47–54 (reprinted in Bagnall [2003] no. 14).

——— 1992b. "Landholding in Late Roman Egypt: The Distribution of Wealth." *JRS* 82: 128–149 (reprinted in Bagnall [2003] no. 12).

——— 1993. *Egypt in Late Antiquity.* Princeton.

——— 2003. *Later Roman Egypt: Society, Religion, Economy and Administration.* Variorum Reprints 758. Aldershot.

Bandy, A. C. 1983. *Ioannes Lydus On Powers or The Magistracies of the Roman State: Introduction, Critical Text, Translation, Commentary, and Indices.* American Philosophical Society Memoirs 149. Philadelphia.

Barber, C. 1990. "The Imperial Panels at San Vitale: A Reconsideration." *Byzantine and Modern Greek Studies* 14: 19–42.

Bardill, J. 1999. "The Great Palace of the Byzantine Emperors and the Walker Trust Excavations." *JRA* 12: 216–230.

Barnes, T. D. 1974. "A Law of Julian." *CPh* 69: 288–291.

——— 1982. *The New Empire of Diocletian and Constantine.* Cambridge, Mass.: Harvard University Press.

——— 1985. "The Career of Abinnaeus." *Phoenix* 39: 368–374 (reprinted in his *From Eusebius to Augustine: Selected Papers 1982–1993,* Variorum Reprints 438, Aldershot, 1994, no. 15).

——— 1993. *Athanasius and Constantius: Theology and Politics in the Constantinian Empire.* Cambridge, Mass.: Harvard University Press.

——— 1996. "Emperors, Panegyrics, Prefects, Provinces and Palaces (284–317)." *JRA* 9: 532–552.

——— 1998. *Ammianus Marcellinus and the Representation of Historical Reality.* Cornell Studies in Classical Philology 56. Ithaca: Cornell University Press.

Barnish, S., A. D. Lee, and Michael Whitby. 2000. "Government and Administration." In Av. Cameron, B. Ward-Perkins, and Michael Whitby, eds., *The Cambridge Ancient History.* Vol. XIV: *Late Antiquity: Empire and Successors, A.D. 425–600.* Cambridge. 164–206.

Barrau, P. 1987. "À propos de l'*officium* du vicaire d'Afrique." In A. Mastino, ed., *"L'Africa Romana": Atti del IV Convegno di studio, Sassari, 12–14 dicembre 1986.* Vol. I. Pubblicazioni del Dipartimento di storia dell'Università di Sassari 8. Sassari. 79–100.

Batiffol, P. H. 1919. *Études de liturgie et d'archéologie chrétienne*. Paris.

Beard, M., J. North, and S. R. F. Price. 1998. *Religions of Rome*. 2 vols. Cambridge.

Bell, H. I., V. Martin, E. G. Turner, and D. van Berchem. 1962. *The Abinnaeus Archive: Papers of a Roman Officer in the Reign of Constantius II*. Oxford.

Berger, P. C. 1981. *The Insignia of the Notitia Dignitatum*. New York.

Blockley, R. C. 1969. "Internal Self-Policing in the Late Roman Administration: Some Evidence from Ammianus Marcellinus." *C&M* 30: 403–419.

———— 1975. *Ammianus Marcellinus: A Study of His Historiography and Political Thought*. Collection Latomus 141. Brussels.

———— 1981. *The Fragmentary Classicising Historians of the Later Roman Empire: Eunapius, Olympiodorus, Priscus and Malchus*. ARCA Classical and Medieval Texts, Papers and Monographs 6. Liverpool.

———— 1983. *The Fragmentary Classicising Historians of the Later Roman Empire: Eunapius, Olympiodorus, Priscus and Malchus*. Vol. II: *Text, Translation and Historiographical Notes*. ARCA Classical and Medieval Texts, Papers and Monographs 10. Liverpool.

Blum, W. 1969. *Curiosi und Regendarii: Untersuchungen zur geheimen Staatspolizei der Spätantike*. Munich.

Boak, A. E. R. 1915. "The Roman *Magistri* in the Civil and Military Service of the Empire." *HSPh* 26: 73–164.

———— 1924. "The Master of Offices in the Later Roman and Byzantine Empires." In A. E. R. Boak and J. E. Dunlap, *Two Studies in Later Roman and Byzantine Administration*. University of Michigan Studies Humanistic Series 14. New York. Part I at 1–160.

———— 1937. "Officium." *P-W* 17.2: cols. 2045–56.

Boeswillwald, E., R. Cagnat, and A. Ballu. 1891–1905. *Timgad, une cité africaine sous l'Empire romain*. Paris.

Bonini, R. 1989. *Ricerche sulla legislazione giustinianea dell'anno 535: Nov. Iustiniani 8: venalità delle cariche e riforme dell'amministrazione periferica*. 3d ed. Bologna.

Boulvert, G. 1970. *Esclaves et les affranchis impériaux sous le Haut-Empire romain: rôle politique et administratif*. Biblioteca di Labeo 4. Naples.

———— 1974. *Domestique et fonctionnaire sous le Haut-Empire romain: la condition de l'affranchi et de l'esclave du prince*. Annales littéraires de l'Université de Besançon 151. Paris.

Boulvert, G., and C. Bruschi. 1982. "Staatsdienst und soziale Strukturen: die Lage der subalternen Provinzbeamten." *Klio* 64: 421–429.

Bowman, A. K. 1985. "Landholding in the Hermopolite Nome in the Fourth Century A.D." *JRS* 75: 137–163.

Bremmer, J. N. 1988. "An Imperial Palace Guard in Heaven: The Date of the Vision of Dorotheus." *ZPE* 75: 82–88.

—— 2002. *The Rise and Fall of the Afterlife: The 1995 Read-Tuckwell Lectures at the University of Bristol.* London: Routledge.

Brennan, P. M. 1996. "The *Notitia Dignitatum.*" In C. Nicolet, ed., *Les littératures techniques dans l'antiquité romaine: statut, public et destination, tradition.* Fondation Hardt, Entretiens. Geneva.

Brock, S. 1990. *St. Ephrem the Syrian: Hymns on Paradise.* New York: St. Vladimir's Seminary Press.

Brown, P. 1971. "The Rise and Function of the Holy Man in Late Antiquity." *JRS* 61: 80–101 (reprinted in his *Society and the Holy in Late Antiquity,* London: Faber and Faber, 1982, at 103–152).

—— 1978. *The Making of Late Antiquity.* Cambridge, Mass.: Harvard University Press.

—— 1981. *The Cult of the Saints: Its Rise and Function in Latin Christianity.* Chicago: University of Chicago Press.

—— 1992. *Power and Persuasion in Late Antiquity: Towards a Christian Empire.* Madison: University of Wisconsin Press.

—— 1995. *Authority and the Sacred: Aspects of the Christianisation of the Roman World.* Cambridge.

Browne, G. M. 1977. "Harpocration Panegyrista." *ICS* 2: 184–196.

Browning, R. 1952. "The Riot of A.D. 387 in Antioch: The Role of the Theatrical Claques in the Later Empire." *JRS* 42: 13–20.

Bruns, G. 1935. *Der Obelisk und seine Basis auf dem Hippodrom zu Konstantinopel.* Istanbuler Forschungen 7. Istanbul.

Brunt, P. A. 1961. "Charges of Provincial Maladministration under the Early Principate." *Historia* 10: 189–227 (reprinted in Brunt [1990] no. 4 at 53–95).

—— 1975. "The Administrators of Roman Egypt." *JRS* 65: 124–147 (reprinted in Brunt [1990] no. 10 at 215–254).

—— 1990. *Roman Imperial Themes.* Oxford.

Burkhalter, F. 1990. "Archives locales et archives centrales en Égypte romaine." *Chiron* 20: 191–216.

Burton, G. P. 1975. "Proconsuls, Assizes and the Administration of Justice under the Empire." *JRS* 65: 92–106.

Caimi, J. 1981. "Ioannis Lydi *de magistratibus* III 70. Note esegetiche e spunti in tema di fiscalità e legislazione protobizantine." In *Miscellanea Agostino Pertusi* I = *Rivista di Studi Bizantini e Slavi* 1: 317–361.

—— 1984. *Burocrazia e diritto nel De magistratibus di Giovanni Lido.* Università di Genova Fondazione Nobile Agostino Poggi 16. Milan.

Calderone, S. 1993. "Costantinopoli: la 'seconda Roma.'" In A. Carandini, L. Cracco Ruggini, and A. Giardina, eds., *Storia di Roma.* Vol. III.1: *L'età tardoantica: crisi e trasformazioni.* Turin. 723–749.

Callu, J.-P. 1969. *La politique monétaire des empereurs romains de 238 à 311*. Bibliothèque des Écoles françaises d'Athènes et de Rome 214. Paris.

Cameron, Alan. 1970. *Claudian: Poetry and Propaganda at the Court of Honorius*. Oxford.

——— 1976. *Circus Factions: Blues and Greens at Rome and Byzantium*. Oxford.

——— 1979. "The Date of the Anonymus *De rebus bellicis*." in M. W. C. Hassall, ed., *De rebus bellicis: Part I, Aspects of the De rebus bellicis: Papers Presented to Professor E. A. Thompson*. BAR International Series 63. Oxford. 1–10 (reprinted in his *Literature and Society in the Early Byzantine World*, Variorum Reprints 209, Aldershot, 1985, no. 9).

——— 1993. *The Greek Anthology from Meleager to Planudes*. Oxford.

Cameron, Alan, and J. Long. 1993. *Barbarians and Politics at the Court of Arcadius*. Transformation of the Classical Heritage 19. Berkeley: University of California Press.

Cameron, Averil. 1975. "Corippus' Poem on Justin II: A Terminus of Antique Art?" *ASNP* 3d ser. 5: 129–165 (reprinted in Av. Cameron [1981] no. 6).

——— 1976. *Flavius Cresconius Corippus: In laudem Iustini Augusti minoris libri IV.* London: Athlone Press.

——— 1980. "The Career of Corippus Again." *CQ* n.s. 30: 534–539 (reprinted in Av. Cameron [1981] no. 8).

——— 1981. *Continuity and Change in Sixth-Century Byzantium*. Variorum Reprints 143. Aldershot.

——— 1985. *Procopius and the Sixth Century*. Transformation of the Classical Heritage 10. Berkeley: University of California Press.

Canto, A. 2000. "Las Quindecennalia de Teodosio I el Grande (19 de Enero del 393 D.C.) en el gran clipeo de Madrid." In M. Almagro-Gorbea et al. (2000) 289–300.

Carney, T. F. 1971. *Bureaucracy in Traditional Society: Romano-Byzantine Bureaucracies Viewed from Within*. Lawrence, Kans.

Carrié, J. M. 1976. "Patronage et propriété militaires au IVe siècle: objet rhétorique et objet réel du discours *Sur les Patronages* de Libanius." *BCH* 100: 159–176.

Casson, L. 1995. *Ships and Seamanship in the Ancient World*. Rev. ed. Baltimore: Johns Hopkins University Press.

Chastagnol, A. 1960. *La préfecture urbaine à Rome sous le Bas-Empire*. Publications de la Faculté des Lettres et Sciences humaines d'Alger 34. Paris.

——— 1965. "Les Espagnols dans l'aristocratie gouvernementale à l'époque de Théodose." In A. Piganiol and H. Terrasse, eds., *Les Empereurs romains d'Espagne. Madrid-Italica, 31 mars–6 avril 1964: Colloques internationaux du*

Centre national de la recherche scientifique. Paris. 269–292 (reprinted in his *Aspects de l'antiquité tardive,* Saggi di storia antica 6, Rome, 1994, at 11–42).

——— 1978. *L'Album municipal de Timgad.* Antiquitas 3:22. Bonn.

——— 1992. *Le sénat romain à l'époque impériale: recherches sur la composition de l'assemblée et le statut de ses membres.* Paris.

Chauvot, A. 1986. *Procope de Gaza, Priscien de Césarée: Panégyriques de l'empereur Anastase Ier.* Antiquitas 1, Abhandlungen zur alten Geschichte 35. Bonn.

——— 1987. "Curiales et paysans en Orient à la fin du Ve et au début du VIe siècle: note sur l'institution du *vindex.*" In E. Frézouls, ed., *Sociétés urbaines, sociétés rurales dans l'Asie Mineure et la Syrie hellénistiques et romaines.* Contributions et travaux de l'Institut d'histoire romaine 4. Strasbourg. 271–281.

Chitty, D. J. 1966. *The Desert a City: An Introduction to the Study of Egyptian and Palestinian Monasticism under the Christian Empire.* Oxford.

Christiansen, P. G. 1969. *The Use of Images by Claudius Claudianus.* Studies in Classical Literature 7. The Hague.

Christol, M. 1986. *Essai sur l'évolution des carrières sénatoriales dans la second moitié de IIIe siècle ap. J.C.* Études prosopographiques 6. Paris.

Chuvin, P. 1990. *A Chronicle of the Last Pagans.* Trans. B. A. Archer, Revealing Antiquity 4. Cambridge, Mass.: Harvard University Press.

Clark, E. A. 1984. *The Life of Melania the Younger.* Studies in Women and Religion 14. New York.

Clauss, M. 1973. *Untersuchungen zu den principales des römischen Heeres von Augustus bis Diokletian: cornicularii, speculatores, frumentarii.* Bochum.

——— 1980. *Der magister officiorum in der Spätantike (4.–6. Jahrhundert): das Amt und sein Einfluss aus der kaiserliche Politik.* Vestigia 32. Munich.

Cockle, W. E. H. 1984. "State Archives in Graeco-Roman Egypt from 30 B.C. to the Reign of Septimius Severus." *JEA* 70: 106–122.

Cohen, B. 1984. "Some Neglected 'Ordines': The Apparatorial Status-Groups." In C. Nicolet, ed., *Des ordres à Rome.* Publications de la Sorbonne, série histoire ancienne et médiévale 13. Paris. 23–60.

Collot, C. 1965. "La pratique et l'institution du *suffragium* au Bas-Empire." *RD* 43: 185–221.

Corcoran, S. 2000. *The Empire of the Tetrarchs: Imperial Pronouncements and Government, AD 284–324.* Rev. ed. Oxford.

Cotton, H. M. 1981. "Military Tribunates and the Exercise of Patronage." *Chiron* 11: 229–238.

Cotton, H. M., W. E. H. Cockle, and F. Millar. 1995. "The Papyrology of the Roman Near East: A Survey." *JRS* 85: 214–235.

Crum, W. E. 1903. "Texts Attributed to Peter of Alexandria." *JThS* 4: 387–397.

Dagron, G. 1969. "Aux origines de la civilisation byzantine: langue de culture et langue d'État." *RH* 241: 23–56 (reprinted in his *La romanité chrétienne en Orient: héritages et mutations*, Variorum Reprints 193, Aldershot, 1984, no. 1).

———— 1974. *Naissance d'une capitale: Constantinople et ses institutions de 330 à 451*. Bibliothèque byzantine études 7. Paris.

———— 1985. "Un tarif des sportules à payer aux *curiosi* du port de Séleucie de Piérie (VIe siècle)." *T&MByz* 9: 435–455.

Daniélou, J. 1950. "L'incompréhensibilité de Dieu d'après saint Jean Chrysostome." *RecSR* 37: 176–194.

de Bonfils, G. 1981. *Il comes et quaestor nell'età della dinastia costantiniana*. Pubblicazioni della Facoltà giuridica dell'Università di Bari 62. Naples.

Deckers, J. G. 1973. "Die Wandmalerei des tetrarchischen Lagerheiligtums im Ammon-Tempel von Luxor." *RQA* 68: 1–34.

———— 1979. "Die Wandmalerei im Kaiserkultraum von Luxor." *JDAI* 94: 600–652.

Deichmann, F. W. 1976. *Ravenna: Haupstadt des spätantiken Abendlandes II. Kommentar Vol. 2*. Wiesbaden.

de Jonge, P. 1948. "A Curious Place in Ammianus Marcellinus, Dealing with Scarcity of Corn and Cornprices." *Mnemosyne* 4th ser. 1: 73–80.

Delbrueck, R. 1929. *Die Consulardiptychen und verwandte Denkmäler. Studien zur spätantiken Kunstgeschichte 2*. Berlin.

Delmaire, R. 1984. "Les dignitaires laïcs au Concile de Chalcédoine: notes sur la hiérarchie et les préséances au milieu du Ve siècle." *Byzantion* 54: 141–175.

———— 1988. "Le personnel de l'administration financière en Égypte sous le Bas-Empire romain (IV–VIe siècles)." *CRIPEL* 10: 113–138.

———— 1989. *Largesses sacrées et res privata: l'aerarium impérial et son administration du IVe au VIe siècle*. Collection de l'École française de Rome 121. Rome.

———— 1995. *Les institutions du Bas-Empire romain de Constantin à Justinien*. Vol. I: *Les institutions civiles palatines*. Initiations au christianisme ancien. Paris.

Demandt, A. 1968. "Die tripolitanischen Wirren unter Valentinian I." *Byzantion* 38: 333–363.

———— 1989. *Die Spätantike: römische Geschichte von Diocletian bis Justinian 284–565 n. Chr.* Handbuch der Altertumswissenschaft 3:6. Munich.

Demougeot, E. 1986. "Le fonctionnariat du Bas-Empire éclairé par les fautes des fonctionnaires." *Latomus* 45: 160–170.

den Heijer, J. 1989. *Mawhūb ibn Manṣūr ibn Mufarriǧ et l'historiographie copto-arabe: étude sur la composition de l'Histoire des Patriarches d'Alexandrie.* CSCO 513, Subsidia 83. Louvain.

de Ste. Croix, G. E. M. 1954. "*Suffragium:* From Vote to Patronage." *British Journal of Sociology* 5: 33–48.

Dimitrov, D. P. 1960. "Le pitture murali del sepolcro romano di Silistra." *Arte Antica e Moderna* 9: 351–365.

——— 1962. "Le système décoratif et la date des peintures murales du tombeau antique de Silistra." *CArch* 12: 35–52.

Döpp, S. 1980. *Zeitgeschichte in Dichtungen Claudians. Hermes* Einzelschriften 43. Wiesbaden.

Downey, G. 1961. *A History of Antioch in Syria, from Seleucus to the Arab Conquest.* Princeton.

Drexler, H. 1974. *Ammianstudien.* Spudasmata 31. Hildesheim.

Drinkwater, J. 1983. "The 'Pagan Underground,' Constantius II's 'Secret Service,' and the Survival and the Usurpation of Julian the Apostate." In C. Deroux, ed., *Studies in Latin Literature and Roman History.* Vol. III. Collection Latomus 180, Brussels. 348–387.

——— 1987. *The Gallic Empire: Separatism and Continuity in the North-Western Provinces of the Roman Empire, A.D. 260–274. Historia* Einzelschiften 52. Stuttgart.

——— 1994. "Silvanus, Ursicinus and Ammianus: Fact or Fiction?" In C. Deroux, ed., *Studies in Latin Literature and Roman History.* Vol. VII. Collection Latomus 227. Brussels. 568–576.

Dubuisson, M. 1991. "Jean le Lydien et les formes de pouvoir personnel à Rome." *CCG* 2: 55–72.

——— 1992. "Jean le Lydien et le Latin: les limites d'une compétence." In *Serta Leodiensia secunda: mélanges publiés par les classiques de Liège à l'occasion du 175e anniversaire de l'Université.* Liège. 123–131.

Duncan-Jones, R. P. 1982. *The Economy of the Roman Empire: Quantitative Studies.* 2d ed. Cambridge.

——— 1990. *Structure and Scale in the Roman Economy.* Cambridge.

——— 1994. *Money and Government in the Roman Empire.* Cambridge.

Dunlap, J. E. 1924. "The Office of the Grand Chamberlain in the Later Roman and Byzantine Empires." In A. E. R. Boak and J. E. Dunlap, *Two Studies in Later Roman and Byzantine Administration.* University of Michigan Studies Humanistic Series 14. New York. Part II at 161–324.

Durliat, J., and A. Guillou. 1984. "Le tarif d'Abydos (vers 492)." *BCH* 108: 581–598.

Dussaud, R., and F. Macler. 1903. *Mission dans les régions désertiques de la Syrie moyenne.* Paris.

Ebersolt, J. 1910. *Le grand palais de Constantinople et le Livre des Cérémonies.* Bibliothèque de la Fondation Thiers 21. Paris.

Eck, W. 1980. "Rom, sein Reich und seine Untertanen: zur administrativen Umsetzung von Herrschaft in der hohen Kaiserzeit." *Geschichte in Köln* 7: 5–31.

——— 1982. "Einfluß korrupter Praktiken auf das senatorisch-ritterliche Beförderugswesen in der Hohen Kaiserzeit." In Schuller (1982a) 135–151.

——— 2000. "Provincial Administration and Finance." In A. K. Bowman, P. Garnsey, and D. Rathbone, eds., *The Cambridge Ancient History.* Vol. XI: *The High Empire, A.D. 70–192.* 2d ed. Cambridge. 266–292.

El-Saghir, M., J.-C. Golvin, M. Reddé, and E.-S. Hegazy. 1986. *Le camp romain de Louqsor.* Mémoires de l'Institut français d'archéologie orientale du Caire 83. Paris.

Elsner, J. 1995. *Art and the Roman Viewer: The Transformation of Art from the Pagan World to Christianity.* Cambridge.

Ensslin, W. 1942. "Palatini." *P-W* 18.2: cols. 2529–60.

——— 1954. "Praefectus Praetorio." *P-W* 22.2: cols. 2391–2502.

Evans, J. A. S. 1996. *The Age of Justinian: The Circumstances of Imperial Power.* London: Routledge.

Fentress, E. W. B. 1979. *Numidia and the Roman Army: Social, Military and Economic Aspects of the Frontier Zone.* BAR International Series 53. Oxford.

Finley, M. I. 1983. *Politics in the Ancient World.* Cambridge.

Fontaine, J. 1978. "Le Julien d'Ammien Marcellin." In R. Braun and J. Richer, eds., *L'Empereur Julien: de l'histoire à la légende (331–1715).* Groupe de recherches de Nice. Paris. 31–65.

Foss, C. 1979. "The *Fabricenses Ducenarii* of Sardis." *ZPE* 35: 279–283.

Foti Talamanca, G. 1974. *Ricerche sul processo nell'Egitto greco-romano.* Vol. I: *L'organizzazione del "Conventus" del "Praefectus Aegypti."* Università di Roma, Pubblicazioni dell'Istituto di diritto romano e dei diritti dell'Oriente mediterraneo 48. Milan.

——— 1979. *Ricerche sul processo nell'Egitto greco-romano.* Vol. II.1: *L'introduzione del giudizio.* Milan.

Frank, R. I. 1967. "*Commendabiles* in Ammianus." *AJPh* 88: 309–318.

——— 1969. *Scholae Palatinae: The Palace Guards of the Later Roman Empire.* Papers and Monographs of the American Academy in Rome 23. Rome.

French, D. R. 1998. "Rhetoric and the Rebellion of A.D. 387 in Antioch." *Historia* 47: 468–484.

Friedländer, L. 1921–23. *Darstellungen aus der Sittengeschichte Roms in der Zeit von Augustus bis zum Ausgang der Antonine.* 4 vols. Ed. G. Wissowa. 10th ed. Leipzig (reprint, Aalen, 1964).

Frier, B. W. 2000. "Demography." In A. K. Bowman, P. Garnsey, and D. Rathbone, eds., *The Cambridge Ancient History*. Vol. XI: *The High Empire, A.D. 70–192*. 2d ed. Cambridge. 787–816.

Fuchs, F. 1926. *Die höheren Schulen von Konstantinopel im Mittelalter*. Byzantinisches Archiv 8. Leipzig.

Gager, J. G. 1992. *Curse Tablets and Binding Spells in the Ancient World*. Oxford.

Garnsey, P. 1970. *Social Status and Legal Privilege in the Roman Empire*. Oxford.

Garnsey, P., and R. P. Saller. 1987. *The Roman Empire: Economy, Society and Culture*. London: Duckworth.

Garnsey, P., and G. D. Woolf. 1989. "Patronage of the Rural Poor in the Roman World." In Wallace-Hadrill (1989) 153–170.

Giardina, A. 1977a. *Aspetti della burocrazia nel Basso Impero*. Filologia e critica 22. Rome.

———— 1977b. "Sulla concorrenza tra prefettura urbana e prefettura dell'annona." *SicGym* 30: 65–74.

———— 1989. *Anonimo: Le cose della guerra*. Fondazione Lorenzo Valla. Milan.

Giardina, A., and F. Grelle. 1983 "La Tavola di Trinitapoli: una nova costituzione di Valentiniano I." *MEFR* 95: 249–303.

Gitti, A. 1932. "L'ordinamento provinciale dell'Oriente sotto Giustiniano." *BMIR* 3: 47–79.

Goffart, W. 1970. "Did Julian Combat Venal *suffragium*? A Note on *C.Th.* 2.29.1." *CPh* 65: 145–151.

Goodburn, R., and P. Bartholomew, eds. 1976. *Aspects of the Notitia Dignitatum: Papers presented to the Conference in Oxford, December 13 to 15, 1974*. BAR Supplementary Series 15. Oxford.

Goodchild, R. G. 1953. "The Roman and Byzantine *limes* in Cyrenaica." *JRS* 43: 65–76.

———— 1976a. "The 'Palace of the Dux.'" In Humphrey (1976) 245–265.

———— 1976b. "The Roman Public Baths." In Humphrey (1976) 175–243.

Gordon, R. 1990. "Religion in the Roman Empire: The Civic Compromise and Its Limits." In M. Beard and J. North, eds., *Pagan Priests: Religion and Power in the Ancient World*. London: Duckworth. 233–255.

Greatrex, G. 1997. "The Nika Riot: A Reappraisal." *JHS* 117: 60–86.

Grégoire, H. 1923. "Miettes d'histoire byzantine (IVme–VIme siècle)." In W. H. Buckler and W. M. Calder, eds., *Anatolian Studies Presented to Sir William Mitchell Ramsay*. Manchester. 151–164.

Grigg, R. 1979. "Portrait-Bearing Codicils in the Illustrations of the *Notitia Dignitatum*." *JRS* 69: 107–124.

Guilland, R. 1948. "Autour du *Livre des Cérémonies:* L'Augusteus, la Main d'Or et l'Onopodion." *REByz* 6: 167–180 (reprinted in Guilland [1969] I 81–93).

———— 1950. "À propos du *Livre des Cérémonies* de Constantin VII Porphyrogénète: Le Delphax." *AIPhO* 10: 293–306 (reprinted in Guilland [1969] I 70–80).

———— 1955. "Études sur le Grand Palais de Constantinople." *Hellenika* 14: 106–122 (reprinted in Guilland [1969] I 56–69).

———— 1958. "Les patrices byzantines du VIe siècle." *Palaeologia* 7: 271–305 (reprinted in his *Recherches sur les institutions byzantines,* 2 vols., Berliner byzantinistische Arbeiten 35, Berlin, 1967, vol. II at 132–161).

———— 1967. "Études sur l'histoire administrative de l'Empire byzantin à la haute époque (IVe–Ve siècles): remarques sur les titres nobiliaires: egrège-perfectissime-clarissime." *EHBS* 35: 17–40 (reprinted in his *Titres et fonctions de l'Empire byzantin,* Variorum Reprints 50, Aldershot, 1976, no. 1).

———— 1969. *Études de topographie de Constantinople byzantine.* 2 vols. Berliner byzantinistische Arbeiten 37. Berlin.

Gutsfeld, A. 1998. "Der Prätorianerpräfekt und der kaiserliche Hof im 4. Jahrhundert n. Chr." In Winterling (1998) 75–102.

Guyot, P. 1980. *Eunuchen als Sklaven und Freigelassene in der griechisch-römischen Antike.* Stuttgarter Beiträge zur Geschichte und Politik 14. Stuttgart.

Haase, R. 1994. *Untersuchungen zur Verwaltung des spätrömischen Reiches unter Kaiser Justinian I. (527 bis 565).* Wiesbaden.

Haensch, R. 1992. "Das Statthalterarchiv." *ZRG* 109: 209–317.

———— 1994. "Die Bearbeitungsweisen von Petitionen in der Provinz Aegyptus." *ZPE* 100: 487–546.

———— 1997. "Zur Konventsordnung in Aegyptus und den übrigen Provinzen des römischen Reiches." In B. Kramer, W. Luppe, H. Machler, and G. Poethke, eds., *Akten des 21. Internationalen Papyrologenkongresses, Berlin, 13.–19.8.1995.* 2 vols. *APF* Beiheift 3. Stuttgart. I 320–391.

Hahn, L. 1907. "Zum Sprachenkampf im römischen Reich bis auf die Zeit Justinians." *Philologus* Supp. 10.4: 675–718.

Harmand, L. 1955. *Libanius: Discours sur les patronages.* Publications de la Faculté des lettres de l'Université de Clermont-Ferrand 2:1. Paris.

Harries, J. 1988. "The Roman imperial Quaestor from Constantine to Theodosius II." *JRS* 78: 148–172.

———— 1999. *Law and Empire in Late Antiquity.* Cambridge.

Heather, P. J. 1994. "New Men for New Constantines? Creating an Imperial Elite in the Eastern Mediterranean." In P. Magdalino, ed., *New Constantines: The Rhythm of Imperial Renewal in Byzantium, 4th–13th Centuries.* Society for the Promotion of Byzantine Studies Publications 2. Aldershot. 11–33.

———— 1998. "Senators and Senates." In Av. Cameron and P. Garnsey, eds.,

The Cambridge Ancient History. Vol. XIII: *The Late Empire, A.D. 337–425.* Cambridge. 184–210.

Hedrick, C. W. 2000. *History and Silence: Purge and the Rehabilitation of Memory in Late Antiquity.* Austin: University of Texas Press.

Hendy, M. F. 1985. *Studies in the Byzantine Monetary Economy c. 300–1450.* Cambridge.

Himmelfarb, M. 1983. *Tours of Hell: An Apocalyptic Form in Jewish and Christian Literature.* Philadelphia: University of Pennsylvania Press.

Hirschfeld, O. 1893. "Die *agentes in rebus.*" *SPAW* 25: 421–441 (reprinted in his *Kleine Schriften,* Berlin, 1913, at 624–645).

Hobson, D. W. 1993. "The Impact of Law on Village Life in Roman Egypt." In B. Halpern and D. W. Hobson, eds., *Law, Politics and Society in the Ancient Mediterranean World.* Sheffield. 193–219.

Holmberg, E. J. 1933. *Zur Geschichte des Cursus Publicus.* Uppsala.

Holum, K. G. 1982. *Theodosian Empresses: Women and Imperial Dominion in Late Antiquity.* Transformation of the Classical Heritage 3. Berkeley: University of California Press.

——— 1995. "Inscriptions from the Imperial Revenue Office of Byzantine Caesarea Palaestinae." In J. H. Humphrey, ed., *The Roman and Byzantine Near East: Some Recent Archaeological Research. JRA* Supplementary Series 14. Ann Arbor, Michigan. 333–345.

Honoré, T. 1978. *Tribonian.* London: Duckworth.

——— 1998. *Law in the Crisis of Empire, 379–455 A.D.: The Theodosian Dynasty and Its Quaestors.* Oxford.

Hopkins, K. 1961. "Social Mobility in the Later Roman Empire: The Evidence of Ausonius." *CQ* n.s. 11: 239–249.

——— 1963. "Eunuchs in Politics in the Later Roman Empire." *PCPhS* 189: 62–80 (reprinted in Hopkins [1978] 172–196).

——— 1978. *Conquerors and Slaves.* Sociological Studies in Roman History I. Cambridge.

——— 1980. "Taxes and Trade in the Roman Empire (200 B.C.–A.D. 400)." *JRS* 70: 101–125.

Humphrey, J. H., ed. 1976. *Apollonia, The Port of Cyrene: Excavations by the University of Michigan, 1965–1967.* Supplements to *Libya Antiqua* 4. Tripoli.

Hunger, H. 1986. "Der Kaiserpalast zu Konstantinopel: seine Funktionen in der byzantinischen Außen- und Innenpolitik." *JÖByz* 36: 1–11.

Hunt, D. 1999. "The Outsider Inside: Ammianus on the Rebellion of Silvanus." In J. W. Drijvers and D. Hunt, eds., *The Late Roman World and Its Historian: Interpreting Ammianus Marcellinus.* London: Routledge. 51–63.

James, S. 1988. "The *fabricae:* State Arms Factories of the Later Roman Empire." In J. C. N. Coulston, ed., *Military Equipment and the Identity of Sol-*

diers: Proceedings of the Fourth Roman Military Equipment Conference. BAR International Series 394. Oxford. 257–331.

Janin, R. 1964. *Constantinople byzantine: développement urbain et répertoire topographique.* 2d ed. Archives de l'Orient chrétien 4A, Institut français d'études byzantines. Paris.

Johnson, A. C., and L. C. West. 1949. *Byzantine Egypt: Economic Studies.* Princeton University Studies in Papyrology 6. Princeton.

Johnson, D. W. 1977. "Further Remarks on the Arabic History of the Patriarchs of Alexandria." *OC 61: 103–116.*

Jones, A. H. M. 1940. *The Greek City from Alexander to Justinian.* Oxford.

―――― 1949. "The Roman Civil Service (Clerical and Sub-Clerical Grades)." *JRS* 39: 38–55 (reprinted in his *Studies in Roman Government and Law,* Oxford, 1968, no. 10 at 151–175).

Jones, C. P. 1978. *The Roman World of Dio Chrysostom.* Cambridge, Mass.: Harvard University Press.

Kalavrezou-Maxeiner, I. 1975. "The Imperial Chamber at Luxor." *DOP* 29: 225–251.

Karayannopulos, J. 1958. *Das Finanzwesen des frühbyzantinischen Staates.* Südosteuropäische Arbeiten 52. Munich.

Kaser, M. 1975. *Das römische Privatrecht II: die nachklassischen Entwicklungen.* 2d ed. Handbuch der Altertumswissenschaft 10:3.3.2. Munich.

Kaser, M., and K. Hackl. 1996. *Das römische Zivilprozessrecht.* 2d ed. Handbuch der Altertumswissenschaft 10:3.4. Munich.

Kaster, R. A. 1988. *Guardians of Language: The Grammarian and Society in Late Antiquity.* Transformation of the Classical Heritage 11. Berkeley: University of California Press.

Keenan, J. G. 1975. "On Law and Society in Late Roman Egypt." *ZPE* 17: 237–250.

―――― 1977. "The Provincial Administration of Egyptian Arcadia." *MPhL.* 2: 193–202.

―――― 1994. "Soldier and Civilian in Byzantine Hermopolis." In A. Bülow-Jacobsen, ed., *Proceedings of the 20th International Congress of Papyrologists, Copenhagen, 23–29 August 1992.* Copenhagen. 444–451.

―――― 2000. "Egypt." In Av. Cameron, B. Ward-Perkins, and Michael Whitby, eds., *The Cambridge Ancient History.* Vol. XIV: *Late Antiquity: Empire and Successors, A.D. 425–600.* Cambridge. 612–637.

Kelly, C. M. 1994. "Later Roman Bureaucracy: Going through the Files." In A. K. Bowman and G. D. Woolf, eds., *Literacy and Power in the Ancient World.* Cambridge. 161–176.

―――― 1998a. "Emperors, Government and Bureaucracy." In Av. Cameron and P. Garnsey, eds., *The Cambridge Ancient History.* Vol. XIII: *The Late Empire, A.D. 337–425.* Cambridge. 138–183.

——— 1998b. "Emperors as Gods, Angels as Bureaucrats: The Representation of Imperial Power in Late Antiquity." *Antigüedad; Religiones y Sociedades* 1: 301–326.

——— 1999. "Empire-Building." In G. W. Bowersock, P. Brown, and O. Grabar, eds., *Late Antiquity: A Guide to the Postclassical World*. Cambridge, Mass.: Harvard University Press. 170–195 (reprinted in G. W. Bowersock, P. Brown, and O. Grabar, eds., *Interpreting Late Antiquity: Essays on the Postclassical World*, Cambridge, Mass.: Harvard University Press, 2001, at 170–195).

——— Forthcoming a. "Bureaucracy and Government." In N. Lenski, ed., *Cambridge Companion to the Age of Constantine*. Cambridge.

——— Forthcoming b. "John Lydus and the Eastern Praetorian Prefecture in the Sixth Century."

Kelly, J. M. 1966. *Roman Litigation*. Oxford.

Kennedy, D. L. 1982. *Archaeological Explorations on the Roman Frontier in North-East Jordan*. BAR International Series 134. Oxford.

Kessels, A. H. M., and P. W. van der Horst. 1987. "The Vision of Dorotheus (*Pap. Bodmer* 29) Edited with an Introduction, Translation and Notes." *VChr* 41: 313–359.

Kiilerich, B. 1993. *Late Fourth Century Classicism in the Plastic Arts: Studies in the So-Called Theodosian Renaissance*. Odense University Classical Studies 18. Odense University Press.

King, C. E. 1980. "The *Sacrae Largitiones:* Revenues, Expenditure and the Production of Coin." In C. E. King, ed., *Imperial Revenue, Expenditure and Monetary Policy in the Fourth Century A.D.: The Fifth Oxford Symposium on Coinage and Monetary History*. BAR International Series 76. Oxford. 141–173.

Klotz, A. 1927. "Lydos." *P-W* 13.2: cols. 2210–17.

Koch, P. 1903. *Die byzantinischen Beamtentitel von 400 bis 700*. Jena.

Kolb, A. 1998. "Kaiser Julians Innenpolitik: grundlegende Reformen oder traditionelle Verwaltung? Das Beispiel des *cursus publicus*." *Historia* 47: 342–359.

Kolias, G. T. 1939. *Ämter- und Würdenkauf im früh- und mittelbyzantinischen Reich*. Texte und Forschungen zur byzantinisch-neugriechischen Philologie 35. Athens.

Kotansky, R. 1991. "Magic in the Court of the Governor of Arabia." *ZPE* 88: 41–60.

Kraus, A. 1960. "*Secretarius* und Sekretariat: der Ursprung der Institution des Staatssekretariats und ihr Einfluß auf die Entwicklung moderner Regierungsformen in Europa." *RQA* 55: 43–84.

Krause, J.-U. 1987. *Spätantike Patronatsformen im Westen des Römischen Reiches*. Vestigia 38. Munich.

Krautheimer, R. 1983. *Three Christian Capitals: Topography and Politics.* Berkeley: University of California Press.

Kruse, H. 1934. *Studien zur offiziellen Geltung des Kaiserbildes im römischen Reiche.* Studien zur Geschichte und Kultur des Altertums 19:3. Paderborn.

Kulikowski, M. 2000. "The *Notitia Dignitatum* as a Historical Source." *Historia* 49: 358–377.

Kunkel, W. 1968–69. "*Consilium, consistorium.*" *JbAC* 11/12: 230–248 (reprinted in his *Kleine Schriften: zum römischen Strafverfahren und zur römischen Verfassungsgeschichte,* ed. H. Niederlander, Weimer, 1974, at 405–440).

Lallemand, J. 1964. *L'administration civile de l'Égypte de l'avènement de Dioclétien à la création du diocèse (284–382): contribution à l'étude des rapports entre Égypte et l'empire à la fin du IIIe et au IVe siècle.* Mémoires de l'Académie royale de Belgique 57:2. Brussels.

Lamma, P. 1947. "Giovanni di Cappadocia." *Aevum* 21: 80–100 (reprinted in his *Oriente e occidente nell'alto medioevo: studi storici sulle due civiltà,* Medioevo et umanesimo 5, Padua, 1968, at 59–81).

Legohérel, H. 1965. "Reparatio Temporum." *Iura* 16: 76–104.

Lemerle, P. 1971. *Le premier humanisme byzantin: notes et remarques sur enseignement et culture à Byzance des origins au Xe siècle.* Bibliothèque byzantine études 6. Paris.

Lendon, J. E. 1997. *Empire of Honour: The Art of Government in the Roman World.* Oxford.

Lenski, N. E. 2002. *Failure of Empire: Valens and the Roman State in the Fourth Century A.D.* Transformation of the Classical Heritage 34. Berkeley: University of California Press.

Lepelley, C. 1979–81. *Les cités de l'Afrique romaine au Bas-Empire.* 2 vols. Études augustiniennes. Paris.

Leschi, L. 1948. "L'album municipal de Timgad et l'''Ordo Salutationis' du consulaire Ulpius Mariscianus." *REA* 50: 71–100 (reprinted in his *Études d'épigraphie, d'archéologie et d'histoire africaines,* Gouvernement Général de l'Algérie, sous-direction des Beaux Arts, Services des Antiquités, Paris, 1957, at 246–266).

Le Vine, V. T. 1975. *Political Corruption: The Ghana Case.* Stanford, Calif.: Hoover Institution Press.

Levy, H. L. 1958. "Themes of Encomium and Invective in Claudian." *TAPhA* 89: 336–347.

———— 1971. *Claudian's In Rufinum: An Exegetical Commentary.* American Philological Association Monographs 30. Cleveland: Case Western Reserve University Press.

Lewis, N. 1976. "*Notationes Legentis.*" *BASP:* 13: 5–14.

——— 1981. "The Prefect's Conventus: Proceedings and Procedure." *BASP* 18: 119–129.

——— 1983. *Life in Egypt under Roman Rule.* Oxford.

——— 1991. "In the World of *P.Panop.Beatty.*" *BASP* 28: 163–178.

Liebeschuetz, J. H. W. G. 1972. *Antioch: City and Imperial Administration in the Later Roman Empire.* Oxford.

——— 1990. *Barbarians and Bishops: Army, Church, and State in the Age of Arcadius and Chrysostom.* Oxford.

——— 2001. *The Decline and Fall of the Roman City.* Oxford.

Liebs, D. 1978. "Ämterkauf und Ämterpatronage in der Spätantike: Propaganda und Sachzwang bei Julian dem Abtrünnigen." *ZRG* 95: 158–186.

Lightfoot, J. B. 1889. *The Apostolic Fathers: Part II S. Ignatius, S. Polycarp.* 3 vols. 2d ed. London.

Lim, R. 1995. *Public Disputation, Power, and Social Order in Late Antiquity.* Transformation of the Classical Heritage 23. Berkeley: University of California Press.

Littmann, E., D. Magie, and D. R. Stuart. 1910. *Syria: Publications of the Princeton University Archaeological Expeditions to Syria in 1904–1905 and 1909: Division III Greek and Latin Inscriptions in Syria, Section A Southern Syria, Part 2 Southern Haurân.* Leiden.

Long, J. 1996. *Claudian's In Eutropium: Or, How, When, and Why to Slander a Eunuch.* Chapel Hill: University of North Carolina Press.

Maas, M. 1992. *John Lydus and the Roman Past: Antiquarianism and Politics in the Age of Justinian.* London: Routledge.

MacCormack, S. G. 1981. *Art and Ceremony in Late Antiquity.* Transformation of the Classical Heritage 1. Berkeley: University of California Press.

MacCoull, L. S. B. 1988. *Dioscorus of Aphrodito: His Work and His World.* Transformation of the Classical Heritage 16. Berkeley: University of California Press.

MacMullen, R. 1962. "Roman Bureaucratese." *Traditio* 18: 364–378 (reprinted in MacMullen [1990] no. 8 at 67–77).

——— 1964a. "Imperial Bureaucrats in the Roman Provinces." *HSPh* 68: 305–316.

——— 1964b. "Some Pictures in Ammianus Marcellinus." *ABull.* 46: 435–455 (reprinted in MacMullen [1990] no. 9 at 78–106).

——— 1976. *Roman Government's Response to Crisis: A.D. 235–337.* New Haven: Yale University Press.

——— 1986a. "Personal Power in the Roman Empire." *AJPh* 107: 512–524 (reprinted in MacMullen [1990] no. 18 at 190–197).

——— 1986b. "Judicial Savagery in the Roman Empire." *Chiron* 16: 147–166 (reprinted in MacMullen [1990] no. 20 at 204–217).

——— 1986c. "What Difference Did Christianity Make?" *Historia* 35: 322–343 (reprinted in MacMullen [1990] no. 13 at 142–155).

——— 1988. *Corruption and the Decline of Rome.* New Haven: Yale University Press.

——— 1990. *Changes in the Roman Empire: Essays in the Ordinary.* Princeton.

Malcus, B. 1969. "Notes sur la révolution du système administratif romain au IIIe siècle." *ORom* 7: 213–237.

Mango, C. 1959. *The Brazen House: A Study of the Vestibule of the Imperial Palace of Constantinople.* Royal Danish Academy, Arkaeologisk-kunsthistoriske meddelelser 4.4. Copenhagen.

——— 1984. "St Michael and Attis." *Deltion tés Christianikés Archaiologikés* 12: 39–62.

——— 1985. *Le développement urbain de Constantinople (IVe–VIIe siècles).* Travaux et mémoires du Centre de recherche d'histoire et civilisation de Byzance, Monographies 2. Paris.

——— 1993. "The Columns of Justinian and His Successors." in his *Studies on Constantinople.* Variorum Reprints 394, Aldershot. no. 10.

Mann, J. C. 1991. "The *Notitia Dignitatum:* Dating and Survival." *Britannia* 22: 215–219.

Marcillet-Jaubert, J. 1980. "Recherches au Qasr el Hallabat." *Annual of the Department of Antiquites Jordan* 24: 121–124.

Marichal, R. 1952. "L'écriture latine de la chancellerie impériale." *Aegyptus* 32: 336–350.

Matthews, J. F. 1974. "The Letters of Symmachus." In J. W. Binns, ed., *Latin Literature of the Fourth Century.* London: Routledge. 58–99 (reprinted in his *Political Life and Culture in Late Roman Antiquity,* Variorum Reprints 217, Aldershot, 1985, no. 4).

——— 1975. *Western Aristocracies and Imperial Court, A.D. 364–425.* Oxford (reprinted with a postscript, 1990).

——— 1989. *The Roman Empire of Ammianus.* London: Duckworth.

——— 1993. "The Making of the Text." In J. Harries and I. Wood, eds., *The Theodosian Code: Studies in the Imperial law of Late Antiquity.* London: Duckworth. 19–44.

——— 2000. *Laying Down the Law: A Study of the Theodosian Code.* New Haven: Yale University Press.

Mayerson, P. 1986. "The Beersheba Edict." *ZPE* 64: 141–148.

McCormick, M. 1985. "Analyzing Imperial Ceremonies." *JÖByz* 35: 1–20.

——— 1986. *Eternal Victory: Triumphal Rulership in Late Antiquity, Byzantium, and the Early Medieval West.* Cambridge.

——— 2001. *Origins of the European Economy: Communications and Commerce, A.D. 300–900.* Cambridge.

McLynn, N. B. 1994. *Ambrose of Milan: Church and Court in a Christian Capital.*

Transformation of the Classical Heritage 22. Berkeley: University of California Press.

Meischner, J. 1996. "Das Missorium des Theodosius in Madrid." *JDAI* 111: 389–432.

Metzger, T. A. 1973. *The Internal Organization of Ch'ing Bureaucracy: Legal, Normative, and Communication Aspects.* Harvard Studies in East Asian Law 7. Cambridge, Mass.: Harvard University Press.

Meyer, M., and R. Smith. 1994. *Ancient Christian Magic: Coptic Texts of Ritual Power.* San Francisco.

Migl, J. 1994. *Die Ordnung der Ämter: Prätorianerpräfektur und Vikariat in der Regionalverwaltung des Römischen Reiches von Konstantin bis zur Valentinianischen Dynastie.* Europäische Hochschulschriften 623. Frankfurt am Main.

Mihăescu, H. 1973. "La lingua latina e la lingua greca nell'Impero bizantino." *A&R* n.s. 18: 144–153.

Millar, F. 1967. "Emperors at Work." *JRS* 57: 9–19.

――― 1983. "Empire and City, Augustus to Julian: Obligations, Excuses and Status." *JRS* 73: 76–96.

――― 1992. *The Emperor in the Roman World (31 B.C.–A.D. 337).* 2d ed. London: Duckworth.

Miller, K. 1916. *Itineraria Romana: Römische Reisewege an der Hand der Tabula Peutingeriana.* Stuttgart.

Mitford, T. B. 1971. *The Inscriptions of Kourion.* American Philosophical Society Memoirs 83. Philadelphia.

Mommsen, T. 1884. "Ordo salutationis sportularumque sub imp. Iuliano in provincia Numidia." *Ephemeris Epigraphica* 5: 629–646 (reprinted in his *Gesammelte Schriften,* vol. VIII = *Epigraphische und numismatische Schriften,* vol. I, 2d ed., Berlin, 1965, at 478–499).

Monks, G. R. 1957. "The Administration of the Privy Purse: An Inquiry into Official Corruption and the Fall of the Roman Empire." *Speculum* 32: 748–779.

Monneret de Villard, U. 1953. "The Temple of the Imperial Cult at Luxor." *Archaeologia* 95: 85–105.

Montevecchi, O. 1936. "Ricerche di sociologia nei documenti dell'Egitto greco-romano." *Aegyptus* 16: 3–83.

Morosi, R. 1977. "L'*officium* del prefetto del pretorio nel VI secolo." *Rom Barb* 2: 103–148.

――― 1978. "*Cancellarii* in Cassiodoro e in Giovanni Lido." *Rom Barb* 3: 127–158.

Müller, C. D. G. 1959. *Die Engellehre der koptischen Kirche: Untersuchungen zur Geschichte der christlichen Frömmigkeit in Ägypten.* Wiesbaden.

Müller-Wiener, W. 1977. *Bildlexikon zur Topographie Istanbuls.* Deutsches Archäologisches Institut. Tübingen.

Niccoli, G. 1976. "Tradizione biografica suetoniana e orientamenti ideologici nei necrologi imperiali di Ammiano Marcellino." *CS* 13.4: 26–36.

Nippel, W. 1995. *Public Order in Ancient Rome.* Cambridge.

Noethlichs, K. L. 1981. *Beamtentum und Dienstvergehen: zur Staatsverwaltung in der Spätantike.* Wiesbaden.

———— 1991. "Hofbeamter." *RLAC* 15: cols. 1111–58.

Nörr, D. 1966. *Imperium und Polis in der hohen Prinzipatszeit.* Münchener Beiträge zur Papyrusforschung und antiken Rechtsgeschichte 50. Munich.

Nutton, V. 1977. "Archiatri and the Medical Profession in Antiquity." *PBSR* 32: 191–226.

Oliverio, G. 1936. *Il decreto di Anastasio I° su l'ordinamento politico-militare della Cirenaica.* Documenti antichi dell'Africa Italiana 2.2. Bergamo.

Orlandi, T. 1971. "Teodosio di Alessandria nella letteratura copta." *GIF* n.s. 2: 175–185.

Pack, R. A. 1935. *Studies in Libanius and Antiochene Society under Theodosius.* Menasha, Wisconsin.

Palme, B. 1999. "Die *Officia* der Statthalter in der Spätantike: Forschungsstand und Perspektiven." *Ant Tard* 7: 85–133.

Paschoud, F. 1979. *Zosime: Histoire nouvelle II.1 (Livre III).* Paris: Guillaume Budé.

Patlagean, E. 1977. *Pauvreté économique et pauvreté sociale à Byzance 4e–7e siècles.* École des hautes études en sciences sociales, Centre de recherches historiques. Civilisations et sociétés 48. Paris.

Patrich, J. 1999. "The Warehouse Complex and Governor's Palace (Areas KK, CC, and NN, May 1993–December 1995)." In K. G. Holum, A. Raban, and J. Patrich, eds., *Caesarea Papers 2. JRA* Supplementary Series 35. Portsmouth, R.I. 70–107.

Patrucco, M. F. 1982. "Social Patronage and Political Mediation in the Activity of Basil of Caesarea." In *Studia Patristica* 17.3, ed. E. A. Livingstone. Oxford. 1102–07.

Pedersen, F. S. 1970. "On Professional Qualifications for Public Posts in Late Antiquity." *C&M* 31: 161–213 (reprinted as *Late Roman Public Professionalism,* Odense University Classical Studies 9, Odense University Press, 1976).

Pedley, J. G. 1976. "The History of the City." In Humphrey (1976) 11–28.

Petit, P. 1955. *Libanius et la vie municipale à Antioche au IVe siècle après J.-C.* Institut français d'archéologie de Beyrouth, Bibliothèque archéologique et historique 62. Paris.

——— 1956. "Recherches sur la publication et la diffusion des discours de Libanius." *Historia* 5: 479–509.

——— 1957. *Les étudiants de Libanius.* Paris.

Pflaum, H.-G. 1948. *Le Marbre de Thorigny.* Bibliothèque de l'École des hautes-études, Sciences historiques et philologiques 292. Paris.

——— 1950. *Les procurateurs équestres sous le Haut-Empire romain.* Paris.

Piganiol, A. 1972. *L'Empire chrétien (325–395).* 2d ed. Rev. A. Chastagnol. Paris.

Piovanelli, P. 1993. "Les origins de *l'Apocalypse de Paul* reconsidérées." *Apocrypha* 4: 25–64.

Potter, D. S. 1990. *Prophecy and History in the Crisis of the Roman Empire: A Historical Commentary on the Thirteenth Sibylline Oracle.* Oxford.

Price, S. R. F. 1984. *Rituals and Power: The Roman Imperial Cult in Asia Minor.* Cambridge.

Puliatti, S. 1980. *Ricerche sulla legislazione "regionale" di Giustiniano: lo statuto civile e l'ordinamento militare della prefettura africana.* Seminario giuridico della Università di Bologna 84. Milan.

Purcell, N. 1983. "The *Apparitores:* A Study in Social Mobility." *PBSR* 51: 125–173.

Purpura, G. 1973. "I *Curiosi* e la *Schola Agentum in Rebus.*" *AGSP* 34: 165–273.

Rémondon, R. 1965. "Militaires et civils dans une campagne égyptienne au temps de Constance II." *JS:* 132–143.

Reynolds, J. M. 1976. "The Inscriptions of Apollonia." In Humphrey (1976) 293–333.

——— 1978. "Hadrian, Antoninus Pius and the Cyrenaican Cities." *JRS* 68: 111–121.

——— 1982. *Aphrodisias and Rome. JRS* Monographs 1. London.

Richard, M. 1941–42. "La lettre de Théodoret à Jean d'Égées." *Les sciences philosophiques et théologiques*: 415–423.

Riepl, W. 1913. *Das Nachrichtenwesen des Altertums mit besonderer Rücksicht auf die Römer.* Leipzig.

Rochette, B. 1997. "Justinien et la langue latine: à propos d'un prétendu oracle rendu à Romulus d'après Jean le Lydien." *BZ* 90: 413–415.

Roda, S. 1986. "Polifunzionalità della lettera commendaticia: teoria e prassi nell'epistolario simmachiano." In F. Paschoud, ed., *Colloque genevois sur Symmaque à l'occasion du mille-six-centième anniversaire du conflict de l'autel de la Victoire.* Paris. 177–207.

Roques, D. 1989. *Études sur la correspondance de Synésios de Cyrène.* Collection Latomus 205. Brussels.

Rosen, K. 1990. "Iudex und Officium: Kollektivstrafe, Kontrolle und Effizienz in der spätantiken Provinzialverwaltung." *AncSoc* 21: 273–292.

Rosenstiehl, J. M. 1990. "L'itinéraire de Paul dans l'au-delà: contribution à l'étude de l'Apocalypse apocryphe de Paul." In P. Nagel, ed., *Carl-Schmidt-Kolloquium an der Martin-Luther-Universität, 1998*. Halle-Wittenberg. 197–212.

Roueché, C. 1989. *Aphrodisias in Late Antiquity. JRS* Monographs 5. London.

Rouland, N. 1979. *Pouvoir politique et dépendance personnelle dans l'antiquité romaine: genèse et rôle des rapports de clientèle.* Collection Latomus 166. Brussels.

Rousseau, P. 1985. *Pachomius: The Making of a Community in Fourth-Century Egypt.* Transformation of the Classical Heritage 6. Berkeley: University of California Press (reprinted with a new preface, 1999).

——— 1994. *Basil of Caesarea.* Transformation of the Classical Heritage 20. Berkeley: University of California Press.

Ruppert, F. 1971. *Das pachomianische Mönchtum und die Anfänge klösterlichen Gehorsams.* Münsterschwarzacher Studien 20. Münsterschwarzach.

Sabbah, G. 1978. *La méthode d'Ammien Marcellin: recherches sur la construction du discours historique dans les Res Gestae.* Collection d'études anciennes. Paris.

Saller, R. P. 1980. "Promotion and Patronage in Equestrian Careers." *JRS* 70: 44–63.

——— 1982. *Personal Patronage under the Early Empire.* Cambridge.

——— 1994. *Patriarchy, Property and Death in the Roman Family.* Cambridge.

Sartre, M. 1982. *Inscriptions grecques et latines de la Syrie.* Vol. XIII, part 1: *Bostra nos. 9001 à 9472.* Bibliothèque archéologique et historique 113. Paris.

Scheidel, W. 2001. "Roman Age Structure: Evidence and Models." *JRS* 91: 1–26.

Scholten, H. 1995. *Der Eunuch in Kaisernähe: zur politischen und sozialen Bedeutung des praepositus sacri cubiculi im 4. und 5. Jahrhundert n. Chr.* Prismata 5. Frankfurt am Main.

——— 1998. "Der oberste Hofeunuch: die politische Effizienz eines gesellschaftlich Diskriminierten." In Winterling (1998) 51–73.

Schubert, W. 1969. "Die rechtliche Sonderstellung der Dekurionen (Kurialen) in der Kaisergesetzgebung des 4.–6. Jahrhunderts." *ZRG* 86: 287–333.

Schuller, W. 1975. "Grenzen des spätrömischen Staates: Staatspolizei und Korruption." *ZPE* 16: 1–21.

——— 1977. "Probleme historischer Korruptionsforschung." *Der Staat* 16: 373–392.

——— 1980. "Ämterkauf im römischen Reich." *Der Staat* 19: 57–71.

——— ed. 1982a. *Korruption im Altertum: Konstanzer Symposium, Oktober 1979.* Munich.

——— 1982b. "Prinzipien des spätantike Beamtentums." In Schuller (1982a) 201–208.

——— 1989. "Zwischen Klientel und Korruption: zum römischen Beamtenwesen." In W. Dahlheim, W. Schuller, and J. von Ungern-Sternberg, eds., *Festschrift Robert Werner zu seinem 65. Geburtstag.* Xenia, Konstanzer Althistorische Vorträge und Forschungen 22. Konstanz. 259–268.

——— 1994. "Kaiser Julian und der Ämterkauf." In R. Günther and S. Rebenich, eds., *E fontibus haurire: Beiträge zur römischen Geschichte und zu ihren Hilfswissenschaften.* Studien zur Geschichte und Kultur des Altertums: Reihe 1, Monographien 8. Paderborn. 197–201.

Scott, R. D. 1972. "John Lydus on Some Procedural Changes." *Byzantina* 4: 439–451.

Seager, R. 1986. *Ammianus Marcellinus: Seven Studies in His Language and Thought.* Columbia: University of Missouri Press.

Seeck, O. 1876. *Notitia Dignitatum accedunt Notitia Urbis Constantinopolitanae et Latercula Provinciarum.* Berlin.

——— 1906. *Die Briefe des Libanius.* Texte und Untersuchungen zur Geschichte der altchristlichen Literatur 15.1–2. Leipzig.

Setton, K. M. 1941. *Christian Attitude towards the Emperor in the Fourth Century Especially as Shown in Addresses to the Emperor.* Studies in History, Economics, and Public Law 482. New York: Columbia University Press.

Sijpesteijn, P. J., and K. A. Worp. 1978. *Zwei Landlisten aus dem Hermupolites (P. Landlisten).* Studia Amstelodamensia ad epigraphicam, ius antiquum, et papyrologicam pertinentia 7. Zutphen.

Silverstein, T. 1962. "The Date of the Apocalypse of Paul." *Mediaeval Studies* 24: 335–348.

Silverstein, T., and A. Hilhorst. 1997. *Apocalypse of Paul: A New Critical Edition of Three Long Latin Versions.* Cahiers d'Orientalisme 21. Geneva.

Sinnigen, W. G. 1957. *The Officium of the Urban Prefecture during the Later Roman Empire.* Papers and Monographs of the American Academy in Rome 17. Rome.

——— 1959. "Two Branches of the Late Roman Secret Service." *AJPh* 80: 238–254.

——— 1962. "Three Administrative Changes Ascribed to Constantius II." *AJPh* 83: 369–382.

Sirks, B. 1993. "The Sources of the Code." In J. Harries and I. Wood, eds., *The Theodosian Code: Studies in the Imperial law of Late Antiquity.* London: Duckworth. 45–67.

Sivan, H. 1993. *Ausonius of Bordeaux: Genesis of a Gallic Aristocracy.* London: Routledge.

Skeat, T. C. 1964. *Papyri from Panopolis in the Chester Beatty Library Dublin.* Chester Beatty Monographs 10. Dublin.

Sly, D. I. 1996. *Philo's Alexandria.* London: Routledge.

Stead, M. 1981. "The High Priest of Alexandria and All Egypt." In R. S. Bagnall, G. M. Browne, A. E. Hanson, and L. Koenen, eds., *Proceedings of the Sixteenth International Congress of Papyrology, New York, 24–31 July 1980.* American Studies in Papyrology 23. Chicago. 411–418.

Stein, E. 1920. "Untersuchungen zum Staatsrecht des Bas-Empire." *ZRG* 41: 195–251 (reprinted in his *Opera Minora Selecta,* ed. J.-R. Palanque, Amsterdam, 1968, at 71–127).

———— 1949. *Histoire du Bas-Empire II: de la disparition de l'Empire d'occident à la mort de Justinien (476–565).* Ed. J.-R. Palanque. Paris.

Stewart, P. 2003. *Statues in Roman Society: Representation and Response.* Oxford.

Stoffel, P. 1994. *Über die Staatspost, die Ochsengespanne und die requirierten Ochsengespanne: eine Darstellung des römischen Postwesens auf Grund der Gesetze des Codex Theodosianus und des Codex Iustinianus.* Europäische Hochschulschriften 595. Bern.

Swift, L. J., and J. H. Oliver. 1962. "Constantius II on Flavius Philippus." *AJPh* 83: 247–264.

Tassi, A. M. 1967. "Costanzo II e la difesa della maestà imperiale nell'opera di Ammiano Marcellino." *CS* 6.2: 157–180.

Taylor, L. R. 1925. "Horace's Equestrian Career." *AJPh* 46: 161–170.

Teitler, H. C. 1985. *Notarii and Exceptores: An Inquiry into Role and Significance of Shorthand Writers in the Imperial and Ecclesiastical Bureaucracy of the Roman Empire (from the Early Principate to c. 450 A.D.).* Dutch Monographs on Ancient History and Archaeology 1. Amsterdam.

Thompson, E. A. 1947. *The Historical Work of Ammianus Marcellinus.* Cambridge.

———— 1952. *A Roman Reformer and Inventor, Being a New Text of the Treatise De rebus bellicis.* Oxford.

Toynbee, J. M. C., and K. S. Painter. 1986. "Silver Picture Plates of Late Antiquity: A.D. 300 to 700." *Archaeologia* 108: 15–65.

Treggiari, S. 1969. *Roman Freedmen during the Late Republic.* Oxford.

Treucker, B. 1981. "A Note on Basil's Letters of Recommendation." In P. J. Fedwick, ed., *Basil of Caesarea: Christian, Humanist, Ascetic: A Sixteen-Hundredth Anniversary Symposium.* 2 vols. Pontifical Institute of Mediaeval Studies, Toronto. Vol. I at 405–410.

Trombley, F. R. 2001. *Hellenic Religion and Christianization, c. 370–529.* 2 vols. 2d ed. Leiden.

Trombley, F. R., and J. W. Watt. 2000. *The Chronicle of Pseudo-Joshua the Stylite.* Translated Texts for Historians 32. Liverpool.

Tsirpanlis, C. N. 1974. "John Lydos on the Imperial Administration." *Byzantion* 44: 479–501.

Turpin, W. N. 1982. "Late Roman Law Codes: Forms and Procedures for Legislation from the Classical Age to Justinian." Ph.D. diss., University of Cambridge.

Urbainczyk, T. 1997. *Socrates of Constantinople: Historian of Church and State.* Ann Arbor: University of Michigan Press.

Valensi, L. 1957. "Quelques réflexions sur le pouvoir impérial d'après Ammien Marcellin." *BAGB* 16.4: 62–107.

Van Dam, R. 2003. *Families and Friends in Late Roman Cappadocia.* Philadelphia: University of Pennsylvania Press.

van de Paverd, F. 1991. *St. John Chrysostom, The Homilies on the Statues: An Introduction.* Orientalia Christiana Analecta 239. Rome.

Vanderspoel, J. 1995. *Themistus and the Imperial Court: Oratory, Civic Duty, and Paideia from Constantius to Theodosius.* Ann Arbor: University of Michigan Press.

van Lantschoot, A. 1946. "Fragments coptes d'une homélie de Jean de Parallos contre les livres hérétiques." *Studi i Testi (Miscellanea Giovanni Mercati I)* 121: 296–326.

——— 1947. "Un texte palimpseste du Vat. copte 65." *Muséon* 60: 261–268.

Veilleux, A. 1980. *Pachomian Koinonia I: The Life of Saint Pachomius and His Disciples.* Cistercian Studies Series 45. Kalamazoo.

Vera, D. 1981. *Commento storico alle Relationes di Quinto Aurelio Simmaco.* Biblioteca di studi antichi 29. Pisa.

Versnel, H. S. 1991. "Beyond Cursing: The Appeal to Justice in Judicial Prayers." In C. A. Faraone and D. Obbink, eds., *Magika Hiera: Ancient Greek Magic and Religion.* New York: Oxford University Press. 60–106.

Veyne, P. 1981. "Clientèle et corruption au service de l'état: la vénalité des offices dans le Bas-Empire romain." *Annales (ESC)* 36: 339–360.

Vincenti, U. 1986. "Note sull'attività giudiziaria del senato dopo i Severi." *Labeo* 32: 55–67.

Vogler, C. 1979. *Constance II et l'administration impériale.* Groupe de recherche d'histoire romaine de l'Université des sciences humaines de Strasbourg, Études et travaux 3. Strasbourg.

Vogt, A. 1935. *Constantin VII Porphyrogénète, Le Livre des Cérémonies.* Vol. I.2: *Commentaire.* Collection byzantine. Paris: Guillaume Budé.

Waddington, W. H. 1868. "Édit de l'empereur Anastase sur l'administration militaire de la Libye." *RA* n.s. 18: 417–430.

——— 1870. *Inscriptions grecques et latines de Syrie.* In P. Le Bas and W. H. Waddington, *Explication des inscriptions grecques et latines recueillies en Grèce et en Asie Mineure III, nos. 1826–2724.* Paris.

Wagner, M. M. 1948. "A Chapter in Byzantine Epistolography: The Letters of Theodoret of Cyrus." *DOP* 4: 119–181.

Wallace-Hadrill, A., ed. 1989. *Patronage in Ancient Society.* London.

—— 1996. "The Imperial Court." In A. K. Bowman, E. Champlin, and A. Lintott, eds., *The Cambridge Ancient History.* Vol. X: *The Augustan Empire, 43 B.C.–A.D. 69.* 2d ed. Cambridge. 283–308.

Wallis Budge, E. A. 1915. *Miscellaneous Coptic Texts in the Dialect of Upper Egypt.* London.

Warmington, B. H. 1956. "The Career of Romanus, *comes Africae.*" *BZ* 49: 55–64.

Waterbury, J. 1973. "Endemic and Planned Corruption in a Monarchical Regime." *World Politics* 25.4: 533–555.

Weaver, P. R. C. 1972. *Familia Caesaris: A Social Study of the Emperor's Freedmen and Slaves.* Cambridge.

Weiss, P. B. 1975. *Consistorium und Comites consistoriani: Untersuchungen zur Hofbeamtenschaft des 4. Jahrhunderts n. Chr. auf prosopographischer Grundlage.* Würzburg.

Whittow, M. 1990. "Ruling the Late Roman and Early Byzantine City: A Continuous History." *P&P* 129: 4–29.

Wickham, L. R. 1983. *Cyril of Alexandria: Select Letters.* Oxford.

Wieber-Scariot, A. 1998. "In Zentrum der Macht: zur Rolle der Kaiserin an spätantiken Kaiserhöfen am Beispiel der Eusebia in den *Res Gestae* des Ammianus Marcellinus." In Winterling (1998) 103–131.

Williams, W. 1967. "Antoninus Pius and the Control of Provincial Embassies." *Historia* 16: 470–483.

—— 1974. "The *Libellus* Procedure and the Severan Papyri." *JRS* 64: 86–103.

Williamson, C. 1987. "Monuments of Bronze: Roman Legal Documents on Bronze Tablets." *ClAnt.* 6: 160–183.

Willis, W. H., and K. Maresch. 1997. *The Archive of Ammon Scholasticus of Panopolis (P.Ammon).* Vol. I: *The Legacy of Harpocration: Texts from the Collections of Duke University and the Universität zu Köln.* Papyrologia Coloniensia 26.1. Opladen.

Winterling, A., ed. 1998. *Comitatus: Beiträge zur Erforschung des spätantiken Kaiserhofes.* Berlin.

Womersley, D., ed. 1994. *Edward Gibbon, The History of the Decline and Fall of the Roman Empire.* 3 vols. London: Allen Lane.

Zuckerman, C. 1998a. "Comtes et ducs en Égypte autour de l'an 400 et la date de la *Notitia Dignitatum Orientis.*" *AntTard* 6: 137–147.

—— 1998b. "Two Reforms of the 370s: Recruiting Soldiers and Senators in the Divided Empire." *REByz* 56: 79–139.

Index

REVEALING ANTIQUITY

G. W. Bowersock, General Editor